CW00515485

5000 Random, Interesting & Fun Facts You Need To Know

The Knowledge Encyclopedia To Win Trivia

Scott Matthews

The more that you read, the more things you will know. The more you learn, the more places you'll go.

- Dr. Seuss

7 BENEFITS OF READING FACTS

1. Knowledge
2. Stress Reduction
3. Mental Stimulation
4. Better Writing Skills
5. Vocabulary Expansion
6. Memory Improvement
7. Stronger Analytical Thinking Skills

ABOUT THE AUTHOR

Scott Matthews is a geologist, world traveller and author of the "Amazing World Facts" series! He was born in Brooklyn, New York, by immigrant parents from Ukraine but grew up in North Carolina. Scott studied at Duke University where he graduated with a degree in Geology and History.

His studies allowed him to travel the globe where he saw and learned amazing trivial knowledge with his many encounters. With the vast amount of interesting information he accumulated, he created his best selling books "Random, Interesting & Fun Facts You Need To Know."

He hopes this book will provide you with hours of fun, knowledge, entertainment and laughter.

If you gain any knowledge from this book, think it's fun and could put a smile on someone's face, he would greatly appreciate your review on Amazon. You can scan the QR code below which will take you straight to the review page!

Table of Contents

Airplanes & Airports

1.   In China, less than 30% of its airspace can be used by commercial airlines. This could be one of the reasons why China's airports are the worst in the world when it comes to punctuality.

2.   Adam Armstrong bought a Ryan air airline ticket in 2015, and by mistake, his surname was misspelled. He chose to change his name instead, because it was more cost effective than just fixing the ticket. The airline charged 220 pounds in administrative fees to alter the ticket, while it was free to change his name, and it only cost 103 pounds to get a new passport.

3.   Each American commercial aircraft is struck by lightning an estimated one time every year. Fortunately, because of improved technology, lightning hasn't caused a single plane to crash since 1967.

4.   China has a shortage of pilots, and as a result, pilots there can make up to $300,000 annually, tax free. A pilot named Jeff Graham said that he used to fly one hundred hours monthly for Southern Air, but now as a carrier pilot in Shenzhen, he makes thrice as much money flying only fifty hours a month.

5.   Commercial flight QF1121 of Qantas Airways was the first one to use sustainable derived bio-fuel in Australia. It took place in 2012, and one of the airplane's engines used fuel made from cooking oil.

6.   The Juan T. Trippe was the first commercial jumbo jet in the world, and was made in 1970. It's now been decommissioned and is in Seoul, South Korea, where it serves as a high concept restaurant.

7.   In order to reduce the risk of collision with planes, US airports use peregrine falcons to keep gulls and geese away from the runways.

8.   Pilots on British Airways once turned back a plane in 2015 when a man took a poop that smelled so bad.

9.   Hassan The Second, the King of Morocco, once escaped death when he was on his Boeing 727 being shot at by assassins. He grabbed the radio and told the assassins in the planes who were shooting at him "stop shooting, the tyrant is dead," which made them stop and disperse.

10.   In 2003, a Boeing 727 was stolen from an Angolan airport by two men. They simply disappeared and were never seen again.

11.   In Arizona there is a place known as the bone yard where about 3,000 military aircraft live, some of them up to sixty years old. They literally just sit there and are occasionally harvested for spare parts.

12.   A study by the BBC was done in 2013 that showed that over 50% of pilots had fallen asleep while flying and almost 30% had woken up to the copilot sleeping as well.

13.   Todu Yamanaka, the CEO of Japan Airlines, earns less than the pilots of the company, takes the bus in to work, and eats in the work cafeteria. He stated that others who seek money first will always fail.

14.   According to US and European laws, travelers whose flight is canceled or delayed must be compensated by the air company. However, only a few of the eligible travelers ask for it.

15.   In the 1940's, planes were a lot more comfortable. The Boeing 377 Stratocruiser, for example, had reclined club chairs throughout the cabin that could adjust into a bed so that each passenger could sleep while on intercontinental flights.

16.   MI-5 once planned to use gerbils to detect terrorists and spies at airports, given that their great sense of smell could acutely detect increased adrenaline in people. However, the project was abandoned when they noticed that the gerbils were not able to tell the difference between terrorists and those who were just afraid of flying.

17.   In May, 1991, the world record for the most people on a commercial aircraft was set when over a thousand Ethiopian Jews had to evacuate to Israel. The flight began with 1,086 passengers but ended up with 1,088 as two women were pregnant and had babies on board.

18.   Jessica Cox from Sierra Vista, Arizona, became the first pilot ever to fly with no arms. She was born in 1983 without arms due to an unusual birth defect.

19.   In the 1980's, in an attempt to save some money, the head of American Airlines at the time, Robert Crandall, decided to remove a single olive from each salad served in first class. It saved them $40,000 that year.

20.   The first female flight attendant ever was Ellen Church, who began flying in 1930. She implemented a plan that required all flight attendants to be registered nurses. However, when World War II began, all nurses were enlisted in the war, so most airlines simply dropped the requirement in order to find any workers.

21.   If you were to be born on a plane flying above the US, you would automatically be given citizenship; however, if you were born over an ocean, it would depend on which country the plane is registered.

22.   In 2006, a woman with a medical condition on a flight from Washington to Dallas was lighting matches to cover her own body odor. As the air staff couldn't detect where the smell was coming from, they were forced to land the plane in Nashville.

23.   Qatar Airways allows you to travel with a falcon in the cabin with the only condition of having less than six falcons in total aboard.

24.   The lightest plane to ever exist is the Bede BD-5 which weighed only 357 pounds (162kg).

25.   On March 27, 1977, one of the deadliest air plane crashes of all time happened on the ground. When the KLM Royal Dutch Airline Boeing 747 started to take off, it crashed into a Pan American World Airways Boeing 747 that was still on the airstrip. The tragedy occurred at Los Rodeos Airport in the Canary Islands, killing a total of 574 people from both planes.

26.   In 1927, American aviator Charles Augustus Lindbergh made the first solo nonstop flight across the Atlantic. The pilot was a polygamist with three other families and wives in Germany and Switzerland.

27.   For a ten hour trip, a Boeing 747 uses 39,000 gallons (150,000 liters) of fuel on average. This means the plane needs a gallon (four liters) for every second that it's in the air.

28.   The largest plane in the Air Force is the Lockheed Martin C-5. It's large enough to transport entire submarines.

29.   The Air lander 10 is the largest airship of the world, measuring ninety two meters (301.7 feet) long. It's filled with almost 1,300,000 cubic feet (37,000 cubic meters) of helium and can reach an altitude of 2.9 miles (4.8 kilometers). The airship has been nicknamed as the flying bum and it can remain in the sky for up to five days.

30.   After terrorist attacks in the US on September 11, 2001, all flights were grounded, except for a single plane that was going to save a person's life. The plane traveled from San Diego, California, to Miami, Florida, transporting an anti-venom for a life threatening snake bite that a man had gotten. The flight was escorted by two fighter jets, and the man's life was saved.

31.   Most foods don't taste too good on airplanes because when you fly, your taste buds along with your sense of smell are impacted. When in a pressurized cabin, your perception of sweetness and saltiness naturally reduces.

32.   Planes don't crash as often as you might imagine. Very few planes ever crash, and when they do, the chances of you dying are about one in eleven million. If you are in a plane and it literally goes down, 95.7% of people in it will likely survive.

33.   In order to scare off birds, the Gloucester-shire Airport in England used to blast Tina Turner music. It was proved to work even better than blasting bird distress calls.

34.   The fastest aircraft made by man is the SR 71 which flew over four thousand missiles while it was in service.

35.   The "Bukken Bruse" flew from Oslo, Norway, en-route to the city of Hommelvik in the same country, on October 2, 1948. Bertrand Russel, a seventy six year old philosopher, upon boarding the aircraft, asked to be seated in the smoking section, saying that "if I cannot smoke, I should die." As the plane landed, the pilot lost control, and it crashed, killing nineteen people who were all sitting in the non-smoking section.

36.   A solar plane that is set to become the first ever solar plane to reach the stratosphere was created by Swiss adventurer Raphael Domjan. It's a sleek white two seater with long wings that are covered with 237 square feet (seventy two square meters) of solar panels.

37.   The shortest commercial flight in the world is only 1.7 miles (2.73 kilometers) in distance. It covers the way between two small Orkney Islands north of Scotland, from the Westray Airport to the Papa Westray Airport. If the wind is ideal, it can take as little as forty seven seconds from start to finish.

38.   Oxygen masks in airplanes aren't actually connected to an oxygen tank. They instead use a chemical reaction to generate it on the spot.

39.   In 1910, the first ever in-flight radio transmission was sent by Walter Wellmen, while he flew across the Atlantic Ocean along with five companions and his cat. The message said: "Roy, come and get this goddamn cat!"

40.   A passenger flight from Moscow to Hong Kong called Aeroflot flight 593 crashed into a mountain range killing everyone on board. Eventually, it was known that the pilot let his children temporarily fly the plane, but his sixteen year old son unintentionally deactivated the autopilot controls. The pilots ended up

over correcting and crashed the plane.

41. One of the world's first private pilots was magician and escape artist Harry Houdini. During his maiden flight in Germany, he actually crashed, but he continued practicing and eventually set his sights on becoming the first man to pilot an airplane in Austria.

42. Javelins are permitted on Delta Air Lines, except for flights departing from or landing in Amsterdam in the Netherlands, or Dublin in Ireland.

43. Any plane that the president of the United States happens to be traveling on at a particular time is given the name Air Force One. Likewise, the Army aircraft that the president is traveling on is called Army One while the helicopter is called Marine One.

44. Jets in the sky leave a white trail across it for the same reason that you can see your breath in the winter. It's carbon dioxide and water creating visible moisture.

45. In 1987, a lifetime unlimited first-class American Airlines ticket costing $250,000 was bought by Steve Rothstein. He flew over 10,000 flights with the same ticket, costing the company some $21 million. The company terminated his ticket in 2008.

46. Air India Flight 216 took off from Evansville, Indiana, and crashed almost immediately, killing the entire University of Evansville basketball team with the exception of one member, on December 13, 1977. The surviving team member wasn't even on the flight. Two weeks after the plane crush, he died after he was hit by a drunk driver.

47. The only airport in the world where a schedule of flights take off and land on a beach is Barra Airport, in Scotland.

48. On July 23, 1983, Air Canada's Flight 143 with sixty nine people on board ran out of fuel at an altitude of seven miles (twelve kilometers). Incredibly, the highly experienced pilot managed to glide the plane down safely and land it without anyone getting hurt.

49. Located in Denver, the Denver International Airport is over twice the size of the whole Manhattan Island. It's America's largest airport, and is home to the biggest jet fuel distribution network on Earth.

50. The last flight of the Concorde jet was in 2003. It could fly at a maximum speed of 1,350 miles (2,100 kilometers) per hour. It could go from London to New York City in about three hours, which was about half the time of other passenger planes.

51. The letter X is used in airport codes such as LAX in Los Angeles and PHX in Phoenix. Previously, there used to be a two-letter system, however, new standards required a three-letter identifier, so airports simply added the letter "X" to avoid changing much.

52. The Guinness World Record for the highest fall survived without a parachute is held by a woman named Vesna Vulovic from Yugoslavia. On January 26, 1972, she was working as a flight attendant when the plane she was aboard blew up; she fell inside a section of the tail unit, falling over 32,800 feet (10,000 meters) over the Czech Republic. She had multiple broken bones, spent sixteen months at hospital, recovered from a twenty seven day coma, and miraculously survived.

53. On July 30, 2016, forty two year old paratrooper Luke Aikens became the first person to jump from an airplane without a parachute or wing-suit in California. He jumped 25,000 feet (7,600 meters) high from the ground, setting a world record for the highest jump. He safely landed in a 100-square-foot (nine-meter-squared) net, which was about one third the size of a football field.

54. The first and oldest running municipal airport in the United States is Albany International Airport. The airstrip was first built in 1908 on an old polo field.

55. The SR71 Blackbird isn't really black, but indigo blue. It has a mixture of microscopic iron ferrite balls, which make the radar signal and heat dissipate.

Amazing

56. The reason snipers usually have an apparatus to help them shoot is because their bullets travel so fast that the rotation of Earth moves the target, hence, snipers need to adjust their aim accordingly.

57. A ten year old boy once saved his grandma's life when she fell unconscious in front of the wheel. He ended up driving the vehicle himself which he said he learned from playing Mario Kart.

58. One of the world's toughest creatures is the microscopic tardigrade, also known as water bear or moss piglet. It can live up to ten years without water and can withstand temperatures as low as -459 degrees Fahrenheit, and as high as 304 degrees Fahrenheit (-272 to 151 degrees Celsius).

59. Dolly the sheep was the first mammal ever to be successfully cloned. It was cloned on July 5, 1996, from an adult cell at the Roslin Institute in Scotland. She was named after Dolly Parton because she was cloned from a mammary cell.

60. As actor Ving Rhames was filming "The Saint of Fort Washington" in 1993, he met a homeless man, and quickly discovered that he was really his older brother named Junior. Junior had been missing since he served in Vietnam, and Rhames' family had been looking for him ever since.

61. UK rapper Mia hadn't had contact with her father since age ten, and she only knew that her father fought in the Sri Lankan Civil War against the government as a Tamil Tiger. To get him to reach out, she named her debut album Arular, after her father. The plan was that he would Google his name, find her music, and reach out. It worked.

62. A seventy seven year old hunter got lost in a forest in Quebec, Canada, near Lac Saint-Jean for two days in September, 2011, and the police search party couldn't find him. His friend, a former wrestling star named Raymond Rougeau, took his seaplane up over the forest, did his own search, and he found the hunter alive.

63. The board game Chess has more possible moves than the number of particles in the universe. For every move you make, it opens up thirty eight acceptable moves. A chess match consists of about forty moves per person, meaning the total number of possible moves equals ten to the power of 126. That also means that there are lots of chess moves that we are yet to figure out.

64. A man from Ohio named Gary Rosheisen, with a tendency to suffer from strokes, attempted to teach his cat Tommy how to dial 911. In 2006, the man fell over from a stroke and the police actually received a silent phone call. When the emergency help arrived at his place, they found the man incapacitated and the cat by the phone.

65. A study conducted at Carnegie Mellon University, in Pittsburgh, concluded that meditating for about half an hour a day for eight weeks can considerably reduce the feeling of loneliness in adults. It also made them feel a lot happier.

66. Jeremy Harper has the world record for the largest number ever counted. He reached one million, taking him three months; he streamlined the whole process online, raising money for charity.

67. Dinosaur fossils have been found on every major continent in the world i.e. Antarctica, Australia, India, and in the far north of Canada.

68. After being offered some pizza, a man who was threatening to jump from the South Carolina Ravenel Bridge, in 2013, was convinced not to jump.

69. In 2013, the first completely blind kayaker to paddle the entire length of the Grand Canyon was Navy Veteran Lonnie Bedwell. He paddled 226 miles (363 kilometers) in a solo kayak for sixteen days.

70. The world record for the longest ice cream man goes to a man named Allen Gans who started in 1947. He serves in the greater Boston area and knows 90% of his patrons by name.

71. A monkey buffet festival is held in Thailand every year. It started back in 1989 by a local businessman, who was looking to boost tourism to the Lopburi Province. The buffet consists of 8,800 pounds (4,000 kilograms) of fruits, vegetables, cakes, candies and more, that are set down in front of temples on tables for the 3,000 monkeys that live in the region. There are also people who dress like monkeys and monkey sculptures.

72. An elderly home in California went bankrupt in 2013 leaving sixteen residents with nowhere to go. All the staff moved on except for Maurice Roland, the cook, and Miguel Alvarez, the janitor, who refused to leave and helped the residents from their own pockets.

73. Saint Augustine is home to Florida School for the Deaf and Blind. The city's Starbucks has employees that use sign language over a two-way video system so that people who are deaf can place their order at the drive-thru.

74. In the Russian Eastern Safari Park they once put a goat in a tiger enclosure that was meant to be food for it, however, instead of the tiger eating the goat, they became friends.

75. A woman named Norma from Michigan was diagnosed with cancer after her sixty seven year old husband died. Instead of getting treatment, she told the doctors: "I'm ninety years old; I'm hitting the road." She then took an indefinite road trip across the US with her retired son and his wife. The journey was documented on Facebook as "Driving Miss Norma."

76. During a tsunami, a baby hippo from Kenya known as Owen was swept away from his mother. The baby hippo then mistook a 130 year old tortoise for another hippo, and the two actually became best friends.

77. On August 16, 1996, a three year old boy fell into a gorilla enclosure at the Brookfield Zoo and lost consciousness. A female gorilla named Binti Jua guarded the kid from other gorillas, held him in her arms, and even carried him to an entrance where zookeepers could easily take him.

78.   Wensleydale Cheese had gone bankrupt three times in a sixty year span and was about to go out of business when it was mentioned in a short animation film that featured Grommet and Wallace. Its sales went up, and the company survived because of the cartoon.

79.   While humans have eighty six billion neurons in their brains, African elephants have 257 billion. So elephants have three times as many neurons as we have, however, our cerebral cortex has three times as many neurons as that of an elephant. In fact, long finned pilot whales are the only mammals that have more neurons in their cerebral cortex than humans.

80.   Iconic actor and martial artist Bruce Lee was extremely fast and accurate. He could toss a grain of rice up into the air and catch it with a set of chopsticks before it hit the ground.

81.   80% of Hong Kong residents flush their toilets using sea water because in the 1950's, they made a separate system of water distribution for that purpose. Sea water is less harmful to some marine life than fresh water, so this helps to protect them.

82.   Tom Harrison, an English police officer, finished the London Marathon on April 29, 2017, after crawling while wearing a gorilla costume for the entire 26.2 mile (42.2 kilometer) distance. He raised $33,650 to conserve gorillas, and the money went to The Gorilla Organization.

83.   Mary Had a Little Lamb, the well-known nursery rhyme, is really based on Mary Sawyer of Sterling Massachusetts, who went to school sometime around 1816, and she did in fact have a lamb that followed her there one day.

84.   Kaylee Foster from Ocean Springs, Mississippi, was named homecoming queen of her high school on September 7, 2018. A little while later, she put her tiara aside, put on a football helmet, and kicked a couple of field goals plus an extra point, helping her school win a game that had gone into overtime.

85.   Scientists in 2016 found the tail of a dinosaur which dates back ninety nine million years. It was perfectly preserved in amber, so it still had its feathers.

86.   Twenty eight year old Marshall Mabey was in Brooklyn, New York, working on a new subway line when air pressure that had built up shot him and two fellow workers out of a tunnel, and upwards through the muddy waters of the east river more than twenty four feet (seven meters) into the air. His two colleagues died, but miraculously, Mabey didn't suffer any serious injuries.

87.   Ellen Gibb of North Bay, Ontario is currently the oldest woman in all of Canada. She's at least 112 years old, has nine grandkids, twenty two great-grandkids, and ten great-great-grandkids.

88.   In the fire service, the Dalmatian was used not just to protect the equipment and carriages from fire, but also to keep the horses calm.

89.   Annie Londonderry bicycled around the world between June, 1894 and September, 1895, becoming the first woman ever to do so. The fact that she learned to ride her bike just a few days before starting her journey makes her accomplishment even more impressive.

90.   The largest land habitat in the world is the Boreal Forest. It spans across Canada, northern American states, Norway, the Southern part of Iceland, Finland, Sweden, Russia, Kazakhstan, and it goes all the way to Mongolia and Northern Japan.

91.   There was a Roman tradition where the leaves of palm trees were laid in the hands of people who won contests, and that's how the underside of our hands came to be known as palms.

92.   When Warren Buffet was only eleven years old, he made his very first investment. He bought three shares of "Citi's Service Preferred" at $38 per share. Later, he sold his shares when they reached $40 and actually regretted it as they later raised to $200 a share. For him, the experience was an early lesson in having patience while investing. He is now worth sixty eight billion dollars.

93.   In 2011, after the Fukushima nuclear disaster occurred, over two hundred Japanese pensioners over the age of sixty volunteered to help tackle the nuclear crisis.

94. In the western Indian city of Amritsar, there is a free kitchen operated by volunteers at the Golden Temple that serves 100,000 hot meals a day and has been doing so for over 300 years.

95. As of 2015, the Guinness World Record for long distance archery is held by Matt Stutzman, a Paralympic, armless archer.

96. The average suit of armor was up to 110 pounds (fifty kilograms) for a medieval knight, so it actually required a significant amount of energy just to walk around wearing such a suit.

97. Bhutan is considered the most eco-friendly country in the world. Once, 108,000 trees were planted to celebrate the birth of its new prince.

98. Thomas Hughes was a British Soldier who threw a bottle with a letter in it to his wife in 1914. It was discovered by a fisherman in 1999 who then delivered it to the soldier's eighty six year old daughter.

99. India-based Graviky Labs makes pens, oil-based paints, and spray paint using pigment from carbon soot-polluted air. A single Air Ink pen can contain thirty to forty minutes of carbon emissions from a single car.

100. A baby kangaroo was found by a man abandoned on the side of the road. The kangaroo walked up to the man, held up his arms, and asked to be picked up. It was named Doodlebug. The rescuer later gave him a teddy bear and he wouldn't stop hugging it.

101. The largest living organism in the world is the armillaria ostoyae, known also as the humongous fungus. It's located in the Malheur National Forest and it covers 2,385 acres.

102. Keikyu Aburatsubo Marine Park is an aquarium located in Japan where you can shake hands with otters.

103. Owls can change eye color from yellow, orange, dark brown, or even black. The eye color suggests what time of the day they prefer to be active and hunt.

104. A personal trainer in 2011 named Drew Manning wanted to prove to his clients it's possible to get back in shape if you are severely overweight. He gained seventy pounds (thirty kilograms) of fat then lost it all again in a matter of six months.

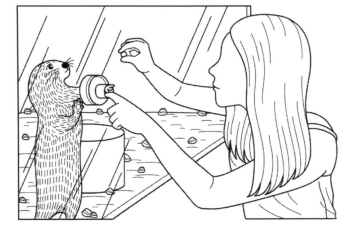

105. As of 2020, there are eleven million millionaires in the US making it the country with the most in the world.

106. The largest leg span of any anthropoid is found in the Japanese spider crab, reaching over 11.8 feet (3.6 meters) in length.

107. In Washing there are pink cherry blossom trees that were gifted by Japan in 1912 as a sign of friendship between the two countries.

108. On the rim of the Kilauea Crater in Hawaii, there is a hotel called the Volcano House Hotel, which opened back in 1846. It had a stone hearth with a fire that burned uninterruptedly for 133 years until New Year's Day in 2010, when the fire was finally allowed to go out.

109. In the Bath River, in the southwest of Western Australia, researchers at Murdoch University in Perth have found goldfish measuring as long as twelve inches (30 centimeters) and weighing as much as 4.2 pounds (1.9 kilograms).

110. A man named Blair McMillan from Canada was worried that his family was becoming too attached to technology so they spent a whole year living like it was the '80s, with old tech such as a boom box, a tube TV and a rotary phone.

111. The Russians and the Finns used to toss living Russian Brown Frogs into fresh milk as a way to preserve it, before fridges were invented. The frog's skin contains antibacterial compounds and peptides that ensured the milk would stay fresh.

112. Since Iceland became an independent republic in 1944, only one person has ever been killed by armed police.

113. An electric catfish exists that's able to produce up to 400 volts of shocks from gland cells on the side of their skin. They have full control of these shocks and use it to stun their prey as well as for defense.

114. There is a forest in Argentina that is shaped like a guitar. Farmer Pedro Martin Ureta planted the 7,000 trees in 1979 as a tribute to his late wife. He has never been able to see it himself from the sky because he is scared of flying.

115. In 2005, a gigantic pink woolen rabbit with its guts hanging out was knitted by the Vietnamese art collective group Gelatin, over a five year period. It was named Hase, meaning hare, and was put on a hill in the Piedmont region of Italy. It's over 200 feet (sixty meters) long and twenty feet (six meters) high. They put it there for hikers to enjoy and it will decay by the year 2025.

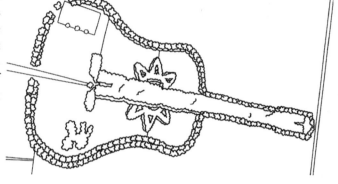

116. At the age of only twenty eight, Beethoven began losing his hearing, so he cut the legs off his piano and began sitting on the floor so he could compose music by feeling the vibrations.

117. Cornell University researchers made the world's smallest guitar, which is about the size of a human blood cell. It was made from crystalline silicon and it has six strings, each about fifty nanometers wide.

118. The only confirmed person in history that has ever been hit by a meteorite is Anne Hodges from Alabama, US. On a clear day in November of 1954, a softball sized hunk of black rock broke through her ceiling, bounced off a radio, and hit her in the thigh while she was having a nap on her couch, leaving a pineapple shaped bruise.

119. An Airbus 321 once made its way from Athens to Zurich carrying a stowaway Greek cat in the undercarriage. It had shock and hypothermia, but incredibly it survived.

120. There are a series of sixty five feet (twenty meter) long concrete arrows all the way from San Francisco to New York City that were created to direct traffic in the air from the pre-digital era.

121. Ingvar Feodor Kamprad, the founder of IKEA, started to work when he was six years old by selling matches. At the age of ten, he used to bike around the neighborhood selling Christmas decorations. Then at the age of seventeen, he was getting money from selling fish and pencils. Finally, after his father gave him a small sum of money for doing well in school, he started IKEA.

122. Fifty four year old Cong Yan from Jilin, China, walked daily with an eighty eight pound (forty kilogram) rock balanced on his head in an attempt to get fit and lose weight.

123. Jason Lewis was the first person to circumnavigate around the globe purely by human power. His journey began in 1994 where he biked, rollerbladed, kayaked and pedaled from country to country, finally ending his trip thirteen years later in 2007.

124. If the New York City subway system was laid end to end, it would stretch from New York City to Chicago, covering 661 miles (1,063 kilometers) of main track.

125. Alex the parrot was the first animal to ask an existential question, which was: "What color am I?" He found out he was grey.

126. There was a man named Malcolm Myatt who hasn't felt the emotion sadness since 2004, after he suffered from a stroke.

127. Mahatma Gandhi was married at the age of thirteen to another thirteen year old girl. They ended up being married for sixty two years.

128. Currently there are over six hundred billion Lego parts that have been created since the inception of the company. That's approximately eighty pieces per person on the globe.

129. In 1860, Valentine Tapley, a pike County farmer and loyal democrat, promised to never trim his beard again if Abraham Lincoln was elected president. He kept his word and his beard grew to 12.5 feet (3.8 meters) long.

130. In 2007, a German shepherd stray dog saved the life of Shannon Lorio after she crashed down an embankment and was thrown through the back window of her car. The dog came from the woods and pulled her by the collar off of the trunk, placing her on the road where she could be seen by passing drivers.

131. In 2011, a team of hackers at MIT turned their Earth and Planetary Science Department building into a giant, multicolored, playable Tetris game. The operation took four years of planning and two months of effort, working every night from ten until five in the morning.

132. A Doberman Pinscher named Khan saved a baby girl from a deadly king brown snake attack in 2007. The dog grabbed the girl by the diaper and fled her to safety, taking a venomous bite to the paw in her place.

133. A man once hit his head while swimming in a shallow pool and awoke with the ability of being able to play the piano skillfully after never having played any instruments before. This condition is a real thing known as Acquired Musical Savant Syndrome.

134. The world's largest pig hairball is at Mount Angel Abbey Museum, in Oregon. The hairball is the size of a football.

135. Photographer Diana Kim from Hawaii had been documenting the homeless for ten years when she found her own father among them.

136. Glass is 100% recyclable and, in fact, it can be recycled limitlessly without any loss in quality or purity. From every ton of glass that is recycled, over a ton of natural resources are actually saved.

137. Pocho was a dying crocodile that was rescued by a man named Chito. After recovering, the crocodile didn't leave and lives with Chito to this day.

138. Daniella Perez, a woman who's in a wheelchair with no feet, won a treadmill and a walk-in sauna in 2015 when she was a contestant on the Price is Right.

139. In 1988, the steamboat Arabia that sank in 1856 was found under almost forty six feet (fourteen meters) of dirt in a field at a farm. Incredibly, many of the objects found were recovered and preserved so well that some of the food was still edible.

140. The world's largest gold crystal was found in Venezuela, years ago, according to scientists at Los Alamos National Laboratory's Lujan Neutron Scattering Center. It's the size of a golf ball, weighs half a pound (227 grams), and is estimated to be worth $1.5 million.

141. The most valuable company to ever exist was the Dutch East India Company in 1637. In today's world, it would be the equivalent of over seven trillion dollars.

142. There is a woman from Serbia named Bojana Danilovic who suffers from a rare brain condition called "Spatial Orientation Phenomenon." The condition causes her to see everything upside down, so she uses a special inverted computer screen and keyboard at work, as well as special work forms that are easier to fill upside down.

143. In Indian culture as well as other parts of the world, there are people who have taken a vow to never sit, lay, or squat for twelve years in order to transport their psyches into a realm of spiritual awareness not experienced by sitters; these people are known as standing babas. They stand before a small hammock in which to rest their arms during the day and torso at night. One of their legs must be on the ground at all times.

144. Lillico is a stray dog that walks up to eight miles (thirteen kilometers) every night to collect a food parcel that she returns and shares with her family, a dog, a cat, and a few chickens.

145. Cecil Chubb bought the Stonehenge for his wife for around ten thousand pounds in 1915, however, she didn't like it so he gave it back to Britain in 1918. Today it's worth approximately a hundred and fifteen million pounds.

146. A boy named Justus Uwayesu was an orphan found living in a garbage dump by Red Cross workers when he was nine in Rwanda. He ended up going to Harvard on a full scholarship studying a Bachelor in Economics.

147. Besides being born on the same day and year, February 12, 1809, Charles Darwin and Abraham Lincoln had other things in common. They both loved Shakespeare, they both lost their mothers at an early age, and they were both abolitionists.

148. A lady named Elvita Adams was saved by a gust of wind when she tried to commit suicide from the 86th floor of the Empire State Building. The strong wind blew her back onto the ledge of the 85th floor.

149. Katherine Johnson was one of the most famous American mathematicians for her generation. Her fascination with counting allowed her to skip ahead in high school at the age of ten, and in 1961, she calculated the trajectory of NASA's first trip into space, and was correct.

150. A fifty six year old Indian woman named Kamla Devi was ambushed by a leopard. She actually managed to kill the animal with the only thing that she had on her: an iron sickle.

151. A normal pregnancy is about 280 days. In 1945, a twenty five year old woman named Beulah Hunter gave birth to a healthy baby girl after being pregnant for 375 days.

152. The largest guitar in the world measures more than 42.6 feet (thirteen meters) long and sixteen feet (4.9 meters) wide, and weighs almost 2,253 pounds (1,023 kilograms). Although the strings are super thick, the same pitch is maintained as if it were a regular-sized guitar.

153. A Malaysian man named Ho Eng Hui, nicknamed "Master Ho," holds the world record for piercing four coconuts with a bare finger. He did it within just 12.1 seconds during an event that took place on April 21, 2011, in the city of Milan in Italy.

154. In Sweden, there are winter concerts where all instruments are made of ice. They are considered some of the rarest instruments in the world and are actually very fragile; just a player's breath risks nudging them out of tune.

155. The Margate Grotto is a series of underground passageways located in Margate, England, that are covered in millions of sea shells. It was discovered in 1835, but it's still unknown how old the grotto really is or who built it.

156. In 2014, during a racing competition, a stray dog named Arthur followed a Swedish racing team through the Amazonian jungle and rivers, completing a 427 mile (688 kilometer) race, just because one of the team members had given it a meatball during one of the earlier halts.

157. In 1848, an ice jam in the upper part of the river from Niagara Falls caused the falls to stay bone-dry for almost forty eight hours. Some people thought of it as a sign that the world was ending and attended special services at local churches. Niagara Falls has the highest flow rate of any waterfall in the world and delivers 4.4 gigawatts of energy to the area.

158. On March 1, 1950, the Westside Baptist Church in Beatrice, Nebraska, was affected by an explosion at 7:25 pm that destroyed the church. That night, the choir practice had been scheduled to begin at 7:20, however, one of the fifteen people who should have been present was injured, and as a result, all of them arrived late that night. Some people thought of it as a divine intervention.

159. In 1928, Madeline Scotto graduated from an elementary school which she came back and taught at as a teacher continuing to work there until 2015, when she was 101 years old.

160. A stray cat became the seeing eye guide for a dog named Terfel who went blind in 2012; the cat uses its paws to guide the dog around the house.

161. A sixteen year old Russian powerlifter, Maryana Naumova, can bench press 350 pounds (160kg).

162. When Jason Padgett was a kid, he had a hard time studying algebra or math. After being attacked outside of a bar however, he started seeing the world in pixelated, geometric shapes. He soon realized about his new ability, understood right away the concept of Pi, and hand drew complex fractals, becoming a renowned math genius.

163. Iron Nun is the nickname given to eighty six year old nun Madonna Buder due to her amazing endurance. She has completed more than forty Iron Man races, which consist of a 111.7 mile (180 kilometer) bike ride, 2.4 mile (3.9 kilometer) swim, and a 26.2-mile (42.2 kilometer) run. She is, in fact, the oldest Iron Man triathlon competitor.

164. The largest weight loss documented for a human was by John Minnoch who weighed 1,400 pounds (635kg) and lost 924 pounds (419kg).

165. Since 1996, Harold Hackett has thrown 4,871 messages in a bottle from Prince Edward Island, Canada. He has actually received 3,100 responses, which represents a 63.6% response rate.

166. Based on the different types of street lamps used to give off different shades of light, it is actually possible to differentiate between East and West Berlin from space.

167. Sean's Bar is a pub located in Athlone, Ireland, that has been open since 900 AD.

168. An Indonesian man named Mbah Gotho claims to be 146 years old. He actually has a photo of his government ID card that shows his birth date as December 31, 1870. He has outlived all ten of his siblings, four wives, and his children.

169. The female with the longest legs in the world according to the Guinness World Records is Russian

Svetlana Pankratova. As of July 8, 2003, her legs measured 4.3 feet (1.3 meters) long.

170. In Buxton, England, a poisonous lagoon at the quarry was dyed black intentionally for safety reasons. The previous lagoon had an azure blue water color so beautiful and inviting, that the warning signs did not keep swimmers out.

171. Irish pirates captured St. Patrick when he was only sixteen years old and later sold him into slavery, where he was held in captivity for six years. During that time, he became deeply devoted to Christianity through constant prayer, and he actually considered his enslavement as God's test of his faith.

172. The oldest message in a bottle spent 108 years, four months, and eighteen days at sea according to the Guinness World Records. The Marine Biological Association in the United Kingdom put the bottle in the sea in November, 1906, and it washed ashore on Amrum Island in Germany on April 17, 2015.

173. Andrej Ciesielski, an eighteen year old tourist in Egypt, was arrested after climbing the Great Pyramid of Giza and taking photos, which he shared with his thousands of followers. He started a trend which other copy cats have begun doing so they can also post to their social media as well.

174. A cat named "Cookie" disappeared on a family trip when they went to the south of France in 2013. Eighteen months later Cookie returned home, dirty and a little skinny, but alive after having travelled over six hundred miles (one thousand kilometers).

175. A hungry sea lion pup once walked into a fancy restaurant in San Diego, California, and sat down at a prime table with an ocean view.

176. A boy named William Kamkwamba built a windmill from bicycle parts, gum trees, and other scraps to power electrical appliances in his home when he was only fourteen years old.

177. 600,000 South Korean students sat for their highly competitive college entrance tests in November, 2016, an event that would determine their future. To ensure that all students got to school on time, business opening hours were delayed, lorries were banned from roads, and construction was stopped. During language tests which required listening, airport authorities shut down all takeoffs and landings for half an hour so the noise wouldn't affect nearby schools.

178. Between January 25 and January 31, 2017, a seventy year old woman named Chau Smith from Independence, Missouri, ran seven marathons in seven days on seven continents.

179. Sam Griner, from the "Successful Kid Memes" group, used his fame to start a GoFundMe page. The site raised nearly $100,000 for his dad's kidney transplant.

180. Disney World is sixty nine square miles (111 square kilometers). That is about the same size as the city of San Francisco and twice the size of Manhattan.

181. President Thomas Jefferson was fluent in English, Greek, Latin, French, German, and Spanish. He also studied Arabic, Gaelic, and Welsh. He remains the most multilingual president of the United States in history.

182. There are plans in Berlin to create a building called "The House of One" which welcomes Jews,

Christians, and Muslims, all under one roof where they can worship their gods together.

183. The world's largest treehouse was built by Minister Horace Burgess outside of Crossville, Tennessee. A still-living white oak tree eighty foot (twenty four meter) tall with a 12.1 foot (3.7 meter) diameter base supports the almost ninety eight foot (thirty meter) tall treehouse and church, while six other oak trees provide additional support.

184. A set of identical twins separated at birth went on to live similarly eerily lives. Both boys were named James but went by the name Jim. They both had a childhood dog named Toy. They both married twice, first to a woman named Linda and then to a woman named Betty. They both had sons named James Alan, both were sheriffs in separate Ohio counties, and both drove Chevrolets.

185. There is a 1966 Volvo with more than three million miles (4,800,000 kilometers) on it. The average lifetime of a car is 150,000 miles (240,000 kilometers).

186. Joao Pereira de Souza, a seventy one year old retired fisherman, was in his home off the coast of Rio de Janeiro in 2011 when he saw a South American penguin stranded on a beach, and saved it. Each year since then, the same penguin, now named Dindim, travels thousands of miles to hang out with Joao for several months, before going back to his colony.

187. In 1978, a US Navy ship, known as the USS Stein, was found to have traces of an unknown species of giant squid attack. Almost all cuts on the sonar dome contained remains of a sharp, curved claw that were found on the rims of the suction cups of some squid tentacles, but some of the claw marks were much bigger than that of any discovered squid species.

188. In 1984, on the upper east side of New York, Todd Berenger launched a restaurant called "Twins" which was staffed by twenty nine sets of identical twins.

189. According to the Journal of Meteoritics and Planetary Science, the blade on the dagger found in Tutankhamun's tomb is made with materials from a meteorite. Scientists performed different tests on the blade to deeply study the elements that composed it. It was found to contain iron, nickel, and cobalt; all materials found in chunks of space rocks.

190. In Nashville, Tennessee, there is a vending machine that dispenses real cars. It has five stories and is fully automated.

191. Between 1932 and 1939, Oskar Speck, a twenty five year old canoeist from Germany, paddled a folding kayak from his home country to Australia just to see the world. He covered more than 31,000 miles (50,000 kilometers).

192. Rosa Zazel Richter was the first human to be cannonballed, back in 1877. She was shot at a distance of about twenty feet (six meters) at Westminster Aquarium in London, England.

193. Shemika Charles, the limbo queen, had been training six hours a day since she was a teenager. In 2010, she set a world record and is now so flexible that she could even limbo under a car.

194. High school student Hayden Godfrey had several jobs while in high school. He saved money for a year and a half and bought a flower for each of the 834 girls at school so no one would miss out and they could all feel joy for the day.

195. The loudest burp ever recorded by a male was 109.9 decibels. It was achieved by Paul Hunn on August 23, 2009, in the UK.

196. Maria and Lucy Aylmer are some of the few world's only non-identical, mixed race twins. One takes after their mother with a darker skin complexion while the other has a fairer skin complexion like her father.

197. Peter Skyllberg survived for over two months when his car was snowed in by staying warm in a sleeping bag and eating the snow.

198. Oysters make pearls as a way to relieve pain. When a grain of sand or debris gets stuck in their bodies, they ease the pain and irritation by coating it with multiple layers of nacre, a mineral that lines the inside of their shells; hence, a pearl begins to form.

199. A British man named Luke Irwin found an amazing discovery buried under his newly-purchased property. While an electrician that he hired was drilling into the ground, he hit a layer of intricate red, white, and blue mosaic tile. It turned out that the house was built on one of the largest and best-preserved Roman villas ever found in Great Britain.

200. A man from Bruceville, Indiana, named Bonny Ver built two roller coasters in his backyard. He named them the blue flash and he built them for his grandchildren with no prior experience, using scrap metal that he collected that he then welded together.

201. Chinese hair stylist Wang Xiaoyu is trained in the art of kung-fu and can actually cut hair while standing on his head.

202. The popemobile is the vehicle used by the pope at public appearances. It has bulletproof glass as well as a handrail for him to hold on to while he stands and waves at the crowd in order to get in and out. It was designed to protect him and be visible at the same time.

203. To raise funds for Glide, an organization that fights poverty, they did an eBay auction where the winner would have lunch with legendary billionaire investor Warren Buffett. Bidding started at just $25,000 and it closed at $3.3 million.

204. Katie and Amy Jones-Elliot are twins, but they were born eighty seven days apart. Their mom, Maria, went into labor on June 1, 2012, when she was only twenty three weeks pregnant, and she birthed Amy. Thirteen weeks later on August 27, her doctors induced labor, and she gave birth to Katie. The twins hold the world record for the longest time between the births of two twins.

205. Employees at a South Carolina 3M plant in 1980 were startled to find out that spools of plastic film, that they used to manufacture stationery, had created a static electricity force-field. The employees were frozen in place and were unable to get close to the machinery. They had to walk backwards to a space where the effects were less serious in order to get away.

206. Lin Ching Lan, a choreographer and dancer from Taiwan, was born deaf, so she feels the vibrations in her feet which come from wooden floors when music plays, and uses it to get her rhythm. She founded a dance troop for the hearing impaired, and she has appeared in a few commercials.

207. The name Jessica was the number one name for baby-girls in America for several years in the 1980's and 1990's, but did you know that it was really created by William Shakespeare? He made it up for his play "The Merchant of Venice." He is also credited with coining popular phrases such as "vanish into thin air," "bated breath," "dead as a doornail," and "kill with kindness."

208. A New York resident named Jeffrey Tanenhaus rented a commuter Citi Bike and rode it 3,000 miles (4,800 kilometers) across America in 2015. He was charged $1,200 in overtime fees, the highest for the NYC Citi Bike.

209. The largest, most extravagant hotel in Las Vegas is the MGM Grand Hotel and Casino. An estimated 15,000 pillow cases are cleaned at the hotel's laundry rooms every single day.

210. The biggest beaver dam to ever be discovered was found in Alberta, Canada, at the Wood Buffalo National Park. Experts claim that it has been under construction from the 1970's, and that several generations of beavers have worked on it so far. It's more than 2,798 feet (eighty five meters) in length, and it's so gigantic that it's visible from space.

211. As an infant, Daniel Kish lost both eyes because of cancer, but he now navigates because he has mastered human echo-location. This means he is able to "see" using sound echoes that bounce off objects, just like how bats do it.

212. There is a 229 feet (seventy meter) underground motel room located in a 65,000,000 year old cave at The Grand Canyon Caverns. It is considered the deepest, darkest, oldest, and quietest, motel room in the world.

213. Charles Joughin, the head baker aboard RMS Titanic, managed to stay cool when the ship struck an iceberg on April 14, 1912. He asked his bakers to distribute bread to passengers on lifeboats as they awaited rescue, and he offered his seat to another person. After a drink, he started throwing chairs into the water, so that those trying to stay afloat would have something to grasp onto. He did go down with the ship and he survived in the freezing-cold water long enough to be rescued.

214. One of the founders of the Kellogg's Company, which makes several popular cereals, John H. Kellogg, wasn't properly educated as a child because his parents didn't believe their kids needed education, as they were certain that Christ would come back before they grew up. Despite that background, John went on to get a medical degree and he founded a food company whose products are eaten in millions of homes.

215. An Aquatic Biologist named Tim Wong, of the San Francisco California Academy of Sciences, personally repopulated and saved the California Pipeline Swallowtail butterfly species by breeding them in a greenhouse behind his house.

216. After Leland Stanford and his wife lost their fifteen year old son unexpectedly, they decided that the only thing they could do for him was to memorialize him. They therefore founded Stanford University, a place where California's children could also be their children.

217. Roger Lausier almost drowned in 1965, but he was saved by a woman named Alice Blaise. Nine years afterwards, Lausier was on a raft on the same beach when he pulled a drowning man out of the water, and he later realized that he had saved Alice's husband.

218. The record for a human intentionally staying awake without the use of any stimulants is held by sixteen year old high school student Randy Gardner. He stayed awake for eleven days and twenty four minutes, in 1965. That's 265 hours straight.

219. On February 2, 2017, a world record for visiting every country in the world in the fastest time was set by twenty seven year old Cassie De Pecol from Connecticut. She left on July 24, 2015, and visited all 196 countries in just eighteen and a half months.

220. In 1984, Jack Lalanne, known also as the "Godfather of Fitness," towed seventy rowboats with passengers in them from Queensway Bridge to the ship Queen Mary while shackled, handcuffed, and fighting winds and currents. He achieved this on his seventieth birthday.

221. The first successful penile transplant was performed on May 15, 2016, in the United States. The recipient was sixty four year old Thomas Manning, from Massachusetts. The surgery lasted around fifteen hours and they used the penis from a deceased donor.

222. Sanduk Ruit, who is a doctor in Nepal, has restored the vision of over one hundred thousand people in the developing world.

223. In October, 2016, in Serbia, a great number of natural snowballs showed up on a beach. They spanned ten miles (seventeen kilometers) and ranged in size from tennis balls to being up to almost one meter wide. It was an unusual phenomenon where pieces of ice were formed and then rolled by wind and water until they became snowballs.

224. "127 Sale" is known as the world's longest yard sale. It took place between August 4 and August 7 of 2016 and extended over 621 miles (1,000 kilometers) throughout four American states: Covington, Kentucky, Gadsden, and Alabama. People selling goods lined the roadside along the US Highway 127 and the Lookout Mountain Parkway.

225. In 1994, a man named Tony Cicoria was standing next to a public telephone when he was struck by lightning. A nurse, who was waiting there to use the same phone, resuscitated him. Shortly after his recovery, he noticed that his head became flooded with music and decided to get a piano; he is now a successful composer and performer.

226. Jadarite is a type of mineral that was discovered in a Serbian mine. It has the same chemical composition as Kryptonite, the one described in the Superman movies.

227. A violin that uses three strands of golden silk spun by an Australian golden orb spider has been developed at Imperial College London. To customize different sounds, the composite material of silk fibers and a binding agent can actually be mixed and used to improve or vary the acoustic properties of the instrument.

228. Bill Morgan, an Australian truck driver, is one of the luckiest people alive. He was involved in a near-fatal truck accident and had a heart attack. He was clinically dead for more than fourteen minutes and survived; he then was in a coma for twelve days and made his way out of it. He then won the lottery twice. With the first winning ticket, he won a car worth $17,000; and during a reenactment for a Melbourne TV show, he purchased another ticket and won a jackpot of $170,000.

229. 105-year-old French cyclist Robert Marchand set a world record on January 4, 2017, for the longest distance cycled in one hour at the Velodrome just outside of Paris. The record was set in the 105+ age category, which was created especially for him. He rode almost fourteen miles (twenty three kilometers) in an hour.

230. A man named László Polgár created a method to raise child prodigies. Later on, he wrote a book on it, married a language teacher, and they both raised the world's best and second-best chess players.

231. There is a picture of a kingfisher diving into water without making a splash. It was taken by wildlife photographer Alan McFadyen after spending 420 hours and taking 720 thousand photos over a six year period.

232. Toldo was a loyal cat from Northeast Italy who visited the grave of his dead owner for more than a year, at times bringing gifts like plastic cups and twigs.

233. On February 5, 1869, the world's largest gold nugget ever was found near Denali, Victoria, in Australia. It weighed 159 pounds (seventy two kilograms) and measured two feet by one foot (0.6 by 0.3 meters). It was shipped to the bank of England after melting it into ingots.

234. In 1985, a hospital collapsed after a magnitude eight earthquake hit Mexico City. Four new born babies were trapped and survived for a week under rubble. They are known as the miracle babies as they survived without human contact, nourishment or water for seven days.

235. On September 9, 1999, at 9:09 AM, Nicholas Steven Waddle was born, also weighing in at nine pounds nine ounces (around four kilograms).

236. About 20,000 bees followed and swarmed a sixty eight year old grandmother's car for two days in West Wales. The bees were actually trying to rescue their queen bee, which unbeknownst to her, had hitched a ride in her Mitsubishi Outlander. Beekeepers were brought in to safely remove them.

237. Belgian national Stefaan Engels, at age forty nine, ran a record setting marathon in 2010 for 365 consecutive days. He started in Belgium and finished in Barcelona, running 9,321 miles (15,000 kilometers), and crossing seven countries along the way.

238. The only man to be struck by lightning seven times according to Guinness World Records was the ex-park ranger Roy C. Sullivan. He suffered a lost toenail, lost eyebrows, a shoulder injury, leg burns, an ankle injury, chest and stomach burns, and had his hair set on fire twice.

239. A dog named Bobby walked over 2,485 miles (4,000 kilometers) across the US to reunite with his owners after he was separated from them on a family road trip.

240. In the Black Sea, there is a particular spot that preserves shipwrecks so well that scientists were able to see the builders' chisel marks in the wood. Forty one well-preserved ships were discovered there, which date back from the 9th century until the 19th century.

241. The longest engagement on record lasted sixty seven years. Octavio Guillen and Adriana Martinez were both eighty-two years old when they finally got married in June of 1969, in Mexico City.

242. In 2005, a newborn baby was abandoned in a forest in Kenya. After two days, a stray dog found the baby and took him all the way back to her own litter of puppies.

243. A man named Larry Walters attached forty five helium-filled weather balloons to a lawn chair and took off from San Pedro, Los Angeles, on July 2, 1992. He flew into controlled airspace near LAX airport and landed forty five minutes later on some power lines in Long Beach. Even though he was unhurt, he had to pay a $1,500 fine.

244. Alex's Lemonade Stand is a foundation started by Alexandra Scott after being diagnosed with neuroblastoma. In 2000, when she was four, she held a fundraiser with a lemonade stand in her front yard and raised $2,000. By the time of her death, in 2004, at the age of eight, she had raised more than one million dollars with the help of supporters from around the world.

245. In 2005, a man named Don Macpherson with a PhD. in glass science was playing ultimate Frisbee one day in Santa Cruz, California, when his friend asked him if he could wear the sunglasses that he made himself. The friend immediately told him that he was no longer color blind.

246. In 2014, the world record for the highest altitude free fall jump was set by American computer scientist Alan Eustace, even though he was in his late 50's. He fell from an altitude of 25.7 miles (41.4 kilometers), reaching speeds of 821.5 miles (1,323 kilometers) per hour. The total descent lasted for four minutes and twenty seven seconds.

247. In 1998, construction worker Travis Bogumill was accidentally shot with a nail gun, causing a 3.25 inch (8.25 centimeter) nail to go right into his skull, which got stuck in the area of the brain that usually involves processing math. After removing the nail, he was completely fine, except his math skills weren't what they used to be.

248. The United States Postal Service handles approximately 47% of the world's mail volume.

249. The North Pole hosts the coldest marathon on Earth every year. Runners have to dress in thermal layers, windproof pants, and goggles due to the extreme temperatures, which are usually below zero when they run the twenty six miles (forty two kilometers).

250. Once a terminal patient was pronounced dead, but brain activity continued for about ten minutes. Doctors from the University of Western Ontario observed the unusual event and had no explanation for it.

251. Robert Landsburg was an American photographer who on May 18, 1980, documented the eruption of Mt. Saint Helens. It dawned on him that he couldn't outrun the clouds of volcanic ash that were coming towards him, so he chose to preserve his record by rewinding the film, enclosing his equipment in its proper case, and then laying his body over the case to protect it. Seventeen days later, he was found dead, but his work was preserved, and it was used by geologists to study key details of the eruption.

252. Dr. Duncan MacDougall from Haverhill once tried to demonstrate that the human soul had weight, so he placed dying patients on a giant scale. Amazingly, at the exact moment of death, there was a slight decrease in weight.

253. A man with a Liverpool FC tattoo on his leg with the club motto "you'll never walk alone" had his lower leg amputated after a combat injury in Afghanistan. The surgery unknowingly cut his tattoo to read "you'll never walk." Luckily, the man got a prosthetic leg and now even runs marathons.

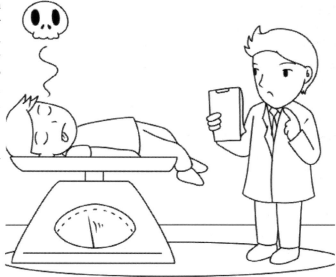

254. In 2012, a cat fell from a nineteen-story window in Boston and incredibly survived. The animal literally only walked away with a bruised chest.

255. Located in a small town just north of Munich, the Von Schesteffan Brewery has been brewing beer uninterruptedly for almost a thousand years, withstanding four fires, three plagues, and a major earthquake.

256. The body of a man and a bear were found dead next to one another in 1883 with the area around them trashed. It's believed that both of them fought till the death.

257. Violet Jessop worked as a ship nurse on the Britannic, the Olympic, and the Titanic. The Olympic collided with a warship and nearly sank. The Titanic hit an iceberg and sank. And the Britannic hit an underwater mine and sank. Yet Violet survived all three.

258. There is a service dog named Opal that not only leads her blind owner around, but she has also become a guide dog to the family's previous guide dog, Edward. Edward had taken care of the owner for six years, but he had his eyes removed after developing cataracts.

259. In theory, a single gram or 0.35 ounces of DNA could hold about 445 exabytes of data, and that's enough capacity to store all the data held by all major tech corporations combined, including Google and Facebook.

260. Dr. Bhakti Yadav is a ninety one year old Indian gynecologist who has been treating patients for decades. She started her career in 1948, just a year after India's independence.

261. In August of 2016, a Tasmanian woman gave birth to her first baby at sixty three years old, making her Australia's oldest new mother.

262. On March 12, 1912, Juliette Gordon Low founded the Girl Scouts in Savannah, Georgia. Today, there are about 2.7 million Girl Scouts, 1.9 million girl members, and 800,000 adult members.

263. Greyfriars Bobby is a dog that sat by his owner's grave in Scotland for fourteen years until he eventually died.

264. Dennis Morin, a fifty four year old from Quebec, used a river board to swim along the Yukon River, covering 1,988 miles (3,200 kilometers) in a mere seventy five days. He swam for six hours per day on average, and he only took ten days off to rest during the whole period.

265. Back in 1962, Tom Monaghan, the founder of Domino's Pizza, met his wife on his very first pizza delivery.

266. The youngest person to ever climb Mount Everest was Jordan Romero, in 2010, at the age of thirteen. While at the summit, he called his mom from a satellite phone and left a rabbit's foot there. He also planted seeds a Buddhist monk gave him at a monastery.

267. A small bird called an Arctic tern was spotted in 2016, migrating from the English coast to Antarctica, and then flying back again. It flew 59,000 miles (96,000 kilometers) in total, which turned out to be the longest recorded migration. That's the same as flying around the Earth's circumference twice, and then adding another 9,900 miles (16,000 kilometers).

268. People in love can simultaneously match their heartbeats simply by gazing into one another's eyes.

269. Scientists discovered an abandoned termite mound in the Miombo Woodland area of Central Africa that is thought to be more than 2,200 years old.

270. A man named Walter Orthmann from Brazil holds the Guinness World Record for the longest career with one company. He started working for Industrias Renaux S.A. back in 1938 and continues to work for the company, which is now called "RenauxView," as of April 2, 2018.

271. Levi Mayhew was a terminally ill six year old boy who gave up his own Make-A-Wish Foundation gift by giving it to a little girl who was writing Levi letters of encouragement. She went to Florida with a cutout photo of Levi on all the rides.

272. Former President Richard Nixon was able to play five instruments: the piano, the saxophone, the clarinet, the accordion, and the violin.

273. A two and a half year old boy named Michelle Funk fell into a creek near her home in Salt Lake City on June 10, 1986. She was rescued an hour later, but she had no pulse and wasn't breathing. Doctors put her on a heart lung bypass machine and rewarmed her blood. Amazingly, when her blood finally warmed to seventy-seven degrees Fahrenheit (twenty five degrees Celsius), she woke up and is still living to this day.

274. James Buchanan, the 15th President of the United States, used to buy slaves with his own money in order to free them.

275. Phyllis Penzo had a humble job waiting tables in Yonkers, New York at Sal's Pizzeria, when in April, 1984, a customer asked her to pick numbers for a lottery ticket. Robert Cunningham, the customer in question, ended up winning a six million dollar prize, and the gentleman that he was, he split the prize with Penzo, giving her three million dollars.

276. The world's largest model railroad is Northlandz in Flemington, New Jersey. It has over eight miles (thirteen kilometers) of track and lifelike scenery, with 3,000 tiny buildings, and over thirty nine feet (twelve meters) of bridges. It has 100 trains, 400 bridges, and over 500,000 tiny trees.

277. The world record for the longest distance pulled by a horse while fully engulfed in flames is held by Joseph Toedtling, from Austria. He traveled 0.3 miles (half a kilometer) completely on fire on June 27, 2015.

278. In 2001, a boy named Jessie Arbogast was attacked by a seven foot (2.1 meter) bull shark. His uncle not only saved Jesse from the shark, but he also dived back in, seized the shark, and wrestled it to shore where a ranger shot it, so they could retrieve the severed arm of his nephew. The arm was pried from its gullet and was placed on ice, then rushed to the hospital. Incredibly, it was sewed back on successfully.

279. Thirty eight year old Shen Sing Sung was at home in High Bay province, China, when, on October 29, 2012, thirty to fifty thugs showed up and attacked him on the orders of a property developer who wanted his land. Shen was a Kung fu expert, and as the thugs forced their way into his house, he bravely fought them off and knocked a few of them unconscious. He succeeded in defending his home as the rest of the thugs retreated.

280. In cities all around the world, street dogs have learned how to navigate through traffic, wait to use crosswalks during a red light, and even ride public transportation.

281. The most credentialed person in history is Michael Nicholson, from Michigan. He has one bachelor degree, two associate degrees, twenty two master degrees, three specialist degrees, and one doctoral degree.

282. The most people that can fit into a classic model Mini according to the Guinness World Records is twenty seven. It was achieved on May 18, 2014, by Dani and the Miniskirts in Brighton, England.

283. A seventy five pound (thirty four kilogram) natural pearl was found by a Filipino fisherman in a giant clam. He kept it hidden under his bed for ten years as a good luck charm. The pearl is 170,000 carats.

284. In Boston Harbor and Massachusetts Bay, the seawater has been found to contain tiny traces of caffeine. There are approximately 140 to 1,600 nanograms in Boston Harbor and five to seventy one nanograms in Massachusetts Bay.

285. Frane Selak has received the name "Fortunate Frank" for his incredible life. Throughout his life, he survived a train crash that killed seventeen, he was blown out of a plane that killed nineteen, and survived a bus accident at the age of four. He has also been in two car explosions, was hit by a bus, and had a close call with a truck. In 2003, he went on to win the lottery.

286. Four year old Marina Chapman was kidnapped from her home in 1954 in Colombia, and was then abandoned in the jungle. That's where she experienced what would put a Tarzan story to shame. Weeper capuchin monkeys took her in and raised her, and she spent the next five years sharing food, sleeping, and battling predators or rival groups of monkeys alongside her adopted wild family.

287. The longest marriage ever recorded lasted eighty six years. The North Carolina couple, named Zelmyra and Herbert Fisher, got married on May 13, 1924, and stayed together until Herbert passed away in 2011, at 105 years old.

288. A man named Bill Haast, aka the snake man, was bitten by over one hundred snakes in his life. He injected himself with snake venom every day for sixty years so he could build up immunity. With his antibody blood, he was able to save twenty one people who had been bitten by snakes.

289. If you gather and melt down together all the gold that was ever mined in the world, it would fill about 3.5 Olympic-size pools.

290. The "Elide Fire Ball" is a fire extinguisher that you just throw or roll at the fire from a safe distance. The ball will self-activate after contacting fire for about three to ten seconds, extinguishing the surrounding area.

291. After watching the movie "Cannonball Run," Ken Imhoff fell in love with Lamborghini cars, so he spent seventeen years building a Lamborghini Countach in his basement. He eventually put the car up for sale on eBay and sold to the highest bidder in Florida for $89,000 US. It cost him $65,000 to build it.

292. Because of the extremely high ductility of gold, a single ounce of gold, which is twenty eight grams, can be stretched into a wire that is about fifty six miles (ninety kilometers) long.

293. Pemba Dorje, a Nepalese climber and also a Sherpa, holds the record for the fastest ascent of Mount Everest. In 2004, he climbed Everest in only eight hours and ten minutes.

Animals

294. The comb and wattles on chickens actually help them stay cool. These are the dangly pieces of red skin under their chins. The blood circulates from the body into the comb and waddle, where the heat can more easily be transferred to the air.

295. Goats are herbivores that are often the target of carnivores. Due to evolution, they have gained horizontal, rectangular slit pupils as a line of defense which helps them run away faster.

296. Studies have shown that crows can be as smart as great apes. They are able to show imagination and anticipation of possible future events as well as being able to solve problems involving abstract reasoning.

297. When put in places without oxygen, naked mole-rats can stay alive for up to eighteen minutes. They can use a process of metabolism that's typically associated with plants, where their bodies start to run on fructose which can be metabolized without oxygen.

298. Certain shark species can live up to a hundred years old. Even though most of them live twenty to thirty years in the wild, some species like the spiny dogfish can live beyond a hundred years.

299. Boa constrictors have a natural ability to sense its prey's heartbeat while killing them. If it senses a heartbeat, the snake will actually add more pressure until it feels no heartbeat at all.

300. Horses have panoramic vision given that their eyes can move independently.

301. The oldest dog ever recorded according to the Guinness World Records was named Bluey, an Australian cattle dog from Rochester Victoria, in Australia. He was born in 1910 and was put to sleep on November 14, 1939, living for twenty nine years and five months.

302. Leeches have interesting bodies. They have thirty two segments each having their own brain, nine pairs of testes, and two sets of reproductive organs.

303. Horses can stand in snow without the cold damaging their hooves or lower limbs because the part of their legs below the knees is just bones and tendons for the most part. If horses are in extremely cold temperatures, their hooves have a mechanism for sending blood that keeps their whole bodies warm.

304. When goldfish stay indoors, they become paler than their counterparts who get natural light regularly. Keeping a pet goldfish in total darkness at all times will in fact result in the death of the chromatophores, which usually produce the pigmentation in the fish, and your goldfish will turn almost white in color.

305. Pope Gregory IX vilified cats in the thirteenth century, by claiming that they were Satan's incarnations. People started to slaughter cats, and as a result, rat populations increased, and ultimately, that contributed to the quick spread of the Black Death.

306. After they are ingested, some insect species, including the pea aphid, will self-destruct by exploding in order to either frighten or kill their enemies.

307. Due to their sonar abilities, dolphins have their own form of X-ray vision. They can use it to see through other sea creatures, and under the sea bed. So if you swim with dolphins, you'll see their skin, but they'll be able to see your skeleton.

308. Unlike our own teeth, Narwhal's tusks are actually soft on the outside and gradually get hard and dense on the inside.

309. Compared to big cats like tigers and lions, dragonflies have more than four times the chance of catching their prey. When dragonflies target prey, it's estimated that they have a success rate of 95% when it comes to catching it, which puts them at the top of the list of the most deadly hunters in the world.

310. Sometimes, male ring-tailed lemurs have what're known as stink fights. It involves applying secretions from their glands onto their comically long tails, and then wafting the foul smelling liquid at their rivals.

311. Because of the position of their eyes on their heads, donkeys have a visual field that covers almost 360 degrees. They can actually see all four of their feet at the same time.

312. The only subspecies of cats that are able to roar are leopards, jaguars, tigers, and lions. The other felines cannot roar because they lack the elastic ligament that connects the bones that support the larynx, which is present in the four subspecies mentioned.

313. Tigers have a reputation as the most vengeful animals in the entire animal world. There are reports of them stalking animals or even humans who have wronged them in one way or another, for several days.

314. When exposed under ultraviolet light, scorpions glow a bright blue green.

315. Bearded vultures like to wear makeup. They modify their appearance by rubbing their necks and heads in iron-rich soil, changing their white color feathers to a bright reddish-orange color. The older and more socially dominant birds wear the most makeup to show off and appear more intimidating to others.

316. The highest percentage of body fat of any animal is found in the blue whale at more than 35%. They can weigh up to 180 tons which would mean sixty three tons of pure fat.

317. Raccoons are extremely intelligent creatures. They can open complex locks in under ten tries and even repeat the process if the locks are rearranged or turned upside down. They can also remember solutions to problems for up to three years.

318. Elephants' tusks can weigh up to 200 pounds (ninety kilograms) and grow up to ten feet (three meters) long.

319. The most efficient swimmers in the ocean are jellyfish, as they consume 48% less oxygen than any other swimming animal.

320. By counting the number of rings on the horns of a mountain goat, you can tell its age. It has an average lifespan of nine to twelve years.

321. In order to blend in with their surroundings, squids, octopuses, and cuttlefish have the ability to change the color of their skin in the blink of an eye.

322. Leopards are solitary animals. They like to hunt and live alone and only get together with other leopards to mate. Moreover, they can eat things that are twice their size.

323. The Bornean bay cat is the rarest cat in the world. There have only ever been twelve captured between 1874 and 2002.

324. Almost every armadillo of the genus Dasypus bears quadruplets.

325. Although flying squirrels cannot fly, they can glide through the air for distances of up to 295 feet (ninety meters).

326. Jellyfish use the same orifice for eating as it does for pooping.

327. Sea scallops have about sixty bright blue colored eyes that help them detect light, dark, and motion.

328. It is known that baby elephants suck on their trunks for pleasure, just like human babies suck on their thumbs.

329. The largest feral hog population in the United States is found in Texas, with nearly 2.6 million wild hogs.

330. The axolotl is a type of salamander that never changes into an adult. For their whole lives, they remain in their larval stage and can even reproduce without reaching the adult phase.

331. The way mosquitoes find their victims is by detecting the carbon dioxide that comes from them. In fact, they can detect it from seventy feet (twenty two meters) away.

332. A grumble is the term used to refer to a group of pugs.

333. On February 18, 1930, Elm Farm Ollie was the first cow to fly in an airplane. She was also the first cow to be milked while flying in an airplane. The stunt was done at the International Air Exposition in St. Louis, Missouri, which is the dairy state of Wisconsin. They honor Elm Farm Ollie every year on February 18, otherwise known as Elm Farm Ollie Day, at the dairy festival in Mount Horeb, Wisconsin.

334. The Bagheera kiplingi is a vegetarian spider that lives in Southeastern Mexico and Northwestern Costa Rica.

335. The hedgehog was named as such because of its unusual foraging methods. When looking for small creatures like insects, worms, centipedes, snails, mice, frogs and snakes, it roots through hedges and undergrowth. In addition, they make a cute little pig-like sound, which is why they are called hogs.

336. Saltwater crocodiles are known to have a bite force of 5,000 psi which stands for pounds per square inch. They are second to the orca whale which can have a bite force of 19,000 psi.

337. There are only two hundred Amur leopard's left on the globe as of 2020. They are a rare subspecies of leopards that are only found in far east Russia.

338. According to an analysis of cat's tongues performed in 2006, their tongues do not have the taste receptors that react to sweet-tasting things. All feline species from the domestic house cat to lions or tigers cannot taste anything sweet.

339. When it comes to resisting nuclear radiation, cockroaches are not the toughest insect. Insects like the flower beetle have been proven to have higher nuclear radiation resistance.

340. The first documented venomous bird was the hooded pitohui bird from Papua New Guinea. The poison found in its feather and skin is the same poison usually found in dart frogs. It's the most powerful natural toxin known to man.

341. If you move a snail sixty five feet (twenty meters) or more, it most likely won't return because it will lose its sense of direction. The homing instincts of a snail only applies to short distances.

342. In order to incubate her eggs, the female Burmese python raises her body temperature by as much as seven degrees warmer than air temperature. To accomplish this, they hiccup repeatedly or have muscle spasms.

343. The only mammals that are capable of flying are bats. To be able to do so, they digest their food extremely fast, sometimes excreting within thirty to sixty minutes after eating, which helps them keep their weight down.

344. According to researchers at the Smithsonian, the brain of the smallest spiders fills up almost 80% of their total body cavity, including 25% of their legs.

345. The largest land crab is the coconut crab, which can grow over three feet (0.9 meters) long. It's also considered as the largest anthropoid, the group that includes insects, spiders, and crustaceans.

346. Pigeons can produce milk to feed their baby squabs.

347. The world's largest living amphibian is the Chinese giant salamander. It can grow up to six feet (1.8 meters) long and can weigh as much as 110 pounds (fifty kilograms).

348. There is a bird named the "Greater Honeyguide" which guides people to beehives. When the honey is taken out, the birds eat what's left in the hive.

349. From 1974 to 1978, there was a four year violent conflict between two communities of chimpanzees in Gombe Stream National Park, in Tanzania. It's known as the Gombe Chimpanzee War.

350. Insects don't breathe the same way that humans do. They have tiny openings in their body walls called spiracles as well as tiny air-filled tubes called trachea, from where they get the oxygen into their tissues.

351. There are some sea species that die soon after giving birth, such as the octopus, the squid, and the salmon. Usually, males die soon after fertilizing the females' eggs, while the females only live long enough to birth their young before dying.

352. Cats have sweat glands, but they mostly sweat through their paws. Because their skin is covered in fur, the amount of cooling that the sweat can provide them is minimal. The paw pads have the most sweat glands, so they sweat there mostly.

353. Cows have more than 800 different blood types.

354. Woodpeckers hit telephone poles and tree trunks with a force that's more than 1,000 times that of gravity, using just their beaks.

355. In the Moroccan sand desert of Erg Chebbi, there is a type of spider called the Cebrennus rechenbergi that uses its legs to do a rolling motion to escape dangerous situations. The spider looks like it's performing acrobatic flips over the desert floor.

356. A mantis shrimp has sixteen photoreceptive cones in its eyes. By comparison, humans just have three, which enable us to see the colors we know. This implies that the mantis shrimp has a considerably larger visual spectrum than we do.

357. Certain species of ants are known to use aphids (tiny sap sucking insects) to collect honeydew, which is released from the aphids' bodies. The ants literally domesticate and guard herds of aphids, and they use their antenna to milk them when they need honeydew for food.

358. If female ferrets don't mate whenever they go into heat, they will die. Estrogen is produced in their bodies in such high amounts when in heat, that it can cause their bone marrow to be progressively depressed, so that their bodies stop making blood cells.

359. Like humans, horses need to bear passports to travel internationally.

360. Fairy flies are the smallest insects known to man, and are native to Costa Rica's temperate forests. They are part of the wasp family, and are so tiny, they are hardly visible. Some are less than 0.0055 inches (0.14 millimeters) in length.

361. The zyzzyva is a beetle from the American tropical region that was discovered in Brazil in 1922, and it's a snouted beetle whose name appears last in several English dictionaries. Some suspect that it was given the name "zyzzyva" just so that it could hold that dictionary position.

362. When female dragonflies don't want to participate in mating rituals initiated by male dragonflies, they have been known to fake their own deaths.

363. Bloodhounds have 230 million scent receptors in the nose, which is about forty times the number of receptors in the human nose. For this reason, bloodhounds became the first animals in America to have their evidence considered admissible in courts of law.

364. Moray eels have a secondary set of jaws that are positioned inside their throats, apart from their standard teeth. The eels would have a difficult time swallowing their prey because they have narrow heads, but they are able to push the second set of teeth forward, using them to grip their prey and pull it inwards to their digestive system.

365. Certain animals engage in locomotor play, which has similarities with the game where children sled down steep slopes.

366. Apart from ostriches, other birds don't have bladders because this helps lower their weight so they can fly. Consequently, they can't urinate.

367. Before female aphids are even a body, many of them are usually already pregnant with their own babies. This is called the telescoping of generations, and it's a natural process that allows insect populations to rise very quickly.

368. A faceless fish was caught in Jervis Bay in May, 2017, by forty scientists from the Australian Government's Commonwealth Scientific. They learned that it was a typhonus nasus A, which was a kind of fish that hadn't been spotted in the area for more than a century.

369. The Hercules beetle, which is named after the demigod, can lift more than a hundred times its body weight, and is native to South and Central America.

370. Peacocks are only male, not female. Peafowl is the right word for the species. The females are peahens, and the males are peacocks. The females don't have the bright blue colors, are smaller than the male ones, and their feathers are usually grey, cream, or brown.

371. The embryo of the red-eyed tree frog has the ability to detect danger when it's threatened by a predator, and it can get itself out from the egg in seconds and drop away to safety, even if there are still several days remaining before it's actually supposed to hatch.

372. The unfertilized date stone beetle has strange breeding habits. It first gives birth to four or five males, mates with the first one, and eats the rest. After that, it gives birth to roughly seventy beetles, both male and females, and the offspring mate with each other.

373. Cicadas are flying insects that originate from Africa. They spend seventeen years of their lives sleeping, and then they wake up, spend a fortnight mating, and die afterwards.

374. Flamingos are tall creatures, standing between 3.94 and 4.92 feet (1.2 and 1.5 meters), but they only weigh between 3.9 and 7.9 pounds (1.8 and 3.6 kilograms). It's because of this remarkably low body density that they are able to stay in the air as they fly at speeds of about thirty seven miles (sixty kilometers) per hour.

375. Even though they look like rodents, elephant shrews aren't categorized as real shrews. They are insectivorous mammals, and they are believed to have more things in common with normal elephants than with actual shrews.

376. In the forests of Central and South America, army ants can build living bridges by linking their bodies to get over gaps and to create shortcuts in the rainforest.

377. There is a rubber-like layer known as eponychium around horse hooves that's meant to protect the womb and birth canals of mother horses from sharp hooves in pregnancy and during birth.

378. Milk from elephant seals has the same consistency as pudding. Its fat content is very high and it's extremely oily. Pups grow from nineteen pounds (nine kilograms) when they're born to 150 pounds (sixty eight kilograms) in a mere three weeks.

379. Flamingos use their webbed feet to stir mud in shallow waters, and they then take mouthfuls of the murk to eat. Their beaks contain a structure that acts as a filter, and extracts creatures such as small fishes, crustaceans, and planktons, which act as food for the flamingos. Flamingos are known for their pink color, but that's not their natural color. In reality, they are pale, almost white in color, but when they ingest beta carotene, which is a natural pigment from the crustaceans and the planktons that they eat, they develop a deeper pink color.

380. Porcupines have a natural buoyancy because they have lots of hollow quills.

381. The northern pseudoscorpion can survive without breathing for seventeen days. They live in the cold Yukon Territory.

382. Chickens are able to detect and see light in color shades better than humans. In addition, they have a better motion sensing ability than we do; this is important for farmers to know because artificial lights need to be avoided as they flicker and it may cause a flock to start fighting each other.

383. A new-born Chinese water deer can be so small and light after birth that you could hold it in one hand; but when they become adults, they can weigh as much as twenty eight pounds (thirteen kilograms) and grow fangs, making them look like a vampire deer.

384. Rabbits eat their own poop daily. They produce something called cecotropes, or night feces, which is some kind of nutrient rich special poop that is passed out of the body like normal stool, but a little different. The poop can later be re-ingested by the rabbit safely so that important nutrients can be reabsorbed.

385. The Leptotyphlops carlae is the world's smallest species of snake. They are found in the Caribbean island of Barbados. On average, an adult is less than four inches (ten centimeters) in length and is as skinny as a spaghetti noodle.

386. There are glands on the slow loris' inner elbow that secrete a poisonous toxin that they can use as both a weapon and a form of protection. The toxin can be sucked into its mouth, which gives it a poisonous bite. It is the only known venomous primate.

387. The humpback whale has black and white patterned undersides, which are distinctive for each whale. The shape and color patterns on their dorsal fins and flukes are equivalent to human fingerprints.

388. Giant anteaters don't have teeth, but they do have large tongues that can grow up to two feet (0.6 meters) in length. Their tongues are covered in tiny spines that point to the back of their throat and are coated with thick, sticky saliva. When they take an insect into their mouth, they crush them against the upper palate to ease digestion.

389. The Ayam Cemani is a type of chicken that is inky black from the tip of its comb to the end of its claws, with blue-blackish skin, jet black eyes, and a black tongue. The bird is covered in shimmering metallic black feathers and even its internal organs are black.

390. Cats have adapted to land on their feet from great heights. When they fall, they reach terminal velocity, turning their bodies so they can twist their paws under the body right before they land.

391. Dogs are able to watch more TV now than in the past, as flat screen TVs flicker at a lower rate at which canines are able to process.

392. Silkie chickens are known for having a calm and friendly temperament. They are considered ideal pets among the most docile of poultry.

393. One in two million lobsters can be blue, one in every three million can be yellowy-orange while white lobsters are one in a hundred million.

394. A study done by researchers at the Australian National University revealed that queen bees and ants can control their colonies' female offspring by emitting a special pheromone. The DNA of their daughters can be altered so the offspring are sterile and remain busy workers. When they are deprived of the pheromone, the worker bees and ants become more self-centered and lazy, and begin to lay eggs.

395. Mice don't really like cheese as much as we believe according to researchers from the UK's Manchester Metropolitan University. They actually have a preference for fruit and grains. The belief of them liking cheese so much was spread via pop culture and cartoons.

396. All members of the cat family, like tigers, have unique scents because their scent glands are naturally individualized. Because of this, cubs can locate their mothers and any cat can identify another individual cat.

397. Based on a study done by Japanese researcher Hiroshi Nittono in 2012, looking at images of cute animals at work, like puppies and pandas, improves your mood and boosts your attention to detail and overall performance.

398. Earthworms are simultaneous hermaphrodites. In other words, they have both male and female reproductive organs.

399. The only two mammals to lay eggs are the duck billed platypus and the echidna.

400. According to National Geographic, 150,000 muscle units are found in an elephant's trunk.

401. Every two hours dolphins shed their entire outer layer of their skin.

402. The leatherback sea turtle has its esophagus lined with papillae, sharp prongs that enable it to dine on jellyfish.

403. According to the Guinness World Records, the smallest dog in terms of length is a female Chihuahua from Florida named Brandy. As of January 31, 2005, she only measured 5.9 inches (15.2 centimeters) from the nose to the tip of her tail.

404. In every 300 calico cats, only one is a male.

405. The vampire fish use their long, sharp fangs to impale their prey. Their fangs can grow as long as six inches (fifteen centimeters).

406. Dolphins aren't able to chew their food. They only use their teeth to grip food that they will shake and rub on the ocean floor to tear it into smaller more manageable pieces.

407. Like humans, cats and dogs can be diagnosed with diabetes. According to estimations, one out of every one hundred dogs that reach the age of twelve years will develop diabetes. In cats, on the other hand, it's estimated that one in every 250 will develop the disease.

408. Skunks are able to spray their victims as far as ten feet (three meters) away.

409. Female loggerhead turtles sometimes return thousands of kilometers back to the beach where they hatch their eggs.

410. The largest rodent in the world is the capybara, which is native of many South American countries. These web-toed creatures can grow more than 4.2 feet (1.3 meters) long and weigh as much as 143 pounds (sixty-five kilograms).

411. Based on research done by the Max Planck Institute for Ornithology in Germany, the frigate bird is able to sleep while it's flying. It sleeps for about twelve seconds at a time, and often with only half its brain. In a twenty-four hour period for example, they can sleep about forty minutes.

412. N'kisi is an African grey parrot that has a 950 word vocabulary. When famous primatologist Jane Goodall went to meet the parrot, N'kisi had previously seen photos of her, so when they first met, N'kisi asked her: "Got a chimp?"

413. Fleas can hitch rides on earwigs to suck bat blood. In 2006, a team of entomologists analyzed the heart of Deer Cave in Malaysia's Gunung Mulu National Park and found earwigs covered in fleas. They found out that the fleas use earwigs as a shuttle to get to the cave's ceiling, where they can feed on the blood of hairless, naked bulldog bats.

414. To make them a little rough, the monarch butterfly has tiny scales of about 0.1 millimeters long that are arranged like roof shingles on their wings. They help to lift the butterfly more effectively. In fact, a group of aero-spaced researchers found that the scales boosted climbing efficiency between 16 to 82%.

415. Elephants have a natural fear of bees, so in developing countries, beehive fences are used to deter elephants, keeping them away from humans. This has reduced issues concerning humans and elephants by over 80%.

416. There's a fish called the black dragon fish that looks very similar to the creature from the Alien movies.

417. A type of frog known as the Southern Gastric-brooding frog turns its stomach into a womb. The female frogs swallow their own eggs and stop generating hydrochloric acid in the stomach so that they don't destroy their developing baby frogs. What's more interesting is that they birth their young ones through propulsive vomiting.

418. All mammals require fresh water in order to survive, including dolphins. It's believed that dolphins possess an advanced filtration system that allows them to extract additional salt from their urine in order to separate it from the saltwater that they ingest.

419. The fastest animal on Earth that travels on two legs is the ostrich. They are capable of running as fast as forty miles (sixty-four kilometers) an hour for brief periods, like when trying to escape from a predator or other danger. If they need to travel long distances, they can reach speeds of thirty miles (forty-eight kilometers) an hour.

420. The largest known beetle in the Amazon rainforest is the Titan beetle, known also as Titanus giganteus, measuring up to 6.5 inches (16.5 centimeters) long. Their mandibles are so strong that they can easily snap a pencil in half.

421. When frogs eat something really nasty, like a poisonous insect, some of them are able to throw up their entire stomachs inside out, so the nasty insect falls out. However, if it doesn't fall out completely, the frog will actually reach up with its forearms and stroke the inverted lining of its stomach, cleaning it off manually.

422. There is a native animal known as the racoon dog that is found only in East Asia. It looks like a racoon but is actually a dog.

423. The largest living beings ever to have lived on Earth are the blue whales. Their tongues alone can weigh as much as an elephant and their hearts as much as a car.

424. Marsha, a stray cat, kept an abandoned two month old baby alive by staying next to him, keeping him warm in freezing cold temperatures overnight.

425. When under threat, the kamikaze ants from Southeast Asia, as suggested by their name, will kill themselves. They have a toxic substance in their heads and in two large glands on the sides of their bodies that are filled with poison. Whenever they feel threatened, they literally explode their heads or rupture their bodies to spray the poison over the predator.

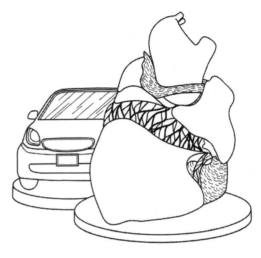

426. When elephants lose their mates, they can actually die of a broken heart. They may refuse to eat or lay down, shedding tears, until they starve to death.

427. In order to supplement its diet, an orca that resides in Marineland, Niagara Falls, has taught itself to throw up fish to entice seagulls to come to the surface of the pool. It then strikes at the birds and eats them. Four other whales living there have seen this trick, and they've started to copy it.

428. Kopi Luwak is the world's most expensive coffee. A cup of it can cost as much as $80. It's made from coffee beans that are partially digested and then pooped out by a creature called the civet. The digestive enzymes of the civet change the structure of the protein in the coffee beans, removing some of the acidity.

429. In the Wolong Nature Reserve in China, there is a center for pandas called the Hetaoping Research and Conservation Center for the Giant Panda. There, researchers would dress up as pandas to prepare panda cubs for their release into the wild. By wearing these costumes, they try to deter the babies from getting attached to humans.

430. Giraffes only need to sleep for thirty minutes a day.

431. Kangaroos often lick their arms until their fur and skin is sopping wet as a way to stay cool in hot temperatures. The wind hitting their arms then causes the saliva to evaporate, cooling them off.

432. Coral is actually an animal species, not a plant.

433. There is a real job position in China as a panda nanny. The job entails spending 365 days a year with panda babies for an annual income of thirty two thousand dollars.

434. In South Africa, elephants are being trained for bio detection. Scientists want to see if they can use their sharp sense of smell to look for poachers, land mines, and explosives. Elephants have 1,948 genes dedicated to smelling, while dogs have 811, and humans less than 400.

435. There is a little mouse-like mammal known as the antechinus that mates so much that it actually kills itself. Males live less than a year, frantically mating like crazy, until their bodies literally start to fall apart.

436. Based on studies performed by researchers at the National Hansen's Disease Program in Baton Rouge, Louisiana, the armadillo is one of the few mammals that harbor the bacteria that cause leprosy.

437. The most valuable cow in the world, Missy, is worth $1.2 million. She produces 50% more milk than other cows and has superior genetics, making her embryos in high demand.

438. In order to help her hatchlings emerge, the Nile crocodile rolls and squeezes her eggs in her mouth.

439. Canine compulsive disorder, or CCD, is a condition that affects dogs that is characterized by excessive repetition of an action or behavior and can vary depending on the context. The condition is actually very similar to human compulsive disorders and is likely to be a coping mechanism for when the dog sees a situation as stressful.

440. Surprisingly, crocodiles have the ability to climb trees and do it regularly.

441. The Bullockornis was a prehistoric bird that grew up to 8.2 feet (2.5 meters) tall and weighed approximately 550 pounds (250 kilograms). It was nicknamed the demon duck of doom.

442. Spiders cannot digest solid food. They need to turn their prey into a liquid form before actually eating them. To do so, they emanate digestive enzymes from their stomach onto the victim's body. Once the enzymes break down the tissues of the prey, they suck up the liquid remains.

443. Before 1900, and according to the Cheetah Conservation Fund, the cheetah population was over 100,000. But from then on, the cheetah has gone extinct in over twenty countries, with only 7,100 cheetahs remaining worldwide.

444. There are over 3,500 species of mosquitoes. They vary in sizes, appetites, and dispositions.

445. There are killer whales living in captivity with dolphins that have learned their complex language, and have started using it with each other.

446. The male African lion uses its urine to mark and protect his territory. The area can be as big as 100 square miles (259 square kilometers).

447. Bedbugs don't have wings so they can't fly or jump. However, they can live for months without food.

448. The first occurrence of identical bird twins ever was reported in the emu.

449. The only iguana in the world that feeds underwater is the Galapagos iguana. They are able to hold their breath for up to half an hour and dive up to 29.8 feet (9.1 meters).

450. An average of 257 gallons (972 liters) of urine is produced by the fin whale each day.

451. Some species of baby whales are born with hair, but they often lose it over the first several days or weeks of birth.

452. About 427 species of mammals, 1,300 species of birds, 378 species of reptiles, and more than 400 species of amphibians live in the Amazon rainforest.

453. The female Tasmanian devil is able to have up to fifty joeys or pups in one litter. They all have to struggle to attach themselves to one of the four available teats in the mother's pouch. Those that don't attach to one don't survive.

454. Bowhead whales are considered as one of the longest-living mammals in the world. In 2007, a whale was caught off the Alaskan coast, having a thirty five inch long head of an explosive harpoon inserted deep in its neck. The projectile was manufactured in Massachusetts around 1890, which suggested that the whale survived a hunt over a century ago.

455. A prickle is the term used to refer to a group of porcupines.

456. On average, a koala sleeps twenty hours a day.

457. In 2001, a study done by Diane Reese of the Osborn Laboratory of Marine Sciences at the New York Aquarium determined that dolphins actually recognize themselves when looking in a mirror; they also notice changes in their appearance. In previous studies, only higher primates such as humans and chimpanzees had demonstrated self-recognition in mirrors.

458. The Secretary bird is a predator bird that kills its prey, mostly poisonous snakes and big lizards, by stomping on its head until it's either incapacitated or dead. Its kick packs a punch of up to 195 Newton, which is equal to roughly five times the body weight of the bird itself.

459. Canada geese generally nest in the same region that their parents did. In fact, they often nest in the same nest every year.

460. Studies performed at Cornell University revealed that the tiger beetle runs so fast, it can no longer see where it's going. So in order to avoid obstacles, it has to use its antennae.

461. There are some whale species that go through menopause, such as the short-finned pilot whale and the orca or killer whale.

462. It's known that elephants can favor one tusk over the other, making one shorter than the other.

463. Newborn giraffes measure about six feet (1.83 meters) tall, making them taller than most humans.

464. Although bison may look slow and not very agile, they can run at thirty five miles (fifty six kilometers) per hour and jump as high as six feet (1.8 meters) off the ground.

465. Ovulation of giant female pandas occurs once a year during the spring, for a period of two to four days.

466. Based on research conducted by Dr. Scott Pitnick of Bowling Green State University in Ohio, the tiny fruit fly, known as Drosophila bifurca, develops big testicles that make up almost 11% of its body weight in order to produce a great amount of sperm. They can even produce sperm that are more than twenty times the size of their own bodies.

467. Crocodiles mainly live in salt or brackish water, while alligators prefer to live in freshwater habitats.

468. The largest egg laid by the whale shark measured twelve inches (thirty one centimeters) long, five inches (fourteen centimeters) wide, and three inches (nine centimeters) thick.

469. It is impossible for cats to move their jaw sideways or grind their teeth because their lower jaws are attached to their upper jaws.

470. A group of flamingos is called a flamboyance of flamingos. Other names to refer to them as a group are a stand, a colony, or a regiment.

471. The largest leatherback sea turtle ever found according to National Geographic was 8.5 feet (2.2 meters) long and weighed 2,019 pounds (916 kilograms).

472. A new species of frog was discovered by scientists in Costa Rica. They called it Diane's bare-hearted glass frog and it looks exactly like Jim Henson's Muppet, Kermit the Frog.

473. There is a rare bioluminescent sea creature called the giant pyrosome that is made up of dozens of smaller creatures that reproduce through cloning. These animals are able to regenerate injured or missing body parts, and live particularly long lives.

474. In June 2016, a leopard shark at the Reef HQ Great Barrier Reef Aquarium, in Australia, had a "virgin birth." Even though she hadn't had any contact with a male shark for years, she ended up laying forty one eggs; three of them hatched into healthy female pups. Virgin births are very rare but aren't unheard of in sharks.

475. Whisker stress is a feeling that cats can experience when eating or drinking out of a bowl that is too small. As whiskers are very sensitive to pressure, any time they come close to something, it triggers a sensation in your cat. If you see your cat trying to scoop out food with their paws, it might mean that they have whisker stress.

476. Cheetah cubs have very long hairs that run from their neck all the way down to the base of their tail. It's called a mantle and it makes a cheetah cub look like a honey badger, protecting them from other animals like lions and hyenas.

477. In the rainforests of Southeast Asia, there are snakes that can fling themselves from trees and fly through the air. They can adapt their body shape to generate the aerodynamic forces needed to fly.

478. Prairie dogs have their own complex language. They have different calls depending on the type of predator and they also make sentences that describe the predator.

479. In order to impress a mate or to get away from a predator, octopuses can break off a limb when fighting. Some of them even eat their own arms once in a while, which some scientists believe may be due to a disease of some sort.

480. Mice can sing just like birds. It's just imperceptible to human ears.

481. One of the most venomous insects in the world is the Maricopa harvester ant. Twelve stings from such ants can kill a 4.4 pound (two kilogram) animal.

482. Oysters are born male, but they can switch their gender and become female when they want to lay eggs, and afterwards, they can either stay female or switch back to male.

483. Seahorse babies have no stomach. Their digestive system has been described as inefficient, meaning that they must eat a lot in order to stay properly nourished. A single seahorse baby can eat as much as 3,000 pieces of food a day.

484. One of the loudest animals on the planet is the blue whale. They emit a series of pulses, groans, and moans that can be heard up to 994 miles (1,600 kilometers) away.

485. In 2002, Daphne Soares from the University of Maryland conducted a study on American alligators. She found that these animals can orient themselves to the ripples created by a single drop of water, even in complete darkness. As their faces and bodies are covered with tiny bumps, they are far more sensitive than our own fingertips.

486. Mr. Splashy Pants is a humpback whale that has been tracked by Greenpeace since 2008.

487. The reason why flamingos are pink is because the algae and crustaceans like shrimp and prawns that they eat contain pigments called carotenoids. Their liver works to break down the carotenoids into pink and orange pigment molecules that get deposited in their feathers, bill, and legs.

488. A study published in the Journal of Science demonstrated that lizards' sleep patterns are very similar to humans'. Researchers put electrodes on five lizards' brains while sleeping. The results showed that they go through slow wave sleep, sharp waves, ripples, and rapid eye movement, or REM sleep.

489. The average sloth travels only 123 feet (38 meters) per day. To put it into perspective, that is less than half the length of a football field.

490. The Tapinoma sessile, also known as the odorous house ant, smells like rotten coconut when their bodies are crushed.

491. The largest snail ever found according to the Guinness World Records weighed two pounds (0.9 kilograms) and measured 15.5 inches (39.3 centimeters) from snout to tail. It was found in Sierra Leone, in 1976, and it was named Gee Geronimo.

492. Elephants are one of the few animals that can feel post-traumatic stress disorder.

493. Lobsters have little urine nozzles under their eyes. When they fight or flirt with each other, they squirt urine at each other's faces.

494. The garfish or needlefish has greenish-blue-colored bones, which is caused by a pigment called biliverdin.

495. Owls have three eyelids. The upper lid closes when the owl blinks; the lower one closes when the owl sleeps; and the third one is a thin layer of tissue that closes diagonally from the inside-out, as a way to clean and protect the surface of its eye.

496. Male kangaroos are able to jump as high as ten feet (three meters) and hop up to thirty seven miles (sixty kilometers) per hour.

497. During spring, when the weather is warm enough, adult muskox can shed up to 7.9 pounds (3.6 kilograms) of underfur.

498. Found in Central and South Africa, the trap-jaw ant can snap its jaw shut at a speed of up to 145 miles (233 kilometers) per hour. To put that into perspective, that's 2,300 times faster than the blink of an eye.

499. There are some insects that don't have noses and use their genitalia to smell instead.

500. In 2006, a study done by Alex Thornton and Katherine McAuliffe at Cambridge University showed how adult meerkats teach their youngest pups how not to be stung by scorpions, one of their main sources of prey. First, they bring dead scorpions to the pups; then they bring ones that are alive but injured; and, eventually, they work their way up to live prey.

501. The snapping shrimp is able to regenerate its snapping claw. If they lose the snapping claw, the missing claw regenerates as a smaller claw, growing to become the new snapping claw.

502. There are some turtles that can breathe through their butts as well as their mouths, such as the Australian Fitzroy River turtle and the North American eastern painted turtle.

503. According to a study done by PhD student Courtney Marneweck, at the School of Life Sciences at the University of KwaZulu-Natal in South Africa, rhinoceroses use communal defecation sites, meaning they poop together. The male rhinos can actually figure out how many other males are around and the reproductive state of female mates from this site.

504. When poison dart frogs are bred in captivity, they are completely non-toxic. In fact, wild caught frogs progressively lose their poisons in captivity. In order to create their toxins, they need certain chemicals that are present in the insects they eat in the wild. So when in captivity, they don't get the same insects as their food, hence they are no longer poisonous.

505. Fish have taste buds on their tongues, lips and bodies. Taste buds need moisture to work and because fish live in water all the time, taste buds can survive not only in the inside of their mouths, but also on the exterior skin of their flanks and fins.

506. Kangaroos cannot move backwards due to their appendages which impede them to move in reverse. However, their muscular legs, big feet, and tails are a great combination for them to move forward and hop effectively.

507. Whale milk contains a high percentage of fat which makes it very thick. In fact, it has the same consistency of toothpaste. The high fat content not only helps nourish the whale calf, but it also prevents the milk from dissolving in the water.

508. The size of a frog's tongue is almost a third of the length of its entire body. If humans had the same sized tongues, they would reach the belly button.

509. Mr. Stubbs, an alligator in Arizona, had his tail bitten off by a bigger alligator, so he had a prosthetic tail made out of silicone rubber that attaches to his back legs with nylon straps.

510. In order to protect their eyes from blowing sand, camels are equipped with three eyelids. The upper and lower eyelids have eyelashes; the third one is a thin membrane that they can see through even in a sandstorm.

511. In 2001, a lion cub, bear cub, and tiger cub were found abandoned in a drug dealer's basement. They were soon adopted by a sanctuary and have lived together ever since, showing a strong friendship among them.

512. Diving bell spiders can breathe underwater by using air bubbles. The bubbles act like mini scuba diving tanks.

513. In 2009, a study led by Deborah Wells of Queen's University, Belfast, discovered that female cats are often right-pawed while males are left-pawed. In humans, testosterone is related to left-handedness, which seems to apply to cats too.

514. The Polypterus is a kind of fish raised by researchers at McGill University in Montreal, Canada. It can breathe air and walk on land using its front fins.

515. Alpacas have been known to die of loneliness. This is why you usually always see them in groups.

516. Starfish, or sea stars, have no brain and no blood. Their nervous system is actually spread through their arms and their blood is filtered sea water.

517. To attract females, the male kangaroos flex their biceps and wrestle other males to show their dominance.

518. Pigs are actually very intelligent animals and have the ability to even manipulate purposefully. For example, they can pinpoint a weak spot, remember it, and use it to their advantage later on.

519. A kindle is the name given to a group of kittens with the same mother.

520. Some cats and dogs can actually be allergic to human dander. Dander is made up of tiny cells shed from hair, fur, or feathers. Although it's known to be related to pets, humans can produce it too.

521. In the rainforests of New Guinea, two new types of ants were discovered by scientists, which were named pheidole viserion and pheidole drogon, after the fire breathing dragons from the fantasy series Game of Thrones. The ants bear a strong resemblance to the dragons because they have blade-like serrations on their backs.

522. On a few occasions, a hen will lay an egg inside of an egg. It occurs when a hen is in the process of forming an egg in her oviduct and a second oocyte is released by the ovary before the first egg has completely traveled through the oviduct and been laid.

523. The maximum lifespan of an olm salamander is over a hundred years.

524. There is a giant American wasp that has a sting so painful that the best thing to do if you're stung is to lie down and scream to avoid further injury.

525. The Malm Whale is the only known mounted whale in the world. It is on display in Sweden's Natural History Museum. It was found stranded on rocks on October 29, 1865, when it swam too close to land in Askim Bay, south of Goteborg. It was over fifty two feet (15.8 meters) long and weighed around twenty five tons.

526. After being decapitated for hours, poisonous snakes could still bite, inject venom, and kill you. According to Steven Beaupre, biology professor at the University of Arkansas, snakes can retain reflexes after death and for venomous snakes, like cobras and rattlesnakes, biting is one of those reflexes.

527. The puffer fish, known also as blowfish, has enough toxins in it to kill thirty adult humans, and there is no antidote. Incredibly, the meat of some puffer fish is considered a delicacy in some parts of the world.

528. The kangaroo rats that live in deserts can go their whole lives without drinking any water. They get enough moisture from their seed diet to survive.

529. One of the two non-human primates that have blue eyes is the blue-eyed black lemur. They are among one of the twenty five most endangered primates. In fact, conservationists think that there are only between 450 to 2,500 in the whole world.

530. Dogs don't feel some emotions such as shame and guilt; however, they do feel sadness when they get shouted at from owners.

531. Instead of front teeth, cows, sheep, and goats all have a tough dental pad below their top lip. This dental arrangement helps them gather great quantities of grass and fibrous plants.

532. Most cats don't like water with the exception of the fishing cat, which is found in India. The main part of the fishing cat's diet is made of fish, so they are experts in swimming and diving, as well as scooping them out with their paws.

533. As they grow, bullfrogs periodically shed their skin at regular intervals. In fact, the old skin is pushed off with their hind legs and eaten by them.

534. Elephants can hold and store on average a gallon (four liters) of water in their trunks.

535. There is a type of fish known as the "barreleye" that has a completely transparent head. It inhabits depths of around 2,000 feet (600 meters) to 2,600 feet (800 meters) where it's almost absolute black.

536. The whale species with the thickest blubber of all is found on the bowhead whale, which lives exclusively in the Arctic. It can get as thick as twenty eight inches (seventy one centimeters).

537. In 2014, a study done by scientists at the University of Wyoming in Laramie revealed that bumble bees can fly higher than Mount Everest. The bees were placed in a Plexiglas flight chamber and the air was pulled out of the chamber by using a hand pump to create the reduced air pressures that the bees would face at high altitudes. The Plexiglas broke before the bumble bees stopped flying.

538. Skunks are actually immune to snake venom.

539. In Japan, the macaque monkeys that inhabit Yakushima Island have been known to ride sika deer around like horses.

540. The first documented case of twin dogs were born via C-section in August, 2016, at Rant en Dal Animal Hospital in Mogale City, South Africa.

541. There is a breed of cat in Turkey known as the "Van Cats" that are pure white in color, have different colored eyes, and love the water.

542. The world's largest sea sponge was found 7,000 feet (2,134 meters) below the ocean surface when

researchers were exploring the northwestern Hawaiian Islands aboard the Okeanos Explorer. It measured twelve feet (3.65 meters) long and seven feet (0.91 centimeters) wide.

543. The largest species of ribbon worms is the boot lace worm. They can grow up to 197 feet (sixty meters) in length, which is even longer than a blue whale.

544. The grasshopper mouse is a type of carnivorous animal that is immune to venom, eats scorpions, and howls like a wolf to claim its territory.

545. Lizards are able to self-amputate their tails for protection and grow them back after a few months.

546. The biologists from the University of North Florida found that male dolphins have lifelong bromances with each other. They team up, acting as wingmen for each other, help herd fertile females and even keep other males from mating with some of them.

547. The hagfish doesn't have bones in its body and has the ability to tie itself into a knot.

548. The French bulldog actually originated in England. It wasn't until English lace makers took them to France where they got their French moniker.

549. Crab claws have muscles so strong that they can produce a pinch force of up to sixty pounds (twenty seven kilograms).

550. Dogs can suffer from tonsillitis; however, they cannot suffer from appendicitis as they don't have an appendix.

551. Given that the platypus has no nipples, the milk basically oozes from their skin.

552. Fireflies are actually beetles, not flies as we may think. Most of them are winged and belong to the same family as the glow worm.

553. There are some marine bird species, like the penguin, that have a supraorbital gland placed just above their eyes which can remove sodium chloride from their blood stream. The gland works just like our kidneys, removing salt, and allowing penguins to survive when they have no access to fresh water. The penguin excretes the salt byproduct as brine through its bill.

554. The Beelzebufo ampinga, known also as the devil frog, may be the largest frog that ever existed according to National Geographic. These beach ball sized amphibians, that are now extinct, grew to almost 1.67 feet (half a meter) long and weighed approximately ten pounds (4.5 kilograms).

555. Based on a study led by zoologist Igor Malyshev, at St. Petersburg State University in Russia, the Australian red kangaroo and the eastern gray kangaroo are almost always left-handed.

556. Most eyes on predators are facing forward while most eyes on prey are on the sides of their head.

557. Years ago, snakes could actually slither and walk because they used to have legs. Eventually, they evolved into legless creatures, although the gene to grow limbs still exists.

558. Bald eagles build nests that are usually about five feet (1.5 meters) in diameter. The same nests are normally used year after year and they can become even bigger, as big as nine feet (2.7 meters), and weigh as much as two tons.

559. The metabolism of hummingbirds is so high that they are always hours away from starving to death.

560. The skunk is not the animal with the strongest smell out there. The lesser anteater gives off a pungent odor that is about four to seven times stronger than that of a skunk. It's so strong that you can smell it up to 164 feet (fifty meters) away.

561. The male emperor moth is able to detect pheromones from the female emperor moth from miles away.

562. The nose of a mosquito, known as proboscis, has forty seven sharp edges on its tip to help cut through skin. They can even cut through protective clothing.

563. The Atlas moth imitates a snake's appearance and behavior in order to defend itself. It has convincing wing patterns and when threatened, it will fall to the ground and flop around to look like a writhing snake.

564. When in danger or frightened, the opossum is known to play dead. It is actually an involuntary reaction, as the animal enters a comatose state as a defense mechanism. Once the fear is gone, they wake up again.

565. A wholphin is a cross between a false killer whale and a bottlenose dolphin.

566. The happier a cow, the more milk it produces. Just calling cows by individual names increases production by 3.5%.

567. Sea otters have skin pockets. There they keep their favorite rocks which they use for cracking open mollusks and clams.

568. Due to having such little mass, ants can't be injured from impact no matter how high a height they're dropped from.

569. The only bird with a bill longer than its body is the sword-billed hummingbird.

570. Archaeologists discovered the bones of a crocodile in 2009 that could gallop. They lived approximately one hundred million years ago along with the dinosaurs, sometimes even eating them.

571. In November, 2016, the world's heaviest earthworm was found in the vegetable garden of a man named Paul Rees in Cheshire County, England. It was named Dave; it measured almost sixteen inches (forty centimeters) long and weighed nearly twenty nine grams, which is almost twice as heavy as any other earthworm ever found.

572. In northeast Illinois, the oldest octopus fossil was discovered which dates back approximately 296 million years.

573. According to the Endangered Species Act of 1973, as of 2016, 1,367 species of animals and 901 species of plants were listed as endangered or threatened.

574. There is a worldwide mega-colony of Argentine ants. In fact, if they traveled to a different continent, they would actually be welcomed by a foreign branch of the colony.

575. The cicada killer wasp is a type of wasp that paralyzes cicadas with its venom and takes it to a burrow. There the wasp lays an egg under its left or right second leg; then when the egg hatches, the larvae eat the cicada, but carefully to still keep it alive.

576. Hawks have up to one million photoreceptors in the retina, so their vision is about eight times more accurate than humans, who only have 200,000 photoreceptors.

577. Shark teeth are coated with fluoride. It acts like toothpaste keeping the shark's mouth healthy and clean.

578. The little brown myotis bat can consume up to a thousand mosquitoes in one hour.

579. Whales fall to the bottom of the ocean when they die. This is known as "a whale fall" and an entire small ecosystem can thrive on the carcass for a few years.

580. The only mammals that don't pee or poo during the winter hibernation months are bears. In fact, doctors have studied how the bears recycle their urine to help human patients with kidney failure.

581. Research shows that ants get self-aware when tiny blue dots are painted on their heads and then placed in front of mirrors. In a study of the twenty four adult ants that were tested, twenty three of them tried to scratch the blue dots off their heads upon looking into the mirror. A total of thirty ants were tested, and they all reacted to the mirror by feeling it with their antennas.

582. A German shepherd called Gunther IV became the richest animal on Earth after he inherited $300 million from his dad, Gunther III, who originally inherited the fortune in 1992 from Carlotta Leibenstein, a German Countess.

583. Scott Bobeck, a vertebrate ecologist at Dickinson College in Pennsylvania, demonstrated in a study that boa constrictors don't suffocate their prey; instead, they cut off their blood supply. When boas tighten their body around the prey, they actually put pressure on the victim's circulatory system, causing their arterial pressures to drop, their venous pressures then increase, and their blood vessels close.

584. There are approximately one thousand different species of bats, and they are spread all over the world, except for desert and polar regions. Bats make up about 25% of all mammals on the planet.

585. The pancake batfish is an actual fish that moves along the seafloor using fins that act like feet and even have elbows. It can jump around like a frog just by flapping its tail. Its long nose can trick prey into coming near its mouth by projecting a lure.

586. Sloths have hair that's so coarse and long, that it's a great place for algae to thrive. The algae works so well as camouflage for sloths, that some of the animals ended up reaching for their own arms thinking they were tree branches, only to fall down to their deaths.

587. Swans only have one partner for their whole lives. In some cases, when one swan dies, its partner dies too from a broken heart.

588. When monarch butterflies experience food shortages, they can become cannibalistic, and they can eat monarch caterpillars or eggs.

589. Pygmy geckos rarely grow to a length of more than 0.95 inches (twenty four millimeters), which means that if there's a torrential downpour in the rainforest, the geckos could easily drown. Thankfully, they are able to float because they're so small and have water resistant skin.

590. The birth control pills used by women have been found to work for female gorillas too, according to research findings. This led many to believe that we have more in common with gorillas than we initially thought.

591. If mother kangaroos feel that the environment around them is too harsh to bring a newborn into, they have the ability to slow the gestation of the baby. They can also tell if the baby is male or female while still carrying it.

592. When alligators and manatees come across each other as they swim in the water, the alligator usually lets the manatee pass first. Even gators that are up to twelve feet (3.7 meters) long have been seen to do this.

593. Dragonflies have had six legs for more than 300 million years, but they are incapable of walking.

594. About 40% of all known types of insects are species of beetles.

595. Seagulls have an advantage over humans because they can drink both seawater and freshwater. They are able to separate salt from sea water, and excrete it through their nostrils.

596. Blue Jay birds have the ability to copy the cries of other birds, including that of the red-tailed hawk. This enables them to keep off predators, or to scare away other birds so they can have a source of food all to themselves.

597. Dogs have a higher likelihood of answering to high-pitched voices, similar to the kind we use to talk to babies, than normal toned voices, according to the University of York researchers.

598. Ribbon worms start eating themselves when they run out of food. According to experts, they can eat up to 95% of their own bodies, and still survive, which makes them highly adaptive creatures.

599. Since 2016, the giraffe is in the vulnerable category on the endangered species list for the first time ever because of years of habitat destruction and poaching.

600. In the tropical forests of Central and South America, there are eagles, such as the harpy eagle, that are so strong, that they hunt and kill sloths and monkeys. The female harpy eagle can actually kill prey that weighs up to twenty pounds (nine kilograms).

601. Black panthers are not a real species. They are actually jaguars or leopards who have melanism, a condition that causes them to have black skin. It's similar to being albino but in reverse.

602. Based on studies performed by biologist Dr. Sandra Goutte of Sorbonne University in Paris, some frogs have developed ultrasonic mating calls that they can use to be heard over rushing water to find a mate.

603. Male platypuses possess venomous spurs; they can even sense electromagnetic fields just like a fish.

604. In the United States, nearly one billion birds die each year due to collisions with glass. Even though most people have seen or heard a bird hit a window, they usually think that it's an unusual event, but the statistics show the opposite.

605. In 2016, Ringling Bros Barnum and Bailey Circus retired all elephants in their show. The animals went to a Florida conservation spot where they actually help with cancer research, as they have a special P53 gene known to help fight cancer.

606. It's known that dinosaurs often used to swallow big rocks, which stayed in their stomach and helped them grind up food.

607. Hippopotamuses are usually vegetarians. However, several times they have been documented cannibalizing one of their own dead.

608. Pizzlies and growler bears are hybrid bears. They are the result of a cross between a polar bear and a grizzly bear. If the father is a polar bear, they are called pizzlies. If the father is a grizzly, they are called growler bears.

609. An epizootic is the term used to refer to an outbreak of disease that affects many animals at the same time.

610. After the movie "Finding Nemo" was released, the demand for home aquariums tripled. The demand was met by large-scale harvesting of fish from the ocean, which devastated clown fish populations.

611. Although penguins cannot fly, they can still get air born by jumping. Some smaller species of penguins can jump as high as ten feet (three meters) in the air.

612. "Puggle" is the name given to a baby echidna or platypus.

613. Although the Darwin's bark spider is small and non-poisonous, it can spin a web sixty five feet (twenty meters) across that is able to span an entire river and it's stronger than Kevlar.

614. If a cat looks at you straight in the eyes and blinks slowly, it's actually trying to tell you that it's in love with you.

615. Dolphins have two stomachs, one for storing food, and the other for digesting it.

616. Large dogs tend to age faster and die younger than small dogs. The reason why is still unclear by scientists.

617. There is a pod of bottlenose dolphins in Laguna, Brazil, that have been helping the fishermen there since 1846. The dolphins herd the fish towards the shore and then let the fishermen know when to cast their nets by signaling to them.

618. If one day you find a stranded dolphin, do not help it to get back into the water. Dolphins sometimes beach themselves purposely because they are sick or injured, beaching themselves to avoid drowning.

619. Okapi is a mammal that has stripes like a zebra and the body of a horse, although it's closely related to the giraffe, not the zebra or horse. Its stripes help break up its body outline, making it hard to find. In fact, the species was so hard to find that Western scientists didn't know about it until 1901.

620. The national animal of Brazil is the jaguar, also known as "Panthera onca," its scientific name. It is the largest carnivorous mammal in Central and South America and it can weigh up to 211 pounds (ninety five kilograms).

621. A study led by Doctor Ronelle Welton from the University of Melbourne concluded that, between 2000 and 2013, horses caused more deaths than poisonous snakes and insects. Horses were actually responsible for seventy four deaths; bees and stinging insects caused twenty seven; snakes also caused twenty seven deaths; and spiders actually killed no one.

622. Instead of having a mouth, the common housefly has an eating tube through which it vomits a drop of fluid from its stomach onto its meal that dissolves the nutrients. It then sucks up the fluid along with the nutrients, leaving behind a great amount of germs.

623. Echidnas have a four headed penis. Also known also as spiny anteaters, they actually don't use their penis to urinate and it only leaves the body during an erection.

624. There is a cat named Artful Dodger in Bridgeport, UK, that takes the bus by himself on a regular basis to travel ten miles to the neighboring town. The driver already knows what stop to let the cat off at and even brings tins of cat food for him.

625. The longest living vertebrate known on Earth is the Greenland shark. It's estimated that they can live 400 years.

626. The longest recorded flight of a chicken is thirteen seconds.

627. One of the rare subspecies of pandas that only exists in the remote Qinling Mountains, in western China, is the quirky brown panda.

628. Queen termites have a really long lifespan. They can live up to fifty years long and are the oldest ones in the colony. They can also produce eggs for up to ten years.

629. Cockroaches have their own personalities and even display different character traits according to researchers from the Université Libre de Bruxelles. Although they are simple animals, they can make complex decisions on survival. One cockroach's decision can even influence others.

630. In order to shred their tails, most species of geckos actually have to have their tails pulled. However, a number of species are able to get rid of their tails at will. In several cases, the tails grow back, but they no longer have the original bone structure and are made of just cartilage.

631. A hoglet is the name given to a baby hedgehog.

632. Female pandas generally give birth to a single cub. If she ends up having two cubs, she will take care of one and abandon the other.

633. The fastest land mammal in the United Kingdom is the European hare. They are able to reach speeds over forty four miles (seventy two kilometers) per hour.

634. Howler monkeys can be heard up to three miles (five kilometers) away when a group lets loose with their howling.

635. Obesity has the same effects in parrots as it does in humans. Even worse, parrots with obesity are likely to get cancer.

636. The nictitating membrane is a third eyelid that dogs have, and according to Deborah Friedman of the American College of Veterinary Ophthalmologists, the membrane has four functions. Firstly, it cleans debris from the dog's eyes. Secondly, it produces one third of the dog's tears. Thirdly, it helps fight off infections; and lastly, it prevents injury to the eye.

637. A West African chimpanzee named Washoe was the first non-human to grasp American Sign Language. She was able to learn just like human infants, by observing and imitating people.

638. A team of Japanese researchers at Keio University in Tokyo successfully taught pigeons to differentiate between Monet and Picasso paintings in the early 1990's. After seeing several works from both artists, the birds could recognize other pieces by the artists, which they have never actually seen before.

639. A super pack of 400 wolves started to attack the village of Vircoyans in Russia in 2011, and within four days, they had killed thirty horses. Local authorities sent out parties of hunters, and they consulted experts who were all mystified as to why the wolves had created such a large pack.

640. Squids have an esophagus that passes through their brain, which is shaped like a donut, and this means that if they swallow large objects, it could literally result in brain damage.

641. Urine produced by the maned wolf has the exact same smell as marijuana. That's because both the animal's urine and the plant contain pyrazine, which gives them their characteristic smell.

642. When hummingbirds breed, they build their nests near hawks' nests, because the hawks, which are larger and stronger, will instinctively protect the eggs from other animals.

643. After sheep are sheared, they no longer recognize each other. At times, they fight each other as if they've never met before.

644. Scientists officially refer to hoofed mammals as ungulates.

645. If you ignore the diseases transmitted by mosquitoes, it would take roughly 400,000 mosquitoes to draw enough blood from a person for it to result in death, and it would require a million mosquitoes to drain all the blood from an average sized person's body.

646. Hawaii was trying to control the rat population in sugarcane plantations, so they set mongooses loose in the fields in 1883. The mongooses didn't solve the problems, because it turns out they are diurnal while rats are nocturnal. Farmers soon realized both animals were a problem, and the population of native birds has drastically fallen since then.

647. Wax worms are newly discovered types of worms that can eat and process polyethylene, the plastic material in shopping bags. Polyethylene makes up 40% of plastics used within Europe, and scientists are hoping wax worms could be used to break down plastic bags that are polluting waterways and overwhelming landfills.

648. The thagomizer refers to the group of four to ten spikes on tails of specific dinosaurs known as stegosauri. It's believed that these spikes were a defense mechanism against predators.

649. Damselflies and dragonflies have a mating ritual where they form their bodies into a heart shape. The claspers at the end of the male's abdomen fit into the grooves on the female one of the same species, and they both bend until they form a heart shape.

650. A walrus can stay up for eighty-four hours without having to sleep.

651. Neil Evenhuis discovered an extinct type of fly which he named Carmenelectra shechisme after Carmen Electra, the model and actress, and he published his findings in 2002.

652. Squids can shoot out water so fast that the squirt can propel them through the air at a speed of up to twenty five miles (forty kilometers) per hour.

653. Domestic cats, bottlenose dolphins, and some other carnivorous animals are unable to taste or even detect sugar or any sweetness because of a genetic mutation.

654. There are species of termites that are natural suicide bombers. When these termites come across a predator that endangers them and their colonies, they hold onto the enemy, then squeeze their own midsection so hard that they burst and die, while sending out sticky, hardening, or toxic substances towards the predator in all directions.

655. The giant African land snails are as big as rats. They can chew through materials such as plaster, and if you drive over one, its shell is strong enough to puncture your tires. They can grow to 7.9 inches (twenty centimeters), live for about nine years, and produce about 1,200 eggs every year.

656. The skeletal remains of the all-time largest rodent in the world was discovered in Venezuela in 2003. It was basically a guinea pig the size of a cow. It lived eight million years ago, weighed 1,500 pounds (700 kilograms), measured 9.8 feet (three meters) long and 4.2 feet (1.3 meters) tall.

657. Some dolphin species are born with hair, which then falls out shortly after birth.

658. The Chan's megastick is the longest insect known to man. These insects, native to Borneo, Malaysia, can grow to over fourteen inches (thirty five centimeters), and they look like long twigs, which allows them to easily hide from predators.

659. The first cheetah race at Romford Stadium, London, was held on December 11, 1937. A female cheetah called Helen raced two greyhounds, attaining a speed of fifty five miles (eighty eight kilometers) per hour, which immediately earned her the title "Queen of the Track."

660. To win mates, male jumping spiders sing and dance. They rub together their two body segments to generate vibrations, which are essentially songs that the females hear through slits on their legs that act as ears.

661. Caterpillars remain in the larval stage for several weeks, within which time they tend to eat more than 27,000 times their own body weight. They also expand in size several times through the molting process, and they can grow to 1,000 times their original mass. Caterpillars have about 4,000 muscles within their small bodies, and by comparison, humans only have 629.

662. The only birds in the world that have calf muscles are the emu birds, which are flightless and are native to Australia. They are famous for their high endurance and speed when running over long distances. Strangely, emus cannot walk backwards, and no one understands why.

663. The "Wraparound" is a spider species in Australia that has the unique ability to wrap its body around small branches to conceal itself from birds and other predators.

664. Grown up goat bucks usually urinate on their own beards, front legs, and even heads before they start a mating ritual.

665. The pistol shrimp is able to stun its prey by using its claws. They have a large claw and when they snap it shut, it creates an intense burst of sound that stuns its prey. In addition, they have a punch that is even faster than a 0.22 caliber bullet, which literally smashes their prey into pieces.

666. "Gnus" are also called wildebeests. They start learning to walk just minutes after birth, and can follow their mothers around and herd in a matter of days.

667. To attract female peacocks, the male ones make fake mating sounds. This makes sexually active females assume that the male is mating, although they aren't. It works by making the females believe that the male one is more genetically fit than his rivals.

668. Male hippos spin their tails around in order to fling their feces. They do this to attract female hippos, and also to mark their territory.

669. Vampire bat saliva contains draculin, a glycoprotein that's named after count Dracula, and serves as an anticoagulant that enables the bats to feed on blood. It's applied through the bat's bite, and it stops blood from clotting, so the bats are able to drink it a lot faster.

670. When ants die, they lay for two whole days on that spot, before the other ants in the colony carry them and put them on a heap of other dead ants.

671. Vinegar eel is a real thing. It's a worm that's one sixteenth of an inch (1.6 millimeters) in length that eats living yeast and bacteria cultures that are used to make vinegar. They are present in unfiltered yeast, and they are often raised as fish feed.

672. Zebras and donkeys can breed with each other. When they do, the resulting crossbreed is called a Zonkey.

673. Chimpanzees can recognize their own fashion trends, according to research done in 2014 at a sanctuary in Zambia. Some chimps started putting bits of glass in their ears in one instance, and the only apparent reason for this was that they wanted to feel like a part of the group.

674. The total weight of all the bones in a pigeon is lower than the weight of its feathers.

675. Nottingham Trent University's Dr. Martin Bencsik discovered that when honeybees bump into each other, they emit vibrations which sound remarkably like whoops. He and his peers believed that the sound indicates that the bees are startled.

676. When male fireflies are fully grown, they never eat their food because they have a strong drive to mate, and they have a short life span to accomplish that. Certain female fireflies can copy the blinking rates of other species of firefly, attracting the males that want to mate, only to end up eating them instead.

677. When cats rub their face on something, they leave their own scent behind as they have glands located around their mouths, chins, inside of their face, neck, and ears. This is called bunting.

678. The urine of bear cats actually smells like buttered popcorn. In fact, their urine has the same compound that is found in buttered popcorn.

679. Berserk male syndrome is a condition that male llamas and alpacas can suffer from. Owners suddenly find their animals wildly charging at them from behind or rearing up at them, screaming, spitting, and biting. It's caused by human over handling and when the alpaca or llama begins to look at their human as a rival.

680. There are some species of turtles where the temperature determines whether the egg will develop into a male or female. In lower temperatures, the egg will develop into a male turtle, while in higher temperatures, the egg will develop into a female.

681. Catfish have about 100,000 taste buds spread all over their bodies, most of them located on their whiskers.

682. Female mosquitoes are the only ones to bite humans and animals. Male mosquitoes on the contrary only feed themselves on flower nectar.

683. Lemurs have extremely bad vision. In fact, they are only able to see in black and white.

684. There is a species of recently discovered nocturnal lizards that are found only on Madagascar. The

Geckolepis megalepis is a kind of fish-scaled gecko and has an amazing defense mechanism. When grabbed by a predator, it can shed patches of skin and scales from most of its body, causing the scales to get stuck in the attacker's mouths.

685. The stripes on tigers are on their skin and not just their fur.

686. Koalas drink water very rarely. In general, the water they drink comes from gum leaves or from dew or rainwater on the surface of the leaves. Over 90% of their hydration is received from the eucalyptus leaves that they eat. They only drink when ill or at times when there isn't enough moisture on the leaves, like during very dry weather.

687. When taken by a predator, most grasshoppers will vomit a repugnant, bitter acidic bile as a last alternative defense mechanism.

688. A bloodhound who hunts by scent is only able to follow the scent of blood that is several days old.

689. The smallest species of armadillo is the pink fairy armadillo. It is only four inches (ten centimeters) long, weighs about a hundred grams, and is pink in color.

690. Platypuses don't have stomachs. In fact, they're not the only animals without one. Others include the echidna and the carp.

691. As a substitute to seeing eye dogs, there are miniature guide horses that the blind can use. Some of the advantages include an average lifespan of thirty years and a 350-degree vision.

692. Female giraffes urinate in males' mouths before mating. From the taste of her urine, the male can conclude if she is in heat or not.

693. The sub-Alpine reaches of Mount Kaputar, Australia, is home of the giant pink slug. They can reach up to eight inches (twenty centimeters) long and on a good day, you can actually see hundreds of them.

694. Based on reports provided by National Geographic, there used to be around 100,000 wild tigers in Asia a century ago. Unfortunately, due to poaching, there are only about 3,200 today.

695. Llamas and alpacas are able to interbreed successfully. Their offspring is called "huarizo."

696. According to a study performed by researchers at the University of Bristol, bees leave a scent on surfaces with their feet. The bees are able to detect the smell and distinguish if it is their own scent, a relative's, or a stranger's.

697. The queen cow of milk production was won by Robert Behnke, a Wisconsin dairy farmer. His cow, Gigi, has produced more milk in one year than any other cow with 8,700 gallons (32,933 liters); three times the national average for a dairy cow to produce in a year.

698. In December of 2016, Wisdom, the albatross known as the oldest breeding wild bird, laid an egg at the ripe old age of sixty-six, at the Midway Atoll National Wildlife Refuge in Hawaii.

699. When cats bring back home a dead animal, they are actually showing its owners how to catch and eat prey, just like they would teach their young in the wild. This is due to their natural role as a mother and teacher.

700. The pill bugs, aka "roly poly bugs," are actually crustaceans. They are related to shrimp and crayfish, they breathe with gills and need humidity and moisture to survive.

701. Lions and jaguars react to catnip similarly to domestic cats, by sniffing, licking and rubbing their chins and bodies on the item that it was sprayed on.

702. The term used to call a group of bears is a sloth of bears.

703. When bats are born, they come out feet first, and in many cases, the mother bat hangs upside down so she can catch the baby in her wings as it exits the womb.

704. In January of 2017, in the Hunan province in southwestern China, an international team of scientists from the United States, France, and China discovered a new species of prehistoric otter that is 6.24 million years old. It was named the siamogale melilutra; it was about the size of a wolf, and weighed around 110 pounds (fifty kilograms). That is almost twice as large as the largest living otter.

705. The opossum is actually immune to bee stings, scorpion stings, rattlesnake venom, and toxins like botulism.

706. The Surinam toad has holes in her back that are used to give birth. They develop eggs embedded in their backs and eventually they hatch and crawl out of the holes.

707. Between 1876 and 2013, the number of attacks reported by great white sharks was 280 globally, and only seventy seven have resulted in a fatality. In comparison, deer kill nearly 200 people a year in the US alone.

708. Bat's wings are actually made up of cartilage with small amounts of calcium. The bones are similar to our fingers, except that they are more flexible.

709. The University of Exeter did studies that found that sharks have their own characteristics and personalities. Some sharks are more social while some are reserved and shy.

710. Caterpillars completely turn into liquid in a cocoon, but when becoming a moth or butterfly, they still remember their life as a caterpillar.

711. Female kangaroos have three vaginas. Two of them are located on the outside and are for sperm, and lead to two uteruses, while the middle one is for giving birth.

712. The female lion does the majority of the hunting. Sporadically, the male will join only when the prey is particularly large, like a buffalo.

713. In 2013, the world's first two-headed sea slug was found by dive master Nash Baiti while on vacation in Borneo. Besides the two heads, it had male and female organs, was bright neon orange and green in color, and toxic.

714. Peregrine falcons are able to bomb their prey from above at up to 199 miles (320 kilometers) per hour.

715. The University of Chicago did a study that found that rats that were trained to press a lever to receive food would stop pressing the button once they found out that another rat would receive an electric shock.

716. A group of buffalos is called a gang.

717. Although hummingbirds cannot walk or hop, they are able to shuffle with their extremely short, weak legs.

718. Male hippopotamuses size each other up by opening their mouths up to 150 degrees and stretching them up to 4.9 feet (1.5 meters) in length.

719. In order to attract a partner, the peacock spider does a little mating dance, with each spider having its own unique style of dance.

720. Bald eagles are able to live for up to fifty years.

721. The Latin word for porcupine literally means "quill pig." There are over two dozen porcupine species known and they all boast a coat of needle like quills. Some of them, like those of Africa's crested porcupine, are nearly a foot (thirty-centimeter) long.

722. A study from biologists at Newfoundland's University suggested that bread is junk food for ducks as it leads them to becoming overweight and disease-ridden.

723. According to the Guinness Book of World Records, the world's tiniest shark is the dwarf lantern shark; a male measures only about 6.3 inches (sixteen centimeters) in length.

724. There is a deep-sea squid called the "Strawberry Squid" that has mismatched eyes and looks like a strawberry. It has one large, light-colored eye that is angled upwards; and a smaller, darker eye that is angled downwards. One eye evolved to look for predators while the other evolved to look for prey.

725. The largest frog in the world is the Goliath frog. It can reach up to 12.5 inches (thirty one centimeters) in length and weigh seven pounds (three kilograms).

726. After being born and within the first ten minutes, a duckling will consider anything that it meets as its parent forever.

727. Female spotted hyenas don't actually have a vagina, but a type of pseudo-penis. They are significantly larger than their male counterparts and are the more dominant ones of the species.

728. Red squirrels are able to make their own mushroom jerky. To keep it better over the winter, they hang fungi out to dry between tree branches. Mushroom jerky is less likely to infect their larder with insect larvae and nematodes.

729. In 1999, Olle Terenius, from the Swedish University of Agricultural Sciences, found out that mute swans can windsurf across water. When these birds want to go fast, they put up their wings and tails to catch a breeze.

730. Throughout Phoenix, Arizona, wild parrots have been spreading and seen for years. Conservationist Greg Clark remarked that these colonies were started in the 1980's when an aviary released a hundred birds after a monsoon. He also pointed out that another aviary released more birds around that time because the owner didn't want them anymore.

731. Most mammals don't live long after their reproductive years are over. Only a few do, such as the killer whale, pilot whales, human beings, and some great apes.

732. Scorpions can live under extreme temperatures. They can even survive being frozen and thawed and extreme heat up to 122 degrees Fahrenheit (fifty degrees Celsius).

733. It's possible for the praying mantises to turn their heads 180 degrees. This ability helps them scan their surroundings using two large, compound eyes and three other simple eyes located between them.

734. The Asian arowana, also known as the dragon fish, is the world's most expensive aquarium fish. The Chinese believe that they bring good luck and prosperity due to its red color and coin-like scales. This fish has sold for up to $300,000.

735. According to neuroscientist Glen Jeffrey from the University College London, the eye color of reindeer changes depending on the time of the year. In the summer they turn golden, reflecting more light through the retina, which helps them deal with the almost continuous Arctic summer daylight. However, in the winter, they turn a deep blue to help them deal with the almost continuous winter darkness.

736. Rats have a really strong sense of smell and have been able to detect buried landmines in the past. For this reason, the US Fish and Wildlife Service is testing the African giant pouched rat to see whether it can help detect illegal shipments of hardwood timber, part of a multi-billion dollar black market industry, as well as pangolins, the world's most poached mammal.

737. In the late summer and fall, blue jays and cardinals go bald. Sometimes they lose all their feathers gradually; sometimes they lose them all at once. They are only bald for about a week until their feathers grow back.

738. A group of mallard ducks were studied and filmed when they were sleeping in a row by researchers at Indiana State University. Scientists found that the ducks on the end of each row had one eye open and half of their brains were still functioning. The reason why was to keep a good look-out for predators and other potential threats to their group.

739. Tonic immobility is a trance-like state where sharks fall when they are flipped upside down. Orcas have figured this out and have been seen in the wild turning great whites over and killing them. It became one of the few instances of something else preying on great white sharks instead of humans.

740. In 1987, there were only twenty seven California condors worldwide. All of them were captured for captive breeding and now, as of 2018, there are 488 of them.

741. The smallest spider in the world, according to the Guinness World Records, is the Patu marplesi, also known as the Samoan moss spider. With a body length of only 0.09 inches (0.25 millimeters), this spider belongs to the group of forty four "midget" species that create the smallest spider webs.

742. The small tropical archer fish has been taught to accurately recognize human faces. When researchers at the University of Oxford displayed two faces side by side on a screen over a fish tank, one familiar and one unknown, the fish was able to recognize the same face 81% of the time in color, and even more accurately in black and white images.

743. The official state animal of California is the grizzly bear. It was designated as such in 1953, more than thirty years after the last one was killed. It was also honored on the state flag.

744. There are only three northern white rhinos left in the world as of June 2018. One male and two other females live in captivity in Northern Kenya. Sadly, despite this, these creatures are still sought after for their horns by poachers.

745. Although camels are thought to live in Australia as an invasive species, some aboriginal recall seeing them in earlier times.

746. Researchers at the National University of Singapore discovered that the Chinese soft shell turtle is able to pee out of its mouth. They noticed that turtles would stick their heads into puddles of water and wiggle their tongues, but they weren't drinking.

747. Wild pigs are considered as one of the most destructive animals in America. They destroy crops, feast on livestock, terrorize tourists, and force other wildlife to flee their homes. They cause more than $400 million in damage each year in Texas alone.

748. Due to the way that horse legs are built, they can actually sleep while standing up. Their legs have ligaments and a structure that allows them to doze off without collapsing.

749. Birds in cities often use cigarette butts for their nests as the nicotine inside them repels parasites.

750. There is a group of blind millipedes that glow in the dark, giving off a neon teal color, in California's Sierra Nevada Mountains. The millipedes have a special type of protein that allows them to produce light from beneath the tough cuticle that covers their bodies.

751. Most mammals have the same number of vertebrae in their necks, which are seven. The only two that do not have exactly seven vertebrae are sloths and manatees.

752. As a self-defense mechanism, the horned lizard has blood-filled sinuses within the eye sockets that squirt blood by swelling and rupturing.

753. A liger is the result of mixing a white lion and a tiger. The world's first ligers were born in 2013, a white lion and a tiger had four male cubs which are now the rarest big cats on Earth.

754. "Frog" is the term given to the underside of a horse's hoof.

755. Masked birch caterpillars use anal drumming to call other young caterpillars to help spin silk for their cocoons and maintain them. To cause the vibrations, they rub hairs on their rear ends against a leaf.

756. The grasshopper mouse defends its territory by standing up on its back legs, and producing a high-pitched howling sound in the same manner as a wolf.

757. Oysters change their sex from male to female and back several times during their lifetime.

758. Giant catfish in parts of Europe have been known to deliberately beach themselves so as to quickly attack birds such as pigeons. After catching the bird, they flop back into the water and drown the bird, just like alligators do.

759. Tigers' night vision is six times better than humans. They have a retinal adaptation that reflects light back to the retina, making their night vision more powerful.

760. It's well documented that ducks sometimes float through tidal rapids in fast flowing river stretches, and upon getting to the end, rush back upstream to do it over again.

761. As a way to thank actor Harrison Ford who narrated a documentary for the London Museum of Natural History in 1994, a spider species discovered in 1993 was named Calponia harrisonfordi. The spider is very tiny, it measures around 0.19 inches (five millimeters) in length, and lives in California.

762. At the back of their nose, dogs have a secondary organ for smelling. It's called the Jacobson's organ, and it boosts the canines' sense of smell so much that dogs have the ability to smell cancer on patients' breaths.

763. The 8998 butterfly is a subspecies of butterfly. Its name comes from its wing markings, which uncannily resemble the number eighty nine on one wing, and the number ninety eight on the other.

764. It's possible for crocodiles to hold their breath underwater for up to two hours. The colder the water, the longer that they can stay under, given that crocodiles use more energy and oxygen in warm water.

765. At one point in time, lemurs in Madagascar were so big that they were the size of today's male gorillas.

766. The tongues of woodpeckers are made up of bone and cartilage. They use them to wrap around their skulls in order to protect their heads. Whenever they peck wood, their tongues absorb the shock that's given to the brain and skull.

767. The tarantula hawk wasp is said to have one of the most painful stings of all known insects. The pain subsides after three minutes, but experts suggest that if it ever stings you, you'd better just lie on the ground, and start screaming. Few people if any are able to maintain their coordination after getting stung, so chances are you'll end up hurting yourself worse as you desperately look for a way to ease your agony.

768. During the cold winters, the Alaskan wood frog shapes itself as a block of ice. It literally stops breathing and its heart stops beating. When spring arrives, the frog then thaws and returns to normal life.

769. The Anelosimus eximius is a breed of social spider that works with others, building some of the largest spider webs in the world. Over 50,000 spiders can live on one web until they eventually outgrow it and have to form new colonies.

770. Rabbits are able to sleep with their eyes open. They go into a trance-like state, which makes them only half asleep. The advantage of this is that, in the wild, it allows them to be more alert and get away from predators in a hurry.

771. There is an animal called the pronghorn antelope which has vision ten times better than the average human. Scientists believe that this animal can see the rings of Saturn on a clear night.

772. Bees can see ultraviolet wavelengths. In fact, they are attracted to flowers because petals have UV patterns on them.

773. According to scientists, studying the earwax of a blue whale can reveal important aspects of its life. The technique is described in the proceedings of the National Academy of Sciences and it's considered a tool to understand the whale's hormonal and chemical biography. It can also provide information about how long discontinued pollutants can still pervade and affect the environment today.

774. Since 2005, thirty six years old Michael Jackson's pet chimpanzee Bubbles has been living at the Center for Great Apes sanctuary in Wauchula, Florida. When Bubbles lived with Michael Jackson, the young chimp slept in a crib and ate candy at Neverland Ranch. However, when it became fully mature and aggressive, he was taken away by an animal trainer to ensure the safety of Jackson.

775. To be born, the babies of a female sea louse actually chew their way out of the mother's insides.

776. Lots of different animal species experience the Coolidge effect. The effect is named after US President Calvin Coolidge, and it refers to a biological anomaly, where males show renewed sexual interest when a new female is added to a group.

777. FIT is a footprint identification technique used by researchers to monitor cheetah populations in the wild. The technique considers every paw print unique to a particular cheetah, and it can be identified similarly to a human fingerprint.

778. A study conducted at Washington University found that rats enjoy being tickled. High frequency recordings showed that they make the same laughing sound during a tickle session than when playing with other rats.

779. Some cats actually love olives as they contain isoprenoids, which are structurally similar to the active chemical in catnip.

780. According to a study led by Doctor Martin Nyffeler, the global population of spiders consumes 400 million to 800 million tons of insect prey per year. To put that into perspective, they consume nearly the same amount of prey as humans consume meat and fish yearly.

781. Lobsters can regenerate lost eyes, claws, and antennae. You can also determine the gender of a lobster by looking at its swimmerets, the small feathery appendages on the underside of its tail. On males, the first pair of swimmerets closest to the body is hard and bony, while on females it's soft and feathery.

782. There are some species of scorpions that can live up to one year with no food or water.

783. Over 300 species of spiders are known to mimic the outward appearance of ants, as a way to get close enough to eat them, or to avoid being eaten by them. It's a phenomenon called myrmecomorphy. These spiders have a false waist and are covered in reflective hair so that they can look shiny like the three-segmented bodies of ants. They also behave like ants by waving their front pairs of legs near their heads like antennae.

784. In order to capture scent particles, snakes and lizards flick their tongues in the air. This basically means that they smell with their tongues.

785. Polar bears have the unique ability to ingest and store very high amounts of vitamin A. The amount is so high that if you ate a polar bear's liver, it's likely that you could die from vitamin A poisoning, also known as hypervitaminosis A.

786. Snowflake is the only known albino gorilla. He was born in the wild but in 1966, he was caught by villagers and lived in the Barcelona Zoo until he died of skin cancer in 2003. Spanish researchers think that Snowflake was the result of inbreeding between an uncle and a niece.

787. A study done by Biology Letters concluded that the duration of time it takes for an animal to yawn predicts the size of its brain and the number of neurons in its cortex. The longer the yawn is, the bigger the brain is.

788. As an adaptation mechanism to dry environments, roadrunners do not need to drink water. Instead they get all of the moisture they need from their food. They're also known to kill and eat rattlesnakes.

789. The larvae of the Middle Eastern epomis beetle socialize in killing frogs, salamanders, and other amphibians that try to eat them. They lure in their prey and encourage them to approach; they attack by striking with double-hooked jaws hanging on and then eat the prey alive.

790. The mantis shrimp can punch fifty times during a blink of an eye, with a speed equal to a bullet. In fact, a blow from a mantis shrimp can easily break through the shell of a crab or mollusk.

791. Every single night orangutans build a brand new nest to sleep. They are made from leaves, branches, and sticks, and are thirty nine feet (twelve meters) off the ground. They have to be sturdy, as the average orangutan weighs eighty four pounds (thirty eight kilograms). Although it is a lot of work to do every day, these animals rarely reuse or even improve an old one, opting instead to start from zero.

792. When a cheetah runs at full sprint, it actually spends more time flying than in contact with the ground.

793. Barn owls are usually monogamous birds. However, a study performed by the University of Lausanne showed that during a year where the bird couples don't have many babies, they may divorce each other and move on to a new mate. The male is often the one to stay at the original breeding ground.

794. Rabbits can die of fright. Loud sounds such as dogs barking, loud music, or screaming can cause a heart attack, putting a rabbit into shock and causing sudden death.

795. Baby kangaroos or joeys can be as small as a grain of rice or as big as a bee at birth.

796. According to PhD candidate Alexis Noel, from the Georgia Institute of Technology, frogs can change the viscosity of their saliva in a fraction of a second. By withdrawing their eyeballs inside of their heads, frogs help create the pressure needed to change the saliva.

797. The honey bee has microscopic short hairs on its eyes called "settey." They help with navigation by catching the wind to help them figure out direction and speed while traveling.

798. The whiptail lizard is the only all-female species as the males are completely extinct. Despite that, they are not hermaphroditic; the females actually lay and hatch from unfertilized eggs.

799. The Basenji is a dog breed that doesn't have the ability to bark, but instead it can produce a yodeling howl sound. It's a small to medium sized, square-shaped dog that is believed to be bred intentionally without the ability to bark.

800. Chinchillas (a type of rodent) don't suffer from fleas. Their fur is so thick and soft that fleas will suffocate if they try to live in it.

801. In 1976, a group of people created the National Fancy Rat Society with the aim to promote the rat as a pet and an exhibition animal.

802. There is a rare species of shark known as the Megamouth shark, which we have only sixty records of since their discovery in 1976.

803. Horses are physically unable to vomit. They have a number of physiological features that ensure that any food they ingest takes a one-way trip. They have, for example, a much lower esophageal sphincter that is much stronger than in other animals, making it nearly impossible to open that valve under backward pressure from the stomach.

804. While flying, albatross are able to sleep. They do this to avoid predators like whales and sharks.

805. The mimic octopus lives in the waters off the Asian coast in the Southeast. It can blend with its environment by changing its color, and it can also copy the physical characteristics and movements of other aquatic animals. It manipulates its body and tentacles to look and move like snakes, eels, stingrays, jellyfish, starfish, and other creatures.

806. Fainting goats exist. There is even a Fainting Goat Festival that is held in Tennessee. These goats are born with a condition called "myotonia congenital," which causes their muscles to tense up for ten to twenty seconds whenever they are spooked, which can cause them to easily faint.

807. In Japan, crows have mastered a new method of cracking nuts. They drop the nuts on the street, wait for a car to run over them, and then retrieve the nuts when they crack.

808. Hummingbirds can only be found in the Western hemisphere. About half of them live around the Equator, while 5% live in the north of Mexico, and about two dozen species live in the United States and Canada.

809. The Tyrannosaurus Rex was closer to us in time than it was to the Stegosaurus. In fact, the Stegosaurus was already a fossil by the time the T-Rex roamed the Earth.

810. The basking shark has a liver so big that it weighs almost a third of its total body weight.

811. Beavers are able to hold their breath underwater for up to fifteen minutes.

812. The opah is the only species of warm-blooded fish on Earth.

813. The largest flying bird in North America is the California condor. Its wingspan can be as wide as ten feet (three meters) from tip to tip and they can fly as high as 15,000 feet (4,500 meters) by catching air currents.

814. In November of 2016, scientists discovered a spider in southwestern China's Yunnan rainforest that can make itself look like a dangling dried up leaf. The leaf-mimicking spider, as it is named, employs a strategy called masquerading, which consists of pretending to look like something else in order to protect itself.

815. One of the most dangerous animals in the world is actually the hippopotamus. Around 500 people a year are killed by hippopotamuses in Africa. These huge animals are capable of running the same speed as humans on land and their jaws are so strong that they could snap a canoe in half.

816. Manatees can actually eat a tenth of their body weight in a twenty four hour period, which can be up to 130 pounds (fifty nine kilograms).

817. In 2009, a fossil of the Titanoboa was discovered. They were the largest snakes that have ever existed, measuring 9.1 feet (2.8 meters) and weighing 2,495 pounds (1,133 kilograms). Given the warmer climate on Earth fifty eight to sixty million years ago, they were able to reach these fabulous sizes. Today, smaller snakes can be found farther away from the equator, while the larger ones are closer to it.

818. Although reindeer and caribou belong to the same species, there are actually differences between them. Caribou, on one hand, are larger and usually are found in North America and Greenland. On the other hand, reindeer are smaller and can be found in Europe and Asia.

819. Jackrabbits are actually hares, not rabbits. They can go as fast as forty miles (sixty four kilometers) per hour and jump as high as ten feet (three meters) in the air.

820. The antlers of a moose can be as wide as six feet (1.8 meters) and weigh as much as seventy pounds (thirty one kilograms).

821. In June of 2015, the pacu fish was found in New Jersey. It's a type of fish native to South America, a flesh-eating kind of piranha known for its unique teeth, which bear a peculiar similarity to human teeth. Luckily, it's considered mostly harmless to humans as it primarily eats plants.

822. The wels catfish is the largest freshwater fish in Europe according to National Geographic explorer Zeb Hogan. It can grow up to fifteen feet (4.5 meters) long, weigh as much as 660 pounds (299 kilograms), and live for decades, even as long as eighty years.

823. Tigers' tongues are very coarse and can actually lick flesh down to the bone.

824. Studies conducted at Turkey's Ataturk University and the University of Manchester have shown that dogs and cats are right or left pawed, just like humans are right or left handed.

825. Rats are extremely flexible and an adult rat can fit through a hole as small as a quarter, or a gap less than one inch (2.5 centimeters) wide. This is how they can easily invade your home without your knowledge.

826. The only member of the canine family that hibernates is the raccoon dog, so it needs to load up on food before winter arrives.

827. Wolves work together and communicate with each other to make decisions as a group. Dogs however operate under a strict hierarchy.

828. Dogs love the herb anise the same way that cats love catnip. In fact, anise is the scent used on the artificial rabbit in greyhound races to get the dogs to run.

829. Chicken eggs as well as other bird eggs have tiny holes or pores on them, which allow baby birds to breathe in oxygen and get rid of carbon dioxide. A chicken egg, for example, has more than 7,000 pores.

830. According to scientist Martin Banks from the University of California, Berkeley, animals with vertical slits as pupils are likely to be an ambush predator. As these animals need to correctly judge the distance between them and their prey, having vertical slits actually optimizes that ability.

831. Owls are actually unable to roll or move their eyes and instead turn their heads in order to look sideways. Some owls are even able to turn their heads up to 270 degrees.

832. One of the most deadly venoms in the world is found in the box jellyfish. Human victims can sometimes drown of heart failure from the pain and shock, and survivors can feel significant pain for weeks after. They also often leave scarring on the body area where the tentacle made contact.

833. The famous sound made by cicadas is actually only produced by males. Their organs have something called tymbals; their muscles pop the tymbals in and out creating that well-known sound.

834. When rabbits are born, they are furless, blind, and too weak to move by themselves. Hares on the other hand are born with lots of hair, can immediately see, and are strong enough to start bouncing around right after birth.

835. Zoe is a very unique white zebra that has light golden stripes and blue eyes due to a condition known as amelanosis. She lives at Hawaii's Three Ring Ranch animal sanctuary.

836. Based on the mood that it's experiencing, the sailfish changes the color of its skin. When they hunt for prey, they become darker. When they are excited or tired, they become neon and copper colored.

837. When dogs are pooping, they feel more vulnerable so they look at their owners for protection.

838. According to records, Australian jewel beetles have been observed to attempt to mate with empty beer bottles instead of females because of the bottle's brown color. This has led to a reduced survival rate for them.

839. The alligators in Southern Florida greatly outnumber crocodiles. It's the only place on the planet where you can find gators and crocs coexisting in the wild.

840. A group of hippos is called a crash. A group of emus is called a mob. A group of crows is called a murder. A group of zebras is called a zeal. A group of apes is called a shrewdness. A group of giraffes is called a tower. And a group of bears is called a sleuth.

841. Honey bees have five eyes: two compound eyes that help them see around themselves at the same time, and three simple eyes situated on the top of their heads that help them with orientation.

842. Guinea pigs are very lonely and social creatures. Hence, in New Zealand, it's illegal to own just one. In fact, they have matchmaking companies that match up your guinea pig if their partner dies, which is part of a sweeping animals' rights legislation that was first introduced in 2008.

843. There are some animals that are immune to the venom of the black widow spider, such as sheep and rabbits.

844. The largest living crocodile in captivity, the Australian saltwater, is eighteen feet (5.5 meters) long according to the Guinness World Records. It's also considered as the most fearsome of today's species; they can live for more than 100 years, grow up to twenty-three feet (seven meters), and weigh more than one ton.

845. If the parents of a baby squirrel die, other squirrels will adopt the baby.

846. In January 2016, a new species of hermit crab was accidentally discovered by underwater photographer Ellen Mueller at the National Marine Park of the southern Caribbean island of Bonaire. It has been called the "Candy Striped Hermit Crab" because its legs look like candy canes.

847. To establish which pets cared more about their owners, Dr. Paul Zack did a neuroscience experiment in 2016 where he checked the levels of oxytocin, the love hormone, in cats and dogs after they played with their owners. He found that the hormone increased by just 12% in cats, but in dogs, it increased by an average of 57%.

848. In order to hide from predators and also sneak up on prey, the praying mantis can actually camouflage itself by changing color. It can vary from dark brown to green to blend in with tree bark and leaves.

849. The largest eyes ever studied in the animal kingdom belong to the colossal squid, measuring almost eleven inches (twenty seven centimeters), almost the same size as a volleyball. In fact, researchers believe that they may be the largest eyes that ever existed.

850. There is a type of bird called "potoos" that use body posture to camouflage themselves in nature looking like the part of a tree stump.

851. The world's slowest mammal is the sloth. Due to its sedentary character, algae grow on its coat giving it a greenish tinge that helps camouflage them in trees.

852. At the Marine Mammal Studies Institute in Mississippi, dolphins were trained to bring trash back that fell into the pools in exchange for fish. Kelly, one of the smartest dolphins, hid pieces of paper under a rock and tore off smaller paper pieces in order to get more fish out of it.

853. About 30% of all the food that Americans eat is actually pollinated by honeybees as well as 85% of all flowering plants. Honeybees are also responsible for 90% of the pollen that is transferred to and from our orchard crops. Unfortunately, 70% of the feral honeybee population has disappeared or died.

854. The largest species of earthworm in the world can measure up to ten feet (three meters) long. It can be found in Gippsland, in southeastern Australia.

855. Sea cucumbers can mutilate their own bodies when feeling threatened, as a defense mechanism. They are able to violently contract their muscles and jettison some of their internal organs out of their anus. The missing body parts are later rapidly regenerated.

856. "Frito feet" is the term coined for when a pet dog's paws smell oddly of corn chips. The yeasty odor is actually caused by bacteria the canine has picked up.

857. Blood type in dogs is different from the types found in humans. Although there are six main blood types, 42% of dogs have the same type, which is universal.

858. There are very few non-extinct mammals that are venomous, and male platypuses are among them. Evidently, their venom causes excruciating pain that is resistant to painkillers and has long lasting effects, but it's non-lethal to humans. They secrete the venom from hind leg spurs during their breeding season.

859. "The Boss" is a big grizzly bear that lives in Bath, Canada. According to residents, he has eaten two black bears; he walks through the town in the middle of the day and has fathered many of the bears that live in Banff, Yoho, and Kootenay National Parks.

860. While in water, fish can actually drown or suffocate. They get their oxygen directly from the water through their gills so if for some reason that water runs out of oxygen, they drown just like an air-breathing animal would.

861. To attract females, male capuchin monkeys urinate on their hands and cover their body with urine.

862. Amazonian butterflies have been known to drink turtle tears so they can receive mineral sodium from them.

863. Mosquitoes use a Zen-like approach of non-resistance in order to survive the impact of raindrops.

864. The fastest shark in the world is the mako shark. It can swim as fast as sixty miles (ninety six kilometers) per hour, while the average shark only swims at a speed of 1.5 miles (2.4 kilometers) per hour.

865. According to a 2010 report, it's estimated that about 30,000 elephants a year are killed by poachers to keep up with the global demand for ivory. As a result, the United States has adopted a near-total ivory ban since July, 2016. In fact, the previous year, more than a ton of ivory was crushed in New York City as part of the US government's effort to crack down on the illegal trade.

866. No two wolves will howl on the same note when howling together. Instead, they harmonize to create the illusion that there are more wolves than there actually are.

867. The Otton frog is a rare Japanese frog species that carries a hidden weapon. They have retractable claws that can shoot out from their thumbs. They use these claws as switchblades to fight and mate.

868. In a single stride, ostriches' long legs can cover nine to sixteen feet (three to five meters). Their legs can also act as powerful weapons. One kick for example can kill a human or a potential predator like a lion.

869. The Meganeuropsis is the largest known insect of all-time. It looks like a dragonfly and measures roughly fifteen inches (forty seven centimeters) long with a wingspan of thirty inches (seventy five centimeters) long.

870. After the death of Meow in 2012, a cat who weighed forty pounds (eighteen kilograms), the Guinness Book of World Records no longer records the heaviest pets in the world to discourage intentional overeating.

871. The dwarf crocodile is the smallest crocodile in the world. It measures about 5.5 feet (1.7 meters) in length and weighs only thirteen pounds (six kilograms).

872. According to a study published by a research team from the University of Florida, bed bugs love the colors black and red, and hate yellow and green.

873. An adult gray wolf can eat more than twenty two pounds (ten kilograms) of meat in only one sitting.

874. Frogs cannot swallow keeping their eyes open.

875. For gorillas, burping is something they do when they feel happy and at ease.

876. Pregnancy in elephants lasts up to 680 days, the longest period known of any animal. Additionally, unlike other animals, elephants are born with an advanced level of brain development and also have a unique cycle of ovulation and hormone levels.

877. Cognitive dysfunction syndrome is a condition similar to Alzheimer that affects dogs. It's estimated that 28% of dogs aged eleven to twelve years old suffer from this. And about 60% of dogs that are fifteen to sixteen years old also present signs of the disease.

878. In Hanahan, South Carolina, there is a 4.9 feet (1.5 meter) long orange alligator living in a pond. Locals named it Trumpigator.

879. When a rain storm is approaching, frogs are known to croak louder. Experts think that because frogs mate and then lay eggs in bodies of freshwater, there are actually more watery places for them to choose from after a heavy rain.

880. Bulls are actually color blind, so it doesn't really matter the color of the matador's cape. It's the motion that attracts the bull's attention to charge, not the color red.

881. The orca that was in the movie "Free Willy," Keiko, was released back into the wild after twenty three years in captivity in 2002. Weeks after its release, it would come back to the Norwegian inlet seeking human contact and give children rides on its back.

882. The largest mouth in the world according to the Guinness World Records belongs to the bowhead whale. It can measure up to sixteen feet (4.8 meters) long, thirteen feet (four meters) high, and eight feet (2.4 meters) wide. Its tongue alone can weigh nearly 200 pounds (ninety kilograms).

883. The teeth of beavers contain iron, so they are capable of cutting through wood easily; this is also why they are orange-colored. Although their teeth look like they are decaying, the iron actually protects them from tooth decay.

884. To help combat the cheetah's stress and focus their wild energy, zoos have begun raising puppies and cheetah kittens together.

885. In order to save the Przewalski's horse from extinction, it was introduced to habits in the Chernobyl area. Because the area has very few if any humans in it, it turned out to be the perfect horse habitat, and the population is thriving.

886. About three million years ago, marsupials made their way into Australia from South America by traveling through Antarctica when it didn't have any ice.

887. The male seahorse becomes pregnant instead of the female. The unfertilized eggs are passed by the female to the sperm producing male, where they are fertilized and then kept in a sealable brood pouch on the male. Ten to twenty days later, the male gives birth to thousands of babies.

888. "Ear furnishing" is the term used to refer to the fur that grows on the inside of the ears of cats.

889. Dalmatian puppies are usually born with solid white coats. The spots are invisible and they appear when the puppies are about ten days old.

890. The nose prints of cats are unique as humans' fingerprints. When cat microchips become useless, nose prints can be used to identify lost cats. Additionally, a cat's sense of smell is known to be fourteen times more sensitive than ours.

891. The highest flying bird ever recorded is the ruppell's griffon vulture. They have been recorded to fly at an altitude of seven miles (eleven kilometers) from the ground. To put it into perspective, the average commercial plane flies at about 5.5-7.4 miles (nine to twelve kilometers) in the air. The vulture, in fact, has developed a special type of hemoglobin which makes their oxygen intake much more effective at those heights.

892. Like humans, koalas have fingerprints; in fact, they are quite similar to human ones. Even through careful analysis under a microscope, it's not easy to differentiate the loopy, whorled ridges on koala's fingers from our own.

893. Cats' eyes have a reddish glow in darkness as a result of light reflecting on a layer of tissue located inside the eyeball behind the retina, that's known as the tapetum lucidum.

894. Racoons that live in the city are very intelligent and have adapted to their environment, learning to open doors and take lids of trash cans.

895. According to different studies, hummingbirds are able to remember migration routes as well as every flower that they have ever visited. The brain in a hummingbird makes up 4.2% of its entire weight; in proportion, it is the largest of any other bird.

896. One of the tiniest known vertebrates is the common pygmy seahorse, or Bargibant's seahorse. It's a camouflage expert and has a maximum length of just one inch (2.5 centimeters).

897. The Wallace flying frog is known to be able to glide from tree branches and glide up to forty nine feet (fifteen meters) by splaying their four webbed feet. As they fall, the skin flaps catch the air.

898. Cats intentionally manipulate people into doing what they want, whether it's to be fed or something else. They make a special kind of purring sound that's similar to a normal purr, but has in it a cry that people find difficult to ignore.

899. Orcas are also known as killer whales and are actually dolphins, not whales.

900. Pregnancy time of gorillas is the same as humans, that is, nine months. However, gorilla babies usually weigh less than human babies, about 3.8 pounds (1.81 kilograms), but their development is around twice as fast.

901. Only one kind of snake has a pair of tentacles at the front part of its head, and it's called a "tentacle snake." The tentacles have the ability to detect vibration and pressure.

902. Although baby hedgehogs are born with quills, they are actually soft and flexible.

903. The spray that comes out of a blue whale's blowhole when it exhales can reach almost thirty feet (nine meters) into the air.

904. In 1998, Fiona Hunter, a researcher at the University of Cambridge, and Lloyd Davis of the University of Otago were the first to report prostitution among penguins and chimpanzees. They were studying the mating patterns of the Adélie Penguins when they noticed that they prostitute themselves for things like stones or food.

905. "Drake" is the name given to a male duck.

906. The emperor penguin can dive up to 1,800 feet (550 meters) underwater which is deeper than any other bird. They can also hold their breath for up to twenty minutes at a time.

907. To help them swallow food, leopard frogs use their eyes. They squeeze their eyes shut, pulling them inwards toward their mouths, and this helps compress food and push it down their throats.

908. The teeth of marine snails are so strong that they are able to clamp onto rocks and grind them down as they feed. They are made from the strongest natural material on Earth.

909. Llamas are pack animals. They can carry up to seventy five pounds (thirty four kilograms) for up to twenty miles (thirty two kilometers). If you overload one however, it will refuse to move and it will lay down and spit or hiss at you until the load is lightened.

910. Rodents cannot vomit due to anatomical constraints. In other words, they simply aren't built with the ability to.

911. Flamingos can fly at a speed of thirty five miles (fifty six kilometers) per hour when flying in a flock. They may seem a bit clumsy in flight because their long necks stretch out in front of their bodies, and their long legs dangle well past their short tails.

912. Every time whales poop, they transport vital nutrients to the warm surface waters, where phytoplankton use the nutrients to photosynthesize and produce oxygen.

913. For around 400 years, pig-tailed macaques have been raised and trained to pick coconuts in Thailand. A male monkey can collect an average of 1,600 coconuts a day and a female can get around 600, while a human can only collect about eighty in a day.

914. Wesley is a golden retriever from Michigan that was outfitted with braces. Due to his crooked teeth, he couldn't close his mouth or chew well.

915. There are some salamanders that have no lungs. They breathe entirely through their skin and the tissue lining in their mouths. In order to respire, their skin and mouths must keep moist, so they are only found in damp areas.

916. Hamsters are able to blink only one eye at a time.

917. When feeling threatened, a group of penguins will put the females and children in the middle and form a huge circle around them, with the males facing inwards and spraying their excrement out to fend off predators.

918. There is a species of immortal jellyfish known as Turritopsis dohrnii. They are called the immortal jellyfish because they don't die, they just revert to their polyp (juvenile) stage over and over again.

919. Snakes are able to predict earthquakes. They can sense a coming earthquake from seventy five miles away (120 kilometers), up to five days before it actually happens.

920. When horses are in a group, they will not go to sleep at the same time; at least one of them will stay awake to look out for the others.

921. Sloths suffer from constipation. They only urinate and defecate once a week.

922. Owls don't have eyeballs but eye tubes instead. Given that they can't move these tubes back and forth, they have developed incredible neck flexibility to be able to see the world around them.

923. There is an extinct species of penguins that were nearly seven feet tall. The species, known as Palaeeudyptes klekowskii or colossus penguins, roamed Antarctica thirty seven million years ago. They weighed about 250 pounds (113 kilograms) and stood about 6.6 feet (two meters) tall, which is the height of the average NBA player.

924. According to scientists, homosexual activity among male giraffes is more common than heterosexual activity. In one study performed in Tanzania and published in Biological Exuberance, 94% of all observed mounting activity was same-sex.

Art & Artists

925. A man-made island was constructed in Mexican waters with 100,000 plastic bottles that helped it stay afloat, by Richart Sowa, a British artist. It is more than eighty two feet (twenty five meters) long, and the Mexican government officially recognized it as an eco-boat.

926. The art masterpiece "Mona Lisa" by Leonard Da Vinci wasn't famous until it was stolen in 1911 from the Louvre.

927. Museo Atlantico is an underwater museum located off the coast of the Spanish island of Lanzarote. It contains the sculptures of British artist Jason de Caires Taylor, which portray our changing and even destructive role in the modern world.

928. David Choe is a graffiti artist who painted Facebook's first office in 2005. He was then paid in shares that are now worth over $200,000,000.

929. The Mona Lisa was once removed from the Louvre Museum so Napoleon could hang it on his bedroom wall.

930. Vincent van Gogh, the renowned Dutch painter, was epileptic.

931. Whenever artist Claude Monet discovered faults in his paintings, he'd immediately destroy them. At one point, he destroyed fifteen of his own paintings right before an exhibition, causing it to be postponed. Those paintings were worth $100,000 according to a newspaper report, and that's more than $2 million in our time.

932. Beethoven was challenged to an improvisation contest by a pianist named Daniel Steibelt. When Beethoven's turn came around, he took the piece, placed it upside down on the stand, and played it. He performed so nicely that Steibelt was furious and he immediately left in the middle of the performance, declaring he would never again perform at an event where Beethoven was also invited.

933. Alfie Bradley, a popular artist, used 100,000 knives to create a twenty three foot (seven meter) tall sculpture, in order to bring attention to the growing rate of knife crimes in Britain. However, the police confiscated his sculpture, and they then joined up with other police stations to collect knives they had taken off the street, which they added to the sculpture and then unveiled it to the public.

934. Dismaland was a 2015 pop-up art exhibition that was created by Banksy in a UK resort, and it stayed open for five weeks. The exhibition featured an apocalyptic theme park, and included displays that critiqued immigrations, consumerism, celebrity culture, and law enforcement.

935. Wolfgang Amadeus Mozart is the full name of the legendary composer, and also an anagram for "German Waltz god," who was well known at the time. Mozart was born in modern-day Austria, although Leopold, his father, was from Osburg, Germany, which means the anagram was strangely prophetic.

936. In August 2016, a huge statue of Pikachu on a defunct fountain was placed in the Coliseum Museum Park in New Orleans, by an anonymous artist.

937. The three wise monkeys actually have names. The see no evil monkey is named Mizaru, the hear no evil monkey is named Mikazaru, and the speak no evil monkey is named Mazaru.

938. Mariusz Kedzierski is a famous photo realistic portrait drawing artist who was born without arms. He refused to give up on his dreams and became an artist who has even won global awards.

939. The older sister of Wolfgang Amadeus Mozart was also a child prodigy. She was named Maria Anna. In fact, they used to perform together until she turned eighteen years old. At the time, a child could perform and tour, a woman, however, risked her reputation, so she never toured again.

940. In 1958, a giant sculpture of an atom called "The Atomium" was built by the World's Fair in Brussels, Belgium, to symbolize the atomic age. It's 335 feet (102 meters) tall and has nine, fifty nine diameter foot (eighteen diameter meter) spheres attached by tubes.

941. Inakadate is a small village in Japan that has reinvented itself by creating rice paddy art. The style of art is created by combining grains of rice in variations to make amazing images.

942. Californian artist Bin Dun creates art by taking photographs of people from the Vietnam War and with the help of sunlight and glass, prints them onto leaves and then casts them in resin.

943. Artist Millie Brown from London creates art by swallowing dead soy milk in a mixture of colors and then vomiting it onto a white canvas.

944. "Red Vineyard at Arles" was the only painting sold by artist Vincent van Gogh during his entire life.

945. In 1984, the famed artist Bob Ross painted a grayscale landscape to show a colorblind man he met that everyone was able to paint.

946. Artist Heidi Hooper from Pennsylvania makes award-winning art out of dryer lint.

947. In 1965, artist Salvador Dali drew a picture of Jesus on the cross and donated it to Rikers Island prison in New York. It hung in the dining hall of the prison for sixteen years, but then it was moved to a Plexiglas case in the lobby because prison administration feared that the prisoners might damage the painting. Surprisingly, it was actually stolen by four prison officials, including a deputy, in 2003.

948. On the sidewalks of Boston there are poems that can only be seen when it rains. They were painted with special waterproof paint, which only appears when wet.

949. In the Hocking Hills Welcome Center in Ohio, there is a Pencil Sharpener Museum. It features a collection of more than 3,400 pencil sharpeners that used to belong to Reverend Paul A. Johnson, who began collecting them in the late 1980's. There are sharpeners of all kinds, from cars, planes, toys, Mickey Mouse, to even US presidents.

950. At the Guggenheim Museum, there's an eighteen karat gold fully functional toilet called America. Created by Italian artist Maurizio Cattelan, the toilet was installed in one of the museum's small single unit restrooms. Visitors are actually encouraged to use it.

951. David Oliveira, a famous Portuguese artist, uses wire to draw in the air and creates sculptures that look like pencil sketches.

952. The artist who painted American Gothic, Grant Wood, used his sister Nan and his dentist Dr. Byron McKeeby as his models. The house actually exists in Eldon, Iowa.

953. According to Vincent van Gogh's brother, his last words were: "The sadness will last forever."

954. Cheese making artists at Dublin Science Gallery made cheese using bacteria from several artists and scientists. The bacteria were collected using sterile cotton swabs from different parts of their body including the belly button, mouth, and even tears.

955. In Peaks Island, Maine, there is a museum entirely dedicated to umbrella sleeves. There are over 700 umbrella coverings that hang from the walls and ceiling.

956. In downtown Austin, Minnesota, there is a museum dedicated to Spam. It has bluegrass instruments made of Spam cans, a Spam rocket, a Spam can conveyor suspended from the ceiling, and a Spam children's play area.

957. An underground chamber containing over 8,000 life-sized warrior figures made out of terracotta clay was found by local farmers when drilling for water in the Shaanxi province of China, in March of 1974. The chamber belonged to China's first emperor Qin Shi Huang, who ordered the construction of the figures back in 246 B.C., in readiness for his own burial; he was only thirteen years old at the time.

958. Photographer Hallgrimur Pierre Helgason once captured stunning images of the Aurora Borealis over Iceland just at the moment they formed the outline of a phoenix.

959. In downtown Dallas, there is a thirty foot (nine meter) tall sculpture of an eyeball. It was created by multimedia artist Tony Tasset, from Chicago, in 2007, and it's located on the grounds of the Joule Hotel.

960. Keisuke Yamada is a Japanese artist who creates incredible carvings out of bananas using only a spoon and a toothpick.

961. In Houston, Texas, there is a museum called the Art Car Museum, also known as the Garage Mahal, which is filled with ornately painted, decorated vehicles. It opened in 1998 and features a bunch of different automobiles ranging from hippy vans to police cruisers.

962. Picasso was once asked "Did you do this?" of his painting "Guernica," a painting of German bombings on the town of Guernica, by a German officer. His response was: "No, you did."

963. Around the year 1500 AD, Leonardo da Vinci made a robot whose exterior consisted of a medieval German-Italian suit of armor, and it had an inner working mechanism. It could sit down, stand up, move its arms, and raise its visor.

964. Johannes Stotter is an artist who spent over four years painting a woman to resemble a parrot.

965. Legendary artist Vincent van Gogh made the majority of his paintings from May, 1889, to May, 1890, during which time he had checked himself into a mental institution in Saint-Rémy-de-Provence, France, called Saint Paul Asylum.

966. Two Spanish brothers from Girona sold a counterfeit Francisco de Goya painting for 1.7 million Swiss Francs to someone claiming to be a Sheik in December, 2014. They later found out that the notes were photocopied, and they were just as fake as the painting.

967. Scissors were invented by Leonardo da Vinci.

968. Instead of paying his secretaries, Salvador Dali chose to offer them commission. As a result, they ended up making seven figures many years later.

969. In the village of Ziembark, Poland, there is a house that is completely upside down. It was designed as an artwork to represent the end of the communist era in Poland, by Polish businessman and philanthropist Daniel Sirpaski. The house was finished in 2007 and took almost five times longer than a conventional house to construct.

970. In front of the National Gallery of Canada, in Ottawa, there is a bronze statue of a spider designed by artist Louise Bourgeois. It's called "Maman" and it cost a whopping $3.2 million. The statue measures thirty feet (nine meters) high, weighs over 13,000 pounds (5,900 kilograms), and has twenty-six white marble eggs in a sack on its underbelly.

971. Leonardo da Vinci was a genius and famous artist in his time. He was also paranoid, dyslexic, and ambidextrous. He could paint or draw forwards with a single hand, and use the other hand to write sentences backwards.

972. When famous artist Henri Matisse was in his 80's and partially bed ridden, he would sketch portraits from his bed by using a 3.9 feet (1.2 meter) long stick with a pencil or piece of charcoal attached to the end in order to reach the paper or canvas.

973. An Ecuadorian artist named Oscar Santillan removed an inch (2.5 centimeters) off England's highest mountain in 2015. Oscar was accused of vandalism and the British demanded that he return the stolen inch.

974. Famous artist Leonardo da Vinci was born out of wedlock, and that's why he never had a last name. The "da Vinci" part of his name actually comes from the town Vinci where he was born, so his name means Leonardo of Vinci.

975. The Moulage Museum in Zurich, Switzerland, is a museum dedicated to wax representations of disfiguring diseases. In the past, civilizations as old as the ancient Egyptians used wax to record how people looked when they died.

976. You can find over 582,000 Buddhas in the Thanboddhay Pagoda Temple in Myanmar.

977. The "London Booster" is a mechanical sculpture which was made by David Cerny to mark the 2012 London Summer Olympics. It's made from a double-decker bus from 1958, and it looks like an athlete with arms that mimic a pushup motion every day at three.

978. An Irish man named Alsan Dixon is known to master the art of the animal selfie. Although pictures look very casual, he sometimes spends hours gaining an animal's trust before a shot.

979. Pablo Diego Jose Francisco de Paula Juan Nepomuceno Crispin Crispiniano María Remedios de la Santísima Trinidad Ruiz Picasso was actually Pablo Picasso's full name.

980. In 2017, Leonardo da Vinci's Salvator Mundi was sold for $450 million dollars at an auction to a prince from Abu Dhabi, becoming the most expensive painting ever sold.

981. The world's first cyborg artist is a man named Neil Harbisson. He has an antenna implanted in his skull, which allows him to hear colors and see sounds. He can also connect to nearby devices via Bluetooth and Wi-Fi.

982. Bob Ross made the "Joy of Painting" series completely for free and only made money from his art supply store.

983. In Boston, there is a Museum of Bad Art. It is the world's only museum that is entirely dedicated to bad art in all of its forms.

984. Chinsekikan is a museum located in Chichibu, Japan, that has almost 2,000 rocks that resemble human faces. The museum's name means "hall of curious rocks."

985. In the 1960's, the Fly Geyser was accidentally created by a power company in Nevada's Black Rock Desert. They did this by drilling into a geothermic pocket that let loose a stream of oil, water, and calcium deposits. Today, it's a vibrant, living sculpture that is always changing due to the colorful algae in the water.

986. Grace Brett is a 104 year old knitter who yarn-bombed her town. She is thought to be the world's oldest street artist.

987. There is a form of art called non visible art. The works are imagined by an artist, then described to an audience. A woman named Amie Davidson bought a piece in 2011 for ten thousand dollars stating that she "really identified with the ideology of the non visible art project."

988. In March 2017, an almost twenty six foot (eight meter) tall statue of King Samotek I, who ruled Egypt from 664 to 610 B.C, was found by a team of Egyptian and German archaeologists. Originally, it was believed to be a representation of Pharaoh Ramses II. The statue is over 3,000 years old.

989. The most visited museum in the world in 2014 was the Louvre Museum, in Paris. It welcomed about 9.3 million visitors, almost as many people as the population of Sweden.

990. Mark Quinn is an artist that creates self-portraits using his own blood as a medium. He casts his own head in plaster mixed with ten pints of his own blood and then immerses it in frozen silicone. He has been doing this every year, since 1991, as a way to preserve the natural aging process as well as a symbol of his alcohol addiction.

991. In 2012, an old bridge in Wuppertal, Germany, was transformed into a massive Lego structure by street artist Megx. He used colored panels to create the illusion of the underside as Lego bricks.

992. Since 1972, artist Michael Heizer has been working on a huge sculpture in the Nevada desert. The piece of art is called "City" and covers an area of 1.2 miles (two kilometers) by 0.2 miles (0.4 kilometers). According to the artist, he got inspired after visiting Yucatan and having studied Chichén Itzá. The work of art won't be open to the public until 2020.

993. The Museo Galileo in Florence, Italy, exhibits Galileo's preserved middle finger. It stands eternally giving the bird in the general direction of the church that once censored his theories, destroyed his good name, imprisoned him in his home, refused for nearly a century to give the man the decent burial that he was due, and for 350 years, neglected to grant him any honor.

994. In 1856, after trick photography was developed, creating headless portraits became a trend that swept through the Victorian era.

Bizarre

995. During World War II, while fighting, Don Karkos was hit with shrapnel that blinded his right eye. Sixty four years later, while working in a barn, a horse head-butted him in the exact same spot, threw him against a wall, and restored his vision all of a sudden.

996. In ancient Greece, an apple used to be thrown at someone to symbolically declare one's love for them. In Greek mythology, the Greek goddess Eris became discontented after she was excluded from a wedding; in revenge, she tossed a golden apple inscribed with "For the most beautiful one" into the wedding party. At that point, it was claimed by Aphrodite, and hence became a symbol for love.

997. In Philadelphia, United States, the Mutter Museum exhibits the body of a woman that was naturally converted into soap because of the chemicals in the soil where she was buried.

998. All tattoos in North Korea must carry praise of the Kim family, or carry a teaching of the state. In other words, they must have a political purpose, for example: "Guard the great leader to our death," or "We are the general's offspring."

999. In Washington State, there is a serious growing problem that involves people leaving their bikes and even cars on ferries. It's a serious concern, because ferry employees have to deal with the possibility that the passengers might have fallen overboard.

1000. Chunosuke Matsuyama, a Japanese treasure hunter, was shipwrecked in 1784 in a south Pacific island so he wrote an SOS message on coconut wood, put it in a bottle, and tossed it into the ocean. The bottle wasn't found in his lifetime, but in 1935, it eventually washed ashore in the exact village where Matsuyama was born.

1001. Hippophagy is the practice or the act of eating horse meat.

1002. Every February there is a hair freezing contest at the Takhini Hot Pools in Yukon, Canada. Visitors dunk their hair into 104 degrees Fahrenheit (forty degrees Celsius) hot water and then let it freeze in the chilly air above, which is usually below negative twenty two degrees Fahrenheit (negative thirty degrees Celsius).

1003. In 2005, there was a murder in Belfast bar where there were seventy one potential witnesses. All of them claimed to be in the four by three toilet when the attack happened.

1004.   Between the 1940's and 1970's, Ivy League schools such as Yale and Harvard attempted to see if there was any correlation between physical attributes and intelligence. They took nude photos of each freshman and some of those pupils include Hillary Clinton, Meryl Streep and George Bush.

1005.   The Foreign Accent Syndrome is an unusual brain disorder that causes people to involuntarily speak in foreign accents.

1006.   In 2008, a meat-scented fragrance for meat-loving men was introduced by Burger King. It was called Flame and it came out for the Christmas season. It was promoted as the scent of seduction with a hint of flame-broiled meat.

1007.   Artful Ashes is a company that will swirl your loved one's cremated ashes with color into a glass decorative as a piece of art.

1008.   The second person to ever go over Niagara Falls in a barrel was Bobby Leach. Amazingly, he survived the stunt, but died ironically fifteen years later while walking down a street in Auckland, New Zealand. He stepped on an orange peel, slipped and fell down, breaking a leg. The leg got infected, had to be amputated, and he died during surgery.

1009.   A study published in the proceedings of the National Academy of Sciences revealed that female named storms have historically killed more people. People don't consider them as dangerous and they don't take the same precautions as the male named storms.

1010.   George Foreman, an Olympic gold medalist for boxing, had five sons whom he all named George.

1011.   Dying in London's Houses of Parliament is actually illegal.

1012.   Studies have shown that the naked mole rat is unable to feel pain, is resistant to cancer, and has extraordinary longevity for a rodent.

1013.   Having Christmas dinner at KFC is so popular in Japan that there are sometimes two hour lines at locations for people waiting to get in.

1014.   As a result of a serious bus accident in March, 2018, an Indian man needed to have one limb amputated. Afterwards, he asked the doctors for a pillow, and after they said they had none to spare, he used his cut off leg as the pillow.

1015.   Terry Davis, a forty eight year old computer programmer with schizophrenia, spent ten years creating an operating system he calls Temple O's. He says he created it so people could use it to communicate with God.

1016.   For a big chunk of his life, Ferdinand Waldo Demara pretended to be other people. The American identity thief moved around a lot starting in 1941, and he impersonated a prison warden, monks, a deputy sheriff and once pretended to be a member of the Brothers of Christian Instruction called Brother John Payne, and ended up founding a college that received a real charter from the state. He also pretended to be a surgeon when he was on a Royal Canadian Naval Destroyer during the Korean War. Although he was a complete fraud, he actually read a textbook and memorized how to perform some surgeries, and he operated on sixteen Korean casualties.

1017.   A monkey called Bobby was arrested by Pakistani authorities in 2011, after it made an illegal crossing into the country from India. Strangely, it became public knowledge that this was done in revenge because at one time, India detained a pigeon which they said was spying for Pakistan.

1018.   Within an hour of getting executed on March 20, 1995, thirty two year old Thomas J. Grosso, a convicted murderer, spent his last words complaining about his last meal. He said that he was given spaghetti instead of the SpaghettiOs that he had ordered, and he wanted the press to know that.

1019.   At one point, musician Kesha asked her fans to send her samples of their teeth. She was making an art piece while she was in rehab battling an eating disorder, and the teeth were to be used to complete the art piece.

1020. A man named Robert Hubbard was executed in 1666 for starting the great fire of London when he claimed that he threw a firebomb through a bakery window. This was even though he was heavily crippled, that bakery didn't have any windows, and it was proved in court that he wasn't even in the country when it happened.

1021. In La Paz, Bolivia, the public water supply was contaminated by metal infused acidic run-off that washed in from old mines, but fortunately researchers discovered an interesting way to filter it; they used llama feces. Bacteria in the feces got rid of most dissolved metals and neutralized the acids.

1022. Roughly 7% of Americans believe that brown cows produce chocolate milk, according to interviews carried out by the Innovation Center for US Dairy.

1023. Adnan and Saina were a couple in a loveless marriage, and in 2007, they both started looking for someone new on the Internet. They both found someone online that they thought could be their soulmate. Upon meeting in person, they realized that they had set up a date with each other. Even after this coincidence, and the affection they had over the Internet, they each accused the other one of infidelity, and they eventually divorced.

1024. The armonica was an instrument made of thirty seven glass bowls that varied in size, were threaded together on a spindle made of iron, and painted in coded colors to identify different notes. Those who played it experienced negative side effects, ringing of the ears, disorientation, and even mental breakdowns.

1025. A website used by Iraqi rebels showed a picture of a captured US soldier on February 1, 2005, claiming that the soldier would be decapitated if certain prisoners weren't released. A little later, American toy maker Dragon Models announced that the supposed prisoner was an action figure that they had created, and not an actual soldier.

1026. The rights to Vantablack, the blackest of all black colors in the world, were bought by artist Anish Kapoor in 2016, so he is the only one that can use it. In response, artist Stuart Semple created the World's Pinkest Pink color pigment, which anyone could buy except for Anish Kapoor.

1027. Back in 1896, a paper in Australia published a claim that sitting inside a dead whale cured rheumatism. Their source was a drunk man who asserted that his joint pain was cured after doing this.

1028. There is a higher likelihood of you dying on your birthday, than on any other day in a given year, according to research done in 2014. This likelihood gets even higher when your birthday is on the weekend.

1029. Revell, a model making company, agreed in June, 2018, to stop making a model of a made-up Nazi UFO called Huanebu II, which, according to the packaging literature, was allegedly the first ship that could go to space. The company got several complaints for the historically inaccurate and ridiculous characterization, and they apologized.

1030. Buzz Aldrin, shortly after returning from the moon and leaving NASA, tried to develop a career as an Air Force test pilot with no success. Later on, he started drinking, had an affair, suffered depression, got divorced, got remarried, got divorced again, and became a Cadillac salesman where he failed to sell a car for six months.

1031. Some criminal cases have not only used fingerprints to solve a crime but also toe prints.

1032. In 2007, Marshall McCue, a researcher from the department of biological sciences at the University of Arkansas, studied snakes and found that intense hunger can cause them to digest their own heart muscle. Nevertheless, immediately after a nutritious meal, snake hearts can actually quickly rebuild themselves.

1033. William Howard Taft, the 27th president of the United States, loved large bathtubs very much. In 1909, he had a huge bathtub built that weighed a ton. It was installed on the USS North Carolina (a navy battleship) for a visit to the Panama Canal. He had another tub installed in the Taft Hotel that was 7.8 feet (2.4 meters) long, 3.9 feet (1.2 meters) wide. Taft used to weigh 339 pounds (154 kilograms).

1034. "Just Enough Room Island" is the official name of an island located in the Thousand Island chain separating Canada and the United States, in the St. Lawrence River. It was purchased in the 1950's by the

Sizeland family, and it has just enough room on its surface for a house, a tree, and a few chairs to sit on the outside.

1035. From 1833 to 1855, Antonio Lopez de Santa Anna was president of Mexico eleven times.

1036. There is a place called Fields of the Wood Bible Park in Murphy, North Carolina, that has a mountain called the "Ten Commandments Mountain," where the Ten Commandments are literally engraved into the side of its grassy slope.

1037. There is a Japanese practice known as "forest bathing" where you just hang out around trees. It's proven to lower blood pressure, heart rate, reduce stress, boost your immune system and increase your overall well being.

1038. The term exocannibalism makes reference to when you eat someone outside your own family or tribe. Endocannibalism on the opposite is when you eat someone from the same community or tribe.

1039. In 1932, Winston Churchill was hit by a car in New York City; he received a prescription for alcohol from his doctor in order to get around the American prohibition. The doctor recommended six shots of alcohol at every meal, stating it was the best solution for the Prime Minister ails.

1040. Due to the intelligence of an octopus, it's actually illegal to perform procedures on them without anesthesia in many countries.

1041. The fear of gold is called aurophobia. People with this phobia may be allergic to gold or they may dislike how gold looks, or what it symbolizes i.e. power or death.

1042. Pinstruck.com is a website where you can anonymously put a voodoo curse on anyone. You are only requested to fill out the description of what they look like, fill out their email, and the service does the rest.

1043. Former President Lyndon B. Johnson loved dogs very much. At his daughter Lucy's wedding, he even tried to sneak in his dog Yuki.

1044. A $15.3 million iPhone was created by UK designer Stuart Hughes for a Chinese businessman. The phone is decorated with 600 white diamonds, the Apple logo is made of solid gold and fifty-three white diamonds, the screen has 135 grams of twenty-four-carat gold and sapphire glass, and the home button is a rare twenty-six-carat black diamond.

1045. A lady in Oregon wanted to give her firefighter friends some work since they hadn't seen a fire in a while so she started one which ended up spreading to seventy seven square miles (200 square kilometers), costing over seven million dollars, and taking sixty days to put out.

1046. Thirteen year old Marie Heffernan was rushed to hospital in Wollongong, Australia, during Christmas dinner in 1972 after she came down with a serious case of laryngitis and bronchitis. Six weeks after that, the condition subsided, but she couldn't speak. Twelve years later, she went into a coughing fit which brought out a ball of dark sludge, and in it was a silver coin. It turned out Marie's mother had placed a coin in the Christmas pudding back in 1972.

1047. Being slightly crossed-eyed was considered a beautiful feature among the Maya people. In fact, parents of babies would hang objects like stones right between their baby's eyes to try to get them to go cross-eyed.

1048. Gangster John Dillinger escaped from a jail in Indiana on March 3, 1934, with the help of a wooden gun that was smuggled into him by one of his attorneys.

1049. Due to mining activities at a local iron mine, the town of Kiruna in Sweden is actually sinking. The authorities are planning on moving the whole city and its inhabitants two miles (three kilometers) to the east.

1050. At the Isle of Wight Zoo, in the UK, there is an exhibition exclusively dedicated to poop. It features feces from both animals and humans. It also features fossilized poop called coprolites that date back 140 million years.

1051. In response to China's worsening air pollution, a Chinese millionaire started selling cans of fresh air for the price of eighty cents a can. Incredibly, he made over six million dollars.

1052. There is a café in Bunkyo, Tokyo, called the Moomin House Cafe that offers coffee, treats, and companionship of huge stuffed animals. They will actually seat you with a stuffed animal if you want so that you don't have to dine alone.

1053. "Extreme Kidnapping" is a company in Detroit where people pay up to $1,500 to get tied up and kidnapped just for fun.

1054. Tying a giraffe to a telephone pole or streetlamp is illegal in Atlanta, Georgia.

1055. There is a condition called puppy pregnancy syndrome where the sufferer believes that they are pregnant with puppies after being bitten by a dog.

1056. The fear of belly buttons is called "omphalophobia." Sufferers of this tend to be afraid to have their belly buttons touched or to touch another person's belly button.

1057. "Bunyadi" is a clothing optional restaurant located in London, England. It costs up to $95 a person for food and drinks; you can choose between clothed or pure naked seating areas where you will be served by semi-nude staff.

1058. It's possible to die from drowning twenty four hours after leaving water. It's known as dry drowning and the victims can be walking and talking while their lungs are actually filled with water.

1059. In Japan, there is a service consisting of hiring a handsome man who will show up at your office, sit down next to you, watch sad videos with you until you cry, and then he will wipe away your tears for you.

1060. In Tenopa, Nevada, there is a clown motel decorated with hundreds of clowns. It's located right next to a graveyard.

1061. There is a museum in Yokohama City, Japan, dedicated entirely to ramen noodles. It's called the Shin-Yokohama Raumen Museum.

1062. Superior canal dissonance is a condition where sufferers can hear their own pulse and their eyes moving in their sockets.

1063. The abnormal fear of beautiful women is called caligynephobia, or venustraphobia, or for short gynophobia.

1064. Genuphobia is the fear of knees. This rare phobia is apparently common in people that have experienced traumatic knee injuries.

1065. In the town of Hakone, in the southeastern part of Japan, there is a spa called "Yunessun Spa House" that offers ramen noodle baths. The bath consists of ramen pork broth and synthetic noodles. It allegedly helps improve a patient's skin.

1066. April 14 is known as Black Day in Korea. On this day, single people who didn't receive anything for Valentine's Day or "White Day" get together dressed in black and eat black noodles together.

1067. In the 18th century, in the Gregorian period, little beauty patches known as mouches were used by women to cover blemishes, like smallpox scars. They would often use small clippings of black velvet, silk, or satin; but those who couldn't afford silk or satin had to use a piece of mouse skin.

1068. Until 1992, electrical appliances were often sold in Britain without plugs on the end of them and consumers had to attach them themselves.

1069. Several prominent people married their first cousins, including Albert Einstein, Charles Darwin, the first prime minister of Canada, John A. Macdonald, and renowned author H.G. Wells.

1070. Papyrophobia is the fear of dry paper. Actress Megan Fox suffers from it.

1071. There is a tradition among the indigenous Sami people of Norway of castrating reindeer using their own teeth.

1072. After collecting unwashed panties that were thrown on stage by women at his shows, musician Frank Zappa had a quilt made.

1073. In China, there's a delicacy called "Virgin Boy Eggs," where the eggs are actually soaked in the urine of boys under the age of ten. The urine is collected from school washrooms and it's strongly believed that eating this can have health benefits. It's possible to buy one for only twenty four cents.

1074. You can buy a wide selection of wigs for your dog from vending machines in Tokyo, Japan. Dog wigs are so popular there that they now offer a large selection in online stores as well.

1075. Scatomancy involves telling a person's fortune by examining their poop, and it's a practice that has existed for thousands of years. Fortune tellers who do this are known as scatomancers.

1076. The irrational fear of clothes is called vestiphobia. People with this disorder experience tremors, difficult breathing, shortness of breath, or heart palpitations when they wear clothes, particularly tight ones.

1077. A pilot named Linda Ducharme held a vow renewal ceremony in 2013 with Bruce, a Ferris wheel that she had already married. She fed a piece of pizza to the Ferris wheel during the ceremony, which was officiated by a Catholic priest who declared "I tie you flesh and steel."

1078. Ireland has some really weird laws that have been in place for centuries. One states that if a leprechaun shows up at your doorstep, you have to share your dinner with him.

1079. On May 20, 2016, a man named Aaron Chervenak drove all the way from Los Angeles to a little chapel in Las Vegas to get married to his smartphone.

1080.   Porphyrophobia is the fear of the color purple.

1081.   In the Island of Tanna, there is a remote village named Yaohnanen where they worship Prince Phillip as a god, and they are currently waiting for him to go there and live among them. A prophet from the island claimed that he had a vision of a great event that would happen in the future and capture the attention of the world.

1082.   "The Boring Conference" is an annual conference where people in the past have given talks on barcodes, sneezing, and the sounds of vending machines, among other boring topics.

1083.   Koumpounophobia is the fear of buttons. Although it is differently manifested in sufferers, some people feel that buttons are dirty and some are afraid of the texture of certain buttons.

1084.   In La Crosse, Kansas, there is a museum dedicated to barbed wire.

1085.   There are coffin clubs intended for senior citizens where they get together and build their own customized coffins.

1086.   Antonio Lopez De Santa Anna, who was a Mexican general in 1838, was hit by cannon fire, so his leg had to be amputated. Four years after this happened, the general did a weird thing; he asked for his leg to be exhumed so it could be buried again with full military honors in a funeral service that included prayers and speeches. It was finally buried under a spectacular monument in Santa Paula Cemetery, inside a crystal vase.

1087.   In Japan, there is a town called "Nagoro" that has more scarecrows than people. The town has around thirty people and over 400 scarecrows.

1088.   "Need a Mom" is the name of a business established by entrepreneur Nina Keneally in Brooklyn, New York. The service involves renting a mom for forty dollars who will listen to you, give you advice, cook, and help you with chores.

1089.   For a short period of time during 1913, it was legal to mail your baby. The only condition was that the baby had to meet the eleven pound (five kilograms) weight limit. This showed just how much rural communities trusted postal workers then.

1090.   Since 1982, Clinton Montana has hosted a five day long festival called the Montana Testicle Festival, and the main event involves competitors eating bull testicles.

1091.   Parthenophobia is a type of social anxiety where sufferers have an abnormal and persistent fear of young girls, specifically virgins.

1092.   The fear of peanut butter sticking to the roof of your mouth is called arachibutyrophobia.

1093.   Miljenko Bukovic, a newspaper vendor from Valparaiso, Chile, adores actress Julia Roberts so much that he had eighty two portraits of her tattooed on his torso. It took him ten years and about 1,800 USD to get them done. In fact, he plans to get more tattoos of the star on his chest, back and arms as long as there is space and he has the money.

1094.   There's a Romanian woman who knitted a vest made out of her own hair. From the age of forty to sixty, she collected all the hair that fell out when she combed it, and at some point, she had enough hair to knit the item, which weighed 2.2 pounds (one kilogram).

1095.   In Essex, England, they have a company that allows you to hire actors to show up at your funeral, so that you can seem more popular than you really were when you were alive. It's called "Rent-A-Mourner," and their actors can come to wakes, and tell stories as though they knew the deceased.

1096.   If you drive too slow in California, you can get a ticket.

Books, Comic Books & Writers

1097. Mark Twain's childhood friend Tom Blankenship was the inspiration for his famous novel character Huckleberry Finn. They both grew up in Hannibal, Missouri, and Tom was four years older than the author.

1098. The legendary villain from the Batman Comics, The Joker, was initially supposed to be stabbed in the heart and killed during his second appearance. However, Whitney Ellsworth, who was the editor at that time, chose to keep The Joker alive, and his character grew to be Batman and Robin's arch nemesis.

1099. A book was returned to the Hereford Cathedral School Library 120 years later in December, 2016, in Hereford England. The book was checked out by student Arthur Boycott, and returned by his granddaughter Alice Gillett.

1100. Humpty Dumpty's character had been presented as an egg in about all mediums since as far back as 1872, even though the nursery rhyme doesn't mention that he is an egg.

1101. Superman was sold to DC Comics by its co-creators Jerry Siegel and Joe Shuster for $130, later earning $25,000 per year for the rest of their lives.

1102. It's possible to buy Harry Potter-inspired makeup brushes. It's a set of five brushes which are modeled after the wands of Harry, Ron, Hermione, Dumbledore, and Lord Voldemort.

1103. Bill Watterson, who created Calvin and Hobbes, rejected about $300 - $400 million worth of revenue when he refused to merchandise or license his creation, because he wanted to preserve the integrity and purity of his comic.

1104. The Disney character Baloo from The Jungle Book looks lazy and mopey because his characteristics were based on a sloth bear, an animal that's native to Nepal and India.

1105. Off the coast of Alaska there are whales that have been alive way before author Herman Melville wrote the classic novel Moby Dick. Melville published his book for the first time on October 18, 1851, and by comparison, many Arctic dwelling whales are more than 200 years old.

1106. Livraria Bertrand is the oldest bookstore on earth that is still operational. It first opened in Portugal in 1732, and it remains the largest and oldest bookstore chain in the country.

1107. Marvel made a very dark one-shot comic book in November, 1995. A fight between superheroes and supervillains ends with "The Punisher" losing his family and he then goes on a one person killing spree, killing all superheroes and supervillains before taking his own life.

1108. Novelist Arnold Bennett stayed at a hotel in Paris, France, in January, 1931, where a waiter warned that he shouldn't drink the water at the establishment. Bennett thought it was clean, and asked for a glassful anyway, but this turned out to be a fatal mistake because a couple of months later he died of typhoid.

1109. A large number of books sold on Amazon have been written by bots. Some include specialized technical and business reports, language dictionaries, and even crossword puzzle books for learning foreign languages. Marketing professor Philip M. Parker created the computer system that can write these books in about twenty minutes.

1110. Adult coloring books are becoming a huge trend and publishers actually struggle to keep up with demand. The books seem to be a way to successfully reduce stress and relieve anxiety. They are even used as rehabilitation aids for patients who are recovering from strokes.

1111. About 17,677 words were used by Shakespeare in his plays, sonnets, and narrative poems. Around 1,700 or nearly 10% of those words were invented by him by simply changing the prefixes and suffixes, connecting words together, borrowing from a different language, or just creating them altogether.

1112. Roald Dahl, the author of Charlie and the Chocolate Factory, invented over 500 new words and character names. Oompa-Loompas and Scrumdiddlyumptious are just a couple of examples. In 2016, the Oxford University Press created the Roald Dahl Dictionary, which features nearly 8,000 real and imaginary words that the author loved to use.

1113. Peter Benchley, the author of the famous books "Jaws" and "The Deep," worked as a speechwriter for President Lyndon B. Johnson.

1114. Mystery writer and playwright Agatha Christie suffered from dyslexia.

1115. F. Scott Fitzgerald, the creator of "The Great Gatsby," died thinking his creation was a failure as he only sold twenty thousand copies the first year.

1116. The world's largest floating bookstore/library is the "Logos Hope." A German charity organization operates it and it has over 6,000 books.

1117. The author of the book "Fight Club" was embarrassed of his own work after he watched the film saying that it was so much better.

1118. The author of the Harry Potter series, J.K. Rowling, also writes crime novels under the pen name of Robert Galbraith. "The Silkworm" and "Cuckoo's Calling" are some of the books that she has published under this pen name.

1119. In the 1970's, famous true crime author Anne Rule once worked at a suicide hotline crisis center with serial killer Ted Bundy. Later she wrote a book about it called "The Stranger Beside Me."

1120. The largest library in the world is the Library of Congress. There are over 838 miles (1,348 kilometers) of bookshelves with more than 162 million items, including more than 38 million books and print materials, 3.6 million recordings, 14 million photos, 5.5 million maps, 7.1 million pieces of sheet music, and 70 million manuscripts.

1121. A French enlightenment writer named Voltaire lived near country borders during the end of his life so that he could make an easy escape to other countries if his writings didn't please authorities.

1122. In "Green Eggs and Ham," Dr. Seuss' best-selling book, there is only one word with more than one syllable, which is the word "anywhere." The book was actually written as the result of a bet, where he was challenged to write a book using just fifty words.

1123. The name of the fictional character James Bond was taken by author Ian Fleming from American ornithologist James Bond, a Caribbean bird expert and author of the Field Guide Birds of the West Indies.

1124. Dr. Seuss' first book was rejected twenty seven times. He was almost ready to give up, but one day he bumped into a friend on the street in New York City, back in 1937, who had just begun working in publishing. Seuss said that if he had been walking on the other side of the street, he probably would have never been a children's author.

1125. The Harry Potter series has been translated into more than seventy languages.

1126. In the original "The Wizard of Oz book," Dorothy's magical slippers were actually silver and not ruby red as in the movie. The color was changed because it was believed that they would be more notable against the yellow brick road.

1127. The last words of famous writer H.G. Wells were: "Go away, I'm alright."

1128. The rights of some Stephen King's short stories are sold by the author for just one dollar. He refers to them as his "dollar babies" and he sells them so that film students can use them to make movies.

1129. More than two million people showed up for French writer Victor Hugo's funeral in Paris, starting from the Arc de Triomphe onwards to his burial site at the Pantheon. He rests in the same Pantheon crypt as Emily Zola and Alexandre Dumas, and most major cities and towns in France have a street named after him.

1130. The renowned author of fantastical horror stories H.P. Lovecraft wrote a whole essay at one point, elaborating on his belief that cats were better than dogs.

1131. The Guinness Book of World Records actually holds the record for being the one book that's most frequently stolen from public libraries.

1132. The "Fat Brad the Cookbook" is a book that contains all the foods that actor Brad Pitt has eaten on screen.

1133. The identity of the unknown wizard at the back of "Harry Potter and the Philosopher's Stone" first edition generated a lot of debate when the book was first released. Thomas Taylor, the illustrator, later revealed he based it on his father after being told to draw a wizard to decorate the back cover.

1134. Benjamin Franklin penned an essay called "A Letter to a Royal Academy" in 1781 as he lived in France as America's Ambassador there, and it was about farting. The essay is more commonly known as "Fart Proudly," and it was his way of expressing his disapproval of how pretentious Academic Societies in Europe had become.

1135. One of the most popular Marvel Comic heroes, Wolverine, is only five feet two inches (1.57 meters) tall, but he weighs 300 pounds (136 kilos) because of the adamantium in his skeletal system.

1136. One of the people who translated the Dead Sea Scrolls, John M. Allegro, was certain that Christianity was based on a fertility cult and the use of psychedelic mushrooms.

1137. In the mid 1990's, DC and Marvel Comics had a crossover event where popular superheroes from both universes clashed. During the series, DC's Flash was challenged to a race by Quicksilver from Marvel.

Flash won the race, but he was disappointed that the two speedsters couldn't be friends.

1138. Nathaniel Hawthorne, the American novelist, inserted the "W" into his last name because he wanted the fact that he was related to John Hathorne, his great-great-grandfather, to remain secret. John Hathorne was a judge during the Salem Witch Trials, and is the only one who didn't repent for his actions.

1139. In The Wizard of Oz, Oscar Zoroaster Phadrig Isaac Norman Henkle Emmanuel Ambroise Diggs is the full name of the wizard. In the original version of the story, he says that he goes by Oz because the remainder of his initials spell out the word "Pinhead."

1140. The Mahabharata is the longest poem ever written, and it's a text that's meant to explain Hinduism principles. It has 74,000 verses, totaling 1.8 million words, and would take you two whole weeks to finish it if you recite it non-stop.

1141. R.L. Stine, the legendary horror writer, started his career by writing comics for Bazooka Joe Bubble Gum; his pen name was Jovial Bob Stein.

1142. There is a three volume book called the "Principia Mathematica" which details the foundations of mathematics. In the book, there is proof that one plus one equals two that is over a hundred and fifty pages long.

1143. Charles Dickens wrote "A Christmas Carol" in only six weeks. In fact, Tiny Tim and Bob Cratchet helped speed up the process.

1144. In 2016, a rare first edition of Philosophiae Naturalis Principia Mathematica by Sir Isaac Newton was sold for $3.7 million.

1145. In the Vietnamese version of Cinderella, known as "Tam Cam," Cinderella cuts her stepsister into pieces, puts the pieces into a jar of food, and sends it to her stepmother to eat, who enjoys it until she finds a skull at the bottom of the jar, and then dies out of shock.

1146. In 1597, a three part book about necromancy and demonology was written and published by King James the first of England.

1147. In 1937, author J.R.R. Tolkien started to write "Lord of the Rings." He finally published them in 1955, eighteen years later after having started.

1148. Originally, Spider-Ham was a spider named "Peter" who was bitten by a radioactive pig, not the other way around.

1149. Casinos are mostly designed in a way to avoid people from turning at a ninety degree angle when they walk. Author Natasha Dow Schull, who wrote "Addiction by Design, Machine Gambling in Las Vegas," states in her book that making these sharp turns forces people to activate the decision-making part of their brains. Hence casinos want you to curve gently when you walk through them.

1150. There is a book named "Becoming Batman - The Possibility of a Superhero." It was published by a neuroscience professor in 2008, exploring the ideas of how much training it would need to become Batman, and if it's even possible to become him in real life.

1151. The acronym SHAZAM shouted to conjure up comic book hero Captain Marvel stands for Solomon, Hercules, Atlas, Zeus, Achilles, and Mercury.

1152. Garfield's illustrator, Jim Davis, almost chooses pizza over lasagna as the character's favorite food, as it was easier to draw, but he ultimately changed his mind. The lovable and lazy cat's favorite dish first appeared in the comic strip on July 15, 1978, where he says: "It's nature's most perfect food."

1153. The "Wreck of the Titan" was a novel written by author Morgan Robertson in 1898. In the book the ship Titan sinks in the north Atlantic after being hit by an iceberg. The story of the sinking is strangely similar to the actual Titanic, which sank just fourteen years after the book was released. Both ships were deemed to be unsinkable, didn't have enough lifeboats, struck an iceberg, and sank and lost more than half of their passengers.

1154. Dr. Ruth, the famous author, American sex therapist, and media personality, was actually trained as a sniper when she was just sixteen years old by the Jewish military organization Haganah, in Israel.

1155. Author Georges Perec wrote a 300-page French book called "A Void" without using the letter "E" even once. The book has since been translated into different languages, by scholars who also managed to avoid using the letter "E."

1156. Author "Virginia Wade" has become renown by writing and publishing Bigfoot erotica novels on Amazon Kindle.

1157. In 1936, the world's largest book called "The Golden Book of Cleveland" suddenly disappeared during some time in Cleveland, Ohio. The book measured 6.88 feet (2.1 meters) by 4.92 feet (1.5 meters) by 3.28 feet (one meter) thick, and weighed 4,993 pounds (2,267 kilograms). To put that into perspective, that's about the same size as a queen size bed.

1158. A hand-written book known as the Voynich Manuscript has 246 pages and many illustrations in approximately 170 thousand characters. Strangely, the script in the book is completely unknown and illegible, so no one has ever been able to read or decipher it.

1159. Writer Charles Dickens always wrote and slept while facing north, and he carried around a compass to ensure that he had his directions right. He held the belief that doing so helped increase his creativity.

1160. In 2009, the Free Little Library, a nonprofit organization, began to operate by offering free books in many little libraries in communities all over the world. Today there are over 50,000 book exchanges worldwide.

1161. In the books written by Sir Arthur Conan Doyle, Sherlock Holmes never says the phrase "elementary, my dear Watson." Basil Rathorn actually said the line in the 1939 film "The Adventures of Sherlock Holmes."

1162. In 1994, Leonardo da Vinci's Codex Leicester notebook was bought by Bill Gates for $30.8 million. Besides adding the item to his personal collection, he used it to also help promote Windows Vista's launch, by using a program called Turning the Pages 2.0 that would let people browse through virtual versions of the notebook.

1163. French philosopher Voltaire was asked to renounce Satan on his deathbed in 1778. He replied: "Now isn't the time to be making new enemies."

1164. Legendary author Ernest Hemingway survived lots of unfortunate things in his life, including two plane crashes. He also suffered from skin cancer, malaria, anthrax, dysentery, hepatitis, pneumonia, a ruptured liver, a ruptured kidney, a ruptured spleen, a cracked skull, and a broken vertebra.

1165. Julio Cortazar published a book named "Hopscotch" in 1966, which is over a hundred and fifty chapters long and makes sense no matter which chapter you begin reading from.

1166. In June 2016, a study performed by researchers from the Yale University of Public Health determined that people who read books live an average of two years longer than those who

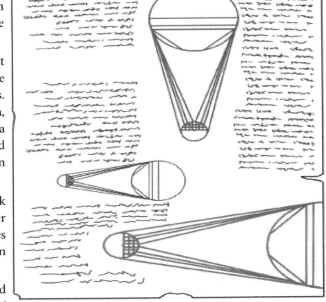

don't.

1167.   The New Testament has been translated into 1,534 different languages. In fact, it's currently in the process of being translated into some 2,659 more languages.

1168.   The tomb of the poet and writer Oscar Wilde in Paris, France, is covered in thousands of lipstick kiss marks left by years of female fans who have visited his grave.

1169.   Jane Austen, the English novelist, is buried at Winchester Cathedral in England, along with the former kings that date back as far as 611 AD.

1170.   In 1905, seventy year old author Mark Twain began to collect young girls from the ages of ten to sixteen for a club, which he called his "angel fish."

1171.   According to historians, William Shakespeare was born and died on the same date. He was born on April 23, 1564, and he died on April 23, 1616.

1172.   On June 8, 1971, seventy two year old author J. I. Rodale died during the taping of the Dick Cavett Show. Before he died, he told Cavett that he was in such good health that he fell down a flight of stairs and laughed the whole way down. He also said that he was going to live to 100.

1173.   The longest mathematical proof in history is 15,000 pages long. It involved more than a hundred mathematicians and took over thirty years to complete.

1174.   Samuel Langhorn Clemens was writer Mark Twain's real name.

1175.   There is a magnetic journal called the Rekonect Notebook where pages can be removed, reattached, or rearranged whenever you want.

1176.   The "Intertidal Zone" is a comic book about tide pool animals written by Stephen Hillenburg, a marine biology instructor at the Orange County Marine Institute. Two years after pursuing a career in animation, Stephen developed the characters from his comic book and turned them into the show "SpongeBob Squarepants."

Buildings & Massive Monuments

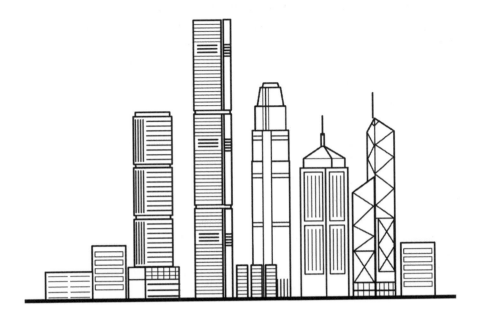

1177. "The Bailong Elevator," also known as the "Hundred Dragons Elevator," is the tallest outdoor elevator in the world. Located in the Province of Hunan, China, it carries tourists 1,083 feet (330 meters) up the side of a massive sandstone column in a mountain range. It's so big that it can carry fifty people at a time.

1178. The biggest cuckoo clock in the world is the one in Triberg Schonach, Germany. Its pendulum is twenty five feet (eight meters) long, and the cuckoo itself weighs roughly 330 pounds (150 kilos).

1179. The first working suspension railway bridge in the world was the Niagara Falls Suspension Bridge. It was operated between 1855 and 1897. It stood over 2.5 miles (four kilometers) above the Niagara River, and it spanned 825 feet (251 kilometers) across the river.

1180. On average, 470,000 people visit the Rockefeller Center on any given weekday, and almost 800,000 during the holiday season.

1181. A ninety year old former monk named Justo Gallego Martinez has been building an unauthorized cathedral in Spain since 1961. He usually works alone for ten hours a day, six days a week.

1182. It cost approximately $25 million to build the Empire State Building. If adding the cost of land, then it's approximately $41 million.

1183. Most people think the England Big Ben in London is the clock and tower. However, Big Ben is actually the name of the large bell.

1184. Originally, James Hoban built the White House between 1792 and 1800. British soldiers torched it down in the War of 1812, and it was reconstructed in 1815.

1185. A real estate developer from Florida Keys named Richter Clyde Perky was trying to get rid of the high mosquito population in the area, so he made an 8.9 feet (2.7 meter) high bat house. He said that the house had everything a bat's little heart might desire, and he hoped that a good amount of animals would move into the house and start eating the mosquitos that were causing a nuisance. Sadly, not even one bat moved into the house.

1186. When the Machu Picchu was constructed, it's estimated that 60% of the works were done underground. This included crushing rocks for drainage and setting deep foundations for the building.

1187. The Brooklyn Bridge in New York was completed in 1883, so it's older than the Tower Bridge in London, which was completed eleven years later, in 1894.

1188. On July 13, 2015, the construction of the world's tallest dam started in the Dadu River, in China. It will be 1,030 feet (314 meters) high and it's expected to be completed in 2022.

1189. Laguna Garzon is a ring-shaped bridge designed by Uruguayan architect Rafael Vinoly on Uruguay's southern coast. The creator's idea is to encourage people to slow down and take in the view.

1190. The country that has the most museums per capita in the world is Israel, with over 200 across the country.

1191. In Sudbury, Canada, there is a thirty foot (nine meter) replica of a 1951 Canadian nickel.

1192. The longest suspension bridge in the world is the Akashi Kaikyo Bridge, also known as the Pearl Bridge, with a total length of 2.4 miles (four kilometers). It spans between the main island of Honshu and Shikoku and the suspension cables used to build the bridge are the same as its length, with a diameter of about thirty five inches (ninety-one centimeters) each.

1193. Beneath the Van Cortlandt Park golf course in the Bronx, there is a gigantic water filtration plant the size of Yankee Stadium that is worth $3.2 billion. The filtration plant can process more than 264.5 million gallons (a billion liters) of water every single day.

1194. Architect Nikola Basic designed a 230 foot (seventy meter) long organ placed on the coast of Zadar, Croatia. The organ has thirty five tubes that make music whenever waves crash into them.

1195. The highest exterior elevator in Europe is the Hammetschwand lift. Located in Switzerland, it connects a rock path with the lookout point Hammetschwand on a plateau overlooking Lake Lucerne. In less than a minute, it takes passengers 502 feet (153 meters) up the summit.

1196. Downey, California, houses the oldest McDonald's restaurant that is still open for business. In fact, it was the third McDonald's ever built and still looks pretty much the same as it did in 1953. Their employees still wear their 1950's uniforms to serve customers.

1197. Residents of the Indian village of Meghalaya grow their own living bridges using the roots of the ficus elastica, or rubber fig tree. Some of their elaborate systems of living bridges are more than 500 years old.

1198. The world's largest cathedral is St. Peter's Basilica, in Vatican City. The structure is 610 feet (186 meters) in length, it has an inside area of more than 163,000 square feet (262,000 square meters), and the main dome is 446 feet (136 meters) high. The cathedral can accommodate 20,000 prayers at one time.

1199. The oldest wooden building in the world is the Pagoda, in Japan. It was built using trees from 600 AD.

1200. The 9/11 Living Memorial Plaza is a monument in Israel designed by Eliezer Weishoff. It's a thirty foot (nine meter) bronze American flag that forms the shape of a flame, representing the flames of the Twin Towers. Its base is made from melted steel from the wreckage of the original World Trade Center. There are plaques around the monument with the names of the victims of 9/11. It was completed in 2009, cost $2 million, and sits on a hill overlooking Jerusalem's largest cemetery.

1201. It took over twenty two years to build the Taj Mahal in India. Construction began in 1632 and finished in 1653. It was built by Emperor Shah Jahan, who was in deep grief over his passing wife, as a tribute to their love.

1202. The Great Sphinx of Giza was constructed out of a single chunk of soft limestone bedrock. This magnificent monument stands over sixty five feet (twenty meters) high, almost 240 feet (seventy four meters) long, and over sixty two feet (nineteen meters) wide.

1203. The only one of the seven wonders of the ancient world that still exists is the Great Pyramid of Giza, in Egypt. The rest were all destroyed, including the Colossus of Rhodes, the Lighthouse of Alexandria, the Mausoleum at Halicarnassus, the Temple of Artemis, and the Statue of Zeus.

1204. In the past, the twenty fourth floor of the Empire State Building was furnished with special comfortable chairs called "nap pods," in which people could take twenty minute siestas.

1205. The Redhorse Osaka Wheel in Japan is a 404 feet (123 meter) Ferris wheel with see-through floors. It is the fifth tallest Ferris wheel in the world and the tallest in Japan.

1206. The Bandra-Worli Sea Link is a massive eight-lane traffic bridge built in India. Every individual cable can support more than 900 tons of weight and, if put together, it could wrap around the whole circumference of the Earth.

1207. To build the Taj Mahal, more than 1,000 elephants were used to transport the materials.

1208. The Rungrado May Day Stadium is the biggest stadium in the world. It's located in Pyongyang, North Korea, and it was completed on May 1, 1989. Although it houses different sporting events, it is more famous for being the place where the annual Mass Games are held, an artistic and gymnastic event with over 100,000 participants in it.

1209. The longest glass sky bridge in the world is in Zhangjiajie, China, which is 1,400 feet (430 meters).

1210. The Shanghai Tower, known for being the world's second tallest building, built the world's fastest elevator in late 2016. According to Mitsubishi, its manufacturer, the elevator moves as fast as 4,000 feet (1,200 meters) per minute, which is forty six miles (seventy four kilometers) per hour.

1211. In the northern Swedish village of Jukkasjarvi, there is a hotel that's made from ice. It was originally made in 1990, and every year, it is rebuilt using ice and snow extracted from the Torne River that passes nearby. It's usually constructed in December, and stays around until April, when it melts away. The chairs, beds, and decorations are all made of ice, and each room is unique.

1212. The Pentagon wasn't meant to look the way it looks today. It was meant to be several stories taller than it is, but due to the country needing steel to build helmets, weapons, amunition and other things for the war, the architectures had to change plans.

1213. The origin of the mortar used in the construction of the Great Pyramids of Giza is still unknown. The material has been analyzed several times and although the chemical composition is known, it cannot be reproduced. It is stronger than stone, and is why it's still holding up today. The pyramids were built sometime between 2540 and 2560 B.C.

1214. Edinburgh Castle, which is the most popular paid tourist attraction in Scotland, was originally constructed on top of a volcano plug. The plug is named Castle Rock and is 350 million years old.

1215. The Dragon Bridge is a steel bridge in Vietnam. It has the shape of the mythical creature, and it includes a head which shoots out jets of water, and fireballs.

1216.   The Manhattan skyline has grown by more than 300 meters in the past one hundred years, and it still continues to grow as more buildings have been planned.

1217.   Although it's claimed the Leaning Tower of Pisa in Italy sank after it was constructed, the structure was never actually straight in the first place. The tower's foundation was set in soft ground, so it never settled properly, and it could never support the tower's weight evenly.

1218.   There are twenty two emojis carved into the concrete façade of a building in Amersfoort in the Netherlands. The design was done by the Attika Architekten Dutch architectural company.

1219.   Diane Hartley, an architectural student, pointed out a flaw in the construction of a New York City skyscraper in 1978, and effectively saved countless lives. If she hadn't discovered the flaw, the fifty nine story structure might have collapsed on everyone inside.

1220.   Located in Hausberg, Bavaria, the Fuggerei is the oldest social housing complex in the whole world, and current renters still pay what used to be paid when the houses were constructed in the 1500's, an amount equivalent to one American dollar.

1221.   In Alaska, attorney and MIT alum Phillip Weidner has built what is called the Goose Creek Tower and what the locals call the Dr. Seuss house. It began as a 39.3 by 39.3 feet (twelve-by-twelve meter) log cabin, but he kept joining one log cabin after the other on top of each other. The log cabins progressively get smaller and the tower has reached almost eighty-two feet (fifty-five meters) tall. The only reason that he stopped was because federal airspace starts at 200 feet (sixty-one meters).

1222.   In 1883, one year after the Brooklyn Bridge opened, twenty-one elephants were led by circus performer P. T. Barnum across it as a way to prove the bridge's strength.

1223.   There is a steel and glass structure called "Tilt" on the 94th floor of the John Hancock Center in Chicago, which allows people to hover 1,000 feet (305 meters) over the city. The structure has three overhead hydraulic actuators that rotate the enclosed moving platform and tilts you out thirty degrees over the edge of the building.

1224.   The seven rays found on the Statue of Liberty's crown represent the seven continents. Each ray measures nine feet (2.7 meters) long and weighs as much as 150 pounds (sixty eight kilograms). Additionally, its overall height is 305 feet (ninety two meters) from its base, and it has a thirty five foot (ten meter) waistline and weighs 225 tons.

1225.   The Tropical Island Resort in Krausnick, Germany, is the world's largest indoor beach. It was built inside an old airplane hangar and has a 50,000-plant forest that spans over a 107,000 square foot (9,940 square meter) area; it has a spa, a waterfall, a whirlpool, and a water slide. In fact, the indoor is so big that it's possible to fly a hot air balloon inside.

1226.   Gustave Eiffel, the designer of the Eiffel Tower, added a secret compartment near the top where he would entertain members of the science community.

1227.   Near Newark, in Ohio, there's a building shaped like a picnic basket. It was built in 1997 by Dave Longaberger, owner of Longaberger Basket Company, to be used as his head office.

1228.   Based on several descriptions, the Colossus of Rhodes, the ancient Greek statue, was about the same height as the Statue of Liberty in New York City.

1229.   There is a large Roman Catholic Church in Barcelona named the Sagrada Famila that began construction in 1882 and won't be completed until 2026.

1230.   In Boyne Valley, Ireland, there's an ancient temple that predates the Great Pyramids of Giza and the Stonehenge. It's known as "Newgrange," and it was constructed by farmers from the Stone Age, about 5,200 years ago. It's a circular grass thatched mound that's 278 feet (eighty five meters) in diameter, and forty four feet (thirteen meters) high.

1231.   The Statue of Liberty was packed in 214 crates containing 350 pieces when it was shipped from France to New York.

1232. A "Bass Pro Shops" mega store located in Memphis, Tennessee, is the sixth-tallest pyramid in the world.

1233. Some buildings in the US, such as the White House, the Empire State Building, the Sears Building, and the Dodger Stadium, are so large that they have their own zip codes.

1234. Since the year 1280, at least four powerful earthquakes have hit the region where the Leaning Tower of Pisa is. In fact, the tower has survived because of the soft soil underneath it.

1235. There is a housing complex in Montreal known as "Habitat 67" which is considered an architectural landmark and is also the most well-known building in the city.

1236. For the construction of the USS New York, in 2005, approximately 6.8 tons of steel was used from the rubble of the World Trade Center towers.

1237. The first and largest stadium ever built in ancient Rome was the "Circus Maximus," which accommodated 150,000 people. However, the massive stadium decayed and quarried off for materials during the sixth century. Today it's a park in Rome.

1238. There is a fifty six feet (seventeen meter) glass structure shaped like a giant high heel shoe built in Chiayi, Taiwan. The structure is a tourist attraction, but it's also used as a wedding hall. It was built in honor of women who suffered from arsenic poisoning from well water that caused gangrene, a condition sometimes known as black feet disease.

1239. The Tower of Hercules, in Spain, is the oldest lighthouse in the world. It was erected in the first century and is still operational.

1240. In the Mojave Desert, California, there is a solar power plant that covers 1.56 square miles (2.5 square kilometers). It's actually the largest solar power plant in the world.

1241. Sudarsan Pattnaik created the tallest sandcastle in the world on February 10, 2017, on Puri Beach in Odisha, India. The sandcastle took nine days to complete, it was forty eight feet (fourteen meters) high and it had a 529 feet (161 meter) wide circular base.

1242. There was a safety net put up under the Golden Gate Bridge while it was being constructed. It saved nineteen men and they became known as the "Halfway to Hell Club."

1243. In 1967, the world's first UFO landing pad was built in St. Paul, Alberta, Canada. The 130-ton structure has a raised platform with a map of Canada imprinted on the backstop consisting of stones provided by each province in Canada. The pad also has a time capsule that is scheduled to be opened on the one hundred year anniversary of the pad's opening, which is in 2067.

1244. Palacio de Sal Resort is a hotel in Bolivia made up of one million fourteen inch (thirty five centimeter) blocks of compressed grains of salt. The furniture is also made out of salt.

1245. In Williamstown, Kentucky, there's a replica of Noah's Ark that was built by the Creationist Ministry. Its dimensions are exactly as indicated in the book of Genesis at 450 feet (137 meters) long, sixty seven feet (twenty meters) high, and forty six feet (fourteen meters) wide. It cost approximately $100 million to make.

1246. Located in Newark, New Jersey, the world's largest indoor farm is 21,024 square feet (6,410 square meter). These types of farms can grow crops without soil, sunlight, and nearly no water. In fact, they use 95% less water than conventional outdoor farms.

1247. In Thailand, there is a temple called "Wat Samphran" that has a giant dragon wrapped around the outside of the building that is about seventeen stories high. On the surroundings, there are also other various animal sculptures, like an elephant, rabbit, dolphins, and other large buildings in the shape of a tortoise.

1248.   With over 17.3 miles (twenty eight kilometers) of corridors, the Pentagon has a total floor area of 2,010,640 square feet (613,000 square meters).

1249.   The largest bridge cables ever made are found in the Golden Gate Bridge. They were so long that they could actually encircle the world more than three times at the equator.

1250.   The Big Ben in London, England, is actually leaning to the northwest by 0.26 degrees, putting it out of alignment at its highest point by 1.6 feet (0.4 meters). This was discovered by the Transport for London when commissioning a report and it's believed that the London clay on which the tower was built is drying out.

Cool

1251. The oldest US retail industry company that is still in business today is Brooks Brothers. On April 7, 1818, the first store opened on Cherry Street in New York City. At that time, it was called H. & D. H. Brooks & Co.

1252. Hotels around the world have black or green arrows positioned around the rooms on places like ceilings and desks. They are known as Qibla pointers, and they are meant to indicate the direction to Kaaba, Saudi Arabia, so that guests of the Islamic faith know how to orient themselves as they pray towards Mecca.

1253. One of the most distinctive things about Ferrari cars is the sound of their engines. The unique sound is made using third and sixth harmonics inside the air tank of the engine. Essentially, Ferrari's are musically engineered to produce great sounds, as you would find in an organ or a flute.

1254. Ben & Jerry showed their support for marriage equality by banning customers in Australia from purchasing two scoops of the same ice-cream flavor at their shops all over the country.

1255. At the 2012 light festival in Belgium, there was a cathedral called the Luminarie de Cagna on display; it was ninety two feet (twenty eight meters) high and lit by 55,000 LED lights.

1256. In 2016, the Sacramento Public Library started a Library of Things. The library allowed customers to check out things like sewing machines and other items that people may find useful but may not need to own for a long time.

1257. For over 175 years, a battery powered bell has been uninterruptedly ringing at Oxford University. Nobody knows what the battery is made of and no one wants to take the device apart in order to figure it out.

1258. The Swedish Number, 46 771 793 336, is a single phone line created by a Swedish tourism agency that connects international callers to randomly-selected Swedish volunteers to chat about whatever they want.

1259. America's most visited national park is the Great Smoky Mountains National Park, located between the border of North Carolina and Tennessee. Just in 2015, it welcomed over ten million visitors.

1260. In 1972, a spaceship house was built by Curtis King for his son in the woods near Signal Mountain, Tennessee, where they lived. It cost $250,000 to build; it has a dropdown staircase and every detail channels futuristic living. He eventually sold the house and it can now be rented by anyone who wants to have a futuristic vacation.

1261.   In Australia, there is a bookstore where books are wrapped in paper with short descriptions. This way they are buying the book without judging it by its cover.

1262. In April of 2016, Inky, an octopus of the National Aquarium in New Zealand, escaped from the aquarium and went back to the ocean. He realized the lid to his tank was left slightly open, so he squeezed out and managed to find his way to one of the drain holes that took him out.

1263. In Finland, there's a Burger King with a ten-person-in-house sauna. The sauna can be rented for three hours at a price of $285 US, and can be used for birthday parties or work events.

1264. The Dog Bark Park Inn is a lodging located in Idaho where guests can stay in the world's largest beagle. The entrance to the body of the beagle is from a second-story deck. It has a loft up another level into the head of the dog, and there is an additional sleeping space and a cozy alcove in the muzzle.

1265. In 1959, Danish fisherman and woodcutter Thomas Dam created the troll doll. Dam wanted to buy a Christmas gift for his daughter Lila, but he couldn't afford any, so he decided to carve a doll out of his own imagination. Other children in the Danish town of Gjøl saw the troll doll and also wanted one. The rest is history.

1266.   The concept of rap-battle has existed since the 5th century. Poets would engage in flighting, a spoken word event where poets would insult each other in verse.

1267.   In MIT, students can meet their physical education quota by sailing, archery, shooting guns, or fencing. Those who do, earn an official Pirate Certificate.

1268.   The sign that looks like a horizontal eight that is used in math where it's referred to as the infinity symbol has an actual name: it's called a lemniscate.

1269.   The biggest snowflakes in recorded history fell from the sky in Fort Keogh, Montana, during a storm in January, 1887. According to a local rancher, they were larger than milk pans, and he did measure one which turned out to be about fifteen inches (thirty eight centimeters) in diameter.

1270.   When birds consume wild chillies, they aren't affected by the heat it gives off. Scientists believe that birds evolved to have this trait so that they could help to spread seeds over a large area through their droppings.

1271.   There is a hiking pathway that makes it possible to walk from one side of America to the other. It's called the American Discovery trail, and it's 6,800 miles (10,900 kilometers) in length, and transects the country from coast to coast, starting at Cape Henlopen in Delaware, and ending at Limantour Beach in California.

1272.   The Aluminum Association claims that about 75% of all aluminum ever made is still being used today. That is because the metal is highly reusable, and efforts have been put in place to recycle it. Aluminum was worth more than gold in the 1850's. A 2.2 pound (one kilo) bar of gold was worth $664 while 2.2 pounds of aluminum was worth $1,200, almost double the value. It's because it was rare to find pure aluminum and it was expensive to extract it from bauxite at the time.

1273.   In The Netherlands, 100% of electric trains have been powered by wind energy as of January, 2017.

1274. In Japan, Kit-Kats coated with edible gold were sold by a Nestle store. They were limited to only five hundred and were sold for the US equivalent of sixteen dollars each.

1275. Level 257 is a Pac-Man-inspired entertainment center in Illinois, with a more than 12,792 square foot (3,900 square meter) playground with bowling, arcade games, and food. The kill screen on Pac-Man is level 256, so level 257 symbolizes the next level of play. It even has a store that sells Pac-Man memorabilia, many of which are only available there.

1276. Beneath the cobbled streets of Belgium City, there's a pipeline that can pump 1,057 gallons of booze an hour, which is the equivalent of 12,000 bottles. It runs a distance of about 1,864 miles (3,000 kilometers) from a brewery in the center of Bruges to a bottling plant on the outskirts of the city.

1277. According to neurologists, every time you avoid acting under anger feelings, you're actually rewiring your brain to be a calmer and more loving person.

1278. There is a reverse color blindness test where only people who are colorblind can actually see what the hidden image is.

1279. Cauliflower creak is actually the name given to the loud creaking sound that cauliflowers create when growing quickly, as their florets rub together.

1280. In Singapore, it's possible to hire a self-driving taxi. They are equipped with a detection system that uses lasers to operate like radar; they also have two cameras on the dashboard to scan for obstacles and detect traffic light changes. During the testing period prior to their release, the cars had a driver in the front who could take over the wheel at any time if needed, and a researcher in the back who would watch the computers.

1281. Our brains have a primal gaze detection system that determines whether someone is staring directly at us or not. So next time you feel that someone is watching you, they probably are.

1282. Seventy year old farmer Winston Howe was married to thirty three year old Janet when she suddenly died. As a last tribute to her, he planted thousands of oak saplings in a six acre field and left a heart shaped point facing towards her childhood home.

1283. There is a prison in Bolivia where inmates live as a society. They have jobs, buy or rent their housing, and often live with their families.

1284. All cars since 2002 are required to have a glow-in-the-dark trunk release lever that opens the trunk from the inside. This is in the event of an emergency.

1285. According to a study conducted by Daniel Buysse, a psychiatrist at the University of Pittsburgh Medical Center, about 2% of the population are considered the sleepless elite. This means that they are night owls and early birds simultaneously.

1286. One aluminum can that is recycled can save enough energy to run a television for three hours.

1287. The rappers Busta Rhymes, Jay Z, DMX and The Notorious B.I.G. all went to the same high school. Jay Z and Busta Rhymes once even held a rap battle in the lunchroom.

1288. Some non-venomous snakes, like the tiger keelback, eat poisonous frogs while being pregnant and then pass the poison onto their eggs, which makes their newborns poisonous when they're born.

1289. The Incas domesticated alpacas more than 6,000 years ago. They were raised for their fleece and, because of its quality, alpaca fiber was reserved exclusively for the elite and nobility.

1290. The Juliet Rose is considered the most expensive rose ever developed. It was created by famed rose-breeder David Austin over the course of fifteen years and it cost nearly £3 million.

1291. Koshik is an Asian elephant that has learned to imitate humans speaking by putting his trunk in his mouth.

1292. Robert Haas managed to capture a picture of a flock of flamingos migrating in the shape of one giant flamingo in the Gulf of Mexico in 2010.

1293. In early January of 2017, the state of Michigan signed a legislation banning the banning of plastic bags. Additionally, it prohibits counties or cities from outlawing disposable cups and other plastic containers. The ban was pushed by the Michigan Restaurant Association because they felt the ban would make it difficult for them to comply.

1294. There is a team of hawks at the Grand Hyatt Cannes Hotel Martinez that have been trained to chase away seagulls that get too close to their dining guests.

1295. On the island of New Guinea, there is a creature called the Prasinohaema skink that has green blood, bones, and tissue. No other vertebrate is known to have green blood, which is extremely toxic to humans.

1296. Sidewalks and streets are heated in Reykjavik, Iceland, to keep them free of ice and snow. Since the installation of these heated roads, over a decade ago, residents have enjoyed significant savings from not having to spend taxpayer money on snow removal services.

1297. There are male geishas known as taikomochi. In fact, the original geishas were only men.

1298. The mailing company UPS began in 1907 with two teenagers, a bike and a hundred dollars borrowed from a friend.

1299. The foxfire diamond is the largest gem-quality diamond ever found. It was found at the Diavik diamond mine above the Arctic Circle in August of 2015. It's a huge 188 carats.

1300. There's a solar facility containing 48,000 solar panels at Walt Disney World in Lake Buena Vista, Florida, that is the shape of Mickey Mouse.

1301. The company "Star Picks" makes some of the most expensive guitar picks, one of which costs $4,674. It's made out of a meteor.

1302. Famous YouTuber KevJumba created a second YouTube channel and donated 100% of its ad revenue to a community in Kenya. The community used the money to build their first secondary school, naming it after him.

1303. Eigengrau is the dark grey color seen by the eyes in perfect darkness. It is actually the result of signals from the optic nerves.

1304. To equal the amount of blood pumped by the heart in the average lifetime of a person, a kitchen faucet would need to be turned on all the way for at least forty-five years.

1305. Jasmine the Greyhound dog was the surrogate mother for eight years in a shelter to over fifty different animals. They included puppies, foxes, chicks, rabbits, guinea pigs, a goose and a deer.

1306. The National Museum of Natural History in Paris studied chimpanzees' behavior in the wild and found that they tend to look both ways before crossing the road. Researchers also found that 57% of the time they would run across the road to be extra safe.

1307. The real name of Sesame Street's Cookie Monster is Syd. In fact, in 2010, Cookie Monster tweeted: "Me wasn't born with name Cookie Monster. It just nickname that stuck. Me don't remember real name. Maybe it was Sydney."

1308. Phoenix Jones was a martial artist who led a superhero movement in Seattle that was actually pretty successful. The group prevented several assaults and robberies until 2014.

1309. There is a special daily wake-up call for spring breakers at the Holiday Inn resort in Panama City Beach, Florida. They blast "Circle of Life," Elton John's hit song from The Lion King musical, at their balconies every morning. The tradition began in 2012.

1310. In 1977, a surfing Santa fifteen cent Christmas stamp was designed by Roger Roberts, in Australia, which caused a lot of controversy and complaints from people around the country. The drawing included a Santa Claus riding a surfboard to deliver presents.

1311. At the Bronx Zoo, for a $10 donation, you can name a cockroach after your partner on Valentine's

Day. The money collected goes to the Wildlife Conservation Society.

1312. If there are any students who are feeling stressed and anxious in the University of Victoria's Law Library, they are able to rent a black Labrador named Echo. You get him for thirty minutes and can take him for a walk or just give him pats.

1313. There is a farm in Albany, Oregon, called "At No Regrets Farm," where you can take a yoga class with goats.

1314. In London, there is a pool suspended between two apartment buildings with transparent sides and floors. You can swim from one building to the other side while enjoying a view of London through almost eight inches (twenty centimeters) of glass casing.

1315. Alfred Heineken created the "Heineken World Bottle" in 1963 in attempts to create a brick that can hold beer whilst also being used to build a house. The project never took off unfortunately, however you can still see a beer brick wall in two places; the Heineken estate and the Heineken museum.

1316. Herbert Hoover, the 31st president of the United States, gave his salary away to charities or as income supplements to his associates.

1317. There is a manufacturer called "Unifi," located in Greensboro, North Carolina, that recycles plastic bottles into polyester yarn to make t-shirts, shorts, or even graduation gowns. In fact, thousands of college students there have actually accepted diplomas while wearing these gowns.

1318. In 2011, a maze was created by farmer Tom Pearcy from York, England, by carving two football-field sized portraits of Harry Potter into a corn field.

1319. In Japan, snow monkeys entertain themselves by making snowballs.

1320. If you're a property owner in New York, you're able to request to have trees planted on your street for free, even choosing which species you want.

1321. Someone has invented tea bags that look like goldfish swimming around in your mug.

1322. Barack Obama personally thanked Japan in 2015 for karaoke, manga, anime, and emojis.

1323. In 2013, the Compassion in World Farming's Good Dairy award was given to Ben and Jerry's for their high quality treatment of their cows. They make sure that their cows get regular massages and their employees get double minimum wage.

1324. There is a US Navy research vessel designed to be capsized vertically. Most rooms there have two doors, one to use when the ship is horizontal and another when it's vertical.

1325. In 2013, a group of footballers were caught being honest when they went into a convenience store that was left open and left cash on the counter for the items they took. The owner of the store was so shocked that he gave them all a fifty dollar gift voucher.

1326. In England, Finland, Germany, and the US, there are playgrounds designed specifically for aging residents. They mainly consist of low-impact exercise equipment designed to promote balance and flexibility. Some of the machines include elliptical machines, static bikes, and flexors.

1327. In Herriman, Utah, there is a replica of Carl Fredricksen's flying house from the Disney Pixar movie "Up."

1328. In Japan, there is a preschool called "The Dai-Ichi Yochien" that has a courtyard that collects rainwater into a giant clean puddle. Kids assisting the preschool are allowed to stomp and splash around in.

1329. Japan has a network of roads that can play music as you drive over them if you go at the correct speed.

1330. Outside of Watson Lake, Yukon, there's a Sign Post Forest. It was started back in 1942 when a soldier named Carl K. Lindley was injured while working on the Alcan Highway. He was taken to the Army air station in Watson Lake to recover, and while he was there, he was homesick, so he decided to place a sign of Danville, Illinois, his hometown. Tourists continued the practice and there are currently about 72,000 signs from around the world.

1331. In Amsterdam, there is a houseboat that works as a sanctuary for rescued cats. The houseboat has become a tourist attraction that receives about 4,500 visitors a year.

1332. It's possible to swim in beer at the Brewer's Starkenberger's Castle, in Austria. They have seven thirteen foot (four meter) pools filled with 42,000 pints of warm beer and some water. People can just sit and relax completely immersed. The beer is rich in vitamins and calcium and it's believed that sitting in it is good for the skin and can help cure open wounds and psoriasis.

1333. In Jerusalem's Valero Square, there are some self-inflating giant flowers where pedestrians can stop for some rest. Installed by HQ architects in 2014, these thirty by thirty inch (nine by nine meter) flowers bloom when someone approaches or when a tram is about to arrive.

1334. "Oo-ko" is the name of a straw goat that Santa rides on in Finland.

1335. There is an annual festival dedicated exclusively to Pikachu in Yokohama, Japan. The Pikachu outbreak is a week-long festival where crowds of dancing Pikachus, along with numerous statues, take over the entire city.

1336. An album called "Wake Up" was released by Pope Francis in November of 2015. It features his speeches set to rock, pop, and Gregorian chants.

1337. Unlike normal tattoos, braille tattoos are not made of ink, but instead are made of metal beads that are put under the skin to create designs of braille messages.

1338. In Marino, Italy, there is a McDonald's where you can have your meal and also check out an ancient Roman road at the same time. The road was actually built between the second and first centuries B.C., but it was only discovered when the McDonald's was being built, in 2014. The road was excavated, documented, and enclosed in a gallery with a glass roof so that customers can look down on it.

1339. After 9/11, the Kenyan Masai gave the United States fourteen blessed cows as a show of sympathy. Cows are considered to be sacred for them and are actually valued above all possessions.

1340. In 2016, Nike created self-lacing shoes, similar to the ones in the movie "Back to the Future."

1341. In July of 2016, in Prince Edward Island, Canada, monks went all around the island and bought up to 600 pounds (272 kilograms) of lobsters and then released them back into the ocean. The purpose of their action was to cultivate compassion for the lobsters and for all beings.

1342. Officially, Harvard is free for those with less than $65,000 in annual family income.

1343. Anke Damask, a German fashion designer, creates clothing out of sour milk. After extracting the strands of protein from the milk, she then spins the fiber into yarn. She uses a type of big noodle machine to mix the ingredients together and it spits out textile fibers from the nozzle at the end.

1344. Some companies in England are now offering pawternity, paid time off to take care of a pet in need.

1345. On Marajo Island, Brazilian police ride water buffalos when they patrol the streets instead of horses.

1346. The WWE superstar John Cena has granted more than 400 Make-A-Wish requests, more than anyone else in the charity's history.

1347. Architects in Iceland wanted utility towers to go beyond their basic functional structures, so they created a design proposal called the "Land of Giants." Basically, it turns electrical pylons into human-shaped sculptures.

1348. In the early 20th century, it was possible to order a kit from the Sears catalog to build a house. Some of the types of constructions offered were small bungalows, large farmhouses, and Queen Anne style homes. All the parts and materials were included in the kit, which were all delivered by train.

1349. In Illinois there is a company called the "Second Chance Coffee Company" that only hires ex-inmates as employees. The company actually conducts FBI background checks to make sure that those seeking employment in the company have actually been to prison.

1350. There is a wine fountain in the town of Caldari di Ortona, in Italy, that stays open twenty four hours a day.

1351. In Norway, there is a sauna that can house 150 people. It's a large timber construction set on a beach, which overlooks the Arctic Ocean.

1352. Pikachurin protein was named by Japanese scientists after the Pokémon character Pikachu because of the character's agility.

1353. All residents of Alaska receive an oil royalty check each year for their share of revenue from Alaskan oil. The payment is usually between one and two thousand dollars.

1354. There's a roller coaster in Japan known as the "Sky Cycle" where you actually have to pedal yourself to propel yourself forward through the track.

1355. In 2014, the largest pyramid constructed with coins was built in Lithuania, made from over a million coins.

1356. In order to help calm anxious mothers, the Hao Sheng Hospital in Japan decorated their maternity ward in 2006 with Hello Kitty-themed murals and items. The cartoon image is on everything, from walls to newborn baby blankets. In the entrance lobby, there's even a giant Hello Kitty figure dressed in a pink doctor's uniform that greets visitors.

1357. Sensor Wake is an alarm clock that uses aromas of your choice to wake you up instead of sounds. You can be delightfully awoken by scents like cut grass, hot croissant, chocolate, espresso, or peppermint.

1358. The toasted selfie is a device introduced by the Vermont Novelty Toaster Corporation. If you send them a selfie, they will print it for you on a selfie toast-producing gadget.

1359. In order to save money on expensive gasoline, Ukrainian drivers are converting their cars into being fueled by wood with burners instead of fuel tanks.

1360. To celebrate the 2016 Cheltenham Festival, designer Alexander McQueen's former apprentice,

Emma Sandham-King, made the world's first Harris Tweed suit, specially designed for a horse. Four weeks and more than eighteen meters of tweed were needed to complete the three-piece suit, which was worn by a racehorse named Morestead.

1361. In 1849, Elizabeth Blackwell was the first woman in the United States to receive a medical degree.

1362. The largest female afro according to the Guinness World Records measures 7.2 inches (18.5 centimeters) high, 7.7 inches (19.6 centimeters wide), and 52 inches (132 centimeters) in circumference. The record was achieved on October 4, 2010, by Eva Douglas in New Orleans, US.

1363. In an attempt to help reestablish some habitats, scientists are using 3D printing technology to create fake reefs. These are less vulnerable to climate change and more durable in changing ocean chemistry.

1364. George Lucas, the creator of Star Wars, made a pledge that stated he'd donate most of his money to improving education. Two years later in 2012, he sold his company Lucasfilm to Disney, and donated most of the money to a foundation that focuses on education.

1365. Since 1947, after the Second World War was over, Norway has sent Britain a giant Norwegian Spruce Christmas tree every year, as a symbol of Norwegian gratitude to the United Kingdom for preserving Norwegian liberty. Londoners gather every year in Trafalgar Square to participate in Christmas carols and to see the tree being lit.

1366. In 2015, the Japanese army created a massive Star Wars sculpture for the yearly Sapporo Snow festival that was made from over three thousand tons of snow.

1367. Almost three quarters of Japanese households use high-tech toilets which eliminate the use of toilet paper and include things such as a seat warmer, self-cleaner, and deodorant spritzer.

1368. A young girl named Michelle Rochon wrote a letter to President Kennedy in 1961 worrying about Santa's safety when the Soviets were testing nuclear bombs close to the North Pole. The president actually wrote back to Michelle stating that he had spoken to Santa and that there was nothing to worry about.

1369. US Senator Gaylord Nelson actually founded "Earth Day" as a way to promote the environmental movement. On April 22, 1970, the first-ever "Earth Day" was held. It has been celebrated on that day every year since.

1370. As the result of people doing the ice bucket challenge, the ALS Association received $101 million in donations. That was a huge amount compared to the $2.8 million raised the previous year.

1371. In Japan, there are special retirement homes for senior dogs. There, they get the proper care and love they need for their last years of life.

1372. To reduce delivery damages, Dutch bike manufacturer VanMoof started printing pictures of flat screen TVs on their bike boxes. Damages went down 70 to 80%.

1373. The tooth fairy is actually a mouse in France. It's known as the "la bon petite souris" and it will take the teeth left under pillows replacing them with cash or sweets.

1374. There are some types of fireworks that can be set off in daylight by using colored smoke.

1375. In the US, there is fully edible six-pack beer can packaging. It was created by the Saltwater Brewery from Florida. It's made from byproducts of the brewing process like wheat and barley, and is fully biodegradable and totally digestible. They are as strong as the plastic ones, but if an animal or bird gets caught in one, they can actually eat it and quickly decompose it.

1376. In Grenoble, France, there are vending machines that will print out a free, quick short story for you to read while you are on the bus or train. Depending on how much time you have to kill, it's possible to print out a one, three, or five minute story.

1377. In Germany's Veltins Arena, there are over a hundred bars that serve beer which come from a three mile (five kilometer) pipeline that links them all. The line can deliver more than 3.7 gallons (fourteen liters) of beer in a minute, from four cooling structures deep underneath the arena.

1378. The "Stuffed Animal Hospital" is a company that operates a literal hospital for stuffed animals. They offer hospital-like services, including rides in ambulances, examinations, hospital name bracelets, and they clean and repair toys to restore their "health."

1379. A farm in Delaware makes mulch out of damaged, retired US paper currency notes. An estimated four tons of the cash is turned to compost each day.

1380. George Barbe, a billionaire from Alabama, had several life sized dinosaurs built and placed over his ten thousand acre home in 1991.

1381. Trains that travel along the Iron Ore Line down to the Swedish Coast generate about five times the quantity of electricity that they use up. That electricity is used to power nearby towns, as well as other trains.

1382. At the Amherst Massachusetts campus of Hampshire College, there's a yearly Easter tradition where students go into the woods in the morning to hunt for "Easter kegs." Senior students work together to purchase beer kegs, take them into the woods, and hide them behind rocks and inside patches of dirt.

1383. Clara da Cruz Almeida, a South African architect, has designed a little portable house. It can be packed into a 258 square foot (twenty four square meter) pod and be shipped anywhere.

1384. National Geographic offers expeditions to exotic places like Antarctica. Anyone who pays for it can join the trip.

1385. Nintendo and Universal have teamed up to create new Nintendo themed areas at Universal Studios in Japan, Universal Orlando Resort, and Universal Studios Hollywood. Visitors there are able to experience what it is like to be inside their favorite video games.

1386. The "Oombrella" is a smart connected umbrella that can predict when it's about to rain and send a notification to your smartphone reminding you to bring your umbrella along. If you happen to forget it in a place, it can send you a notification via Bluetooth that you forgot it before you get too far.

1387. A Canadian woman originally from Iraq, known as Basma Hameed, learned how to tattoo so she could cover the burn scars she received on her face when she was a child. The results were impressive and now she runs a business that helps other burn victims by tattooing discolored scars to match their own skin tone.

1388. Caromont Farms in Esmont, Virginia, once posted a message on its Facebook page asking for volunteers to snuggle with baby goats. The sign up list filled up immediately.

1389. In Sweden, there is a hotel called the "Jumbo Stay," which has been converted from a 747 jumbo jet. It has thirty three rooms that are sixty four square feet (six square meters) wide and ten feet (three meters) from floor to ceiling, equipped with flat screen TVs, access to Wi-Fi, and private or shared showers and toilets in the corridor.

1390. Numi is a type of toilet made by Kohler, which has a heated seat, foot warmers, lights, and

Bluetooth technology.

1391. In Japan, a daruma doll or gold doll is a handmade wishing doll that keeps you focused on your goals in five steps. Step one is you establish a particular goal. Step two is you draw one on daruma's blank eyes to signify your commitment, and then write down your goal on the heart painted on the back of the doll for extra commitment. Step three is you place daruma somewhere that is visible in your home or office to remind you to stay focused on your goal. Step four, once you've achieved your goal, draw in daruma's other eye to say thank you. And step five, write the goal you achieved on the back of the doll if you didn't, of course, already in step two. If having a new goal, then you get a new daruma doll, and repeat the process again.

1392. People over fifty who suffer from diabetes are given medals in the United Kingdom for their courage and perseverance of living with diabetes.

1393. Territorio de Zaguates, meaning land of the strays, is a territory in Costa Rica where you can hike for free with dogs. It is basically a huge no-kill dog shelter.

1394. The largest gingerbread house in the world was created in 2013 in Bryan, Texas, according to the Guinness World Records. It was fifty nine feet (eighteen meters) long, thirty nine feet (twelve meters) wide and nine feet (three meters) high. The entire house was edible, and in total, all baking ingredients used made up over thirty five million calories.

1395. In Chongqing, China, there is a zoo called the "Lehe Ledu Wildlife Zoo" where visitors are placed in cages instead of the animals. The cages are stalked by lions and tigers, so the guests are warned to keep their fingers and hands inside the cage at all times.

1396. Rage Yoga is an actual yoga class that's offered in Calgary, at the Dickens Pub. Participants perform traditional yoga poses which are combined with heavy metal rock, as people scream vulgarities and make lewd gestures such as the middle finger.

1397. President Gerald Ford's seventeen year old daughter, Susan Ford, hosted her high school prom on May 31, 1975, at the White House. The senior prom for Holton-Arms School turned out to be the only one ever to take place at the presidential mansion.

1398. "Noix de Vie," which translates to "nuts of life," is a mouse-sized French shop located on the side of a building in Malmo, Sweden. Right next to it there is a similarly-sized Italian restaurant Il Topolino, which means "Mickey Mouse." They were both built into the wall of a building by an artist called Anonymouse.

1399. The deepest mail box in the world is in a small Japanese fishing town called Susami, according to the Guinness Book of World Records. It's an old-school red mailbox that's located thirty two feet (ten meters) under water, and divers often place waterproof letters there and they are then collected in regular intervals. The mailbox is quite active, as it receives one to five thousand pieces of mail annually.

1400. When Donald Duck turned fifty in 1984, he was given a birthday parade in Disney World. The parade float included live ducks that wore party hats, and they were covered with a plexiglass barrier.

1401. American businessman Russ George partnered with Haida Salmon Restoration Company in October, 2012, to pour a hundred tons of iron sulphate off the British Columbia, Canada coast, into the

Pacific Ocean. This was done to boost the growth of planktons which are known to absorb carbon dioxide from the air.

1402. The world became increasingly more generous between 2001 and 2011, as per the 2012 Giving USA Report. Charitable giving around the globe grew by 240% within that decade.

1403. In the UK, you can get your ashes baked into a vinyl record by a company called "And Vinyly" after you are cremated. The record can even contain songs you like, your own voice, or an audio version of your will.

1404. In Lancaster, California, there is a musical road that was created as a TV ad for Honda. The road is cut into groves that when traveling about fifty miles (eighty kilometers) per hour, it will play William Tell's Overture.

1405. Nat-2 is a German sneaker company that has created the first vegan wooden sneaker. They are made of up to 90% real sustainable wood, which is applied to an organic cotton and vector engraved in a way that the material bends and becomes soft and flexible, like fine leather.

1406. There is an annual sidewalk egg frying contest held in Oatman, Arizona, on the 4th of July. Contenders have to fry two eggs using only solar power in a period of fifteen minutes. Mirrors, magnifying glasses, and aluminum are allowed for use to help speed up the process.

1407. Kakslauttanen Arctic Resort is a hotel in Finland that offers accommodation in glass igloos.

1408. According to the Guinness World Records, 1,416 Toyota cars were parked together at Kuznetsova airport, in Russia, on June 7, 2014, to create a giant Toyota logo, breaking the previous world record held by Subaru. The exhibition was intended to introduce a new Toyota dealership in the area.

1409. In the Netherlands, there is McDonald's that has a place mat called a McTrax, where you can make music while you eat. The way it works is by placing your phone on the mat, getting an app, and then composing your music including your voice.

1410. In California, there is a replica of the 1948 original In-N-Out Burger at its original location on the intersection of Francis Guido and Garvey in Baldwin Park. It contains a cigarette machine, the original potato dicer, and a frying station.

1411. In Pune, India, there is a school that encourages students to preserve water by pouring leftover drinking water from their bottles into a large tank before they go home every day. The water is then used for watering plants and trees or for other non-drinking purposes.

1412. The seaside resort of San Alfonso del Mar, in Chile, houses the largest pool of the world. It was built in 2006 and is 114 feet (thirty five meters) deep. Around sixty six million gallons (249 million liters) of water is needed to fill it in.

1413. Chocolate Avenue is a street in Hershey, Pennsylvania. The avenue runs past the original Hershey's Chocolate factory and it has street lights shaped like Hershey Kisses.

1414. College student Dave MacPherson was the very first guest to enter Disneyland. He didn't ride a single attraction that time because he had to get back to school. However, he was awarded a life-long ticket to Disneyland with up to three guests. The ticket was later extended to include Disney parks around the world.

1415. Women named Isabella get a free lifetime admission to the "Isabella Stewart Gardner Museum" in Boston.

1416. McDonald's has Happy Meal boxes in some locations in Sweden that can fold into virtual reality viewers that are called Happy Goggles.

1417. There are some traffic lights in Germany that have touch screens installed where you can play pong with pedestrians across the street from you.

1418. The American company Creative Home Engineering specializes in making hidden rooms for your home. There is a room that even requires a chess board played in a certain combination in order to it.

1419. There is a cafe in Hong Kong called "Rabbit Land." It has bunnies that customers can pet, most of which were abandoned by their previous owners. It caters to people who don't have space for their own rabbit.

1420. In the Sacred Valley, in Peru, there is an accommodation facility called "The Skylodge Adventure Suites" that offers a unique chance to sleep in a completely transparent hanging bedroom capsule over 1,000 feet (305 meters) above the valley floor. The capsules measure 23.9 feet (7.3 meters) in length and 7.8 feet (2.4 meters) in height and width; it has four beds, a dining area, and a bathroom.

1421. In Paris, a law was approved that allows anyone to plant an urban garden anywhere within the city.

1422. There is a vending machine in Istanbul that gives water and food to dogs in exchange for recyclable bottles.

1423. The "Ruggie" is an alarm clock device disguised as a rug. It has a sensor that will only turn off the alarm once you have stepped on it for at least three seconds, forcing you to get out of bed. It also has speakers that will deliver motivational quotes that you can choose to start your day right.

1424. Located in Tokyo, Butler Café is staffed by waiters who are all butlers. You can ask them to address you as "Princess" or "Prince," and they'll comply.

1425. The first robot-run hotel is named the Henn-na Hotel, meaning "strange hotel" in Japanese. Customers are greeted by multilingual robots at the front desk that help them check in or check out. At the coat room, a robotic arm stores your luggage for you and the porter robots carry them to your room.

1426. They are currently developing a new kind of cheerleading called Paracheer. The idea is that athletic teams made up of individuals both with and without disabilities will perform routines that involve dancing, jumping, and creative stunts.

1427. Located in Oak Bluffs, on Martha's Vineyard, the Flying Horses Carousel is the oldest carousel in the United States. It was built in 1876 and it's still running. It is one of the twenty surviving carousels that include a ring machine and people who grab the ring get a free ride.

1428. "Momentary Ink" is a company that prints temporary tailor-made tattoo designs, lasting three to ten days. The idea is that you try it out before you really commit to one.

1429. There is a sixty acre forest near Walt Disney World which has the largest hidden Mickey Mouse; the forest has over 50,000 pine trees.

1430. It's possible to see coral reefs and underwater sea life by using Google Maps.

1431. After banning alcohol in the Indian village of Marottichal, residents began playing chess as a substitute for drinking. The village is now known as Chess Village due to its near 100% chess literacy.

1432. In South Korea, there is a fake prison where stressed-out business people and students check themselves in in order to relax and find relief. There, mobile phones or clocks are not allowed and it's also forbidden to talk to other inmates. Their menu is rice porridge for breakfast and a steamed sweet potato with a banana milkshake for dinner.

1433. In Port Vila, Vanuatu, at the Hideaway Island Resort and Marine Sanctuary, there is an underwater post office, the only one of its kind in the world. Snorkelers and divers can post special waterproof postcards in ten feet (three meters) of water.

1434. A picture of a nine year old boy named Daniel Cabrera, from the Philippines, doing his homework in the street, assisted by the light of a local McDonald's became so viral that donations around the world were sent including money, school supplies, and a college scholarship to both him and his family.

1435. Giraffe Manor is not only a giraffe sanctuary in Kenya, but it's also a hotel where guests can hang out with giraffes and feed them from their windows.

1436. Xiong Shulhua, a millionaire Chinese businessman, demolished entire rundown huts in his native village and decided to build luxury flats. Later he gave the keys to the residents for free.

1437. The "Taxi Fabric Project" in Mumbai, India, has upcoming designers reupholster and transform taxi cab interiors.

1438. American President Calvin Coolidge had a pet raccoon named Rebecca. She was originally supposed to be eaten at their 1926 White House Thanksgiving dinner, however, the family found her to be friendly and docile, so they decided to keep her as a pet instead.

1439. In 2012, a chain of 228 people paid for the customer behind them at a Tim Hortons in Winnipeg. The act of kindness and generosity lasted for about three hours, after someone broke the chain by paying only for their coffee and not the customers behind them.

1440. Every December since 1960, between finals and the end of the semester, volunteers at a dorm at the University of Illinois will sing you a Christmas carol upon request. All you have to do is call Dial-A-Carol at (217) 332-1882, any time and any day after finals and before the end of the semester, and they will sing you a carol.

1441. In China, in order to draw tourists to the panda base in Chengdu, a large panda bear conservation facility, a panda themed subway train was created.

1442. "FrankenStrat" is a guitar created by musician Eddie Van Halen, combining different parts of the instrument from various places. This was his attempt to have the classical sound of a Gibson mixed with the physical attributes of the Fender.

1443. "Shewee" is a portable urination device that allows women and girls to urinate while standing and without removing any clothes.

1444. In New York, when the Rockefeller Center Christmas tree is taken down each year, it's used as lumber for Habitat for Humanity, a non-profit charity.

1445. In 1998, a professor of cybernetics at Reading University named Kevin Warwick became the first technical cyborg of the world. He had a radio frequency ID implanted in his arm and could turn on the lights by snapping his fingers.

1446. There is a new dining craze known as "Dinner in the Sky" where you actually eat your food suspended 197 feet (sixty meters) above the ground in a racing chair. It is already available in fifteen countries around the world.

1447. A shoe made exclusively from ocean trash, including gill nets and beach litter, was released by Adidas in 2015. The company stated: "there is no shortage of material to produce this line."

1448. Photographer Andrew Suryono was under heavy rain when he noticed an orangutan using a leaf for shelter. He quickly took the shot that made him earn an honorable mention in the 2015 National Geographic photo contest.

1449. In Singapore, there exists a floating stage above water that can hold up to 9,000 people. They use the stage for things such as concerts, soccer, and a place of celebration.

1450. Tokyo has a hedgehog café with twenty to thirty friendly hedgehogs of different breeds that you can actually spend time with and even take home. It's the world's first café place of its type.

1451. The original floats used by Macy's during the Thanksgiving Parade were released into the air after the parade because Macy's didn't know what to do with them. The floats however, included a ticket that would fall to the ground after they popped. People who found a ticket could redeem it for a prize at the store.

1452. Diggerland is a kind of adventure park in England, where visitors can drive and operate real tractors, dump trucks, and other full-size construction machinery.

1453. In Collinsville, Illinois, there is a sixty nine foot (twenty one meter) tall ketchup bottle, which is the largest of the world, perched on the top of a hundred (thirty meter) foot tall steel tower. It's the water tower at the Old Brooks Ketchup Plant and Headquarters, and Collinsville holds the World's Largest Ketchup Bottle Festival every single year.

1454. In 2006, Branson, Missouri, held the annual Discover Santa Convention with workshops, vendor fairs, events, and networking. More than 300 Santas showed up and it was the first true modern day Santa convention.

1455. Bug Racer is a toy car powered by a live cricket. You can watch the cricket drive through a see-through windshield.

1456. The biggest fortune left to a charity was by a lady named Margaret Anne Cargill who left stocks that totaled six billion dollars.

1457. Subsix is a restaurant located around twenty feet (six meters) below the surface of the Indian Ocean, in the Maldives. You can sit near floor to ceiling glass windows and watch schools of fish and more than ninety coral reef species while you eat.

1458. There is a restaurant in Kochi, India, called "Pappadavada" that has placed a functioning fridge outside where customers can leave leftovers for other people in need.

1459. Rap artist Nelly has been secretly offering college sponsorships for two kids every year for the last decade.

1460. In the early 1980's, a fourteen-carat gold Lego brick was given out to those employees who had worked at the Germany Lego Factory for over twenty five years. Today they are valued at over $15,000.

1461. There is a twenty year old anonymous British man from Birmingham, UK, who wears a Spiderman costume at night and helps homeless people by buying them food from the supermarket.

1462. In the Russian city of Yekaterinburg, there is a giant granite ball which was painted to look like a giant Pokeball.

1463. The largest collection of snow globes according to the Guinness World Record belongs to Wendy Suen from Shanghai, China. As of November 27, 2016, she had gathered more than 4,059 of them; she started her collection back in 2000.

1464. Australians have a Christmas song where Santa's sleigh is pulled by six white kangaroos. Their names are Jackaroo, Curly, Bluey, Two-Up, Desert-Head, and Snow.

1465. Pope Benedict XIV is actually a licensed pilot. He is able to legally fly small engine planes or helicopters.

1466. Rajendra Singh from India is known as the water man of the country. He managed to revive five rivers and brought water back to 1,000 villages in India using native water preservation techniques.

1467. Blind mothers are now able to have a three dimensional ultrasound of their unborn child printed to get a better sense of the image thanks to 3D printing.

1468. A pineapple takes about eighteen months to bloom when planted from a sucker. However, if you plant the top of the pineapple first, it will take two and a half years to produce a bloom.

Countries & Cities

1469.   Colombian island Santa Cruz del Islote is the most densely populated island on the planet. It measures about 0.0074 miles (0.012 kilometers) and it is home to over 12,000 people.

1470.   In Japan, there is a ninja school that was opened by Nagoya Castle where tourists can take an hour lesson from Hatori Hanzo and the ninjas. The group of men and women dressed in ninja outfits give lectures on things such as ninja weapons.

1471.   In Canada, since the end of World War II, thousands of unnamed lakes have been named after fallen soldiers.

1472.   One of the highest literacy rates in the whole world is found in Cuba, at 99.8%.

1473.   Divorces were unlawful in Ireland until 1995, when a referendum was held on the issue, 50.28% of people wanted it legalized and 49.72% didn't, a margin of only 0.56%.

1474.   Legal TV networks in North Korea only show state sanctioned local programs, and apart from a closed domestic network, the Internet doesn't exist there. As a result, very few North Korean citizens are informed about world events, apart from what the state propaganda media tells them.

1475.   During Father's Day in Germany, dads get temporary freedom from parental duties, instead of breakfast in bed and new ties. The dads go around in groups, wearing odd clothes and dragging along wagons full of alcoholic drinks. The day is also called accident day, because traffic accidents increase three fold because of drunk fathers on the roads. Some local governments tried to ban the German Father's Day tradition in 2012, but state courts stopped the bans, saying that the fathers had the constitutional freedom of action, and that drinking beer was a component of the country's culture.

1476.   Inside Denmark, it's legal to desecrate the Danish national flag, also called the Dannebrog, e.g. by burning it. However, it's unlawful to desecrate or burn flags of other countries, the European Council, or the United Nations, because that is perceived as a threat.

1477.   In Germany, it's illegal to kill a vertebrate without a proper reason, so all animal shelters in the country are no-kill shelters.

1478.   Lichtenstein and Haiti used to have the same exact flag until 1936, when both countries showed up in Germany for the Berlin Olympic Games. A year later, Lichtenstein decided to distinguish itself by adding a crown to its flag.

1479. There are 10,685 beaches in total in Australia, which means if you tried to go to a new beach in the country every day, it would take you more than 29 years to visit them all.

1480. Before Lisbon was Portugal's capital city, Rio de Janeiro used to have that role. Portugal was the only country in Europe whose capital city wasn't actually located on the continent.

1481. Iranians have nose surgery at a higher rate per capita than any other country in the world. Iran has a population of seventy seven million, and it records 200,000 nose jobs a year, four times the rate in America.

1482. The city of Tokyo in Japan has more people living in it than the whole population of Canada.

1483. The only state in America that requires US flags sold within its borders to be made in America is Minnesota.

1484. The largest country in the western hemisphere is Canada. It also has the longest coastline.

1485. There are no snakes native to Ireland, New Zealand, Iceland, and Newfoundland.

1486. The only country in the world that denies divorce to the majority of its citizens is the Philippines. Couples can ask for legal separation, which will allow them to separate their possessions and live apart, but it does not legally end the marital union. Hence remarriage is not permitted.

1487. Approximately half of the world's zippers are made by the Japanese company YKK.

1488. Rossi is the most common surname in Italy, followed by Russo, and Ferrari.

1489. The importation or sale of gum is illegal in Singapore, unless you have a medicinal reason for needing it.

1490. The countries Saint Lucia, Colombia, and Jamaica are the only places in the world where the boss is more likely to be a woman than a man.

1491. Close to 100% of eligible North Korean voters turn out to cast their ballots although there is only a single candidate to consider.

1492. Speeding fine tickets in Finland are calculated based on a percentage of the person's income, so some Finnish millionaires have faced fines of over $100,000.

1493. Tipping in Japan can actually be considered rude. If you do decide to tip something, the correct protocol is to place the money in a tasteful, decorative envelope, seal it, and then hand it to the recipient with a slight bow.

1494. Canada is the country to consume the most donuts and has the most donut shops per capita of any country in the world.

1495. The smallest independent state in the world is Vatican City. In fact, they even have their own national soccer team.

1496. Capri-style pants took their name from the Isle of Capri in the Gulf of Naples, Italy.

1497. In the 1970's and 1980's, skateboarding was banned in Norway for eleven years. The country's Environment Ministry considered the hobby as too dangerous for children.

1498. France exists in twelve time zones if you count the territories under its control, which is more than any other country. The US is in eleven time zones, and Russia is in nine.

1499. Bangladesh and India had a land dispute which, oddly enough, was settled by global warming in 2010. The two countries both claimed to own New Moore, a little island at the Bay of Bengal. Global warming caused sea waters to rise and permanently covered the island. Unless you have diving gear, you can't access it anymore.

1500. America has over 6.9 million vending machines, which is more than any other country in the world.

1501. The border between America and Canada is the exact site of the "Haskell Free Library and Opera

House," which has two unique addresses; one address is in Derby Line in the State of Vermont, and the other, in Stansted in the Quebec Province. The library and stage are on the Canadian side, while the entrance and most of the seating areas are on the American side. It's possible to borrow a book in one country, then sit down and read it in a different country, all within the same room.

1502. Luxembourg has the best-paid teachers on the planet. Their starting salaries are equivalent to US $80,000 and their annual salaries can go as high as $130,000.

1503. Hawaii is the only state in the United States that grows coffee.

1504. The only capital city in the world that does not have traffic lights is Bhutan, in the Himalayas. Instead, there are policemen standing in little pavilions who direct traffic with hand motions.

1505. On January 12, 2011, forty nine out of the fifty states in the United States had snow on the ground, which was about 71% of the country. The only state without snow was Florida.

1506. Besides sinking about one to two millimeters per year, Venice, Italy, is also tilting slightly to the east.

1507. The first nation to make it illegal to strike a child as a form of corporal punishment was Sweden, back in 1979. Since then, many other countries in Europe, Africa, and the Americas have implemented this prohibition.

1508. According to NASA, the most lightning-prone place in the world is Lake Maracaibo in Venezuela. Storms light up the skies almost 300 nights each year.

1509. In Turkey, there's a city called Batman in the province of Batman that even has a river named the Batman River.

1510. There are only two countries in the world whose flags don't have the color red, white or blue. They are Jamaica and Mauritania.

1511. As of December, 2016, the largest city in the United States, and one of the few cities in the entire world, to rely solely on green energy to power its municipal facilities was Las Vegas.

1512. More than seventy five film festivals are held in Toronto, Canada, each year.

1513. In some parts of India, both Muslims and Hindus have a ritual that dates back 500 years, which consists of dropping their babies from the roof of a temple to a sheet held taut by men on the ground. The ceremony is considered to bring good health and good luck.

1514. The United Kingdom has a right to roam, which allows public access for walking in leisure to spots like mountains, moors, heaths, and downs that are privately owned.

1515. Torn bank notes in Australia are worth half of the proportion of the note left, so half of a $20 bill is actually $10.

1516. The largest falcon hospital in the world is in Abu Dhabi, housing more than 6,000 falcons.

1517. In the Northwestern Territories in Canada, license plates are shaped like polar bears.

1518. In South Australia, it is against the law to disrupt a wedding or a funeral.

1519. The maximum life sentence in Norway is only twenty one years, except for genocide in war crimes. Despite this, the nation has one of the lowest recidivism rates in the world at 20%. In contrast, the United States has one of the highest with 76.6% of prisoners rearrested within the following five years.

1520. In Tennessee, it is against the law to sell bologna on Sunday.

1521. The place on Earth where the most twins are born is Nigeria.

1522. The popular known Panama hats are actually made in Ecuador, not in Panama.

1523. In 2014, the American Psychological Association conducted a survey that revealed that the most stressed out people in America are millennials, which are people between the ages of eighteen and thirty five, parents with kids under eighteen, and low-income families. The survey determined that the main source of stress was money.

1524. In China, people who are caught cheating on exams are banned from repeating the test for several years. Also, if someone is caught facilitating mass cheating or paying someone to take the test for them, they can be sent to prison for seven years.

1525. The North American bison is the official mammal of the United States. After years of campaigning by conservationists, President Obama finally signed a National Bison Legacy Act into law in May of 2016. This is the first official mammal recognized by the federal government.

1526. In Japan, on Valentine's Day, it's actually women who do the gift giving. Men have the choice to reciprocate or not a month later, on "White Day."

1527. The first country to ban plastic plates, cups, and utensils was France. The regulation is actually part of the country's energy transition for Green Growth Act, which is the same legislation that outlawed plastic bags in grocery stores and markets.

1528. The first Latin American country to ban hunting as a sport was Costa Rica, in 2012.

1529. In the Canary Islands, there is a restaurant called "El Diablo" where food is served with the geothermal heat from an actual volcano.

1530. The official national animal of Scotland is the unicorn. It was used in an earlier version of William the First's Scottish Code of Arms and, since then, it evolved into the respected symbol the country sees it as today.

1531. People in Australia are twenty times more likely to drown than be bitten by a shark. In other words, an Australian is significantly more likely to win the top prize in the lottery than being involved in a shark accident of any type.

1532. The Japanese national anthem is only five lines long.

1533. Canadian currency has tactile marks on them that allow the blind and visually impaired to identify the bills by touch.

1534. The "Ilha da Queimada Grande," or "Snake Island," is an island in Brazil covered in deadly snakes, which remains untouched by humans. This reptile is responsible for 90% of snake bite related fatalities in Brazil and they're so dangerous that the Navy has forbidden anyone from landing there.

1535. In Copenhagen, there are more bicycles than people and five times as many bicycles as cars. Over 50% of city residents travel by bicycle and over 41% arrive at their place of work or study by bike.

1536. The town of Viganella, in Italy, does not get any direct sunlight for eighty three days during winter due to the surrounding mountains. Residents there have set up a giant, computer controlled mirror on the top of the mountainside to reflect the sun's rays onto the town.

1537. The only continent that has no spiders is Antarctica.

1538. Pig Beach is an island in the Bahamas populated entirely by pigs and it's possible for visitors to arrange a day to go swimming with them.

1539. Tian Zi is a ten story hotel in Langfang, China, that is made up of three Chinese gods: Shou, the symbol of longevity; Fu, who stands for good luck; and Lu, who represents prosperity.

1540. Off of the coast of Iceland, there is a natural rock formation that looks like a huge elephant.

1541. Collingwood in Ontario, Canada, holds the world's largest Elvis festival, welcoming around 30,000 visitors every year. There is an Elvis impersonator competition and vendors sell Elvis memorabilia.

1542. There is an Indonesian island where babies who die before growing their teeth are placed inside the trunk of a growing tree. The hole is then sealed and as the tree begins to heal, the child is believed to be absorbed. Within a single tree, there may even be dozens of babies inside.

1543. City street number seventy seven, in Reutlingen, Germany, is the narrowest street in the world. It ranges from just 12.2 inches (thirty one centimeters) at its narrowest to 19.6 inches (fifty centimeters) at its widest. It was built in 1727.

1544. "The Channel," also known as the "Tunnel" or "Chunnel," is a thirty one mile (fifty kilometer) long tunnel that connects the United Kingdom to Europe, located underneath the English Channel. The trip underneath through the channel takes only about thirty minutes while an entire trip from London to Paris is only two hours and fifteen minutes.

1545. The holly plant used as a decoration at Christmas time is known as the "Christ thorn" in Scandinavia. People there think that it represents the thorns that Jesus wore when he was crucified, and the berries are the drops of blood.

1546. In Tianducheng, China, there was a ghost town built in 2007 that looks just like Paris. It even includes a 354 foot (107 meter) replica of the Eiffel Tower. They have replicas of Italian, German, and English towns, but they are also deserted.

1547. There are houses made within caves known as Yaodong in Northern China, where forty million people currently reside.

1548. On March 29, 1867, 586,000 square miles (943,000 square kilometers) of land was bought by the United States at the northwestern tip of the North American continent from Russia, which is the current state of Alaska. They paid $7.2 million dollars, which equals to about two cents per acre.

1549. The least densely populated territory in the world is Greenland with only 0.6 people per square mile (0.02 people per square kilometer). In fact, the entire population is only about 56,000 people.

1550. Antarctica has no time zone. Scientists who live there while doing research usually go by the time zone from their home land. In addition, daylight savings is useless, as most of the area experiences twenty four hours of sunlight during the summertime and twenty four hours of night during the winter. It's almost the same in the Arctic, although most of the North Pole is nothing but water and sea ice.

1551. In Finland, there are more saunas than cars. Most countries in the world usually view a hop in a sauna as a luxury, however, the Finnish consider their weekly sauna trip as a necessary right, along with food, rye bread, and vodka.

1552. Vehicles without drivers cannot exceed sixty miles (ninety six kilometers) per hour in California. Companies who make autonomous cars, like Google, have the technology to make them go much faster, but must limit them based on the laws.

1553. In Japan, Bitcoin became a legal method of payment on April 1, 2017. It's only considered a method of payment however, and not a currency.

1554. The only country in the history of the modern world to gain independence against its own will is Singapore.

1555. In the state of Maryland in the US, there are no natural lakes. All lakes found there are man-made by damming rivers.

1556. The Japanese invented a pot known as the Kuru-Kuru Nabe, which stirs the contents in the pot by itself when the water inside gets hot enough.

1557. Kodinhi is a village in Kerala, India, with a high occurrence of multiple births. There are 2,000 families in the village and around 200 pairs of twins. There is still no scientific explanation for this.

1558. Hawaii is the only American state that is not geographically located in North America, the only one to be entirely surrounded by water, and the only one that does not have a straight line as a boundary.

1559. In Thailand, people are not allowed to have over 120 playing cards thanks to a 1935 law known as the Playing Cards Act. Anti-gambling laws in Thailand are quite strict. Virtually all forms of gambling are banned.

1560. In Lexington, Kentucky, residents can pay parking tickets with canned food donations during the holiday season.

1561. France has so many castles that some of them are up for sale cheaper than two-bedroom apartments in big cities like New York and Sydney.

1562. In the Czech Republic, there is a church made entirely of bones called the Sedlec Ossuary, featuring a collection of dismembered and bleached human remains. It contains the remains of between 40,000 and 70,000 people, a lot of whom died during the plague in 1418 and during the Hussite Wars of the 15th century. It's located under the cemetery church of "All Saints" and has a variety of objects such as candelabras, candle holders, and chalices made from bones.

1563. It's illegal to look for a moose from an airplane in Alaska.

1564. In France, it is against the law that grocery stores throw away edible food. Instead, they have to donate edible, unused food to charity or other facilities that process it into animal feed or compost.

1565. The first nation to start switching off its FM radio network and taking the jump to digital technology was Norway.

1566. Declawing your cat is illegal in most European countries, including Britain. In Israel, for example, if you're caught declawing a cat, you can be sent to prison for a year and be fined twenty thousand dollars. Over thirty other countries, including Scotland, Italy, and New Zealand, have also followed suit.

1567. In Japan, nearly 1,500 earthquakes are recorded every year.

1568. In the last sixty years, Mexico City has sunk more than 32.1 feet (9.8 meters). This is because 70% of the water people rely on is extracted from the aquifer located below the city.

1569. Ground bees in China can be used as a natural remedy for a sore throat.

1570. In Peru, it's a New Year's tradition to give and wear new yellow underwear. It actually represents luck and happiness.

1571. The national animal of North Korea is the Chollima, a mythical winged horse.

1572. After calculating population density, unemployment rates, hours worked, and other factors, a study conducted by the real estate website Movoto found that Florida is currently America's most stressed-out state.

1573. The first parliament in the world to be completely powered by solar energy is Pakistan's Parliament.

1574. Approximately one million people live in nuclear underground bunkers in Beijing, which have been transformed into housing units. They were originally built in the late 1960's and 1970's, in anticipation of the devastation of the Cold War nuclear fallout.

1575. The first major US city to require that all new buildings have solar panels installed on the roof was San Francisco.

1576. The closest state in the United States to Africa is Maine.

1577. The largest country in the world that has no rivers is Saudi Arabia.

1578. In an effort to fight obesity, the government from Mexico City offers a free subway ticket to each person who does ten squats. Currently, 70% of the adult population is overweight.

1579. In Wood Buffalo National Park in northern Alberta, Canada, there is a beaver dam so large that it can be seen from outer space. It spans 2,789 feet (850 meters) across.

1580. In Tasmania, they have an extra day off known as Easter Tuesday. It's not celebrated anywhere else.

1581. The state of Wyoming produces nearly 40% of all coal production in the United States.

1582. The fourth largest island in the world is the Republic of Madagascar, with an area of 364,000 square miles (586,000 square kilometers). The other three larger islands are Borneo, Greenland, and New Guinea.

1583. In 2015, in an effort to boost consumer confidence and spending, a program called "Fresh Start" was launched by Croatia. The program helped to wipe away debt for 60,000 low income Croatians who had been struggling to pay their bills. The state, along with firms and banks, agreed to forgive up to 60,000 kuna, or 8,830 dollars per citizen.

1584. On September 5, 1698, Russian Czar Peter the Great, in an attempt to impose a more Western way of living, enforced a beard tax on all Russian men because European men were usually clean shaven. For centuries, Russian men had worn long flowing beards and a lot of men considered it a sin to shave, so it was very difficult for some to remove their beards. The tax was up to 100 rubles, which represented a small fortune in those days, and it affected mostly the upper classes. Peasants, however, were allowed to wear beards in their villages but, if they were entering the city, they had to pay a one kopek coin.

1585. The world's longest highway is in Australia which has a total length of nine thousand miles (fourteen thousand kilometers).

1586. After the winter ice melts, Lake Michigan in Traverse City becomes so clear that you are able to see shipwrecks 298 feet (91 meters) below the water.

1587. In Sri Lanka, elephants are sacred animals. In fact, they are protected under the Sri Lankan law and killing one carries the death penalty.

1588. In Japan, the Japanese Anniversary Association officially recognized May 9 as Goku Day. In Japanese the number five is pronounced "go" and the number nine is pronounced "ku."

1589. In Canada, lawn darts with pointy, elongated tips are banned.

1590. The only countries to have both Mediterranean and Atlantic coastlines are Morocco, France, and Spain.

1591. There is a famous Mosque in Iran known as "Nasir Al-Mulk Mosque" for its amazing stained glass windows. When the sun shines through them during the day, the inside of the mosque looks like a kaleidoscope.

1592. Approximately 3.1 billion people a year are transported by the Tokyo subway system.

1593. Between 2010 and 2015, the population in China actually shrunk by one million people.

1594. In Southeast Asia, around sixty million people rely on the Mekong River Base for food. In fact, the river is home to more giant fish than any other river on Earth.

1595. "Eureka, I have found it" is California's state motto. It refers to the discovery of gold and it appears on the state seal.

1596. Liberia, Burma, and the United States are the only three countries in the world that don't use the metric system.

1597. There is a marine park in Japan that has little holes in the otter enclosure so that visitors can shake their hands.

1598. In Sweden, blood donors are notified via text message whenever their blood helps save a life.

1599. In Denmark, if you buy a new car, you have to pay a registration tax on the new vehicle of 150%. The tax was actually reduced by the Danish government from 180%. This was all part of its 2016 budget.

1600. In some countries such as Britain, Ireland, Norway, Iceland, and New Zealand, police officers are

unarmed when they are on patrol. In fact, they are only equipped with guns under special situations. This is rooted in the belief that arming the police with guns causes more violence than it prevents.

1601. The Yakuza is known as Japan's largest organized crime syndicate. During both the 1995 and 2001 Japanese earthquakes, they provided food, water, blankets, diapers, and other supplies to those in need. They even had a faster response time than the Japanese government.

1602. The only official place on Earth named "Earth" is in a town called Texas.

1603. The space between New York City in the United States and London in the United Kingdom increases by 0.98 inches (2.5 centimeters) every year, according to National Geographic. The cities are essentially drifting apart.

1604. Dull, Boring, and Bland Day are annual holidays on August 9, that were jointly created by the American City of Boring in Oregon, a Scottish town called Dull, and the Australian city of Bland.

1605. The "Interstate Mullet Toss" is a charity function that's hosted along the Florida-Alabama border annually, and it attracts thousands of spectators who pay money to literally throw dead fish from one state to the other one.

1606. In the same vein as the White House in Washington D.C., the Korean president resides in the Blue House, which gets its name from the roof made of about 150,000 blue tiles.

1607. In Coloma, a town in California, the living are outnumbered by the dead by a ratio of one to 1,000. The town has a population of only 1,600, but it's home to 1.5 million grave markers.

1608. In lots of places in Europe and the US, people celebrate "Put a Pillow on Your Fridge Day" on May

29. You merely have to place your pillow on your fridge, and it's believed that you'll get prosperity and good fortune as a result.

1609.   It's illegal to have domestic rabbits for pets in Queensland, but all other Australian states permit it. You can be fined $45,000 for violating that law.

1610.   A census conducted in 2012 shows that in the South Atlantic British territory of the Falkland Islands, there are only 2,932 permanent residents, but there are more than half a million sheep. This means that for every single person, there's about 167 sheep.

1611.   "AKA Hoverboards," a type of motorized self-balancing scooters, are actually illegal in New York City.

1612.   In Hawaii, it is illegal to own a hamster, gerbil, or ferret. It's also forbidden to own an alligator, a piranha, or a toucan.

1613.   Montpelier, Vermont, is the only state capital in the United States without a McDonald's.

1614.   There are over three million lakes in the state of Alaska. In fact, 86,000 square miles (138,000 square kilometers) of Alaska is covered by water.

1615.   Zalipie is a village in southeastern Poland where all the cottages are painted with floral designs. Over a hundred years ago, women used to paint over the dark spots of soot that were caused by their fires with paintings of flowers, and the tradition continues to this day.

1616.   Based on a Gallup poll, New Hampshire is the least religious state in the United States as of February, 2016. The poll showed that only 20% of people in New Hampshire are actually religious.

1617.   There is an annual beauty pageant held in the village of Ramygala, Lithuania, where the contestants are goats. Nearly 500 people attend the parade in honor of the goats, a traditional symbol of the northern village.

1618.   Reindeer's antlers in Finland are sprayed with reflective paint by herders so that they won't cause as many traffic accidents.

1619.   The Florida city of Key West was frustrated that it was being treated as a foreign country with border patrol blocks everywhere, so on April 23, 1982, it seceded from the United States, becoming a conch republic. The newly created country then declared war on America, surrendered in less than a minute, and then applied for a billion dollars of foreign aid almost immediately. Interestingly, the strange plan worked, and they soon removed the annoying roadblocks from the city.

1620.   The left hand is unclean according to Indian culture because it's used to wipe the bottom, while the right hand is used to greet others and eat food. When in India, only use your right hand to greet people, receive items, and exchange cash.

1621.   The Photoshop Law is a regulation adopted by Israel in March of 2012. The law specifies that fashion and commercial models should have a body mass index (BMI) of at least 18.5. To put it into perspective, a healthy BMI is between 18.5 and 24.9.

1622.   Utah reduced the state's homelessness in 2005 by 78% by providing homeless people apartments and social workers, which cost them less money than yearly ER visits and jail stays.

1623.   Oymyakon, in Russia, is considered the coldest village of the world. In January, the average temperature there is 123 Fahrenheit (minus fifty one degrees Celsius), while the lowest temperature ever recorded was 159 Fahrenheit (minus seventy one degrees Celsius) in February.

1624.   As of 2020, there are twenty three countries that don't have any military. Some of these countries include the Vatican, Iceland, and Costa Rica.

1625.   Conservationists in South Africa are infusing a special red dye into the horns of live rhinos. The mixture renders the horn completely useless to poachers that are trying to sell it commercially and also has a toxin making it dangerous for human consumption.

1626. In Norway, it's illegal to neuter your dog, except in extreme circumstances. They believe in social neutering and training.

1627. Since 1979, no one has been reported to die from a confirmed spider bite in Australia. Deaths by spiders actually occur more when you are surprised by them, e.g. when you are driving.

1628. The Witwatersrand Basin in South Africa, which is 2.7 square miles (4.3 square kilometers) deep, has produced more gold than any other continent. About 50,000 tons have been extracted over a course of 120 years, which is nearly half the gold ever mined.

1629. The city of Jericho, located in modern day Palestinian territory, is the oldest city in the world, and it dates back 10,000 years.

1630. The state of Virginia has a law that allows people to legally hunt raccoons on Sunday, provided that it's all done before 2:00 am.

1631. 95% of all people in Suriname live along the country's northern coast. That's because 91% of the whole country is a dense jungle.

1632. Students in Sweden are literally paid by the government to go to school. Students between the ages of sixteen and twenty are paid a monthly salary that ranges from $570 to $693.

1633. Because of high levels of carbon dioxide, Tasmania Island has what could be the cleanest air in the whole world.

1634. Children in Nigeria don't have as much access to cookies as those in the west, so Nigeria's version of Sesame Street has a character named Zobi the Yam Monster who is the equivalent of the Cookie Monster.

1635. The New Madrid region close to the Mississippi River in what's modern day Arkansas was hit by an earthquake on February 7, 1812, after several months of tremors. They estimated that it was an extremely powerful 8.8 magnitude earthquake that literally forced the Mississippi river to flow upstream for a little while.

1636. When trains run late in Japan, transit staff show up at the stations to apologize to commuter passengers and issue them with train delay certificates.

1637. National Jealousy Day is celebrated in Finland every year on November 1, and it's a holiday where everyone's taxable income is publicly revealed at eight in the morning.

1638. The Puck Fair is one of the oldest annual festivals in Ireland, and it happens between August 10 and 12, in Killorglin Town. During the event, they always capture a wild goat from the mountain and carry it down. It's then crowned King Puck, and it's put on a pedestal in a small cage for the duration of the festival, before they let it go free.

1639. California generated so much solar power in 2016 that they literally paid Arizona to take the surplus.

1640. Lots of people relocate to Florida after retirement, and the trend is so popular that by 2030, an estimated one out of four Florida residents will be over sixty five years old.

1641. The sixth most populous Peruvian city is Iquitos, which serves as the capital of the Loreto Region and Maynas Province. Although it has 470,000 residents, the city is only accessible by air or by river. It's the biggest city in the world that can't be reached by road.

1642.   As a result of an ad campaign that ran in 1967, residents of Piscataqua village in Ecuador voted in a foot deodorant called "Pul Vapes" during a mayoral race.

1643.   The country with the youngest population in the world is Niger. It has eighteen million citizens, and almost half of them are under the age of fifteen. That's because the country has an oddly high fertility rate of 6.6 children for every woman.

1644.   The first president of Equatorial Guinea, Francisco Macias Nguema, changed the country's motto to "There's no other god than Macias Nguema." He did that in 1978, and was overthrown and killed the next year.

1645.   In 1998, Florida passed a law that mandated that all state-funded preschools and daycare facilities should play classical music for the kids. They originally thought that the Mozart effect would contribute to the development of the children's minds, but although that effect was disapproved, the law still remains in place to date.

1646.   If you come across Bigfoot when you are down in Texas, you have a legal right to shoot him dead, according to state laws. On the other side, there are some places such as Skamania County in Washington where it's legally forbidden to kill a Sasquatch.

1647.   To combat speeding drivers, inhabitants of a village named Hopeman, in Scotland, have been posing as police officers using speed guns by arming themselves with hair dryers and reflective vests.

1648.   European settlers gave Argentina its name because they suspected that there were hidden riches within the mountains. The word Argentina loosely translates to "silvery" in Italian. There was a legend about a hidden mountain of silver in that land at the time.

1649.   In most cultures, sticking out one's tongue is considered a sign of distaste. However, in Tibet, it has the opposite meaning, because sticking your tongue at someone is considered good manners.

1650.   The Republic of Nauru has the biggest percentage of obese citizens as per the World Health Organization. Around 94.5% of their entire population is overweight according to a 2007 report. The United States is ninth in terms of obesity, with 74.1% of people being overweight.

1651.   One of the oldest cities in the world is Jerusalem which has been attacked over fifty times, destroyed twice, and captured and then recaptured over forty times.

1652.   In rich countries, obesity is more common among the less educated. In poor countries on the contrary, obesity is common among the highly educated.

1653.   During the 1997 Asian financial crisis, Koreans donated billions of dollars' worth of gold jewelry to help pay down the country's international monetary fund debt, which enabled them to pay off the debt ahead of schedule. Citizens were asked to donate their gold jewelry by the government, and many did so by donating heirlooms, wedding rings, trophies, and small gold figurines. Within a few months, about 227 tons of gold was collected.

1654.   In December of 2000, the Netherlands became the first country to legalize same sex marriage. Today over twenty three major countries have legalized it, including Canada, England, and the United

States.

1655.   In Japan, if you are in someone's home, you need to wear slippers when walking around. Not only that, but there is one pair to be used around the house and another pair just for the bathroom.

1656.   The state slogan for New Hampshire is "Live Free or Die" and is written on all car license plates. Ironically these licenses are made by the prisoners of the state.

1657.   South Korea has a population of almost fifty million people. About 20% of them have the family name of Kim; that's over ten million people.

1658.   In Peru, the inhabitants of the Chumbivilcas Province celebrate a tradition on Christmas, where all the men settle grudges with each other by calling them out and having a fist fight. Afterwards they all go have drinks together to numb the pain and start the New Year together.

1659.   Lyme disease got its name from Lyme, Connecticut, as it was the place where researchers found a large number of children suffering from juvenile rheumatoid arthritis, back in 1975.

1660.   On July 4, 2016, the practice of daylight saving's time was annulled by Egypt, three days before it was due to start.

1661.   One of the most rare blood types, type O, is shared by every single person by the Bororo people, an indigenous race in Brazil.

1662.   In March of 2017, the iconic rock formation known as the Azure Window, a tourist attraction in Malta, collapsed into the sea after being there for thousands of years.

1663.   An underpass intended for the blue feathered korora penguins was built in the south island town of Oamaru, in New Zealand, so that they can get to their nesting sites every night.

1664.   The only two countries to depict the outline of their nation on their flags are Cypress and Kosovo.

1665.   Argentina had five presidents during the last week of 2001 and first week of 2002. The string of presidents started when Fernando de La Rua resigned in December of 2001. The last of the five was appointed in January of 2002 during major protests.

1666.   The lowest graduation rate in Canada is found in Nunavut, in the Northwest Territories, where only 57% of students actually finish high school.

1667.   There is an underground town in Australia where all inhabitants, around 200 people, live in abandoned opal mines. Residents there have electricity and plumbing facilities, and it's known that they find great quantities of opal when renovating.

1668.   Only military and government officials can own motor vehicles in North Korea.

1669.   Ding Dong is a town located in Bell County, Texas.

1670.   "The Glory Hole" is a drain hole with a diameter of seventy two feet (twenty two meters) situated in Napa, California, in the Monticello Dam.

1671.   In Egypt, every president that has held the position has died in office or been arrested into military custody.

1672.   Whittier is a town in Alaska where almost everyone works under the same roof. Inside the fourteen story building, there is a school, police station, bed and breakfast, and two convenience stores.

1673.   In Vietnam, eating still-beating hearts of live cobras is considered a delicacy.

1674.   The only US state that considers cannibalism illegal is Idaho. In fact, a ban was created in 1990 after spreading fear that cannibalism would present itself in ritualized practices.

1675.   In Sarasota, Florida, they have an Amish beach called "Pinecraft," which allows folks who like a simpler life to take in the sun on the sand while sticking with their traditional values and lifestyle choices. It's a literal Amish paradise, and probably the only one of its kind anywhere in the world.

1676.   The Mama Zebra Program is a project developed in Bolivian cities where a team of young people dress in zebra costumes and dance in the streets to make drivers and pedestrians aware of traffic rules. The zebra was picked because of the pattern of the zebra crossing.

1677.   In Bavaria, Germany, the medieval town of Nordlingen is situated entirely inside a meteorite crater. It's 15.5 miles (twenty five kilometers) across and it's estimated to have formed 14.5 million years ago.

1678.   The African Union is planning to have a single continent-wide currency modeled after the Euro. The most popular proposed name for the currency is the "Afro."

1679.   In 2017, the celebration of Valentine's Day was banned in Pakistan by the Islamabad High Court.

1680.   The country with the highest rate of recycled bottles in the world is Finland where over 90% of plastics and cans are recycled and almost 100% of glass bottles are recycled.

1681.   Since 2010, Japanese population has shrunk by one million people; as a result, the government has started to set up speed-dating events. According to economists, younger generations are losing interest in getting married and starting a family.

1682.   Spain offers citizenship to the descendants of those Spanish people who came to the Americas running away from the Inquisition.

1683.   Western hairstyles that included ponytails, mullets, and elaborate spikes were banned by the Iranian government in 2010.

1684.   In an effort to reduce rampant speeding in Arnprior, Scotland, local authorities had the lines on the road repainted to look wiggly. The twisting lines haven't reduced the speeding, but they have really upset local residents.

1685.   The most polluted river in the world is the Citarum River located in Indonesia which contains dyes, chemicals and various other substances.

1686.   The only quadripoint on Earth where four different countries meet is in Africa among the countries of Namibia, Botswana, Zimbabwe, and Zambia.

1687.   There are no felon voting restrictions in the states of Maine and Vermont. This means that even current inmates can vote.

1688.   In Aberdeen, Washington, which is Kurt Cobain's hometown, there is a sign welcoming visitors that says "Come As You Are," after Nirvana's hit song.

1689.   In Icelandic folklore, the Yule Cat is a vicious creature that hunts and eats people who did not receive any garments or clothes to wear for Christmas.

1690.   The province of Newfoundland was once an independent dominion that functioned much like its own country until 1934. On March 31, 1949, it became a part of Canada, after a referendum where 52% of voters supported joining the country.

1691.   In 1971, women in Switzerland were conceded the right to vote. From all the way back to 1291, the men of Switzerland exercised their democratic right to deny voting rights to their mothers, daughters and sisters.

1692.   The US is the only country worldwide that prints all its currency in the same size and color. Consequently, 3.3 million blind and visually-impaired Americans depend on someone else to identify the denomination of each bill.

1693.   In the Czech Republic, the representation of Santa Claus or Father Christmas doesn't exist. However, children there believe that Baby Jesus brings them Christmas gifts.

1694.   In the United States, the average dental student graduates with over $261,000 of debt. That is actually four times more from what it used to be in 1990.

1695.   There is a school located in Atule'er village, in southwest China, where some students between the ages of six and fifteen have to climb a cliff about 2,624 feet (800 meters) high in order to get to the school, taking about ninety minutes to do so.

1696. On June 24 every year, people in the Philippines hold the Roasted Pig Parade to celebrate the feast of Saint John the Baptist. They roast pigs and then dress them up with sunglasses, bridal attire, or even wigs.

1697. "Marmot Day" is Alaska's own version of Groundhog Day, as there are no groundhogs in the region.

1698. Every August 31 since 1922, El Salvador has held an annual tradition called "Los Bolos del Juego," or balls of fire, where two groups of young people throw flaming balls of old cloth and wire that are soaked in gas at each other.

1699. India and Colombia are the two countries with the most public holidays. Per year, they both have eighteen holidays.

1700. There is not a single land snake in New Zealand. They do have sea snakes however.

1701. In 2017, RAND conducted a study that showed that 60% of American adults suffer at least from one chronic condition, and 42% suffer from more than one. This actually represents hundreds of billions of dollars spent on healthcare every year.

1702. Sweetwater, in Texas, holds a three day rattlesnake round-up every single spring. Snake hunters bring in their catches, which end up being thousands of snakes, for which they are paid five dollars for every pound (0.45 kilograms). The tradition began back in 1958 by the Junior Chamber of Commerce as a way to address the overpopulation of snakes.

1703. The largest bonfire ever was held in Norway, on June 27, 2016, which measured 155 feet (forty seven meters) in the air.

1704. The national animal of Indonesia is the Komodo dragon.

1705. Australia has more wild camels that any other place in the world, including the Middle Eastern region. The high camel population has in fact become such a serious issue, that the government now spends tens of millions of dollars dealing with it.

1706. The Ministry of Environment, Energy, and the Sea in France is working on paving over 599 miles (965 kilometers) of road with solar panels. They expect that, in around five years, it will provide cheap and renewable energy to five million people.

1707. Having a dried llama fetus under the foundation of their homes is considered good luck for most Bolivian families. The animal fetus can usually be found at Bolivia's witch's market where you can also get toad talismans, owl feathers, and stone amulets.

1708. In 1915, the city of San Diego experienced a severe drought. At one point, they hired a rain maker named Charles Hatfield, who referred to himself as a moisture accelerator, to solve the problem. He claimed to have concocted a chemical cocktail that would be released into the air and cause rainfall. Finally, on January 1, 1916, heavy rains started to fall on the city and prolonged for over a month, causing flood damage and almost fifty deaths. Eventually, the city declared the rain and floods were an act of God, so Hatfield was never paid for the job.

1709. Kamikatsu, a small Japanese town, has been trying since 2003 to become the country's first zero-waste community. They already recycle 80% of their waste and currently have thirty-four different recycling categories.

1710. The toothpick capital of the world is considered to be Strong, in Maine. Up until 2003, they manufactured 90% of the US supply of toothpicks, producing twenty million toothpicks a day.

1711. During summer, Alaska has as much as twenty hours of sunshine per day. This allows them to grow vegetables of gigantic proportions, like 137 pound (sixty two kilogram) cabbages, sixty four pound (twenty-nine kilogram) cantaloupes, and thirty five pound (sixteen kilogram) broccoli.

1712. Iceland has about 1,300 different types of insects, but no mosquitoes at all. However, the neighboring countries of Greenland, Scotland, and Denmark all have mosquitoes.

1713. According to the provincial government in Alberta, Canada, the region has been rat-free for more than fifty years. Even though it's known that rodents do enter through trucks, trains, and on foot, they are almost always alone; hence they cannot breed to create more.

1714. Since 2005, people in Estonia have been able to vote via the Internet.

1715. Disposable diapers in Norway are the cheapest in all of Europe. In fact, many Russians smuggle them over the northern border.

1716. Approximately 40% of Vietnamese people share the same last name, with Nguyen being the most popular last name, while the top fourteen most popular names make up 90% of the population. Compared to the United States, the top fourteen last names in the country only makeup fewer than 6%.

1717. There is a weight loss competition in Dubai called the "Your Child In Gold." The competition aims to fight early aged obesity and the winner receives eighty eight pounds (forty kilograms) in gold.

1718. All countries worldwide use the Gregorian calendar, except for Ethiopia, Iran, and Afghanistan.

1719. Since 2003, happy hour has been illegal in the Republic of Ireland according to their Intoxicating Liquor Act.

1720. In some states of the United States it is against the law to take a selfie at the voting booth. People can be fined or even face jail time if doing so.

1721. Mexico's official legal name is the United Mexican States, a name that even today is still used by the country's government.

1722. The only continent that doesn't have rabies according to the World Health Organization is the Antarctic. About 95% of human deaths that occur in Africa and Asia are actually caused by rabies.

1723. An average of $1,100 per year is spent by Americans on clothes for themselves.

1724. The longest coastline in the United States belongs to Alaska at 6,640 miles (10,683 kilometers) long.

1725. Almost half of the world's population is at risk for malaria, according to the World Health Organization. In 2015, for example, there were about 212 million malaria cases and approximately 429,000 deaths. Out of those, 90% of malaria cases and 92% of malaria deaths were found in sub-Saharan Africa.

1726. In 2014, the number one cause of death in the United States, according to the Center of Disease Control and Prevention, was heart disease with over 600,000 deaths, followed by cancer, with 591,000.

1727. International Redhead Day, also known as "Roodharigendag," is an event held every year in Breda, a small town in Holland, on the first weekend of September. Natural redheads come by the thousands to take part in demonstrations, lectures, and workshops, all centered around having red hair.

1728. Located in the southern Pacific Ocean, the Pitcairn Islands are a British overseas territory with a population of about fifty people, most of them descending from nine mutineers of the Bounty ship in 1789. People who are under sixteen years old require a prior clearance before visiting.

1729. The law in Indiana stipulates that the coroner has to be elected into office because they vest the authority to arrest sitting sheriffs. The law originates from the twelfth century, because the British king was worried at the time that sheriffs and other officials were becoming too powerful. He chose the coroner to monitor the officials, and in fact, the name coroner came about because coroners represented the crown.

1730. The world's biggest meat eaters are Australians, followed by Americans. On average, Australians consume 200 pounds (ninety one kilograms) per year, while Americans consume just a bit under that at 198 pounds (eighty nine kilograms) a year.

1731. "Sock City" is another name given to the town of Detang in China, as they produce eight billion pairs of socks every year. This represents one third of the socks made worldwide.

1732. The population density in Siberia is less than eight people per one square mile (2.5 square kilometers). Although Siberia covers 77% of all of Russia and has an area of more than fifty times that of the UK, it is barely populated.

1733. The highest life expectancy in the world is found in Japan, at almost eighty four years on average. Okinawa Island has much to do with it as it's known for having some of the longest-living people in the entire world. The island houses thirty four centenarians per 100,000 people, which is more than three times the rate of mainland Japan.

1734. In Bangalore, India, there is a lake called Bellandur Lake. It is so toxic that it's covered in froth and sometimes bursts into flames. The foam on it is the result of toxic water which has a high amount of ammonia and phosphate, and very low dissolved oxygen, as the result of many years of untreated chemical waste going into it. Given the amount of grease, oil, and detergent in the froth, it often catches fire.

1735. Cyber-homeless refers to a class of people in Japan who live at cyber cafes, as they are a cheaper alternative for housing. The cyber cafes offer free showers to customers and also sell underwear.

1736. In San Francisco, there is a fire hydrant that survived the 1906 earthquake, helping firefighters to save the mission district. In memory of the event, it was painted gold.

1737. The average American consumes between 149 and 169 pounds (sixty eight and seventy seven kilograms) of refined sugar every year, according to the Department of Agriculture. This means that for every American who eats 4.4 pounds (two kilograms) of sugar a year, there is one who eats 293 pounds (133 kilograms) a year.

1738. Since 2017, San Francisco is the first city in the United States to offer free college.

1739. In California, the breeding of killer whales in captivity is now illegal. They have also banned killer whales to perform in shows just for entertainment.

1740. In Japan, October 10 is considered Tom Cruise Day, as per a 2006 declaration. The Japan Memorial Day Association said that the actor received that honor because he visited the country more often than any other Hollywood star.

1741. All citizens' tax returns in Norway are publicly available as they are posted online, showing their total income and total taxes paid. So if you want to gossip on your neighbor or any other person's income, you can do it; the only thing is that they will receive an email letting them know that you were snooping.

1742. There is a small village in India called "Shani Shingapur" which has three hundred buildings that have no doors to them. People leave their businesses, homes and schools open as they believe anyone who does steal anything will face seven years of bad luck.

1743. In 1922, a referendum to ban alcohol took place in Sweden, but it failed with 51% of the voters choosing against it. The decision was split between the sexes with 63% of women voting for the prohibition and 63% of men voting against it.

1744. In 2015, Japan finally lifted its sixty seven year old ban on dancing that ruled after World War II. They prohibited dancing in venues without a special dance license. Originally the law intended to crack down on dance halls that were often a hotbed for prostitution.

1745. In Peru, vultures are equipped with GoPros and GPS trackers to help find illegal trash dumps.

1746. In 1979, the residents of Naco, Arizona, and Mexico, had a volleyball match over the fence of the border that divides them. From then on, it has become an annual tradition.

1747. In February 2017, a survey based on Venezuela's living conditions showed that almost 75% of the population lost an average of at least 18.9 pounds (8.6 kilograms) in 2016, due to a lack of proper nutrition because of the economic crisis.

1748. Pointing the sole of your feet or shoes at somebody is considered an insult in Buddhist and Muslim countries.

1749. Beer cans in Japan have braille on them saying that it's alcohol. Sometimes it says the manufacturer's name as well.

1750. The "Royal March" is Spain's national anthem. It has no lyrics.

1751. The proportion of the world's population over sixty years old, according to the World Health Organization, will nearly double from 12% to 22% between 2015 and 2050. In addition, about 80% of those older people will be living in low and middle income countries.

1752. As of 2016, there are about 35,402 people living with HIV in Atlanta, Georgia, according to AIDSVu. The majority of them are men.

1753. In Korea, there is a culture called fan death, which means that a running electric fan in a closed room with unopened windows will be fatal. Although there is no evidence to support this belief, Korean people do believe it.

1754. Germans consume the highest volume of candy per capita in the world, with each person eating twenty eight pounds (thirteen kilograms) of sugar, chocolate and gum candy on average.

1755. According to the annual statistics of the American Cancer Society, the death rate from cancer in the United States has gradually declined over the past two decades, falling 23% from its peak in 1991 all the way up to 2012. This translates to about 1.7 million deaths averted.

1756. More than 70% of all rail journeys in the United Kingdom either start or finish in London.

1757. Lawyers were actually banned from the state of Georgia from 1733 to 1755. In fact, they were considered pests and the scourge of mankind. At the time, it was believed that every person was perfectly capable of pleading their own case when required.

1758. New Zealand has two official national anthems of equal importance. One is "God Defends New Zealand" and the other is "God Save the Queen." The latter has been New Zealand's official anthem since 1840, but it's rarely sung in the country.

1759. In Iceland, a highway construction project was stopped in 2014 because some people protested the potential destruction of a church that's only attended by elves, which was along the path of the construction. The city actually had to facilitate the church, which only appears as a gigantic boulder to the naked human eye, to be safely moved out of the way with a crane, before the construction could go on.

1760. "Hikikomori" is a kind of condition suffered by around a million people in Japan, mostly men, who have locked themselves in their bedrooms for years, resulting in social and health problems.

1761.   There are some countries where you can purchase beer with your meal at McDonald's, such as Germany, France, Greece, Portugal, South Korea, and Austria.

1762.   The entire European Union is smaller than Canada alone. In fact, Canada is thirty three times bigger than Italy and fifteen times bigger than France.

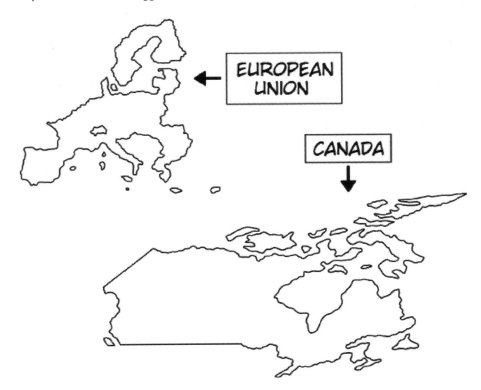

1763.   Given the negative effects on their textile industry, Kenya, Uganda, and Tanzania proposed a ban on the importation of second hand clothes and garments in 2015, as it put thousands of people out of work.

1764.   In 2011, a seventy five year old lady accidentally cut off the whole country's Internet in Armenia when she cut an underground cable when she was looking for copper.

1765.   In 1910, New York became the first state in America to create a law against drunk driving. It was then followed by California and eventually every other state in the country.

1766.   In Ukraine, along the Dnieper River, one of the earliest house structures ever has been found. They are huts that date back to between 23,000 BC and 12,000 BC. They were made of mammoth bones and large pits have been found near them that contain stone tools, bone fragments, and ash.

1767.   Rhode Island and Providence Plantations is actually the full official name of the state of Rhode Island. In 2009, the general assembly voted on whether to keep the original longer name or its shortest form. Even though they decided to keep the original name, nobody really uses it.

1768.   About 45.8 pints of ice cream per year is eaten by the average US citizen, which is more than any other citizen in the world. After the United States, Australia and Norway are second and third respectively to eat the most ice cream in the world.

1769.   In Kansas, there is a state law that requires that all pedestrians crossing a highway at night must wear tail lights on themselves.

1770.   Pieces of land are being given to businesses and entrepreneurs in Dalhousie, New Brunswick, Canada. The value of the land varies from $20,000 to $50,000.

1771.　In Russia, giving your date a dozen roses is considered a faux pas. For happy occasions, you give an odd number of flowers while for condolences an even number.

1772.　The Hogwarts Express is a real train that you can ride in Scotland. The name of the train is "The Jacobite" and it's also known for running on the most beautiful railway route in the UK.

1773.　The Auto Insurance Center decided to rank American states with the highest selfies taken while driving in 2016. After looking through more than 70,000 Instagram posts, they discovered that California had 2.53 driving selfies for every 100,000 residents, making it number one in the whole country.

1774.　Although the population of Finland is only 5.3 million, there are approximately two million saunas in the country. People there can basically go to their favorite sauna whenever or wherever they want.

1775.　The first transgender school has opened in Kochi, India. The school is named Sahaj International. The school aims to offer equal opportunities for transgender students, who had dropped out of other schools due to discrimination.

1776.　The Chinese population's demand for surgical masks has increased due to the bad air pollution. They have even become a fashion statement with designer brands coming out with their own masks.

1777.　In 2017, the world's first hydrogen powered zero emission train was put into service by Germany. The non-electric network trains are powered using a hydrogen fuel cell, which only emits steam and water.

1778.　Traquair Castle is the oldest inhabited house in Scotland. It's located less than thirty miles (forty eight kilometers) from Edinburgh and it has been lived in for over 900 years. It was initially a hunting lodge for the kings and queens of Scotland.

1779.　The wind phone is a phone booth located on the top of a hill that overlooks the Pacific Ocean and Otsuchi town in the northeastern part of Japan. It's there to "connect" family members to their loved ones who lost their lives in the 2011 earthquake and tsunami that hit the coastline of Japan.

1780.　You can purchase meat from cow-bison hybrids in twenty one of fifty American States. The hybrids are called "beefalos."

1781.　There are countries with literacy rates of almost 100%, such as Andorra, Finland, Greenland, Lichtenstein, Luxembourg, and Norway. In general, governments of these countries require by law that every young child shows a compulsory attendance within its school systems. Moreover, some provide free schooling up to the secondary level of education and, along with a higher percentage of its GDP being allotted for the education sector, has resulted in higher literacy rates.

1782.　The first country to offer free public transit to its residents is Luxembourg. The main goal is to relieve big traffic jams for commuters as the country has the highest amount of cars in relation to its population in the European Union.

1783.　In Stanley Park, Vancouver, there is a cannon that goes off every night at exactly 9:00 pm. It was installed in 1898 by the Canadian department of Marine and Fisheries to warn fishermen that the nightly fishing was now closed. It's overlooking Coal Harbor in the downtown skyline.

1784.　The first US states to require a driver's license were Massachusetts and Missouri, back in 1903. It wasn't necessary to pass a test however, you just needed to have one.

1785.　Located off the coast of Antarctica, the Elephant Island has elephant moss growing on it that is over 5,500 years old.

1786. In southeastern Indonesia, the Korowai and Kombai indigenous tribes live in homes that are atop of trees. The houses are often built between twenty feet (six meters) and eighty two feet (twenty five meters) above the ground, but they can go as high as 164 feet (fifty meters). The reason they build them that high is to protect themselves from animal attacks, to avoid the flood during the rainy season, and to be a post guard during conflict that may occur among tribes.

1787. In Japan, there is an S&M gym called "Himitsu No Gym," which translates to "Secret Gym." There your personal trainer is a professional dominatrix who controls your diet and workout. A trial session can cost around ¥7,800 (seventy one dollars).

1788. Bringing bears to the beach is considered illegal in Israel.

1789. Countries located in the Bean Belt, basically the tropics, are the main producers of most of the world's coffee, with Brazil ranked as the biggest coffee-producing country in the world.

1790. The country that eats the most macaroni and cheese in the world is Canada.

1791. In 1826, Scotland attempted to replicate the Parthenon, but bigger and cheaper. The construction was never completed and is now nicknamed "Scotland's Disgrace".

1792. In Portugal, writing in red ink is considered rude.

Crime, Drugs & Prison

1793.   An inmate named Robert Gleason was a murderer who told the guards he would continue killing other inmates until he received the death penalty. He was granted his wish in 2013.

1794.   In a court in France, on January 9, 1386, a pig was found guilty of murdering a child and it was then executed by hanging. The pig was found next to the dead child, so it was officially arrested and imprisoned in a human jail before it was sentenced to death by a real life judge.

1795.   Some rich people in China have avoided going to prison by paying body doubles to take their place. They essentially hire other people to serve their prison sentences.

1796.   Michael Cicconette is a judge known for giving out unusual punishments to guilty defendants. One punishment he gave was to a woman who tried to escape paying a taxi fee by making her walk thirty miles within forty eight hours.

1797.   In Finland, there is a prison where a yellow picket fence is the only thing that keeps the prisoners in.

1798.   In the UK, if a person is caught injuring or killing a swan, or stealing one of their eggs, they could be fined or even sent to prison for up to six months.

1799.   Based on a study conducted by Fight Crime, approximately 60% of boys who were classified as bullies in grades six to nine were convicted of at least one crime by the age of twenty four, while the other 40% had three or more convictions.

1800.   The prisoners in California have the choice to fight forest fires if they want and a lot of them take on the role. It reduces their sentences, allows them to be outdoors, and also pays better than other jobs they're offered.

1801.   Halden Prison, a Norwegian prison in Halden, is an institution that is genuinely devoted to the rehabilitation of people rather than punishing them. Even the most dangerous criminals in there have flat screen TVs in their cells, as well as suite showers, and cozy fluffy towels.

1802.   A CIA officer named William Kampiles was unhappy with his rank, so in November, 1977, he quit his job and took a manual for a secret satellite project with him, which he sold for $3,000 to the Soviets. Hoping to impress his former bosses, he went back to the CIA, confessed what he had done, and asked if he could be a double agent. The CIA wasn't amused, so they arrested him and he served an eighteen year sentence in federal prison for espionage.

1803.   In 1991, there was uncontrolled flooding that caused The Oceanos, a cruise ship, to start to sink. The captain and crew abandoned the ship first, leaving passengers on board without sounding the alarm. Moss Hills, an entertainer aboard the ship, used the radio to call mayday, and everyone was saved. The crew were charged with negligence.

1804.   The Gulabi Gang or Pink Gang, in India, is a gang of women who stand up to abusers in the country. It was founded in 2006 and is based in Badousa. With more than 400,000 members, it helps bring abusers and corrupt policemen to justice. Registered women are given a small ID card, wear a distinctive pink uniform, a pink sari, and for 500 rupees a year, they also get a stick to carry.

1805.   On January 2nd, 1902, a bill that would criminalize people who had drunk too much and were trying to flirt in a disorderly way to get women's attention was introduced by State Assemblyman Francis G. Landon of the Duchess. Offenders could actually be sent to prison and fined up to 500 dollars.

1806.   In 2013, on New Year's Eve, a cat was found wandering around the gate of the medium security prison Judge Luiz de Oliveira Souza in Rio de Janeiro, Brazil. The weird thing about it was that two concrete drill bits, a headset, a memory card, a cell phone, three batteries, and a mobile phone charger were all attached to the cat's body.

1807.   On December 31, 1946, a man named Alphonse Rocco claimed to be a detective and gave a pedestrian a camera, asking her to take a picture of a suspect. It turned out, the detective was a gangster, the suspect was his ex-wife, and the camera was a concealed shotgun firing via the shutter button.

1808.   The NYPD has undercover cop cabs. Safe exchange zones have been created by some police stations; these zones are designated areas for trades arranged through Craigslist and similar sites.

1809.   A report issued by Michael Gibson Light, a doctoral candidate in the University of Arizona's School of Sociology, concluded that ramen noodles are now more popular than tobacco as currency in US penitentiaries centers.

1810.   There was a belief that Communist firing squads were not permitted to shoot at an image of their leaders. For that reason, Russian criminals used to get tattoos bearing the images of Lenin and Stalin so they wouldn't get shot.

1811.   Pablo Escobar was a drug lord in Colombia who offered to pay the country's $20 billion foreign debt to avoid being extradited to the US.

1812.   According to estimates, the Mexican Drug Cartel Caballeros Templarios, or "The Knights Templar," makes around $152 million a year.

1813.   Fourteen year old teenager Al Capone was expelled from school for hitting a female teacher and he never went back.

1814.   Mexican drug cartels made half a trillion dollars in 2019. To put things into perspective, that's more than what Walmart earned.

1815.   Joe Munch was given the shortest jail sentence in history of only one minute in jail. His crime was being drunk and disorderly, but the judge didn't want to punish him, just "teach him a lesson."

1816.   Up until 2013, drug trafficking in Singapore was punished with a mandatory death sentence. As far as harsh drug laws are concerned, Singapore had and still has some of the toughest out of any country in the world.

1817.   Officers in Quebec arrested four men in 2012 for robbing a warehouse and attempting to steal six million pounds of maple syrup worth eighteen million dollars.

1818.   The Grandpa Gang was a group of men that committed the biggest bank robbery in the history of England. The oldest gang member was seventy nine, and the thieves ran off with more than $200 million in jewelry and cash.

1819. The word mafia is not mentioned even once in the 1972 mafia classic "The Godfather," because of threats from the actual mafia. Albert Ruddy, who produced the movie, got the green light from mafia boss Joseph Colombo to make it after he and Paramount Studios agreed to remove the word entirely from the script, and to donate the money made during the premier to the hospital building fund of the Italian American Civil Rights League.

1820. Michael Anderson Godwin was on death row in South Carolina, when one day in 1989, he decided to multitask by peeing and repairing his prison cell TV at the same time. He bit into a wire which was still connected to the TV, and he accidentally electrocuted himself, essentially turning his toilet into something of an electric chair, like the one that was waiting for him.

1821. The Elgin Federal Prison Camp closed in 2006, but during its operations as a minimum security prison, it was said to be so comfortable and cozy that it was nicknamed "Club Fed."

1822. Al Capone, also known as Scarface, was an American gangster who was known to send flowers to rival gang members' funerals. One time he even spent five thousand dollars for a single funeral.

1823. Animal abuse is now being tracked by the FBI the same way they track homicides and assaults. The logic behind it is that if you abuse animals, there is a good chance that you would do the same to a person, so they have classified animal cruelty as a group A felony.

1824. In 1818, treadmills were created with the aim of punishing English inmates.

1825. It's considered illegal to wear a bullet resistant vest in New Jersey when committing a violent crime.

1826. In Indiana prisons, they give death row inmates their meal of choice two or three days prior to execution because most of them are rarely hungry on the day they know they'll die.

1827. Renowned gangster Al Capone left prison in 1939 after which he was treated for paresis at Union Memorial Hospital for some time. When he was discharged, Capone gave two weeping cherry trees to the hospital as a sign of appreciation.

1828. A Taliban commander named Mohammed Ashan turned himself in at a checkpoint operated by Afgan soldiers in April, 2012, hoping to claim the one hundred dollar reward they had offered for his capture. He didn't get his reward, but he was arrested.

1829. Alcatraz was a maximum high security federal prison that was home to the most notorious criminals, but it was also known for the great food that it served its inmates. Murderers serving more than one life sentence often ate baked meat croquettes, beef steaks, and cupcakes with icing. They were permitted to eat as much food as they wanted, provided they didn't leave any waste behind.

1830. Drug smugglers dropped approximately eighty eight pounds (forty kilograms) of cocaine into the Chattahoochee National Forest in Georgia, in 1985. A black bear stumbled upon the drugs, ate all of them, and died a while later because of a serious overdose. The bear got the nickname Pablo Escobar.

1831. On September 21, 1990, the Shiawassee Police Department in Michigan staged a fake wedding where the bride and groom were undercover cops who invited local drug dealers to their big day. At the reception, they busted them all at once.

1832. Gangaram Mahes was a homeless man in New York throughout the 1990's who would get sent to prison on purpose so he could receive three meals and a clean bed.

1833. In Japan, death row prisoners aren't told the date of their execution, so every single day they wake up wondering if today may be their last.

1834. During Hurricane Katrina, hundreds of inmates were left to die in their cells because officials abandoned Orleans Parish Prison.

1835. In the United States, the first drug law was to forbid Chinese opium dens.

1836. Colombian drug lord Pablo Escobar got to build his own prison in 1991 known as La Cathedral. It had a soccer field, a giant dollhouse, a bar, a Jacuzzi, and even a waterfall. He was caught torturing his guests after thirteen months of being there. After that, he was back on the run.

1837. In order to taunt police, a convicted pedophile named Christopher Paul Neil posted a picture of himself with a swirl effect on his face. The image, however, was unswirled by Interpol revealing his face, and he was arrested.

1838. A French woman named Nadine Vaujour was so determined to get her husband out of jail that she learned how to fly a helicopter to get him out. She succeeded in picking him up off the roof, however, she was arrested shortly after.

1839. Because of a toothache, a Swedish inmate escaped from prison in 2013 and went to a dentist to get it fixed. After the pain was treated, he turned himself back into the police. His sentence of one month was only increased by a day.

1840. Kowloon Walled City in China existed from 1810 to 1993. Before the city was demolished, it was controlled by triads with thousands of people involved in drugs, gambling, and prostitution.

1841. The final words of murderer Gary Gilmore actually inspired Nike's slogan, Just Do It. Before being executed by firing squad, his final words were "let's do it." Advertising executive Dan Wieden modified it and pitched it to Nike, creating their iconic slogan.

1842. Poppy seed consumption can actually produce positive results during drug screening tests.

1843. Al Capone was in the business of used furniture, at least according to the business card that he carried around. Whenever he encountered law enforcement authorities, the gangster would hand out his card, and explain that he was merely a second-hand furniture seller.

1844. In 2010, a biker gang in Denmark called "Black Cobra" once took 120 boxes of almond tarts, punsch rolls, apple crowns, and brownies from a delivery truck.

1845. In Liechtenstein, the incarceration rate is nineteen people for every one hundred thousand. The country's population is only thirty seven thousand meaning they only have seven people in their jail.

1846. In Alaska, there was a serial killer man named Robert Hansen. He used to kidnap young women and take them to his cabin. Later, he would release them into the woods and hunt them down with a rifle and knife. Hansen was convicted in 1984 and died in 2014.

1847. China is actually monitoring and testing their sewage for traces of drugs that are excreted through urine. According to officials, a drug manufacturer was already caught and arrested by using this technique.

1848. In Honolulu, Hawaii, stealing spam is starting to be considered a form of organized crime, as the number of cases has greatly increased in the last years.

1849. In 2017, a plot to steal legendary racing pioneer Enzo Ferrari's body from a cemetery was stopped by the Italian police. The group of thieves planned to ask for money in exchange for the body. Ferrari died in 1988 at ninety years old.

1850. Ted Bundy, a notorious serial killer, shockingly served as the assistant director of the Seattle Crime Prevention Advisory Commission. He was even the author of a pamphlet instructing women on rape prevention.

1851. One of the main reasons why the police still use horses today is because they offer an important height advantage. Officers can easily overlook large crowds of people as well as move through them, something that they are not able to do if they were to be on foot or in a car.

1852. From the 1980's until the 1990's, the Italian mafia trafficked nuclear waste and ended up dumping it in Somalia.

1853. In July of 2018, a horn shark was stolen by three thieves from an aquarium in San Antonio. They masked it as a baby before putting it in a stroller and wheeling it out. Eventually, two of the thieves confessed to the police and were sentenced.

1854. Pablo Escobar had his own private zoo with about 200 animals. He used his drug planes to smuggle many of the animals into the country.

1855. In 1999, a man named Cornelius Anderson helped in robbing a Burger King and was sentenced to serve thirteen years in prison, but no one ever came to collect him so he continued on living his life. Twelve years later the police were preparing for his release only to realize that they never arrested him to begin with.

1856. Doctor Fareed Farah, an oncologist from Michigan, was sentenced to forty five years in prison after finding out that he had milked 553 cancer patients for millions of dollars. He was accused of overtreating, undertreating, misdiagnosing, and even administering treatment to people that never had cancer in the first place.

1857. Nightclub owner Ruth Ellis was the last woman to be executed for murder in Great Britain, on July 13, 1955. She was hanged for killing her boyfriend. The death penalty for murder was actually banned in England, Scotland, and Wales in 1965.

1858. Despite having DNA evidence of the suspect, German police could not prosecute a 6.8 million dollar jewel heist because the DNA belonged to identical twins; police could not prove to whom the DNA belonged to.

1859. Steven Jay Russell has escaped from prison four times. The first time, he simply walked out. Upon recapture, Russell lowered and paid his bail by pretending to be a judge, escaped his next capture by impersonating a doctor, and did so again by faking his death. He eventually received a 144 year sentence that he is still serving.

1860. In 2010, a serial killer named Rodney Alcala was his own attorney for his trial case. In a deep voice, he would interrogate himself on the witness stand addressing them to Mr. Alcala, and then answer them himself in a normal voice.

1861.　John Dillinger was actually a professional baseball player before he became a criminal and a famous bank robber. He played shortstop for Martinsville Athletics.

1862.　In Scotland, there are three verdicts instead of two under the court of law: guilty, not guilty, and not proven.

1863.　In 1982, Tylenol murders in Chicago killed seven people. No suspect was ever caught or charged for the crime.

1864.　In 1928, the last conviction in the United States for blasphemy took effect in Little Rock, Arkansas, to atheist activist Charles Lee Smith. A sign in the storefront window read: "Evolution is true, the Bible is a lie, God's a ghost." He was condemned to ninety days in jail and had to pay a fine of $100.

1865.　Between 1934 and 1938, while gangster Al Capone was imprisoned in Alcatraz for tax evasion, he was permitted to play the banjo in the prison band that he helped form due to his good behavior. The band was named Rock Islanders and they performed every Sunday for the other inmates.

Entertainment Industry

1866. The Ku Klux Klan was sending out a very racist and homophobic phone message while impersonating the charismatic Mr. Rogers, a PBS show character in 1990. Fred Rogers, who starred as Mr. Rogers in the show, had to sue the organization to make them stop. The KKK was forced by a judge to stop, and ordered to hand over tapes with the message.

1867. There was a pine tree planted in Los Angeles in memory of George Harrison, a member from the Beatles, that ended up dying due to an infestation of beetles.

1868. "Star Wars: The Force Awakens" had an incredible opening weekend in movie history with a total of a whopping $247,966,675.

1869. Matthew Knowles, Beyoncé's father, used to manage his daughter and the other members of Destiny's Child. He made the girls run a mile while singing so that they could perform on stage without getting exhausted.

1870. For the Disney's "Toy Story" movie, the original concept of Woody wasn't going to be of him as a cowboy. Instead, Woody was going to be a ventriloquist dummy that was really cruel to the other toys. Later, the creators realized that people don't want to watch a movie about a character so cruel and they changed him to a cowboy.

1871. Singer Bono got his stage name when friends started to call him "Bonavox," the name of a hearing aid store in his neighborhood, and he kept the name since that time. In Latin, Bonavox means "good voice."

1872. When sixteen year old actress Judy Garland filmed "The Wizard of Oz" as the main character Dorothy, she was put on a strict daily diet of chicken soup, black coffee, and eighty cigarettes.

1873. Judge Judy makes $47 million a year, which means she's the highest paid star on TV irrespective of genre. She also only works fifty two days a year, meaning she receives $900,000 for every single episode of her show.

1874. When Michael Jackson finished performing at his concerts, he had to get smaller sized clothes, because he sweated so much during the performances that he lost weight and literally shrunk in size.

1875. The face on the mask worn by Michael Meyer in the Halloween film series actually belongs to William Shatner. The prop department for the Halloween franchise simply took a Captain Kirk mask, painted it white, and gave it to the horror film killer character to wear.

1876. Actor Anthony Hopkins went to London in 1973, looking for a book that was the basis of a movie he was in. He couldn't find a copy of "The Girl from Petrovka" at any store there. He finally gave up, but as he sat on a bench waiting for the train home, he found a copy of that book, left unattended, right next to him. Later, in 1975, he met George Feifer, the author of the book, and was surprised to find the author didn't even have a copy himself. It turns out he had given his copy to a friend after scribbling some crucial notes on the margins, but the friend had lost it. Amazingly, the copy that Hopkins found was the same one that Feifer had lost.

1877. Charles Gusman, a famous radio announcer, was lying on his deathbed on October 18, 2000, when his daughter reminded him that he had always wanted his last words to be memorable, so he took off his oxygen mask and whispered: "And now, for a final word from our sponsor!" Those turned out to be his last words.

1878. After comedian Jack Benny died on December 26, 1974, he kept reminding Mary Livingstone, his wife, just how much he cared for her. Mary got a long stemmed rose every day from Benny's estate, until nine years later, when she too passed on.

1879. Actor Tom Hanks was meant to use his real natural accent in the movie Forrest Gump. However, child actor Michael Conner Humphreys, who played the younger Gump in the movie, wasn't able to adapt Tom Hanks's accent, so Hanks chose to take up the boy's Mississippi accent for uniformity.

1880. The popular sitcom "Friends" had a few different working titles before they settled on its name. They included: Insomnia Café and Across the Hall.

1881. Author George R. R. Martin, who wrote the books upon which HBO's Game of Thrones is based, made a cameo on the unaired pilot of the show as a nobleman wearing a large hat. He however didn't repeat his role when they had to reshoot the scenes.

1882. Comedian Charlie Chaplin was given an honorary Oscar for his contribution to film in 1972, during the 44th Annual Academy Awards. During the event, he showed up in the United States after staying away for twenty years because he was labeled a communist. As he went to stage, he was welcomed with a twelve minute standing ovation from the audience and celebrities. This still stands as the longest Oscar in history.

1883. Jennifer Lopez dropped her second studio album J-Lo in January, 2001, the same time her movie The Wedding Planner came out, and she became the first woman in history to have a number one movie and a number one album at the same time, and in the same week.

1884. Stephen King's "The Shining" was inspired by the Stanley Hotel in Colorado, and the hotel is now embracing the fame it gained from the movie. They play the movie so frequently in the hotel that channel forty two is dedicated to it, and in all the 160 guest rooms, the movie is played on an endless loop.

1885. The movie "La La Land" broke a record in 2017 by winning all seven of its Golden Globe Award Nominations. The awards included Best Motion Picture, Musical or Comedy, Best Director, Best Screenplay, Best Score, and acting awards for its actors.

1886. In the movie "Star Wars Episode IV: A New Hope," Darth Vader only appears on screen for a total of twelve minutes.

1887.   On August 29, 1966, the Beatles' final live concert was held at Candlestick Park, in San Francisco, California. Even though the park's capacity was 42,500, only 25,000 tickets were sold. Tickets cost between four dollars and fifty cents and six dollars and fifty cents.

1888.   Iggy Pop has a pet cockatoo named Biggy Pop. They like to do things together like sleep, snuggle, and even listen to rock classics.

1889.   The sons of adventurer Bear Grylls are named Jesse Marmaduke and Huckleberry.

1890.   A round-trip ticket on Virgin Galactic's Spaceship Two Rocket Plane costs $200,000. Actor Ashton Kutcher was the 500th person to purchase a ticket.

1891.   When Satsuki Mitchel found out that her fiancé Daniel Craig ran off with Racel Weisz in 2010, she spent a million dollars on his credit card in revenge.

1892.   The first lyrics to The Beatles song "Yesterday" were "scrambled eggs." One morning Paul McCartney woke up with the melody in his head, so as a way to remember the melody until the lyrics could be written for the tune, he went around the house just humming "scrambled eggs, baby I love scrambled eggs."

1893.   The biological father of Steve Jobs was an immigrant from Syria.

1894.   Simon Cowell, from X Factor and American Idol, worked as a runner on the set of the movie The Shining.

1895.   In Atlanta, Georgia, a Miss Klingon Empire beauty pageant is held as part of the annual tech tracks convention. The participants all wear Klingon costumes and makeup, and are judged on beauty, talent, and personality.

1896.   To create the voice of Chewbacca from Star Wars, bear vocalizations, as well as the sound of walruses, badgers, and the howls of sick animals were used.

1897.   Willard is actually the first name of actor, producer, rapper, and songwriter Will Smith; not William as many believe. His full name is Willard Carroll Smith Junior.

1898.   The suit used by Jim Carrey to play The Grinch was covered in yak hairs that were dyed green and sewn onto a spandex suit.

1899.   The first video of a black artist to air on MTV was Billy Jean by Michael Jackson.

1900.   The youngest person to ever host Saturday Night Live was actress Drew Barrymore, on November 20, 1982, at the age of seven.

1901.   The Guinness World Record for the most words in a single song is held by Eminem's Rap God. Released in 2013, the rapper spits out 1,560 words during its six minute and four second run time song. That's an average of 4.3 words per second.

1902.   The first American film to show a toilet flushing on screen was Alfred Hitchcock's thriller "Psycho."

1903.   Prince, Madonna and Michael Jackson were all born in the summer of 1958 within two months of each other, and they are all from the Great Lakes region.

1904.   Illusionist David Copperfield was the first in his line of work to get a star on the Hollywood Walk of Fame. Additionally, as a solo performer, he has sold more tickets than any entertainer throughout history.

1905.   Throughout his career, Elvis Presley only did a single commercial. He recorded a jingle for Southern Made Donuts. He was a regular customer at the store, and that was where he began his storied love for donuts.

1906.   Frankie Munez, the star of "Malcolm in the Middle," had such damaging memory loss that he doesn't recall starting in the show. His girlfriend maintains a journal of the things they do every day to help him remember and cope with his condition.

1907.   The US Mint was angered by Twentieth Century Fox in 2007, when the company used real American currency for an advertising stand for the movie "Fantastic Four: Rise of the Silver Surfer." 40,000 real California Statehood quarters were modified by adding an image of the Silver Surfer and a website link, and then put into circulation. The mint had to make it clear that it was against the law to advertise on real currency.

1908. Wayne McClarin, also known as the Marlboro Man, died of lung cancer on July 22, 1992. Although he was famous as a spokesman for the popular cigarette company, some of his last words were: "Take care of the children, tobacco will kill you, and I'm living proof of it."

1909. Randy Savage, aka Macho Man, was named Randy Poffo at birth, and he played in the Cardinals Minor Baseball League before he became a wrestler.

1910. In Mr. Rogers' Neighborhood, the character of Officer Clemmons was portrayed by Francois Clemmons between 1968 and 1993. Francois was the first black actor to have a recurring role on children's TV.

1911. The TV show Gunsmoke ran for twenty years and spun off several TV movies, and in all that time, the character Marshal Matt Dillion killed 407 people in total.

1912. There's a real mall in the basement of singer Barbra Streisand's house. You can buy vintage shoes and clothes, antique dolls, and real movie costumes at the mall.

1913. Indian musician Daler Mehndi wanted to prove that his videos weren't just popular because they featured pretty women, so he created one that only featured himself. It turned out to be a great hit in the country and it even became a viral meme.

1914. The movie "Van Wilder," starring Ryan Reynolds, was released in 2002 and it's based on the real life of Bert Kreischer, a stand-up comedian who spent six years as an undergraduate at Florida State University.

1915. When Orson Wells, the legendary movie director, made the classic movie Citizen Kane, he was just twenty five years old.

1916. Mark Hamill would never have gotten the role of Luke Skywalker had it not been for Robert Englund, who portrayed Freddy Krueger in "The Nightmare on Elm Street" films. Englund was briefly considered for the part of Han Solo in Star Wars, and coincidentally, Hamill was crashing on his couch. Englund urged Hamill to audition for Skywalker, and that's how he got the iconic role.

1917. The Wrecking Crew drummer Hal Blaine is the most accomplished drummer in the history of rock and roll. He's played drums of forty number one hit singles, 150 top ten hits, and more than 35,000 songs. He has performed with dozens of musicians, including Elvis Presley, Nancy Sinatra, Steely Dan, The Beach Boys, John Denver, The Monkees, and Simon and Gurfunkel.

1918. The popular song "Hey Ya!" was released by the band Outkast on September 9, 2003, and it quickly got to number one on the music charts. It contained a lyric that asked people to "shake it like a Polaroid picture," forcing the real Polaroid Company to send out a warning telling people to avoid shaking self-developing pictures after taking them, to avoid ruining them. The company Polaroid still used the song's popularity to rekindle people's perception of their camera and other products.

1919. Nick Cave, the Australian musician, wrote a follow-up to the successful 2000 movie Gladiator, and it centered on the main character Maximus, who after dying, went to the afterlife and tried to kill a rogue god, before he came back to earth to lead a revolt. Filmmaker Ridley Scott has confirmed that he is working on a Gladiator sequel, but it won't be about Cave's story.

1920. Singer Freddie Mercury's birth name was actually Farrokh Bulsara, and he was born in Zanzibar, an Island in East Africa.

1921. When they were casting for the role of James Bond in Casino Royale, Henry Cavill got the part, but producers wanted a Bond who looked older, so they went with Daniel Craig.

1922. Assad, who was an infant at the time, was featured as an executive producer on his father DJ Khaled's tenth studio album named "Grateful," which came out on June 23, 2017. DJ Khaled watched his son's reactions while producing the music. He claims that when the child threw up on him while they listened to the track "Shining," he immediately knew it would be a big hit.

1923. The longest song ever to be on the Billboard Hot A Hundred was Guns N' Roses' "November Rain," which plays for eight minutes and fifty seven seconds.

1924. Bounty, the replica ship used in the film Pirates of the Caribbean, sank off the coast of North Carolina during Hurricane Sandy.

1925. Instead of the classic solid bronze, twenty four karat gold-plated statuettes, Academy Award winners were given plaster statuettes for three years during the Second World War. That's because there was a metal shortage at the time, but when the war ended, the winners were asked to return the plaster Oscars in exchange for the classic versions.

1926. Twisty the Clown was so scary in "American Horror Freak Show" that some crew members would have to leave the set at times while others said they had nightmares after filming.

1927. Vin Diesel was only seven years old when he got his first acting gig. His friends and him were breaking into a theater to vandalize it when a lady stopped them and offered them a script and twenty dollars each if they attended rehearsals everyday after school.

1928. "Bill Haley and His Comets" was the first rock 'n' roll group to play at Carnegie Hall, in May 1955.

1929. Originally, Walt Disney's Goofy was called Dippy Dog; it was first introduced to audiences in Mickey's Revue.

1930. Tony Lommi started down-tuning his guitar after an accident that cut the end of his two fingers off. As a result, Black Sabbath's signature sound was born.

1931. The actor Sean Bean was so afraid of flying that when they had to fly to certain locations for the Lord of the Rings, he traveled by sky lift and walked the rest of the way.

1932. Frank "Rocky" Fiegel, a local tough guy from Chester, Illinois, was the inspiration for the character of Popeye. His appearance and looks were replicated very similarly to the real Popeye.

1933. After the movie Rocky IV came out, there was a joke going around Hollywood that since Rocky had no more opponents left to fight, he'd have to fight an alien for the fifth film. Writers John and Jim Thomas played on this joke which ended up becoming the plot for the movie Predator.

1934. The most expensive silent film ever made was the 1925 released film Ben Hur. It cost between four to six million dollars at that time.

1935.   Dudeism is a religion that came from the movie "The Big Lebowski," which promotes the practice of being cool headed, going with the flow, and taking it easy.

1936.   The Muppet Show once received a letter from a man telling them that the Swedish chef doesn't actually speak Swedish. The head writer wrote back by saying: "Thank you for bringing this to our attention. We were going to fire the chef on the spot, but he has a wife and family, and promised to take Swedish lessons."

1937.   When Andy Garcia was born, there was a tennis ball sized lump on his shoulder which turned out to be an undeveloped conjoined twin. The actor eventually had surgery to get rid of the lump.

1938.   The older brother of actor Matthew McConaughey, Michael, also known as Rooster, named his son Miller Lite after his favorite beer.

1939.   Actor Michael Clarke Duncan, who played John Coffey in the movie The Green Mile, previously worked as the bodyguard of Queen Latifah, Will Smith, Martin Lawrence, and Jamie Foxx.

1940.   Steven Victor Tallarico was the birth name of Steven Tyler, from the band Aerosmith.

1941.   Oscar winners are requested to sign a waiver by the Academy of Motion Picture Arts and Sciences promising to give the Academy first right of buying back the trophies for $1.

1942.   The creator of Star Wars, George Lucas, convinced actor Carrie Fisher to wear no underwear because it doesn't exist in outer space.

1943.   A typical Rihanna hit single can cost around $75,000 to make and another million to promote it, although it only takes about fifteen minutes to write the lyrics.

1944.   No two female characters speak to each other in the whole "The Lord of the Rings" trilogy.

1945.   In theater, it is commonly thought that peacocks, or more specifically peacock feathers, bring bad luck to actors. There are a number of tales from veteran actors about sets collapsing or forgetting their lines when a peacock feather was onstage. It stems from the fact that the blue and green design resembles an evil eye.

1946.   The actress Halle Berry was named after "Halle's Department Store" which was a local icon in the state of Cleveland where she was born.

1947.   All members of the band "ZZ Top" have beards, except for one whose last name is Beard.

1948.   The band members of Good Charlotte were known to protest against KFC's treatment of chickens, however, after 2013, they appeared in several KFC commercials in Australia and even tried to set a new world record for eating KFC on Australia's Got Talent.

1949.   Writer, actor, and comedian Dan Akroyd suffers from Asperger, a form of autism. One of his symptoms is having an obsession with ghosts and law enforcement, which resulted into the idea of the "Ghostbusters" film.

1950.   According to the former US President Bill Clinton, the Netflix series "House of Cards" is 99% real.

1951.   While filming the movie "Apocalypse Now," the production cast design decided to use real bodies instead of fake ones. It was only when the odor became too strong that the rest of the cast found out about it.

1952.   In the 1990's, the King of Pop Michael Jackson wanted to play Spiderman so badly that he discussed purchasing Marvel Comics with Stan Lee. No agreement was made.

1953.   Beyonce was making about $4 per second in 2014.

1954.   In the movie "Back to the Future," the time machine was meant to be a refrigerator, however, it was changed to the car as the writers thought that kids would lock themselves in a fridge recreating the scene.

1955.   Musician Pharell Williams was fired from three different McDonald's stores when he was only seventeen for stealing nuggets and being lazy. Later on he created a jingle with Justin Timberlake called "I'm Lovin' It."

1956.   In the 1990's, the movie Wayne's World was filmed in only thirty four days, extremely fast if compared to today where most movies take many months or even years to film.

1957.   In 2009, three masked criminals unknowingly broke into Swedish actor Dolph Lundgren's home. The intruders tied the actor up and then threatened his wife. But soon, they realized who owned the house when finding a family picture and immediately ran away.

1958.   The animated film "Sleeping Beauty" took several years to complete. Walt Disney even got bored of it at some point and actually redirected his energy into the creation of Disneyland. In fact, the iconic Sleeping Beauty's castle was built at the center of the park as promotion for the movie's eventual debut, which was four years later.

1959.   In 2013, Shawn Mendes, the award-winning Canadian singer/songwriter, got his start performing covers of famous songs on the social media platform Vine. Today, he is considered one of the 100 Most Influential People in the World according to Time Magazine.

1960.   In the movie "The Dark Knight Rises," the plane that crashed with the help of computer generated special effects actually did crash the next year, killing two people on board.

1961.   The "Toy Story" character Buzz Lightyear was actually named after astronaut Buzz Aldrin, the second astronaut to walk on the moon.

1962.   The reality show "The Voice" not only shapes participants to become new singing stars, but also rejuvenates the careers of its celebrity judges.

1963.   When Rolling Stones bassist Bill Wyman was fifty two, he married eighteen year old Mandy Smith, but they got divorced after a year. Later, Bill's thirty year old son, Stephen, married Mandy's mother, aged forty six. If Bill and Mandy had remained married, Stephen would have been his father's father-in-law and his own grandpa.

1964.   In 1923, the original Hollywood sign was erected. It was placed there as an outdoor ad campaign for a suburban housing development called Hollywoodland. In 1949, the sign was restored and shortened to just Hollywood.

1965.   According to Netflix, in 2015 alone, their users streamed 42.5 billion hours of programming, which is an increase from the twenty nine billion hours of the previous year. As of 2020, there are 167 million subscribers worldwide.

1966.   In 1980, music star Paul McCartney was arrested and then deported from Japan for trying to smuggle in nearly half a pound of marijuana in his baggage. In fact, he spent nine days in the Tokyo narcotics detention center.

1967.   On May 8, 2010, actress Betty White hosted Saturday Night Live. She was eighty eight years old at the time, becoming the oldest person to host the show.

1968.   In 1999, PETA conferred a humanitarian award to actor Steven Seagal for preventing the export of baby elephants from South Africa to Japan.

1969.   "Keeping Up with the Kattarshians" is a real round the clock live streamed show where four kittens, that are yet to be adopted and are living in a large dollhouse, are being filmed using GoPro cameras.

1970.   Norville "Shaggy" Rogers is actually Shaggy's full name in the Scooby-Doo cartoon.

1971.   The actor Don Johnson once asked famous journalist Hunter Thompson what the sound of a one handed clap sounded like. Thompson responded by reaching over and slapping Don over the head.

1972.   Jonah Hill wanted the role in "The Wolf of Wall Street" so bad that he accepted the position for only $60,000. For his role he received an Oscar nomination for the best supporting actor.

1973.   A twelve year old boy was punched by Zach Braff for spraying fake paint on his Porsche as part of a prank on the show Punk'd. The scene had to be cut out.

1974.   Before becoming an actor, Liam Neeson was a teacher and did it for a few years before he got fired.

A fifteen year old boy pulled out a knife in class so he punched him in the face.

1975. Martha Steward once dated Anthony Hopkins, but after watching "Silence of the Lambs," she broke up with him, as she was unable to avoid associating Hopkins with the character of Hannibal Lector.

1976. When Demi Lovato and Selena Gomez were kids, they both appeared on the TV show "Barney and Friends." In fact, the long-time friends were regularly shown together dancing and singing on screen.

1977. Musician David Grohl was admitted into hospital after overdosing on a drug. That drug was caffeine. He consumed too much coffee while recording his new album.

1978. During a basketball game, teenager Mick Jagger bit off the tip of his tongue when he collided with another player. From then on, he spoke and sang with a less posh accent and more of a street accent.

1979. Steven Spielberg was rejected three times by the admission's officer when he applied for Cinematic Art School. When he was awarded his honorary doctorate from that school, he said he'd only accept it if it was personally signed by that admission's officer, which it was.

1980. Five hundred stormtroopers were placed on the Great Wall of China by Disney to promote Star Wars the Force Awakens.

1981. Actor Tom Cruise is not as tall as you think. He is only 5.6 feet (1.7 meters) tall.

1982. The animators of the "How to Train your Dragon" movie had to attend flight school in order to help them capture the realism of flying creatures soaring through the clouds.

1983. Paul McCartney's mother was a midwife in charge of the maternity ward at the Walton Hospital Liverpool. In fact, she had the privilege of giving birth to Paul in a private ward. Her ambition for her son was that he would become a doctor.

1984. The animal rights group PETA once suggested the band the "Pet Shop Boys" to change their name to "Rescue Shelter Boys," as a protest against the cruel conditions of many pet shops. Although Neil Tennant and Chris Lowe refused to change it, they did think that the request raised an issue worth talking about, as they mentioned in a post on their website.

1985. In the 1973 movie "The Exorcist," the green vomit that comes out of Regan, played by actress Linda Blair, was actually a combination of split pea soup and oatmeal.

1986. The youngest individual winner of a Grammy is Country singer LeAnn Rimes. She was fourteen years old when she won her first two awards in 1997: "Best New Artist" and "Best Female Country Vocal Performance."

1987. The first black woman to appear on the cover of the "Sports Illustrated" was supermodel Tyra Banks, in 1997.

1988. The ashes of actress Carrie Fisher, known as Princess Leia from the Star Wars franchise, were placed in a gigantic Prozac pill urn. During her life, she openly battled with drug addiction and suffered from mental disorder. The urn was actually purchased by Carrie herself; it was an antique porcelain pill from the 1950's, and was one of her favorite prized possessions.

1989. In the Rugrats movie, rapper Busta Rhymes actually voiced Reptar.

1990.   Dolly Parton, the famous country singer, is Miley Cyrus' godmother.

1991.   The actor who played the creepy little kid in "The Shining," Danny Lloyd, stopped his acting career as he grew up and went on to actually become a professor, teaching biology in Louisville.

1992.   The movie "Straight Outta Compton" wasn't shown in Compton because the city has no theaters.

1993.   The first actor to appear on the cover of Time Magazine was Charlie Chaplin, on July 6, 1925.

1994.   Director David Fincher wanted Ben Affleck to wear a Yankees cap for a scene while filming "Gone Girl." Affleck, a huge fan of the Red Sox, refused. After a four day production halt, they finally came to an agreement that he would wear a Mets cap.

1995.   On March 27, 1973, actor Marlon Brando declined the Academy Award for best actor for his performance in "The Godfather" film. Native American actress Sacheen Littlefeather went in Brando's place. According to her, Marlon would not accept the award as he was protesting Hollywood's portrayal of Native Americans in the movie.

1996.   The record for one of the largest casts ever is held by the movie Gandhi. Just in the funeral scene, more than 300,000 people were used as extras.

1997.   Oscar the Grouch from Sesame Street wasn't always green; he was originally orange.

1998.   The monkey in "Hangover 2" is the same one seen in "Night at the Museum." His name is Crystal and he's featured in twenty five other movies as well. He was awarded the Poscar in 2015, which is an Oscar for animals.

1999.   Elvis Presley made his first and last Grand Ole Opry appearance on October 2, 1954. Seemingly, his gyration-filled performance was not received well and one of the officials there apparently told him to not quit his day job, which was driving trucks.

2000.   After the movie "Cannibal Holocaust" was released in 1980, the director had to prove in court that the actors were indeed still alive and didn't die during the movie.

2001.   Chuck Lorre, the creator of "The Big Bang Theory," and "Two and a Half Men," also wrote "The Teenage Mutant Ninja Turtles" theme song.

2002.   Back in 1995, Dwayne "The Rock" Johnson used to play football for the CFL's Calgary Stampeders. That was before he went into wrestling and acting.

2003.   The tumbler for the Dark Knight trilogy is not a CGI model; it's actually a working vehicle.

2004.   The most famous opera singer of the late Victorian period was Dame Nellie Melba. Melba toast and peach melba are actually both named after her.

2005.   In the movie Jurassic Park, the sound of Velociraptors talking back and forth to each other was actually the sound of mating tortoises.

2006.   Muhammad Ali once invited Billy Crystal to join him for a run at the local country club. Billy accepted, however, couldn't go because the country club didn't allow Jews. Ali never went back to that club.

2007.   Edith Macefield was an eighty four year old lady who refused an offer of a million dollars from a building developer to move, so they built around her house instead. The movie "Up" was inspired by this story.

2008.   Whenever Mr. Rogers fed his fish on the TV series "Mr. Roger's Neighborhood," he said out loud that he was doing it. This was because of a letter he got from a blind five year old fan, who was concerned about the fish, and wanted to make sure they were attended to.

2009.   Pierce Brosnan performed in a circus for three years as a fire eater, before he became the actor who played Remington Steel and James Bond.

2010.   Jackie Kennedy, former First American Lady, actually won an Emmy for her televised tour of the White House in 1962.

2011.   Artist Michael Pangrazio created the matte painting used to film the warehouse scene in "Raiders of the Lost Ark." It was painted on glass and the live action shots were actually done through a hole in it. It took him three months to complete it.

2012.   In the Back to the Future trilogy, Donald Trump was actually the inspiration for the character Biff Tanned.

2013.   Henry Cavill was playing World of Warcraft when he got a call from Zack Snyder for the role of Superman. He almost missed the call because of the game.

2014.   Jean-Claude Van Damme was the original actor behind the scenes shot for the movie Predator. Because he didn't like the suit that he had to wear, he was then replaced by actor Kevin Peter Hall.

2015.   From the Spongebob Squarepants movie, David Hasselhoff owns a fourteen feet (four meter) tall replica of himself.

2016.   While filming Disney's Napoleon and Samantha, eight year old actress Jodie Foster was attacked by a lion and briefly carried in its mouth. She has had a fear of cats ever since.

2017.   When he was a teenager, actor Tom Cruise was a student at a Franciscan seminary. In fact, he aspired to become a priest before he went into acting.

2018.   Gordon Matthew Thomas Sumner is actually the real name of musician and singer Sting. The nickname Sting was given by band leader Gordon Solomon of the Phoenix Jazzmen because he would perform on stage in a sweater that made him look like a giant bee.

2019.   The role of Gandalf in the Lord of the Rings trilogy was offered to actor Sean Connery, in exchange of $10 million and 15% of box office takings for all three movies. The actor, however, rejected the offer because he didn't understand the script.

2020.   The most recorded song in history is "Yesterday" by The Beatles, written by Paul McCartney. More than 4,000 versions of the song have been recorded.

2021.   In the 1996 movie "Twister," the sound for the tornado was recorded from a camel's moan which was then slowed down.

2022.   When actress Sissy Spacek played the role of a teenager in the movie Carrie, she was actually twenty six years old. The movie was based on Stephen King's first novel.

2023.   On June 17, 2007, the Czech TV weather report was hacked by an art collective known for pulling off elaborate pranks. The group replaced the weather image with a live nuclear blast complete with mushroom cloud, giving the illusion that there was an actual nuclear bomb going off right there at that moment live.

2024.   In March of 2017, in commemoration of artist David Bowie, a set of royal stamps became available for people in Britain to use. He is actually the first single artist to have this honor.

2025.   In 2002, a HIV-positive character was created by Sesame Workshop to be in the cast of the South African co-production of Sesame Street. The Muppet was a five year old female kid who contracted the disease through a tainted blood transfusion. The purpose of this was to promote tolerance and reduce the stigma associated with being positive with HIV/AIDS.

2026.   Playboy founder and Playboy Bunny creator, the late Hugh Hefner, has an actual species of bunnies named in his honor. It's a marsh rabbit native to the Southeastern United States named Sylvilagus palustris hefneri.

2027.   The singer Eric Clapton who he thought was his mother when he was young, turned out to be his grandmother, and his sister turned out to be his real mother. His mother had him when she was sixteen and single, so his grandparents raised him as their own child.

2028.   Roger Ebert, a film critic, was the co-writer of a film called "Up," a movie about a murder mystery that involved a caricature version of Adolph Hitler, who lived in Northern California.

2029.   Buddy Holly and the Crickets played at the Apollo Theater in Harlem, New York, becoming the first white band to ever play at the venue. The guy who booked the band thought they were an African-American R&B group called "The Crickets," but they turned out to be three white guys from Texas. When they discovered the error, it was too late to change things up, so Buddy Holly and his band took the stage to a rocky start, but they finally won over the audience.

2030.   Actor John Ritter showed his testicles on camera by accident in "The Charming Stranger," an episode of Three's Company. The sitcom episode first aired on December 20, 1983, and it ran on TV for seventeen years, until a Nickelodeon viewer raised an alarm in 2001.

2031.   Actor Dwayne Johnson has a beard in the 2014 film Hercules, which isn't really his own, but is a prosthetic made of yak hair.

2032.   When "Hey Jude" was recorded by The Beatles, Paul McCartney accidentally played the wrong piano note and he gasped "Effing hell!" which you can actually hear at the 2:56 to 2:58 mark of the song. John Lennon thought it would be hilarious if it stayed in the song buried in the background where people wouldn't hear it but they'd know it was there.

2033.   Alan Rickman looks realistically terrified in the movie "Die Hard" when his character falls to his death because they dropped him earlier than he knew they would. He was to fall twenty five feet (seven meters) onto an airbag on the count of three, but he was let loose on the count of one because the director wanted an authentic reaction.

2034.   Beatles member John Lennon frequently visited a Liverpool orphanage in his youth, and that was the subject of the hit song "Strawberry Fields Forever."

2035.   Joaquin Phoenix had the last name Bottom, but after his family broke free from a cult called "The Children of God," they changed their surname to Phoenix, after the mythical bird that rose from the ashes.

2036.   To prepare for his role as James Dean in the 2001 biographical TV film, actor James Franco, who was previously a nonsmoker, started smoking two cigarette packs a day. He also learned to play guitar, ride a motorbike, and even stayed away from friends and family so he could get into the right mindset to play the role. He won a Golden Globe for the performance, so his efforts paid off.

2037.   From 1969 to date, musician Willie Nelson has only used one guitar. It's an old Martin N-20 that has developed a large hole after years of use. Nelson named it after Roy Rogers' horse Trigger.

2038.   Tom Scholz and his band "Boston" recorded their debut album "More Than a Feeling" inside his basement, and he handed the tracks to the studio, who thought they had been recorded in a professional studio. Today, the album has sold a total of seventeen million copies.

2039.   "Memento," the neo-noir psychological thriller movie made by Christopher Nolan, and released on September 5, 2000, is regarded by some experts in neurology as one of the most realistic depictions of anterograde amnesia throughout the history of motion pictures.

2040.   Steven Spielberg and Amy Irving had a prenup in place, but when they got divorced, the judge tossed out the prenup and awarded Amy a $100 million settlement. This was mostly because the prenup was written on a cocktail napkin.

2041.   There are seventeen fictional characters who have their own stars on the Hollywood Walk of Fame. They include Mickey Mouse, Shrek, Donald Duck, Bugs Bunny, Snoopy, Woody Woodpecker, and Godzilla.

2042.   Every single restaurant that appeared on season two of Kitchen Nightmares is now closed.

2043.   Paul Walker actually owned the blue Toyota Supra that he drives off in at the end of Fast and Furious 7.

2044.   The actor who voices Darth Vader, James Earl Jones, began to stutter as a child, and it got so serious that, at times, he couldn't talk to anyone but himself and close family members. When the stutter persisted in his high school years, his English teacher advised him to memorize speeches and sign up for oratorical competitions, and that's how he succeeded in curing his stutter.

2045.   Chaim Witz was originally the name of Gene Simmons from Kiss. He was born on August 25, 1949, in Haifa, Israel.

2046.   The sorcerer's name in Disney's "Fantasia" is Yen Sid; the name is actually Disney spelt backwards. This is because Walt Disney himself was a great inspiration for the character.

2047.   When actress Charlize Theron was fifteen years old, her mother shot and killed her alcoholic father in self-defense.

2048.   Before legendary actor Christopher Walken started his acting career, he worked as a circus owner's apprentice. During shows, he acted as the lion tamer performing alongside a lioness named Sheba.

2049.   On August 1, 1981, MTV played on air the first ever video, which was "Video Killed the Radio Star" by the Buggles. The very first original broadcast is available on YouTube.

2050.   In 2016, Jackie Chan won an honorary Oscar, becoming the first Chinese actor in history to receive the award.

2051.   Fan-made short Lego films were incorporated into the Lego movie plot. You can see them in the scene where the citizens discover their creativity.

2052.   The first ever character to fart in a Disney movie was Pumbaa.

2053.   Sir Patrick Stewart, the actor that plays Professor X in the X-Men series, began losing his hair at the age of eighteen. He thought that no woman would ever be interested in him again. He's now married happily to his third wife.

2054.   Beatles' singer Roy Orbison had pretty bad eyesight and needed thick glasses. During his 1963 tour with the band, he forgot his glasses on a plane before a show, which forced him to wear his ugly prescription sunglasses that night. The look, however, ended up becoming his trademark.

2055.   In an attempt to convince Robin Williams to agree to voice the role of the genie in Disney's Aladdin, the filmmakers produced animated clips of the character saying lines from the comedian's standup performances.

2056.   Pingu, the Swiss Claymation children's TV character, doesn't just speak gibberish, he actually speaks a specific nonsense language called Grammelot. The language has been around since the sixteenth century, and was used by clowns in theaters.

2057.   Elvis Presley had a great love for animals. He had a chimpanzee named Scatter among countless other pets over the course of his life, including dogs, horses, birds, and more.

2058.   Before becoming an actor, Chris Pratt worked as a waiter at the Bubba Gump Shrimp Company in Hawaii. While working there, he was discovered by actress and director Rae Dawn Chong.

2059.   Steven Tyler, the lead singer of Aerosmith, started Janie's Fund to support programs offered at youth villages to help girls overcome deep trauma of abuse and neglect. It was named after his song "Janie's Got a Gun."

2060.   The letter "T" was the first letter Vanna White ever turned on the game show Wheel of Fortune.

2061.   The song "Gangsta's Paradise" by Coolio is one of their few songs to not feature any profane words because it was the only way that Stevie Wonder would authorize the sampling of his song Pastime Paradise.

2062.   Ellen DeGeneres was asked to play Phoebe in the show Friends, but she declined before Lisa Kudrow was cast for the part.

2063.   Robert De Niro was considered an extreme actor for his time because he learned to box for the movie "Raging Bull" and actually got a taxi license for his role in the movie "Taxi Driver."

2064.   Thurl Ravenscroft was not only the voice of Kellogg's Tony the Tiger, but the one who sang "You're a mean one, Mr. Grinch" in the original "How the Grinch Stole Christmas movie."

2065.   Actress Carrie Mulligan and singer Marcus Mumford of Mumford & Sons were childhood pen pals who lost contact. Each of them found fame on their own and both were reintroduced to each other as adults, falling in love and eventually getting married.

2066.   "High School Musical," the successful Disney movie, started out as a 1999 script with the title "Grease Three." The idea was for Justin Timberlake and Britney Spears to have leading roles as the children of Sandy Olsson and Danny Zuko from the 1978 film Grease.

2067.   On February 11, 1964, The Beatles performed at the Washington Coliseum in the United States. The son of venue owner, Harry Lynn, claims that the building had a strong urine smell that night because some ladies who attended the concert wet themselves because they were so crazy about seeing The Beatles.

2068.   Singer Frank Sinatra couldn't get ringside tickets to the Mohammed Ali vs. Joe Fraser fight, which was then billed as the fight of the century, so the singer struck a deal with Life Magazine to work as their photographer, and he got his ringside seat, right in the press box. He took pictures of the fight, and four of them were used in the magazine, including one that was on the cover.

2069.   Velociraptors are portrayed as larger than humans in the Jurassic Park film franchise, but the fact is that they were really the size of domestic turkeys, and it's possible that they even had feathers.

2070.   Originally released in 1993, the hit song "Whoomp, there it is" still makes about $500,000 annually. It has been called both the best and worst song of the 1990's.

2071.   Elvis Presley was figuring out plans for his first European tour when he died. Outside the United States, he only held five music events, and they were all in Canada.

2072.   After Disney wrapped up the show "Boy Missed World," they forbade the cast from taking any keepsakes, but Rider Strong, whose character was Shawn Hunter, stole his leather jacket from the set. He later left the jacket in a parked car in NYC and it was stolen.

2073.   Hollywood visionary Stuart Freeborn made Yoda for the movie "Star Wars Episode Five: The Empire Strikes Back," by modeling the sage green Jedi master's character from a composite of his own face and that of scientist Albert Einstein.

2074.   Ed O'Neill, best known for his acting roles on Modern Family and Married with Children, is a black belt Brazilian Jiu Jitsu fighter. He got his black-belt in 2007, and he has more than twenty two years of practice in the martial art.

2075.   Jack Black got addicted to cocaine when he was fourteen following his parents' divorce. Thankfully, he got sober after seeing a therapist at Poseidon, a Los Angeles school for troubled teens.

2076.   The Powerpuff Girls, the animated girl superheroes, were originally created by Craig McCracken as a college project. At the time the project was named "Whoopass Stew."

2077.   To bring attention to the issue of unequal pay, a brief episode of Batman was made in 1973, starring Adam West. Robin and Batman were tied up close to a time bomb, and Batgirl, played by Yvonne Craig, came in and stated that it was too late, and that she made less money than Robin did, which wasn't right, or in accordance with the Federal Equal Pay Law.

2078.   The Simpsons character Krusty the Clown was originally supposed to be Homer disguising himself in a clown costume, the inside joke being that Bart loved Krusty but hated Homer.

2079.   When filming "The Hunger Games: Mockingjay," according to Liam Hemsworth, fellow actor Jennifer Lawrence would intentionally eat something gross, like tuna or garlic, whenever the two had to kiss.

2080.   When making Spiderman Homecoming, the 2017 Marvel blockbuster, Tom Holland was trolled by Michael Keaton, who kept quoting lines from his movie, The Dark Knight. In one specific fight scene, as Spiderman (Holland) punched Vulture (Keaton), Keaton turned around and whispered "I'm Batman" in a dark tone, which threw Holland off.

2081.   Mars Needs Moms, an animated motion picture film from Disney, cost $150 million to produce, but only made $6.9 million when it debuted domestically at the box office. Its opening was the 12th worst of all time.

2082.   From two feet (sixty one centimeters) away, Bruce Lee could strike you in just 500th of a second.

2083.   Sony BMG tried to keep its copyrighted music from being pirated from 2005 to 2007 by putting a legal rootkit on twenty two million CDs they had produced. When the discs were inserted into computers, the rootkit software modified the computer's operating system to make copying the CD almost impossible, and users couldn't delete the program. The software also sent users' music listening habits back to Sony, so ironically, the rootkit created to prevent copyright infringement, wound up being a copyright infringement.

2084.   Pattie Boyd was married to the late Beatles band member George Harrison, and was the inspiration for the song "Something." Interestingly, she's also the inspiration for "Layla," the hit song by Eric Clapton, in which Clapton admits that he's in love with his friend's wife.

2085.   Legendary director Stephen Spielberg had been named in forty two Academy Award acceptance speeches as of February, 2015, more than any other filmmaker.

2086.   "The Contest," an episode of the sitcom Seinfeld, was named the all-time best TV episode by TV Guide in 2009 in addition to winning an Emmy award for writing when it originally aired. The whole episode revolved around masturbation, but the topic was never mentioned directly, and euphemisms weren't used either.

2087.   The vast majority of the Muppets of the Muppet Show or Sesame Street are left handed. This is a result of the fact that most puppeteers are right-handed. They therefore tend to use their right hand to control the puppets' mouths, and the left hand to control the puppets' left limb or hand rod.

2088.   Matt Groening, creator of the animated series The Simpsons, told the writers of the show in a meeting in the early years, that if the character Marge ever let her hair down, people would learn for the first time that she has rabbit ears.

2089.   William Shatner, the iconic Canadian actor, revealed that he and his fellow Star Trek actor, DeForest Kelly, avoided talking to each other for two years, after he laughed upon hearing Kelly's sad story about Emily, his Chihuahua, who ran into a sprinkler head on and was killed instantly.

2090.   Hollywood star Morgan Freeman was in a car accident in 2008, where he broke his elbow, arm, and shoulder. He was in surgery for four hours, but afterwards, his left fingers remained paralyzed. He has to keep wearing a compression glove so that blood keeps flowing in his hand.

2091.   Danny DeVito voiced the main character in "The Lorax," which was released in 2012. The actor also voiced the same character in the Italian, Spanish, German, and Russian dubbed version of the animated film.

2092.   Paranormal Activity, the horror movie, made $194 million, although it was filmed with a budget of just $15,000.

2093.   Several famous musicians could neither read nor write music when they first became famous singers. They include Elvis Presley, Michael Jackson, Eric Clapton, Jimi Hendrix, and Eddie Van Halen.

2094.   Donnie Yen, the action star, was outside a nightclub one evening when he was attacked by eight gang members who started harassing his girlfriend. He tried to stop them, and ended up sending all of them to the hospital.

2095.   It took Lady Gaga ten minutes each to write her sounds "Just Dance," and "Born This Way." Both songs hit number one on the charts.

2096.   Because of a glitch in the Canadian iTunes Store in 2014, Taylor Swift accidentally launched a song called Track Three. Although it was only eight seconds of static, the song immediately reached the top of the music charts.

2097.   Elvis Presley's dark-slicked hair is one of the most recognizable things about him, but he was really a natural blonde. He chose the raven-black dyed look because he thought it made him appear edgier.

2098.   Of the four Metallica band members, three of them divorced their wives while they were producing the Black album. The band believes that this contributed to the moody feeling reflected in their tracks.

2099.   Instead of an actual belly button, model Karolina Kurkova has a smooth indentation on her navel area, a result of a surgery she had in her infancy. They often Photoshop a belly button onto her photos to hide this.

2100.   Hayley Atwell, who portrays Marvel character Peggy Carter in the Captain America movies, took a driver's license photo in April, 2015, while wearing her full movie makeup.

2101.   The word "Beastie" in the band name The Beastie Boys is short for "Boys Entertaining Anarchistic States towards Inner Excellence."

2102. The Ewoks' language was created by Ben Burtt, a sound designer for the Star Wars franchise. It's mostly a bunch of Tibetan phrases and a little Nepalese.

2103. Within the time that they were starring as brother and sister on the Showtime program Dexter, Jennifer Carpenter and Michael C. Hall started going out, got engaged, became married, and got divorced.

2104. Renowned musician Yo-Yo Ma accidentally left his cello, which was 266 years old and worth $2.5 million, in a taxi trunk in 1999. The police were able to find it at a garage in Queens, right on time for a concert scheduled for that night.

2105. Ninety five year old actress Betty White holds the Guinness record for the longest TV career for a female entertainer, starting her career back in the 1950's.

2106. The KLF, a British electronic band, declared that they were quitting the music business on February 12, 1992, at the Brit Awards. At the end of their set, Bill Drummond shot a machine gun with blanks over the heads of the bewildered audience. After the ceremony, he and fellow bandmates left a dead sheep at the doorway, with a note that said: "I died for you, bon appetit."

2107. Will Ferrell refused to take twenty nine million dollars to make a sequel for Elf. He thought that if the movie wasn't great, he couldn't deal with being criticized by people who'd think he'd just made the movie for the cash.

2108. Rock band Blink 182 was originally called "Duct Tape."

2109. During the 2007 writer's strike, the Late Show staff was actually paid out by David Letterman's own pocket.

2110. Kim Kardashian used to be Paris Hilton's personal assistant back in the mid-2000's.

2111. Leonidas is depicted as a young man of about thirty in the Battle of Thermopylae in the movie 300, however, in reality he was closer to sixty.

2112. In the movie "Saving Private Ryan," some combat scenes looked so realistic that veterans actually had to leave the movie theaters during the opening scene; they stated that it was the most realistic depiction of combat that they had ever seen.

2113. The idea for the movie "The Human Centipede" came from a joke between the director and writer on what should happen to child molesters.

2114. In the movie Alfred Hitchcock's "Psycho," the blood in the famous shower scene was actually Hersey's chocolate syrup. At the time, this was the usual substance for blood in black and white films.

2115. None of the members of The Beatles could actually read music. Music for them was a discovery process and did not involve any books.

2116. Horror movie soundtracks sometimes involve infrasound, which is sound below the range of human hearing; although we can't hear it, it's possible to feel it. Infrasound has been proven to induce anxiety, heart palpitations, and even shivering.

2117. The longest running Broadway of all show performances is "The Phantom of the Opera." As of 2015, the show has had over 11,000 performances since its conception in 1988.

2118. Samuel L. Jackson used to be Bill Cosby's camera stand-in on "The Cosby Show" before he became a movie star.

2119. The guitarist from the band Queen, Brian May, actually has a PhD in astrophysics. He put aside his academic pursuits for three decades to become a rock star; in 2007, he returned to school to complete and receive his degree.

2120. The average a musician makes for every thousand dollars worth of sales in the industry is roughly twenty three dollars.

2121. Dwayne "The Rock" Johnson created a motivational alarm clock app that helps you get out of bed and meet your personal goals. There are twenty five ringtones to choose from that were created by The Rock himself and it has no snooze button. Among the ringtones there's one, for example, that is just a mash up of sounds that come from his dog, a couple where he just keeps repeating the words beep and ring-ring, and another where he smashes a harp.

2122. The island on the TV show "Gilligan's Island" was created in Hollywood, in the middle of an artificial lake in CBS's studios. The set cost $75,000 to build and it had artificial palm trees mixed in with real plants and flowers.

2123. Elvis Presley had a twin brother who died at birth. His name was Jesse Garon.

2124. While director James Cameron was editing the Titanic, he taped a razor blade to the side of the computer with instructions that said: "Use only if the film sucks." However, the film went on to gross a total of $1.84 billion worldwide.

2125. A few days after the release of "The Marshall Mathers LP 2" album by Eminem, his childhood home that is on the cover strangely caught fire and was left in ruin.

2126. Before Hugh Jackman took up the role of Wolverine in X-Men, he didn't know that they were an actual animal.

2127. Daniel Radcliffe celebrated winning his role in Harry Potter by watching an extra episode of Fawlty Towers and staying up half an hour longer than usual.

2128. The richest superhero to exist is Black Panther who has an estimated net worth of five hundred billion dollars. Bruce Wayne only has a net worth of eighty billion while Tony Stark's estimated net worth was one hundred billion dollars.

2129. Actor John Ratzenberger, known for his role as Cliff Clavin in the TV hit Cheers, is the only actor who has voiced characters in every single Pixar movie.

2130. Jackie Chan is the best paid actor in Asia.

2131. The jingle "State Farm like a Good Neighbor" was written by singer Barry Manilow. He was only paid $500 for it.

2132. Samuel L. Jackson was one of the ushers of Martin Luther King Jr's funeral.

2133. Renowned actor James Franco is a doctoral candidate at Yale University. Starting in 2012, he has also been giving film classes at the Faculty of Theater, Film and Television at UCLA.

2134. George R.R. Martin, the creator of Game of Thrones, was so impressed by Jack Gleeson's portrayal of Joffrey in the series that he sent him a letter which said: "Congratulations on your marvelous performance, everyone hates you."

2135. The actor Peter Meyhew, who played Chewbacca in the Star Wars films, had to be escorted by crew members dressed in brightly colored vests while shooting in the forest of the Pacific Northwest, to ensure that he wasn't shot by hunters who would mistake him for Bigfoot.

2136. Neo, the lead character in the movie "The Matrix," was actually offered to Will Smith, but he turned it down to do "Wild Wild West" instead.

2137. Nicholas Cage once woke up at home in the middle of the night and found an almost naked man wearing only a leather jacket eating a fudgesicle in front of his bed. After that, the actor could no longer live in that house and later moved to the Bahamas.

2138.   In the 1984 movie "Indiana Jones and the Temple of Doom," the name of the bar in the opening fight scene is Club Obi Wan. The name was based on the character Obi-Wan Kenobi from the "Star Wars" films, also directed by George Lucas.

2139.   Harrison Ford used to be a carpenter prior to becoming a superstar actor. He was working for famous producer Fred Roos, fixing a door in a location where George Lucas was holding casting meetings for Star Wars. He randomly auditioned for the role of Han Solo, got the part, and shortly after became famous.

2140.   Mel Gibson, who has won two Oscars, has a rare birth defect which affects about one in 600 newborns called horseshoe kidney. His two kidneys fused before he was born, forming a horseshoe or U-shape.

2141.   The first role that actor Brad Pitt played was a chicken. He wore a chicken suit to bring customers to a restaurant called El Pollo Loco in Hollywood. Today the fifty six year old actor has now been in more than seventy movies and won an Academy Award out of five nominations.

2142.   The only person to have won British Academy of Film and Television Arts Awards in black and white, color, HD, 3-D, and 4k was broadcaster and national historian Sir David Attenborough.

2143.   In 2000, Justin Timberlake's leftover French toast was actually sold on eBay. Nineteen year old Kathy Summers paid $1,025 for it. The famous singer finished a breakfast interview at the studio of New York area radio station Z100, and the DJ put it on eBay shortly after he left.

2144.   Actor Tom Cruise, who is also a Scientology front man, split up with all his three ex-wives Nicole Kidman, Mimi Rogers, and Katie Holmes when they turned thirty three. The number thirty three is considered the "master teacher" in the scientology faith, and it represents true love, altruism, and increased positive energy.

2145.   Actor Chuck Norris and Bob Barker, the iconic host of "The Price is Right," have trained karate together for eight years.

2146.   On June 9, 1946, the first car television commercial was aired. It was for Chevrolet.

2147.   Ryan Gosling and Rachel McAdams didn't like each other when filming The Notebook. But after finishing filming the movie, they fell in love and dated for four years.

2148.   Beatles' band member George Harrison wrote a letter to actor Mike Meyers expressing how much he loved watching the Austin Powers movie, and that turned out to be his last letter.

2149.   The horse head used when filming "The Godfather" was actually a real one. Actor John Marley was not informed beforehand, so his scream was authentic, not scripted at all.

2150.   Famous actor Joe Pesci from hit movies such as "GoodFellas" and "My Cousin Vinny" released a rap song called "Wise Guy" in 1998. He said that originally he wanted to be a musician, but his father pushed him into acting.

2151.   Director and daughter of Francis Ford Coppola, Sofia Coppola, actually appeared in all three of her father's Godfather movies.

2152.   In 2027, the autopsy report for Elvis Presley is expected to be unsealed for the first time, which will be fifty years after his death.

2153. Back in 2007, late night talk show host Conan O'Brien was being stalked by a priest, who was later arrested. The priest was writing threatening notes on parish letterheads, contacting his parents, and showing up at his studio. He even referred to himself as "your priest stalker."

2154. The shark prop used in the 1975 movie "Jaws" was named "Bruce" by Steven Spielberg after his lawyer.

2155. In the 2015 Disney film "Moana," retired NFL safety Troy Polamalu had a minor speaking role.

2156. All members of the Wu-Tang Clan are in the top twenty artists with the biggest vocabularies in the world.

2157. In order to make the World War II movie "Fury" more realistic, actor Shia LeBeouf cut his own face and had his dentist pull out one of his teeth.

2158. On July 1, 1941, the first ever TV commercial was shown in the United States. It was a shaky ten-second commercial for Bulova Watches, which was aired just before a Brooklyn Dodgers and Philadelphia Phillies baseball game.

2159. Will Smith got so attached to the German Shepherd in "I am Legend" that he asked if he could buy her, but the dog owner refused.

2160. The ex-wife of singer Freddie Mercury, Mary Austin, is the only person who knows where the singer's ashes are laid to rest as she buried them herself. She has said that she will never reveal where they are buried.

2161. Chicken Run is the highest grossing stop motion animation film starring Mel Gibson. It was filmed in the year 2000.

2162. Jerry Springer, talk show host and the king of racy TV, used to be in politics. As a matter of fact, he was the Mayor of Cincinnati for an entire year, from 1977 to 1978.

2163. The 1942 musical film "Holiday Inn," starring Bing Crosby, gave the name to the popular Holiday Inn Hotel chain.

2164. The last woman over forty years old to have a number one song and Billboard Hot 100 chart as a lead artist is singer Sia, with the song "Cheap Thrills." Before her, the last woman to do so was Bette Midler, in 1989, with the song "Wind Beneath My Wings," when she was forty three years old.

2165. The artist who has performed the most concerts in Madison Square Garden than any other singer is Billy Joel.

2166. Viggo Mortensen, who starred in "Lord of the Rings," actually bought the two horses he rode when making the movies. He also bought the one he rode at the set of Hidalgo.

2167. The "water phone" is an instrument that makes many of the scary sounds that you hear in thriller and horror movies.

2168. Justin Bieber's single "Baby" is the most disliked music video on the Internet. It has over 9.9 million dislikes on YouTube and over two billion views.

2169. The Warner Brothers started creating short animations to promote the music they owned in the early 1930's. They're known as "Looney Tunes."

2170. The first primetime TV show to have a sound of a flushing toilet was "All in the Family." Before, it was actually taboo to even show a bathroom on TV.

2171. The role of James Bond was offered to Liam Neeson who was up for the role, but had to turn it down as his girlfriend at the time said she wouldn't marry him if he took it.

2172. Elmo testified in front of the Congressional subcommittee on Education Appropriations back in 2002, where he advocated for music research funding and more instruments for schools. He also went to the White House for an education event.

2173. In May of 2007, a course on creating and maintaining a personal brand was actually co-taught by supermodel Tyra Banks at Stanford's Graduate School of Business.

2174. In 2016, Drake actually beat Michael Jackson's record for the most American Music Award nominations in one year. He had thirteen nominations, beating Jackson's record of eleven from 1984.

2175. After the shooting of the 1970 film "The Private Life of Sherlock Holmes," starring Sir Christopher Lee, a movie prop of Nessie that sank to the bottom of Loch Ness was made.

2176. In 1949, actor Ricardo Montalban was the first person to perform "Baby, It's Cold Outside," in the musical romantic comedy film "Neptune's Daughter." The actor is better known for playing the iconic villain Khan in the original Star Trek television series.

2177. "Ed, Edd, Eddy" was the last major cartoon show to utilize traditional animation techniques before CGI was introduced in subsequent shows.

2178. Hopeful contestants are not allowed to compete on "Wheel of Fortune" or "Jeopardy!" if they have already competed on any other national game show.

2179. Actress Candace Bergen didn't receive a single penny from her father while his ventriloquist dummy got $10,000. In reference to the dummy, he said: "The dummy had been my constant companion from whom I have never been separated, even for a day."

2180. When the CEO of Sesame Street, Gery Knell, was asked if Ernie and Bert were gay he responded: "they're not gay, they're not straight, they don't exist below the waist."

2181. Elvis Presley once gave his limo driver a gift of the exact same limo that he had been driving Elvis in.

2182. Bradley Cooper's dream as a child was to train as a ninja and wanted his father to send him to Japan so he could learn to become one.

2183. By combining the sound of an elephant call with a car driving on wet pavement, sound designer Ben Burtt created the distinctive sound for the TIE fighter from the "Star Wars" movies. According to the book "The Sounds of Star Wars," the sound of the engine was supposed to imitate the German junker bombers that would use sirens to scare civilians during raids.

2184. The only musician in history to be inducted into the Rock and Roll Hall of Fame three times is legendary guitarist Eric Clapton. The first time was in 1992, when he was a member of The Yardbirds. The second was in 1993, when Cream was inducted. And the third time was in 2000, when he was inducted as a solo artist.

2185. Edward Nigma or E. Nigma was Riddler's real name in the Batman stories. He also has some other aliases such as the Prince of Puzzlers, the Crown Prince of Conundrums, and the Wizard of Quiz.

2186. Before even thinking of starting an acting career, Idris Elba used to be a drug dealer. He would sell marijuana while he was a bouncer at the popular club Carolines. Celebrities who went regularly to the nightclub, like D.L. Hughley and Dave Chappelle, simply knew him as the doorman.

2187. Actor Christian Bale had to lose sixty three pounds (twenty nine kilograms) for his role in "The Machinist." His daily diet consisted of one can of tuna, an apple, black coffee, and water.

2188. After the release of the 1996 horror movie "Scream," Caller ID tripled in the United States. The film was about a killer who would anonymously call his victims before attacking them.

2189. Actress Lucille Ball from the hit show "I Love Lucy" found out that she was pregnant during season two of the show. CBS agreed to write her pregnancy into the show, but the network considered that the word pregnant was too vulgar, so they used instead the word expecting.

2190. Michael Jackson wanted to make a Harry Potter musical, but author J.K. Rowling turned down the offer as she later confessed on Oprah Winfrey.

2191. Mike Kroeger named his band Nickelback after his cashier experience at a Starbucks. Many customers used to pay $1.50 for a coffee that cost $1.45, so he always had to give them a nickel back.

2192. After graduating from high school at the age of sixteen, Jessica Alba was already a successful actress.

2193. During the Wheel of Fortune's 30th anniversary, aired on May 30, 2013, thirty year old woman Autumn Erhard won the top prize of one million dollars.

2194. Actor, comedian, and writer Stepehn Colbert also exists in the Marvel Universe. He helped defeat a villain with spiderman and also ran for president.

2195. Toto, from the "Wizard of Oz," was paid $125 per week. This was more than the Munchkin actors were paid.

2196. Elvis Presley failed music class in high school.

2197. In 2016, a teacup and saucer used by Lady Gaga sold at an auction for almost $74,000. The cup was marked with her lipstick bearing the Japanese message: "We pray for Japan" along with her autograph. The money went to charity.

2198. Around five million dollars an episode and more than 100 million dollars overall were turned down by Jerry Seinfeld just to run a tenth season of Seinfeld. The amount was three times more than anyone on television had ever been offered at the time.

2199. Jim Henson, the Muppets creator, believed in allowing a character to grow organically. His viewpoint was that each Muppet had a distinct personality. He even thought that it was the job of the puppeteer to uncover it.

2200. The song Sussudio by Phil Collins was based on a made up word. When he couldn't think of actual lyrics to fill the line, he just left it in as the chorus and title.

2201. Kanye West invited Seth Rogen to give him feedback on all his tracks on his new album when Rogen released a parody on the "Bound 2" music video.

2202. Joe Dougherty provided the original voice of Porky Pig; he also had a stutter familiar to the character on screen. However, he was unable to get his own stuttering under control and missed cues, hence causing delays. In 1937, he was replaced by legendary voice actor Mel Blanc, who took over the role for fifty two years.

2203. In Australia, Weird Al Yankovic's song "Eat It" reached number one on the music charts, while Michael Jackson's song "Beat It" surprisingly only went as high as number three.

2204. The phrase "hakuna matata" was trademarked by Walt Disney Company for clothing, headgear, and footwear.

2205. The producers of the Disney film "The Lion King" asked the musical group Abba to write the songs, but they turned it down as they were not available. They ended up asking their second favorite choice, Elton John.

2206. As Mel Brooks, the legendary filmmaker and comedian, placed his handprints in his Hollywood Walk of Fame star, he added an eleventh prosthetic finger to one hand.

2207. Katy Hudson was the name of singer Katy Perry's debut album. She originally went by this name and although the album was overall well-reviewed by critics, only 200 copies were sold. The record label she recorded it on eventually had to close, and Katy Hudson became who we all know as Katy Perry today.

2208. When Twitter first came out, Adele was known for tweeting while drunk. She is not allowed to send out her own tweets anymore.

2209. The magician Teller from Penn and Teller began performing in silence. In his youth, he used to do shows at college fraternity parties and found out that if he stayed quiet throughout the act, he was least likely to get beer poured on him or heckled. Penn Jillette never knew how to play poker until eight days before his appearance on the show Celebrity Poker Showdown in 2004.

2210. Actor Charlie Sheen once spent over six thousand dollars to buy twenty five hundred seats at a baseball game in attempts to catch a home-run ball.

2211. Peter Robbins, the original voice actor of Charlie Brown, is currently in prison for threatening the manager of a mobile home park that he lived in.

2212. As of 2020, the highest grossing movie of all time surpassing Avatar from 2009 is "Avengers: Endgame." It brought in a little under $2.8 billion at the box office around the globe.

2213. The sports television channel ESPN is actually owned by Disney with a majority ownership of 80%. Disney also owns Pixar, ABC Broadcasting Company, Lucasfilm, Marvel, A&E, and the History Channel.

2214. When singers Taylor Swift, Miley Cyrus, and Katy Perry met in a dressing room at the Grammy Awards, Katy asked the other two for locks of their hair. They both obliged, and Katy wrapped both clippings in a ribbon, and put them in her handbag.

2215. The independent Disney princess Merida from the animated movie Brave is the only Disney princess who neither sang nor had a love interest in her movie.

2216. During his college days at William and Mary, comedian Jon Stewart was a walk-on soccer player. He even scored the only goal in the game that drove the team to the NCAA tournament.

2217. "The Lion King" was originally called "The King of the Jungle." The Disney team later learned that lions don't live in jungles, so they renamed it.

2218. During the filming of Rocky IV, Sylvester Stallone spent nine days in intensive care at hospital because of Dolph Lundgren. During a fight scene, Dolph hit him so hard in the chest that the pericardial sac around his heart swelled up, which impeded the beating of his heart and caused his blood pressure to skyrocket to 290.

2219. The last verse of the hit song "Sitting on the Dock of the Bay" was whistled by singer Otis Redding because he didn't have the words written for it when it was recorded. His plan was to fill in the verse, but he unfortunately died in a plane crash three days after recording it. The producer, however, decided to leave the whistling in.

2220. Actress Margaret Hamilton, who is mostly remembered for playing the scary wicked witch in The Wizard of Oz and terrifying children everywhere, was actually a kindergarten teacher before she started her acting career.

2221. Throughout the filming of "The Hobbit" trilogy, twenty seven animals died on set. Some of them fell into sink holes while other smaller ones, like chickens, were killed by unsupervised dogs. As a result, PETA made a global protest on the trilogy.

2222. "Somebody to love" was Freddy Mercury's favorite song, however, he didn't tell anyone that because he didn't want everyone to know he liked his own music.

2223. The powerful drum reverb entrance in the song "In the Air Tonight" by Phil Collins was actually an accident. While Collins was playing drums for another song for Peter Gabriel's third solo album, the reverse talk back was unintentionally activated and left on.

2224. The only entertainer to have all five stars on the Hollywood Walk of Fame is actor-singer Gene Autry. One for radio, one for recording, one for motion pictures, one for television, and one for live theater performance.

2225. In the film adaptation of the videogame Super Mario Bros, actor Tom Hanks auditioned for the role of Mario.

2226. In the film "Pulp Fiction," the scene where John Travolta gives the adrenaline shot to Uma Thurman's chest was shot in reverse with the actor pulling the needle away. A fake chest was bought from a special effects company by director Quentin Tarantino, but he later decided just to use that trick instead.

2227. Beach Boys drummer Mike Love is the uncle of NBA all-star Kevin Love of the Cleveland Cavaliers.

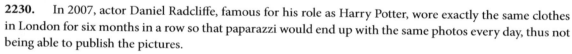

2228. Whenever actor Kevin Bacon is invited to a wedding, he always bribes the DJ not to play the song "Footloose." The reason behind is that he does not want to upstage the bride and groom on their big day.

2229. When Chrissy Metz was cast as Kate on the show "This Is Us," her contract obliged her to progressively lose weight over the span of the show. She accepted those terms, and many fans have been inspired to take the journey with her, towards a healthier self.

2230. In 2007, actor Daniel Radcliffe, famous for his role as Harry Potter, wore exactly the same clothes in London for six months in a row so that paparazzi would end up with the same photos every day, thus not being able to publish the pictures.

2231. Independent Studio Services makes a prop beer that is used in several movies and television shows. It's called Heisler Beer or Heisler Gold Ale, and it has appeared on "Beerfest," "Brooklyn Nine-Nine," and "Parks and Recreation."

2232. The first-ever toy advertised on TV was Mr. Potato Head, back in 1952. Almost two million were sold in the first year alone.

2233. Actor from the hit television show "The Office," Rainn Wilson, had a pet sloth while he was growing up.

2234. Dexter Holland, the lead singer of the famous punk band The Offspring, is also a molecular biologist. He attended the University of Southern California where he received his master's degree. In fact, he had to withdraw from his PhD. program candidature due to the success of the band.

2235. When filming Django Unchained, actor Leonardo DiCaprio, who plays Calvin Candie, smashes his hand on a dinner table and accidentally crushes a stemmed glass with his palm. His hand started to bleed, but the actor finished the scene and gave an amazing performance. Director Quentin Tarantino decided to include the scene in the movie.

2236. The singer of "Ex's and Oh's," Elle King, is actor Rob Schneider's daughter.

2237. Singer Johnny Cash received death threats from the KKK. The group saw a picture of him with his first wife and thought she was black; she was actually an Italian American woman.

2238.	In 2001, actor Russell Crowe was informed by the FBI that the Al-Qaeda terrorist group was planning to kidnap him as part of a cultural destabilization plot. During the filming of his movies "A Beautiful Mind" and "Master and Commander: The Far Side of the World," he required extra security; in fact, he was followed around by the FBI for almost two years.

2239.	The oldest working American actor today is Norman Lloyd, at 104 years old. He first appeared on screen during the Great Depression when he was just a teenager, and he has been working for eighty eight years. Originally he wanted to become a tennis champion.

2240.	The only four musical artists or groups who have a Billboard Top 40 single from the 1980's, 1990's, 2000's, and 2010's are Michael Jackson, Madonna, U2, and Weird Al Yankovic.

2241.	Shooting the film Super Mario Brothers was so laborious that Bob Hoskins and John Leguizamo, the lead actors, would get drunk between scenes.

2242.	The character Gonzo, in the film "Muppets from Space," was an alien and his family came to Earth to throw a party for him. They later ask him if he could go back with them to space and even though he initially agrees, he later changes his mind to be with his Muppet friends.

2243.	Fake snow was commonly used in place of the real thing during the early days of Hollywood. Foamite, the material used in fire extinguishers, was used and mixed with sugar, water, soap flakes, corn flakes painted white, marble dust, salt and flour, and even cancer causing material asbestos.

2244.	Whenever Dwayne "The Rock" Johnson goes to a film set, he travels with his own private gym which comprises more than 39,000 pounds (18,000 kilograms) of equipment, and requires more than a hundred people to assemble.

2245.	Since 2008, singer Rihanna has had her own holiday in her home country of Barbados, which is celebrated on February 22. It's called Rihanna Day, and Prime Minister David Thompson even announced it at an awards ceremony.

2246.	The only artist to top the charts as a solo artist, duo, trio, quartet and quintet is Paul McCartney.

2247.	Some of the stars that have joined the infamous "27 Club" are Jimi Hendrix, Janis Joplin, Kurt Cobain, Brian Jones from the Rolling Stones, Amy Winehouse, and Jim Morrison. They all were twenty-seven years old when they passed away.

2248.	During the filming of The Hobbit, Sir Ian McKellen actually broke down and cried after he had to film in front of a green screen and not other actors stating: "This is not why I became an actor."

2249.	In 1999, actor Christian Bale played Jesus Christ in a movie called "Mary, Mother of Jesus," made for television. According to Rotten Tomatoes, it had a 48% audience score.

2250.	In 2013, Ed Sheeran's The A Team received a Grammy nomination. Elton John suggested having Ed give a performance opening at the awards show, but he was told he was not high profile enough. To solve the problem, Elton decided to perform with Ed.

2251.	Lena Headley, who plays Cersei, and Jerome Flynn, who plays Bronn on the HBO Series "Game of Thrones," are never put on the same scene together because they dated in real life and had a terrible break up. They both have contracts with the show, which stipulate that they can't ever be in the same room at the same time.

2252.	The ideas for the movies "Wall-E," "A Bug's Life," "Monsters Inc.," and "Finding Nemo" were created in one meeting at the Pixar office.

2253.	In Carnegie Hall, first-time stagehands get paid an average of $400,000 a year.

2254.	The Hunger Games is banned in Vietnam. The movie was considered as too violent by the Vietnamese National Film Board, so they unanimously voted for it to be banned.

2255.	Peter Weir, the Truman Show director, wanted to place secret cameras behind the scenes in movie theaters, so that the projectionist could cut the film at some point during the movie and have the audience watch themselves, and then he would cut back to the movie.

2256.　Shigeru Miyamoto, the Super Mario creator, said that he did not like the 1993 film adaptation of it given that it was very similar to the videogame.

2257.　Actor Kurt Russell smashed an authentic Martin guitar from the 1870's during the filming of the movie "The Hateful Eight." The guitar was on loan from the Martin Guitar Museum and it was supposed to be switched out for a prop before he smashed it. Unfortunately for the actor, no one told him.

2258.　Despite the huge success of the music band "The Beatles," who sold more than 1.6 billion singles in the United States, 600 million albums worldwide, and won eight Grammy Awards, none of the members could actually read music. Music for them was a discovery process and did not involve any books.

2259.　In the original Halloween movie, the mask that Michael Myers wore was actually a $2 mask of William Shatner from Star Trek. The mask was painted in white, the hair was teased, and the eye holes were reshaped.

2260.　In every scene of the Fight Club movie, there is a Starbucks coffee cup.

2261.　Cordozar Calvin Broadus Jr. is the real name of rapper Snoop Dogg. His mother thought he looked like Snoopy from the Peanuts and that's where his nickname comes from.

2262.　The tradition of hand and footprints in front of Los Angeles Chinese Theater actually started by accident when silent film actress, Norma Talmadge, stepped on wet cement.

2263.　It took Pixar three years to study the physics of curly hair in order to correctly recreate Merida's hair in the movie "Brave."

Food & Drinks

2264. In 1961, Haagen-Dazs ice cream was founded in the Bronx, New York, by Reuben and Rose Mattus, two Jewish-Polish immigrants. They invented the Danish sounding name as a tribute to Denmark's exemplary treatment of the Jews during the Second World War, and included an outline map of Denmark on early labels.

2265. French fries drizzled with two kinds of chocolate sauce were introduced by McDonald's Japan in January of 2016. Unfortunately, it only lasted for a limited time.

2266. There are approximately 40,000 different types of rice worldwide.

2267. The "Down Cafe" is a cafe opened in Istanbul in 2011. They only recruit waiters between the ages of eighteen to twenty five with Down syndrome.

2268. In 1965, a team of university physicians in Florida were approached by a University of Florida's football assistant, coach of the Florida Gators, who wanted to find out why his players were being affected by the heat and heat-related illnesses. After several studies, they ended up creating the drink Gatorade that balanced carbohydrates and electrolytes. The drink was named after the Florida Gators football team.

2269. Tayto Park is a theme park in Ireland which is owned by and named after a potato chip brand, Tayto crisps. It is located right across the street from the enterprise's manufacturing plant. All guests are given a small packet of Tayto crisps when visiting the park.

2270. For most of the 20th century, beer with more than 2.25% alcohol was banned until March 1, 1989, which is now celebrated every year as "Beer Day."

2271. There are over thirty eight million sandwich combinations offered by Subway.

2272. Of all the calories consumed by humans across the world, approximately 20% of it all comes from eating rice.

2273. Coca-Cola wanted a newly shaped soda bottle design in 1915, so they told competing glass makers to create a bottle that was so distinctive, that people would recognize it if it was broken and lying on the ground, or if they felt it in the dark. The winning design was from the Root Glass Company which made the ribbed bottle shaped like a cocoa bean that the soda company is widely known for today.

2274. Chef George Crum of the Moon Lake Lodge Diner invented potato chips in 1853. A customer at the diner in Saratoga Springs, New York, insistently declined batches of French fries claiming that they were too thick for him to eat. Chef Crum, in retaliation, made fries that were paper thin and fried them excessively so they couldn't be cut with a fork.

2275. There is a fruit that looks like a white strawberry and tastes like a pineapple. It's called pineberry.

2276. Lexus once partnered with Huy Fong Foods to create a customized 2017 Lexus Sriracha IS. It's a Sriracha-themed car where even its paint has Sriracha in it. It has all kinds of Sriracha-themed details including a trunk filled with forty three bottles of Sriracha for emergencies.

2277. According to the executive director from the Washington State Potato Commission, potatoes have almost all the nutrients that humans need to survive. To prove this, he ate nothing but potatoes for sixty days in a row and was just fine.

2278. In 1998, as an April Fools prank, Burger King released the Left-Handed Whopper, a solution for the 1.4 million left-handed customers that visit the restaurants every day. Burger King said that all the ingredients were rotated 180 degrees to suit the left-handed burger connoisseur. The very next day, only a few people actually showed up to order the special burger.

2279. In the Philippines, they have banana ketchup. During World War II, there was a shortage of tomatoes, so they had to use bananas as a replacement. It's made from mashed bananas, sugar, vinegar, and spices.

2280. A thirty nine year old man named Dan Janssen from Maryland, USA, has only eaten pizza for all his meals for the last twenty six years.

2281. To hide imperfections on pistachios' shells caused by their processing, they used to be dyed with red food coloring, the same food dye that enhanced the appearance of pastries and decorations. However, it didn't last very long as the contact with moisture transferred the dye from the nut to the mouths of people, which they didn't like.

2282. Most energy drinks don't actually have as much caffeine as coffee. A large coffee at Starbucks has over three hundred milligrams of caffeine whereas the average can of energy drink has only eighty.

2283. Boiled, fried or even raw tuna eyes are considered a delicacy in Japan.

2284. Pizza Hut has unveiled the world's first working DJ turntable made from a pizza box in the United Kingdom. It was created alongside Cambridge-based printed electronics firm Novalia. When you unfold the box, you can play music.

2285. In 1996, McDonald's opened their first ski-through fast food restaurant in Sweden. People can actually ski up to the counter, order food, and ski off. It is called McSki.

2286. Potato Parcel is a company based in Canada that will send a potato with a message written on it for anyone you want. For just $10, they will print anything you want on it, from "Congrats on the baby!" to "I still love you."

2287. In Vienna, there is an orchestra that only performs with instruments that are fabricated entirely from vegetables. It's called the Vegetable Orchestra, and its specially made instruments utilize a wide range of vegetables to produce exceptional unique sounds.

2288. Cashews belong to the same family as poison ivy and poison sumac. It contains powerful chemical irritants that are found in the shell oil; for this reason, you can only buy cashews already out of the shell.

2289. "Double Or Muffin" is a muffin shop located in San Francisco that will double your muffin order for free if you flip a coin and it lands on heads.

2290. China consumes 1.6 billion pounds (726 million kilograms) of tea every year, which is more tea than any other country in the world.

2291. Nabisco, the name of the biscuit company, is actually short for National Biscuit Company.

2292. The filling placed between Kit Kat chocolate bars wafers are made of other Kit Kats. When the bars are made, their exterior is examined, and those with lots of air bubbles and other deformities are crushed into crumbs and used to create new chocolate bars.

2293. A pineapple is not just one fruit, it's technically multiple fruits. It forms when a cluster of flowers form one berry each, and the berries compress and merge to form a pineapple.

2294. Ketchup was originally marketed as a medicine, which happened after an 1834 publication claimed tomatoes could treat digestive problems.

2295. James Monaghan and his brother Tom bought a pizza restaurant named DomiNick's for a mere $500, and eight months later, James traded his shares to his brother in exchange for a second hand Volkswagen Beetle. Thirty eight years later, Tom sold 93% of that business for a billion dollars, and we now know it as Domino's Pizza.

2296. Crickets have double the protein that beef has, and it also has five times the magnesium, and three times the iron.

2297. The video game company Atari was founded by Nolan Bushnell, who later sold it, and used his profits to found the Chuck E. Cheese franchise.

2298. McDonald's and Walt Disney Company had a cross-promotion deal which Disney sought to end quietly in the summer of 2006, because they wanted to distance themselves from McDonald's, which is accused of contributing to America's childhood obesity epidemic.

2299. Claud Hatcher, an American business, was buying syrup in bulk, when he was denied a discounted rate, so he swore to create his own soft drink and never buy a Coca-Cola again. He kept his promise by creating Royal Crown RC Cola.

2300. Bacardi, the spirit company, was established in 1862, and since then has been owned by the same family for seven generations. It's currently the largest privately held company of its kind in the whole world.

2301. Cheerios maker General Mills created Millenios, a limited edition box of the original product, in 1999. The box contained the classic donut-shaped cereal along with new whole-grain bits with a number two shape. At the back of the box was a message urging people to use it as a time capsule, along with suggestions of things to put in the box.

2302. In Britain, sausages are called bangers because they often burst open when they are pan fried. This nickname was first used around the time of the First World War.

2303. A Cheeto sold on eBay for about $100,000 in February, 2017, after a bidding war that lasted 132 episodes, all because it looked like Harambe.

2304. A British supermarket franchise called "Iceland Foods Limited" made a line of food products called "Wacky Veg" in 1997, in an effort to get children to eat healthily. The line included peas that were baked bean flavored, carrots that were chocolate flavored, sweet corn with pizza flavor, and cauliflower with cheese and onion flavors.

2305. According to the Guinness World Records, the heaviest chocolate bar ever made was created by Thorntons in Derbyshire, UK, on October 7, 2011. The bar measured twelve feet by fourteen feet by one foot thick (3x4x0.3 meters), and it weighed 12,770 pounds (5,800 kilograms).

2306. The Center for Retail Research in Britain concluded that the most stolen food item in the world is cheese. According to this institution, 4% of all cheese sold was actually stolen.

2307. The largest gingerbread man ever made, according to the Guinness World Records, was made by IKEA in Oslo, Norway, on November 9, 2009. It weighed 1,400 pounds (650 kilograms) and was all baked in one piece.

2308. According to studies conducted by the Chinese Academy of Medical Sciences, people who have spicy foods six to seven times per week have a 14% lower risk of premature death for all causes, compared to people who eat spicy foods once a week or less.

2309. Nuts are very beneficial to our health. Twenty grams of nuts a day can reduce the risk of heart disease by almost 30%, the risk of premature death by 22%, and the risk of cancer by 15%.

2310. Ghost peppers can actually burn a hole in your esophagus because it's so hot. Its heat is measured at one million units on the Scoville Scale, a measure of capsaicin per mass, which is the chemical compound that imbues peppers with heat. To put it into perspective, a regular jalapeño is only about 2,500 on the scale.

2311. Tomatoes have around 25% more genes than humans. While a simple tomato has approximately 31,760 genes, a human has about 20,000. Nevertheless, the amount of genetic material does not indicate how advanced an organism is.

2312. The golden silk orb weave spider's web is so strong that it can capture birds. They're also known for eating the bird.

2313. The German chocolate cake didn't originate in Germany, as the name suggests. It's a creation from the United States that contains the key ingredients of sweet baking chocolate, coconut, and pecans. The cake was named after Sam German, who created the mild dark baking chocolate bar for Baker's Chocolate Company in 1852.

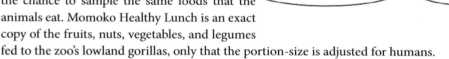

2314. In Tokyo, visitors at the Ueno Zoo get the chance to sample the same foods that the animals eat. Momoko Healthy Lunch is an exact copy of the fruits, nuts, vegetables, and legumes fed to the zoo's lowland gorillas, only that the portion-size is adjusted for humans.

2315. There is a type of red banana that exists that tastes super sweet, creamy, and a little bit like raspberries.

2316. The world's first 3D printing restaurant is Food Ink. All the food, utensils, and furniture are actually produced through 3D printing. Using fresh and natural ingredients, the edible art is prepared by the finest chefs.

2317. The average strawberry is covered by approximately 200 seeds.

2318. Fruitarianism is a subgroup of veganism. The diet basically consists of fruit and possible nuts and seeds. In fact, there are some fruitarians that will only eat what would naturally fall from a plant.

2319. There is a strain of seaweed that tastes like bacon when cooked that even has twice the nutritional value of kale, discovered by researchers at Oregon State.

2320. "The Scent of First Love" is a strawberry found in Japan that is white in color and has red seeds. They are sweeter and richer than usual and cost up to four dollars for one berry.

2321. Grapefruit juice affects the activity of certain enzymes that are responsible for breaking down many prescription drugs. The fruit contains compounds that block the enzymes, reducing the enzyme's ability to break down the drug. In consequence, blood levels of the drug may rise, resulting in a risk of new or worsened side effects.

2322. Storing bread in the fridge instead of at room temperature makes it go stale six times faster.

2323. Baby carrots are just regular carrots. They are cut and peeled to make those bite-sized pieces.

2324. An SPF 30 sunscreen that smells like fried chicken was released by KFC, in August of 2016. It went out to promote their extra crispy recipe.

2325. The record for producing the world's longest pizza was set in Naples, Italy. It measured about 6,081 feet (1,854 meters) long and had about a hundred chefs working on it together for eleven hours. To make it, it took two tons of flour, 1.6 tons of tomatoes, a ton of cheese, and fifty two gallons (200 liters) of olive oil.

2326. In Japan, it's possible to buy a pyramid-shaped watermelon. They can cost $500 each however.

2327. McDonald's for the first time in over forty years closed more stores than it opened in 2015 in the United States.

2328. There are only two restaurant chains in the US that offer antibiotic-free meat: Panera and Chipotle.

2329. According to the EWG Shopper's Guide to Pesticides in Produce, strawberries have the highest concentration of pesticides with a single sample of strawberries that show twenty. On the contrary, sweet corn and avocados have the lowest.

2330. To make egg yolks look more orange, marigolds and other plants that contain the pigment xanthophyll are added to chicken food.

2331. For the third year in a row, a restaurant called "Gaggan" has been crowned the best restaurant in Asia. The one page menu consists of twenty two emojis, each representing a different dish.

2332. Shamans in Mexico started using Coca-Cola for their rituals to heal worshippers. When Pepsi found out about this, they offered commission to Shamans to begin using Pepsi instead.

2333. Sweety con Nutella is a Nutella burger sold by McDonald's in Italy. It consists of Nutella spread between a hamburger bun.

2334. A bubble gum flavored broccoli was once created by McDonald's to get kids to eat more vegetables. However, testing on children didn't go well; in fact, the candy flavored vegetable only caused confusion in the kids.

2335. Huy Fong Foods, the makers of Sriracha hot sauce, chose a green cap for their bottle of Sriracha to represent a fresh chilli stem.

2336. According to the Guinness World Records, on May 31, 2014, 104 volunteers at the Deer Run Camping Resort in Gardners, Pennsylvania, made the largest s'mores ever, weighing 267 pounds (121 kilograms).

2337. In the late 1990's, a vending machine that could automatically raise prices for drinks in hot weather was created and tested by the Coca Cola Company.

2338. Originally Twinkie filling was banana-flavored. But during World War II, there was a banana shortage so vanilla became the standard flavor.

2339. 8% of all global manufactured salt is used for de-icing roads, while only 6% goes for human consumption.

2340. In 1932, M&M Mars invented the original Three Musketeers candy bar in the United States. It was originally packaged as three individual mini bars of chocolate, vanilla, and strawberry nougat; hence the name.

2341. The gelatin that is produced as the result of boiling the bones, skin, and hides of animals such as cows and pigs is actually used to make Jell-O. In fact, people have been eating it since 1897 and it accounts for about 80% of the gelatin market.

2342. The shorter term for Canadian oil is canola, created by the Canadian Oil Industry in 1978. Originally, canola oil was called "the rapeseed oil," but the name resulted in negative connotations, hence the organization decided to rename it.

2343. A study published by Vegetarian Times concluded that 3.2% of US adults follow a vegetarian-based diet, which is about 3.7 million people.

2344. The spiciest chips in the world are the Carolina Reaper Madness chip. It is so spicy that it is sold as a single and comes in a coffin shaped package. The reaper pepper actually holds the Guinness World Record for the hottest chilli pepper on Earth, and the Carolina Reaper Madness chip is also seasoned with ghost peppers and chipotle seasoning.

2345. The best selling beer in America is Bud Lite, followed by Coors Lite, and then regular Budweiser.

2346. Tuna imported to the US from Thailand is up to 40% illegal or unreported, followed by 45% of pollock imports from China, and 70% of salmon imports.

2347. A contest in 1948, called the "Chicken of Tomorrow," was created to develop a superior chicken for its meat. The winner of that contest is most of the chicken we eat today due to its superior genetics.

2348. From 2010 to 2015, the sodium content of thirty three Taco Bell menu items was secretly reduced by the company by 33% and nobody noticed.

2349. The oldest and most difficult pasta to make is Italian pasta su filindeu, also called "The Threads of God." The recipe is 300 years old and only three women know how to make it in the remote town of Nuoro, on the island of Sardinia.

2350. Pickles are served with sandwiches in restaurants because the acid in the vinegar works as a palate cleanser.

2351. To hard-boil an ostrich egg, it can take from ninety to 120 minutes.

2352. Smoked bats are considered a delicacy in Indonesia.

2353. In Italy, there is a vending machine named "Let's Pizza" that can create a fresh pizza in three minutes with custom toppings.

2354. In August 2016, a limited edition Swedish Fish Oreo cookie was released by Nabisco. It's the regular chocolate cookie but filled with a red Swedish Fish flavored cream.

2355. The Sobrino de Botin is the world's oldest restaurant, located in Madrid, Spain, and was founded in 1725 by French cook Jean Botin and his wife.

2356. The cartoon on the Cap'n Crunch cereal is not really a captain, but a commander. Real captains have four stripes on their sleeves, but the cartoon only has three which makes him a commander.

2357. In Hong Kong, there is a KFC that offers lickable edible fingernail polish in two different flavors: "original" and "hot and spicy."

2358. According to a 2014 report from the United States Department of Agriculture, the average American consumes up to 170 pounds (seventy seven kilograms) of refined sugar every year.

2359. Gympie Gympie is a bush that's known to sting anyone who touches it by delivering a potent neurotoxin. The fruit however is edible if the stingers are removed.

2360. Based on research done by the Royal Society for Public Health, approximately 800 additional calories a week are consumed by the average UK commuter while traveling to and from work, as a consequence from consuming mostly unhealthy snacks.

2361. The fear of cooking is called mageirocophobia. It's a very common affection that can take many forms, although it is only considered a phobia when it's severe enough to interfere with daily life.

2362. In 1934, Hawaiian Punch was originally developed as an ice cream topping. Later on, it became the tropical fruit drink when consumers discovered how good it was when mixed with water.

2363. A hamdog is a hamburger and hotdog combination with a special shaped bun, created by Australian Mark Murray.

2364. In 1974, Gerber baby products tried to market meals in a jar, like creamed beef and beef burgundy, aimed at college students and young adults. Unfortunately, the product failed.

2365. The creator of Wendy's, Dave Thomas, worked at KFC before he started, and was the one who designed the signature KFC bucket.

2366. In the 1940's, the first beer ever to be sold in a six-pack was Pabst Blue Ribbon Beer.

2367. The most expensive potato chip in the world is crafted by a Swedish brewery. It costs $56 for a set of five or $11.20 per piece. They are made from special potatoes that are hand-harvested, and come in five flavors: matsutake mushrooms, truffle seaweed, crown dill, Leksand onions, and Indian Pale Ale.

2368. Italian wine company Torti Winery has teamed up with Sanrio, the company that created the Hello Kitty character, to create a line of Hello Kitty wine. It is a blend of Pinot Noir and Chardonnay. According to Torti, every grape is handpicked.

2369. An indoor farm was created in Japan that has the ability to create ten thousand heads of lettuce in a day, using 99% less water than an outdoor farm.

2370. The swiftlet's nest is made out of the bird's own saliva. In some Asian countries, the bird's nest is boiled into a soup and it's considered a delicacy. A single bowl of soup can cost $100.

2371. Acqua di Cristallo Tributo a Modigliani is the most expensive bottle of water in the world priced at sixty thousand dollars for twenty five ounces. It comes from either Fiji or France and is contained within a twenty four karat solid gold bottle.

2372. The "M's" in M&Ms stand for the last names of their founders: Mars and Murray. It's the same thing for the Mars bar itself, even though it wasn't originally named by its creator Frank Mars, but by his son Forrest Mars.

2373. In the late 1700's, many Europeans thought that the tomato was poisonous. In fact, it was nicknamed the "poison apple" because wealthy people were dying after eating them. However, the reason they died was because they were eaten off of pewter plates, which were high in lead content, so the combination of the lead and acid from the tomatoes caused lead poisoning. As a result, the tomato was feared in Europe for more than 200 years.

2374. Honey reaches the bloodstream within twenty minutes after swallowing it.

2375. A ten-pack of Juicy Fruit gum was the first product to be sold by scanning a barcode. The transaction occurred at 8:01 am, on June 26, 1974, at a Marsh Supermarket in Troy, Ohio.

2376. The world record for the most tomatoes harvested from a single plant in one year is held by a tomato tree in Epcot's land pavilion, in Florida. It had a one year harvest of 32,000 tomatoes, which weighed a total of 1,150 pounds (522 kilograms).

2377. The most expensive bottle of white wine according to the Guinness World Records is the Chateau d'Yquem from 1811. It was sold by the antique wine company for $117,000 to Christian Vanneque on January 18, 2011.

2378. Coffee beans are not beans, they are actually fruit pits.

2379. Kawaii is a cooking trend in Japan. It's a form of miniature cooking where people create mini edible cuisine using little stoves, pots, pans, and cooking utensils, as well as real-life ingredients that are cooked over a candle flame.

2380. Carmine is a type of food coloring extracted from female cochineal insect shells boiled in ammonia or sodium carbonate solution. It is actually used in more things than you might think, like ice cream, yogurt, candy, and red fruit drinks.

2381. There is a cereal cafe in London known as The Cereal Killer Café where you can eat hundreds of different kinds of cereal from around the world.

2382. If you add cold cream to your coffee, it actually keeps it warmer longer, compared to just having black coffee.

2383. The temperature of milk that has just been freshly milked from a cow is 100 degrees Fahrenheit (37.8 degrees Celsius).

2384. One of the very first soup kitchens was actually started by gangster Al Capone in Chicago, back in 1931.

2385. A pastrami-flavored pilsner was created by Shmaltz Brewing in collaboration with Barcade. It's a beer made with authentic pastrami notes, including ingredients like a pinch of kosher salt, a dash of pepper, and smoke.

2386. In 1964, in Hamilton, Ontario, the first Tim Hortons Donut Shop opened. Coffee and doughnuts would cost only ten cents each. The apple fritter and the dutchie are two of the original doughnuts that were offered from its opening.

2387. The Heart Attack Grill is a restaurant in Las Vegas that offers the burger with the most calories in the world. According to Jon Basso, the owner, the Octuple Bypass Burger is 20,000 calories. The restaurant ended up making national headlines for killing its customers.

2388. When you eat oysters, they are usually still alive. Since they go bad relatively quickly, they are served while still living so that they stay as fresh as possible.

2389. Stilton cheese can't be created within Stilton village because of European Union rules. Only the English counties of Derbyshire, Leicestershire, and Nottinghamshire can use that name as per the protected designation of origin, according to British government guidelines.

2390. The full name of the Captain Crunch mascot is Captain Horacio Magellan Crunch, and he has a ship that is known as S.S. Guppy.

2391. The Snickers Bar made by the chocolate company Mars was named after the favorite horse of the family that owned the company.

2392. The word fruit refers to the component of a plant which comes from a flower, and the part that contains seeds. The remaining parts, including leaves, stems, and flower buds, are considered vegetables. Therefore, beans, tomatoes, cucumbers, and avocados are all fruits.

2393. Kidney beans contain toxins when they are still raw, and eating just four or five of them can result in symptoms that present in one to three hours. The symptoms may include abdominal pain, diarrhea, overwhelming nausea, and vomiting. The toxins become inactive when the beans are cooked.

2394. A conservation group called Oceania released a report in 2013 claiming that about one third of all fish served in sushi restaurants and sold in stores aren't really the kind the buyer thinks they are. Because of the wrong labeling, you might be eating king mackerel while thinking it's white tuna.

2395. Although ketchup can expire, the acidity of the vinegar, tomatoes, and the sugar used to make it gives it a rather long shelf life. If a can remains sealed, it can stay good for about two years past the indicated expiry date.

2396. Based on studies made by Australian researchers at the Commonwealth Scientific and Industrial Research Organization, drinking a cup of Asian pear juice before drinking alcohol can result in reduced hangover symptoms the very next day.

2397. It's possible to buy snake wine in some countries like China, Vietnam, and throughout Southeast Asia. The alcoholic drink contains a whole venomous snake in the bottle and also includes insects, herbs, and other animals.

2398. Red Bull grew so much in 2019 that they almost sold as many cans of its drink than people on the planet. They sold 7.5 billion cans and the world population is 7.8 billion.

2399. Approximately forty six million turkeys are eaten every Thanksgiving in the United States.

2400. There is only one McDonald's in the US as of 2020 that still serves pizza, which is located in Orlando, Florida.

2401. "Bib-Label Lithiated Lemon-Lime Soda" was originally the name given to 7 Up. The drink was invented in 1929 by Charles Leiper Grigg. One of its main ingredients was lithia, a naturally occurring substance found in minute quantities of bubbling waters fed by underground springs. Lithia is better known as lithium, a drug used to even out mood swings.

2402. Shishito Pepper is a well-known pepper grown in Japan. Only one out of every ten is spicy, but there is no way to know which one is spicy beforehand.

2403. Numerous research papers have shown that coffee can prevent cancer, reduce the chance of getting diabetes, and improve your overall health.

2404. The main source of Vitamin C for the Inuit people is found in narwhal (a type of whale) skin. In fact, there is as much Vitamin C gram for gram in narwhal skin as there is in an orange.

2405. It's a tradition to eat something called Kivia at Christmas time in Iceland. The dish is made from the raw flesh of little auks, a type of Arctic bird. The birds are previously buried whole in seal skin for several months until they have reached an advanced stage of decomposition.

2406. Until 2011, beer was not considered an alcohol in Russia. It was in fact classified as a soft drink because it had less than 10% alcohol, so it could be bought by anybody from street kiosks, at railway stations, or at twenty four hour corner shops, just like any fruit juice or mineral water.

2407. The highest priced beef in the world is Wagyu beef. It's priced at $50 per 3.5 ounces (a hundred grams) of the meat itself, but a rib steak will set you back $3,200.

2408. H2NO was an upselling campaign that was once launched by Coca-Cola, the soft drink giant. The campaign had a website that trained waiters to talk customers into buying sodas instead of asking for free water.

2409. Bjorn De La Cruz, who co-owns the Brooklyn based Manila Social Club and is an executive chef there, created a gold-dusted twenty-four karat doughnut that's served with Cristal Champagne and costs $100.

2410. The killing of sharks for their fins has reduced by 50% thanks to conservation campaigns led by Yao Ming, the retired NBA star. Various surveys have shown that in China, 91% of people currently support the ban on consumption of shark fins.

2411. In Salt Lake City, University of Utah researchers found a correlation between the size of people's utensils, and how much food they consumed. The bottom-line is that the bigger your fork, the less you eat.

2412. Two million out of the twenty one million cases of diabetes that are projected to develop in America by 2020 might be prevented if people quit taking drinks with artificial sweeteners, according to a study done by Cambridge University researchers in 2015.

2413. Guava is a super fruit. It has four times the Vitamin C in an orange, more potassium than a standard banana, and compared to pineapples, it has four times the fiber and three times the protein.

2414. Bees are the only animals on the planet which create food that is consumed by humans.

2415. The Jägermeister emblem represents the Patron Saint of Hunters, Saint Hubertus, who lived in Germany in the seventh century.

2416. Kit Kat bars became a big hit in Japan partly because by sheer coincidence, "Kit Kat" sounds like "Kitto katsu," a Japanese phrase that means "you will certainly win." So people in Japan believe that this chocolate brings good luck.

2417. You can keep apples from browning by using lemon juice. It prevents the reaction that turns apples brown, which is between oxygen in air and polyphenol oxidase, an enzyme found in apples.

2418. The Kroger Company made the largest strawberry shortcake in the world in 2014. It was 2,073 square feet (192 square meters) in size, it weighed 21,500 pounds (9,780 kilograms), and it contained more than a ton of real strawberries, and whipped and glazed toppings.

2419. "The Modern Toilet" is a restaurant in Taipei, Taiwan, that has a gross theme, which it pushes to the extreme. Their food is served in bowls in the shape of toilets, and their drinks are distributed in urine sample bottles. Their menu offers food like stuffed brown sugar poop pancakes, poop meatballs, and patrons eat while seated on toilets.

2420. When you sprinkle a pineapple with salt, it becomes sweeter. It's because table salt is mainly sodium chlorine, and the sodium is effective in lowering bitterness levels in foods, so it makes the pineapple less bitter.

2421. Portobello, cremini, and the button mushrooms are actually the same type of mushroom, and are just at different states of maturity.

2422. Campbell Soup offers a watercress and duck gizzard flavored product in Hong Kong, China, and a cream of Chile poblano flavored product in Mexico.

2423. Richard Montanez was a janitor working at a factory floor, when the idea for Frito-Lay's Flamin Hot Cheetos came to him. He invented the product, and today, he works at Pepsi-Co as an executive vice president.

2424. The flame and fury PF 24-007 peach is the biggest kind of peach in the world. They were originally grown in Colome, Michigan, at Paul Friday Farms. When mature, they measure three inches (7.6 centimeters) in diameter.

2425. Disneyland sells almost three million churros at their parks every year.

2426. Compared to coffee, apples are more effective in waking you up during the morning. The fruit gives you glucose, which energizes the body, and provides fuel to the brain.

2427. The most expensive bottle of vodka in the world costs almost four million dollars. It's filtered through sand and created from crushed up gems and diamonds.

2428. In the 1930's, McDonald's started off selling hotdogs from a cart. Today, the fast food giant sells seventy five hamburgers every second of every day.

2429. In 2016, Budweiser changed its name to America. Labels on all bottles and cans were changed, with images and phrases related to the United States. The controversial campaign was called "America in

Your Hands" and it ran from May 23 to November, 2016.

2430. In March of 2017, a hamburger sold at a charity auction in Dubai for $10,000. It contained seven beef patties, one for each of the emirates in The United Arab Emirates, aged cheddar cheese, and veal bacon strips in a saffron brioche bun.

2431. In some parts of South Asia, Africa, and China, monkey brains are considered a delicacy and an easily digestible substance. It's often given to children, and there are even entire cookbooks dedicated on how to cook them.

2432. Guolizhuang is an exotic restaurant in Beijing; its menu consists almost entirely of penis and testicle dishes.

2433. Colonel Sanders used to make surprise visits to KFC restaurants. If he wasn't happy with the quality of food, he would throw everything on the ground and curse at the employees.

2434. Out of all the peaches in the world, China is responsible for producing 58%. With a worldwide production of twenty five million metric tons, that represents about 14.4 million metric tons.

2435. The most popular fruit in the world is tomato.

2436. The "coco de mer" is the largest fruit in the world and it belongs to the palm tree family. The fruit weighs about 92.5 pounds (forty two kilograms) while the seed weighs 37.4 pounds (seventeen kilograms). It's also known as the sea coconut or the double coconut.

2437. Green bell peppers are just less mature, less ripe versions of red, orange, and yellow peppers.

2438. Some people refer to cranberries as bounce berries because they actually bounce when they are ripe.

2439. Before modern refrigeration existed, people in Russia and Finland used to put Russian brown frogs in their milk to keep it fresh. According to organic chemist A.T. Lebedev, from the Moscow State University, the frog's skin secretions are loaded with peptides and anti-microbial compounds.

2440. Research conducted in 2012 by the Monell Chemical Sense Center shows that steak and wine taste great together because they are on opposite ends of the culinary sensory spectrum, a contrast that's pleasing to the palate.

2441. The top selling product at Walmart is bananas. The company sells around 999,102,136 pounds (453,592,370 kilograms) of bananas per year worldwide. That's 31.9 pounds (14.5 kilograms) every second of the day.

2442. Margarine is naturally white. When it was first introduced, thirty two states had imposed color constraints on it. Vermont, New Hampshire, and South Dakota all passed laws demanding that margarine be dyed pink. Other states proposed it be colored red, brown, or black. The reason behind it was that butter makers didn't want it to be yellow, as it was already the color of butter.

2443. Turophobia is the fear of cheese.

2444. About 554 million tacos from the fast food chain "Jack in the Box" are eaten every year according to the Wall Street Journal.

2445. People's obsession with bacon over the past decade has led to some really strange bacon products, such as bacon ice cream, bacon lollipops, bacon mayonnaise, bacon chocolate bars, and bacon gumballs.

2446. Durian is a type of fruit from Asia that smells so bad that Singapore banned it on their Rapid Mass Transit systems. The odor is described as turpentine and onions garnished with a gym sock, according to food writer Richard Sterling.

2447. There are 3D printers that can print food. The "Foodini Food Printer" can print anything from pizza to burgers to chocolate, using fresh ingredients.

2448. Until the 1970's, the bluefin tuna was considered a trash fish and it was used to make cat food or hauled off to the dumps. It had such a bad reputation in Japan that they called it "nekomatagi," which translates to food too low for even a cat to eat.

2449. In the Philippines, Balut is considered a national delicacy. It consists of a fertilized duck egg or duck embryo that is boiled and then eaten from the shell.

2450. Methyl anthranilate is the chemical used to flavor grape Kool Aid. Other uses of the chemical involve protecting crops such as corn, rice, and sunflowers as well as golf courses. It's also known to be used as a bird repellent.

2451. Methodes champenoise is a double fermentation process used to create champagne. The technique creates a lot of carbon dioxide that leads to an internal pressure of around five to six atmospheres, which is the equivalent of over eleven pounds (five kilograms) of weight on the glass. As a result, champagne bottles are much thicker and heavier, and their corks are held on by wire cages to prevent premature cork popping.

2452. Bloom is a natural protective layer that coats eggs, sealing the pores to diminish moisture loss and preventing the development of bacteria.

2453. In 2016, garlic flavored black Doritos were introduced in Japan, right before Halloween. The bag is black and it features a haunted house, bats, and a Dracula graphic.

2454. "Rigatoni con la pajata" is a classic Roman dish consisting of the intestines of an unweaned calf that was only fed on its mother's milk. The intestines become a thick and creamy cheese-like sauce after they are cooked, which is then served with tomato sauce and rigatoni.

2455. In Thailand, rats are considered a delicacy.

2456. Glycyrrhizin is a substance contained in licorice root that is about fifty times sweeter than sugar.

2457. Chips have a vanishing caloric density that tricks our tongue and brain into thinking that we haven't actually eaten anything. This is why it's so easy to eat a full bag of them without even noticing.

2458. McDonald's takes approximately 7% of all potatoes grown in the United States and turns them into french fries.

2459. Musa Velutina is a type of banana. They are pink and peel themselves when ripe. Although they are often grown as ornamental, they are still edible; the flesh is soft and sweet, but the seeds are quite hard and can even chip a tooth.

2460. To prevent rigor mortis, beef carcasses are given electrical stimulation before they are slaughtered and skinned.

2461. In 2012, wine producer Ian Hutcheon launched the world's first meteorite-aged wine at his Tremonte Vineyard in the Cachapoal Valley, in Chile. It's a Cabernet Sauvignon called Meteorite that was aged with a 4.5 billion year old meteorite from the asteroid belt between Mars and Jupiter.

2462. Potato chips cause significantly more weight gain in people than most other foods, according to a

2011 Harvard study.

2463. In January 2017, a craft beer maker known as the Veil Brewing Company in Richmond, Virginia, created a new beer that was infused with Oreo cookies. They took their chocolate milk stout and conditioned it with hundreds of Oreo cookies, naming it "Horn Swaddler Chocolate Milk Stout with Oreos."

2464. Back in 1920, Hans Riegel created the gummy bear candies, initially called dancing bears. They were originally made out of licorice.

2465. In 1927, Pez was invented in Vienna, Austria, as a breath mint. The name is actually an abbreviation for the German word "pfefferminz," which means peppermint.

2466. The very last McDonald's hamburger and fries sold in Iceland is on display at a bus hostel in Reykjavik. You can watch real-time footage of it over a live stream. It has been there since October 30 of 2009 when a man bought it and left it there.

2467. A rainbow grilled cheese sandwich is one of the specials at the Chomp Eatery Restaurant in Los Angeles. In the sandwich, the blue tastes like lavender, the green like basil, the red like tomatoes, and the yellow tastes like plain cheese.

2468. Cheetos Burrito was a new product released by Taco Bell in August of 2016. It was a burrito stuffed with seasoned meat, buttery rice and a cheese sauce and Cheetos that cost just a dollar.

2469. Expiration dates for bottled water actually applies for the bottle, not for the water itself.

2470. Kinder Surprise, the candy-filled eggs made by Italian company Ferrero, are actually illegal in the United States. According to the US Food, Drug and Cosmetic Act, all candies embedded with non-nutritive objects are banned in the country. If you bring these candies into the United States, you can be fined up to $1,200 per egg.

2471. Around two billion people in the world eat insects as part of their everyday diet. They are known to contain high amounts of protein and are usually inexpensive. The only region where they are not consumed is in the West.

2472. If you want to speed up the ripening process of green tomatoes, you can place them with a ripe banana or apple in an enclosed space. Furthermore, there is a gas called ethylene that helps speed up ripening, which is used commercially with tomatoes and other fruits that are picked green before shipping and then ripened for sale.

2473. Since 1954, more Burger King fast-food places have burned down than any other fast food chain.

2474. There are differences among jam, jelly, marmalade, and preserves. Jam is a thick mixture of fruit, pectin, and sugar that's boiled rapidly until the fruit is soft, but thick enough to spread easily. Jelly is different in that it's made from sugar, pectin, acid, and fruit juice that turn into a clear spread. Marmalade is a spread made from the peel and pulp of citrus fruit which is cooked for a long time. And finally, preserves are chunks of fruit that are surrounded by jelly.

2475. In the early 1900's, celery was a popular delicacy among many Americans. Restaurants would offer it in many different ways, such as mashed celery, fried celery, and celery tea. Kalamazoo, Michigan, was also known as the celery capital of the world.

2476. Don Gorski, a sixty four year old man from Wisconsin, ate the 30,000th Big Mac of his life on May 4, 2018. Don holds the world record for being the single person who's consumed the highest number of Big Macs, and according to him, the sandwiches make up ninety to 95% of the food he eats daily.

2477. Yao Ming, the retired NBA All-Star basketball player, has his own winery in Napa Valley. It opened in 2009 as Yao Family Wines; they make ultra-premium wines and it's open from ten to five for tastings.

2478. Named after RnB singer Luther Vandross, the Luther Burger is made of a Krispy Kreme donut with bacon and cheese. It's rumored that the singer invented the burger himself when he was short on hamburger buns.

2479. Maple Taffy is a Canadian candy that's made by pouring hot maple syrup onto fresh snow. The cold from the snow quickly thickens the syrup that creates a soft candy.

2480. During the 2008 Olympics in Beijing, China, seahorse kebabs and deep-fried scorpion were among some of the eating options offered to visitors.

2481. In a medium McDonald's chocolate milkshake, there are 630 calories. The same calories are found in an average meal.

2482. In China, it's possible to buy baby pears shaped like Buddha. The farmers actually clamp a mold onto a growing fruit to get the shape. There is also a company called "Fruit Mold" that makes heart-shaped cucumbers, square watermelons, and other more deliciously weird shapes.

2483. Eggplant is actually a fruit, not a vegetable. In fact, it is considered a family of the berries.

2484. In 2016, McDonald's in Japan started selling pumpkin spice fries. They are called the Halloween Choco-Potato; they are french fries drizzled with a pumpkin spiced and chocolate sauce.

2485. A food and brand lab study of 497 diners conducted by Cornell revealed that customers who order their dinner from a heavy server ordered significantly more food, were four times more likely to order dessert, and ordered 17% more alcohol.

2486. Until 1964, when Teressa Bellissimo invented the buffalo wing at her restaurant in Anchor Bar in Buffalo, New York, chicken wings used to be throwaway parts of the chicken in restaurant kitchens. Today wings are actually the most popular and expensive part of the chicken in the United States.

2487. In 2013, in an attempt to make French fries healthier, Burger King introduced satis-fries, a low calorie alternative. Customers, however, preferred the full fat version and Burger King had to dismiss the item the following year.

2488. Eel's blood is poisonous, that is why it's always cooked before eating. Just a small amount of eel's blood can kill a person. In consequence, raw eel should never be eaten.

2489. In the United States, apples that are sold in stores can be up to one year old.

2490. Watermelon is 92% water. It's a great choice to stay hydrated and is also low in calories.

2491. One of the best ways to retain vitamins and nutrients in food when you cook it in a microwave is by placing a small amount of water inside.

2492. In Australia, a beer was created by "Seven Cent Brewery" using the yeast isolated from the belly button lint of its brewers.

2493. In the 1960's, Dr. Pepper was marketed as a warm holiday drink. The idea was to heat it up in a saucepan until it lost all of its carbonation and then pour the warm and sweet beverage over a lemon.

2494. It's possible to purchase different wedding e-cards from Domino's pizza to give to someone. Some of the cards they offer are a $25 gift of pizza called "the post-honeymoon adjustment to real life because washing the dishes is the worst." There is also a $15 married but chill option.

2495. "Charles Entertainment Cheese" is the full name of Chuck E. Cheese.

Funny

2496. In 1980, there was a siege in the Iranian embassy in London. When the armed men were given the choice of which hostage would be released, they chose Ali Guil Ghanzafar, whose snoring wasn't letting the terrorists get any sleep.

2497. 170 soldiers from Switzerland were on a nightly training march on February 28, 2007, when they got lost, and accidentally invaded Liechtenstein, a small neighboring country. The soldiers retreated back to Switzerland immediately after learning where they were, and their government later apologized. A Liechtenstein spokesperson responded by saying: "No problem, these things happen."

2498. Fourteen squirrels were caught and detained by Iranian Intelligence officers in July, 2007, because they suspected that the squirrels were spies. The agents thought the squirrels looked like they were carrying sophisticated Western spy equipment, and that they were sent to undermine the Islamic Republic of Iran.

2499. A forty nine year old resident of Leicester, England, named Tim Price was frustrated with receiving endless calls from telemarketers, so, in 2012, he changed his surname to "PPPPPPPPP Price." His reason for adding nine Ps to his name was that he wanted to make it hard for marketers to pronounce it when making calls.

2500. A man drunkenly rode a horse on the freeway in 2015, and he got arrested. He told the police that his horse knew the way home, so the sheriff determined that the incident didn't count as a DUI.

2501. In 2011, Hamish Blake, a comedian from Australia, joined the New York bodybuilding Championship after he was jokingly challenged to do it. Amazingly, Blake ended up winning a medal because he was the only contestant in the over 200 pounds weight category.

2502. The creators of the Anti-Piracy ad were issued a fine in 2012 for using music that was stolen on their ad.

2503. When syphilis occurred, many countries named it after another one. The French called it the Spanish disease, the Japanese called it Chinese Pox while the English called it the French disease.

2504. A man tried to sue Pepsi in 2012 when he said he found a dead mouse in his Mountain Dew. Pepsi won by saying that a mouse would have dissolved in a Mountain Dew after thirty days and that the man's drink was purchased after seventy days of being manufactured.

2505. A company in Texas once conducted a survey where they asked participants to try three different wines labeled California, Texas and France. Most people said the French wine was the best, but in reality, all three wines were from Texas.

2506. Iran tried to create a new world record for the longest sandwich ever made in 2008, however, failed when the spectators started eating it before it was measured.

2507. In 1972, nine time Olympic champion Mark Spitz told the Russian swim team coach as a joke that his mustache increased his speed in the water, deflecting water away from his mouth. The next year every Russian swimmer had grown a mustache.

2508. IKEA once gave away cribs to Australian couples that could prove that their babies were born on November 14th, that is, exactly nine months after Valentine's Day.

2509. Slovakia and Slovenia are so frequently confused that the staff of Slovak and Slovanian embassies get together once a month to exchange wrongly addressed mail.

2510. Ephebiphobia is the irrational fear of being near, among, or in the company of teenagers.

2511. Police in Ireland noticed that a serial traffic offender named Prawo Jazdy was racking up parking and speeding tickets by the dozens in 2009. After more than fifty tickets were issued to people with that name, the police learned that Prawo Jazdy means "driver's license" in Polish. The officers were looking at the wrong part of the license.

2512. Even though modern Eskimos still mostly live in sub-zero temperatures, they now use fridges. Unlike other people who use fridges to keep food cool, the Eskimos use them to keep food from freezing.

2513. A twelve member jury was going to court to adjudicate over a lawsuit filed against Otis Elevator Company, on November 3, 1986, when the elevator they were using broke down and was stuck. That particular elevator was an Otis elevator.

2514. The Tsar of Russia outlawed the sale of alcohol on July 31, 1914, in preparation for what became the First World War. This however, ended up destroying the state's budget, because a third of all the money made by the Russian government was from the sale of alcohol.

2515. The Restaurant of "Order Mistakes" was a pop-up dining establishment that showed up in Tokyo, Japan, between June 2 and June 4, 2017. The owners only employed people who had dementia to work as waiters and waitresses, and it left too many patrons having a lot of fun and laughter as they were served things they didn't order.

2516. Some hair salons in the UK have designated quiet chairs in their shops. It's usually a single chair set aside for anti-social customers who want their haircut and colored without having to make small talk.

2517. In the 1830's, in Germany, a naturalist called Vernos was arrested for heresy after he claimed that he could transform caterpillars into butterflies.

2518. At the Washington National Cathedral's Northwestern tower, high up amongst the grotesque gargoyles, there is a stone carved Darth Vader head. That's because when the tower was built in the 1980's, the Cathedral had a contest where children submitted designs for statues. A kid named Christopher Rader submitted the Dark Lord of Sith, and he came in third, so his entry was added up there.

2519. A surprisingly large number of people around the world claim to suffer from cenosillicaphobia, which is the fear of one's beer glass being totally empty.

2520. Between 1913 and the late 1970's, American high schools required all boys to swim in the nude.

2521. Molehill Town in West Virginia decided to change its official name to "Mountain" in 1949, because they thought it would be funny to "make a mountain out of a molehill."

2522. Moonshiners made illegal alcohol in secret locations, such as meadows and forests, during prohibition. To get the police off their scent, they would sometimes put on special footwear known as cow shoes, which would leave behind marks that looked like cow hoof prints instead of human footprints.

2523. Confetti manipulation is illegal in Mobile, Alabama, in all its possible forms. It's illegal to possess, store, use, manufacture, sell, offer to sell, give away, or even handle confetti.

2524. Bruce Wayne, aka Batman, is part owner of the Daily Planet where Clark Kent, aka Superman, works. So basically Batman pays Superman's salary.

2525. The earliest "your momma joke" was written on a tablet 3,500 years ago by a student in ancient Babylon.

2526. Back in the 1920's, there were beach police whose job was to go around measuring women's swimsuit lengths to check that no one was wearing a swimsuit with a questionable length. If a woman didn't meet the established length, she would be forced to cover up, was sent home, or was even arrested in some cases.

2527. In 2001, the Russian space agency was paid one million dollars by Pizza Hut to send a pizza to the International Space Station.

2528. If someone has a hard time waking up, someone invented a sonic grenade alarm clock that might do the job. You just need to pull the pin, toss it into their room, and run for cover. It emits an ear splitting noise that only turns off when putting the pin back in.

2529. "Schimpf-los," which means "swear away," is a German hotline where people can call after a stressful day to let off some steam.

2530. Listerine ads popularized the phrase "always a bridesmaid, never a bride." The ads used to show a lovelorn woman unable to find a husband due to her halitosis. The term halitosis was also made up in the same ads.

2531. In 2015, a man skipped out on his bill at a Houston restaurant and later was seen running into an empty building across the street. After arriving at the building, the police officers jokingly called out "Marco," to which the suspect accidentally replied "Polo." He was immediately detained.

2532. A teen from Georgia was arrested for stealing a goat in 2015 after confessing he wanted to take a girl out, asking her "would she goat to prom with him."

2533. The lead singer of the black metal band "Hatebeak" is a parrot.

2534. A Russian Soviet star, which is a highly revered symbol for communism in the country, was once vandalized by being painted to look like Patrick, the cartoon starfish from the kid's show Spongebob Squarepants.

2535. In Mexico City, there are special bins where you can put your dog poo in it and get free Wi-Fi in exchange. The more poo, the longer the free Wi-Fi.

2536. On April 1, 1996, Taco Bell created a marketing gimmick which was a hoax. The full page ad appeared in six major newspapers announcing that they had purchased the Liberty Bell to help the national debt. The ad went on to say that it would now be called Taco Liberty Bell.

2537. The traffic in London is so slow that it moves at the same speed as horse drawn carriages from over a hundred years ago.

2538. A faraday cage was built into the ceiling of the Gin Tub in Brighton, England, to block cell phone reception. The owner wanted his customers to socialize the old-fashioned way by actually speaking to each other.

2539. Before Super Bowl 51, Zoo Atlanta located in the Roger Williams Park Zoo in Providence, Rhode Island, made a bet that if their team lost, they would name a baby animal after the winning team's quarterback. That year, the New England Patriots beat the Atlanta Falcons; hence a Madagascar hissing cockroach was named Tom Brady by the zoo staff.

2540. In High Wycombe, UK, there is a tradition that dates back to medieval times where the mayor is weighed in full view of the public to see whether or not they have been getting fat at the taxpayers' expense.

2541. There is an alternate Barbie doll with a regular nineteen year old body. She's named the Lammily doll, has cellulite, brown hair, stretch marks, acne, and freckles.

2542. In December of 2016, a warning to motorists was issued by the Alberta parks system in Canada because there was an aggressive moose going around licking the sides of cars for salt.

2543. From 2015 to 2018, there was a serial pooper that had pooped on at least nineteen cars that the police were on the lookout for. He was never caught and although he didn't cause any damage, he did leave a big mess.

2544. Jimmy Connors beat Vitas Gerulatis in tennis sixteen times before he lost. When Vitas finally won, he said: "Nobody beats Vitas Gerulaitis seventeen times in a row."

2545. Monkeys have been trained by researchers to recognize themselves in mirrors. One of the first things they did when being in front of the mirror was to check out all the places on their bodies that they have never seen before, especially their genitalia area. Monkeys were contorting and spreading their legs in front of the mirror to get a better look at all unseen corners of their bodies.

Lammily Doll

2546. "Skeletons in the Closet" is the name of a gift shop at the Los Angeles County Coroner's Office.

2547. In China, there are parking spots designated just for women drivers that are 50% larger than normal spaces. Additionally, they are outlined in pink and have ladies' bathroom style symbols on them.

2548. Residents of the village of Shitterton in England, tired of people stealing the sign of the village name, placed a one and a half ton block of stone with the name inscribed upon it.

2549. In Singapore, it's illegal not to flush the toilet. If you forget to flush it, you will be fined $150. It's even known that police officers do check.

2550. On February 13, 2017, a study released by Netflix revealed that almost half of streaming couples around the world have cheated on their significant other by watching a show ahead of them without their knowledge.

2551. "Mutton shunters" was the name given to police in Victorian times.

2552. Christian Poincheval created a variety of pills that made people's fart smell like roses or chocolates, in 2014. He named the chocolate one "Father Christmas Fart Pill."

2553. Tunarama is an annual festival celebrated in Port Lincoln, Australia. The main event is the world championship tuna toss competition. The one who can throw their tuna the farthest is the winner.

2554. In South Korea, there is a plastic surgery called smile lipping, where both corners of your mouth are raised in order to give you a permanent smile.

2555. "Pennywise Poo Poo Butt Inc." is the corporate name for Blink-182 which they chose so their accountants and managers would have to say that while doing business.

2556. Cheetos Company joined the beauty market in 2016 when they produced a perfume called "Cheeteau" that smelled like Cheetos and retailed for nineteen dollars. They also produced a Cheetos themed bronzer that supposedly gave users the "Cheetos-kissed glow."

2557. In 2014, Jason Willis, a thirty one year old American from Waterford, Wisconsin, was banned from the Internet after sending a naked man to a neighbor's house using a Craigslist ad.

2558. Kiran Cable, a twenty year old man from South Wales, spent so much time with his girlfriend that his friends said that he actually disappeared from their lives. After eighteen months of unreturned calls and emails, Cable's friends decided to surprise him with a mock funeral that included a coffin, a hearse, and even a eulogy.

2559. In Hong Kong, you can have a "McWedding." For $1,200 you can get food, drinks, and apple pies for fifty people.

2560. There is a tradition in Denmark where those who are still single when turning twenty five are doused in cinnamon.

2561. Richard Feynman, a famous American physicist, was named the world's smartest man by Omni Magazine. His mother was actually quoted as saying: "If that's the world's smartest man, God help us."

2562. Stephen Hawking's son, Tim Hawking, once added swear words to his dad's voice synthesizer as a prank.

2563. Bill Gates used to be so addicted to Minesweeper that he actually had to uninstall it on his own computer because he was playing it too much.

2564. If you search the number 241543903 on Google images, you get a bunch of pictures of people sticking their heads in a freezer.

2565. In 1987, to commemorate a visit by Pope John Paul II, the Hollywood sign was changed to Holywood. The prank, however, was undone before the pope arrived in LA.

2566. Police in Athens, Greece, have the authority to strip a driver of his or her license if they think he is poorly dressed or unbathed.

2567. When his own mobile phone rang during court proceedings in 2013, Raymond Voet, a judge from Michigan, held himself in contempt of court and imposed a twenty five dollar fine on himself. From that day, Voet has put up a notice at his courtroom stating that any attendant whose electronics disrupted proceedings would be held in contempt, and that he himself wasn't an exception.

2568. "Hangover Helpers" is a company that, for $20 a person, makes your hangover go easy. They will bring you Gatorade, cook you a homemade burrito for breakfast, clean the room where your party was held in, and do all the dirty dishes.

2569. "Cabbages & Condoms" is a chain of restaurants in Bangkok, Thailand, with condom-themed decoration. There, instead of offering you an after dinner mint, you get a condom on the way out.

2570. A woman named Lina Poulsen, from Sweden, found her wedding ring sixteen years after she lost it, growing on a carrot in her garden.

2571. In Las Vegas, it's illegal to pawn your dentures because they are considered under the law as prescribed medical devices.

2572. In Basel, Switzerland, in 1474, a rooster laid an egg, and as a result the whole community panicked because they believed it was Satan's work. The rooster was put on trial, found guilty and burned alive, but they later discovered that it was just a hen that looked remarkably like a rooster.

2573. According to an analysis conducted by Swift Key, Canada uses the poop emoji more than any other country in the world. In France hearts are number one, while Australia leads the world in alcohol and drug related emojis.

2574. Author Michael Crichton suspected that his Harvard English professor was giving him unfair grades, so to prove his suspicions, he submitted a George Orwell essay as his own. The professor gave the essay a B minus.

2575. The company that made the game "Cards against Humanity" wanted to protect people from the madness of Black Friday shopping in 2014, so they chose to avoid putting out a new product, and instead, they sold and sent out 30,000 boxes containing bull excrement.

2576. There has been a real court case called Batman V Commissioner, but it wasn't the Dark Knight suing the head of the Gotham Police force. A farmer called Ray Batman was attempting to appeal a decision by the IRS to increase his tax.

2577. The Barbie Liberation Organization was a group of activists and artists who, in 1993, performed surgery on about 300 to 500 dolls, switching the voice boxes inside the G.I. Joe and the Barbie figures, returning all the toys to the stores afterwards. G.I Joes were reportedly saying things like "the beach is a great place for the summer," while Barbies were saying "vengeance is mine."

2578. In New York State, you legally have to let a buyer know if a house is considered haunted before you sell it to them.

2579. According to a survey conducted in the US, 51% of people consider that sharing a Netflix password with a significant other means the relationship is serious.

2580. Tony Fernandez, the CEO of Air Asia, once made a bet with Sir Richard Branson on who would be the winner of the 2010 Grand Prix in Abu Dhabi. Richard lost and had to work as a female flight attendant on Air Asia.

2581. In 2015, a teenager often broke into homes in Colorado to steal snacks, specifically Hot Pockets, and to watch Netflix. No cash or other valuables were ever stolen, only snacks and Netflix.

2582. It was illegal to show your face in Chicago if you were ugly before 1974.

2583. On January 9, 1493, when sailing near the Dominican Republic, three mermaids were supposedly seen in the water by famous Italian explorer Christopher Columbus. He described them as being not half as beautiful as they are painted. The creatures turned out to be manatees.

2584. The Nigerian police force once arrested a goat as one of the suspects for attempted armed robbery.

2585. One of the best vasectomy doctors found in Austin, Texas, is named Dick Chop.

2586. In July 2016, after a night of drinking with friends, thirty three year old British man Simon Smith changed his name to Bacon Double Cheeseburger.

2587. On the top floor of the US Supreme Court Building, there is a basketball court named "the highest court in the land."

2588. As of 2012, in Italy, it's illegal to tell a man that he has no balls, since it hurts male pride.

2589.   Cecil Chao, a Hong Kong billionaire, once offered one hundred and twenty million dollars to anyone who could turn his lesbian daughter straight.

2590.   The Comedy Wildlife Photography Awards is an annual photo contest that exhibits the funniest animal wildlife pictures that photographers accidentally or intentionally have captured throughout their career.

2591.   An April Fool's Day joke turned awry in 2013 when two DJs in Florida told fans that their taps were emitting dihydrogen monoxide. This resulted in serious panic, and the DJs were suspended until they paid a fine. The funny part is that dihydrogen monoxide is actually supposed to come out of taps and is just a different way to say water.

2592.   In 1891, electricity was first introduced to the White House. The then President Benjamin Harrison and his wife refused to touch any of the light switches because they were afraid of being electrocuted, so they had employees follow them around the White House to turn the switches on and off for them whenever they entered or left a room.

2593.   William Morrison was a dentist who invented cotton candy, something notoriously bad for your teeth.

2594.   In 2015, a man named Torkel Kristoffers was arrested for kidnapping. It turned out that his neighbors didn't recognize him with his new beard that he grew while taking time off of work, so they alerted the authorities as soon as they saw a stranger getting into Torkel's place.

2595.   In 1948, a local man named Tony Signorini would put on a pair of 29.9 pound (13.6 kilogram), three-toed shoes and walk along the beaches in Florida at night, creating huge footprints in the sand. Locals believed that a 14.7 foot (4.5 meter) tall penguin was roaming the beaches until the mystery was solved in 1988.

2596.   In Japan, the workers of Maruyama Zoo were attempting to get two hyenas to mate for four years until they realized they were both males.

2597.   A woman from Missouri named Edie Simms got herself arrested by the police so that she could cross "get arrested" off of her bucket list. The police officers were happy to handcuff her and take her to the police station so she could reach her goal.

2598.   The "Hizamakura Lap Pillow" is a cushion pillow shaped like a woman's legs wearing a mini-skirt. It was created by Makoto Igarashib, in Tokyo, Japan, and you can lay your head down on it for maternal feelings.

2599.   When General Motors revealed the Camaro name in 1966, Automotive Press asked Chevrolet product managers what a Camaro was. The answer was: "it's a small vicious animal that eats mustangs."

2600.   There is an unnamed species of octopus that is so cute that scientists are pushing to have it named "Opisthoteuthis adorabilis."

2601. In 1997, a man in Frankfurt, Germany, went to the police to report his car stolen. Twenty years later, the car was tracked down by the police, finding out that the man just forgot where he parked it, and he just assumed it was stolen.

2602. After the incident where a shoe was thrown by a journalist at George W. Bush during his last visit to Iraq, the town of Tikrit in Iraq erected a six foot (two meter tall) monument to the shoe.

2603. In Scotland, there is an island called "The Island of Discussion" where, historically, those with different arguments and points of view were sent. They would take with them cheese and whiskey to sort out their problems and couldn't leave until they came to a mutual agreement on the subject.

2604. As of 2018, there are 328 girls in the United States with the name ABCDE according to Vocative.

2605. The Dulle Griet is a bar in Belgium that requires customers to give the bar one of their shoes if they want to drink any of their house beer; the reason behind this is to avoid tourists from stealing their beer glasses. The shoes are then placed in a basket and raised up to the ceiling, which has now become a popular attraction.

2606. In 2004, Barbie and Ken broke up after being together since 1961.

2607. In 2005, comedian Tim FitzHigham rode across the English Channel in a copper bathtub for charity, setting a world record as the first bathtub crosser of the English Channel.

2608. In Australia, there is a cave called "Well It Wasn't There Last Year Cave."

2609. The fear of long words is called "hippopotomonstrosesquippedaliophobia."

2610. In order to pass the height requirements of 5'8" (1.76 meters), sumo wrestlers in Japan used to get silicone implants on top of their heads.

2611. One of the oldest jokes in recorded history was found from 1900 B.C., in ancient Sumeria. The joke translates to: "Here's something that has never happened from the beginning of time; a young wife farting in her husband's lap."

2612. Ferret-legging used to be a sport in the past, where a ferret was strapped in a contestant's pants, without wearing any underwear. The competitor who could stand the teeth and claws the longest would win.

2613. In 1989, on April Fools' Day, Richard Branson created a hot air balloon to look like a UFO and hired a dwarf to wear an ET costume and scare anyone who came near it.

2614. A woman once took part in a search for a missing tourist in Iceland. Hours later she realized she was the missing person everyone was searching for.

2615. 50,000 people signed a 2015 petition to drop the name Australian Dollar, and to adopt "Dollarydoo" as the official name of Australia's currency. The term Dollarydoo originates from an episode of the Simpsons.

2616. A man in China once spent forty thousand dollars in 2014 to buy out all the seats in two IMAX theaters because an ex-girlfriend from seven years earlier dumped him for not being able to afford movie tickets.

2617. In Japan, it's possible to buy a fan just for your armpits. The cooling device was developed by gadget-maker named "Thanko." It's a small fan that clips onto your sleeve to deliver cool air to your armpits for five to nine hours. Although it's a battery-run device, you can also connect it to your PC or a battery pack.

2618. In 1945, during President Andrew Jackson's funeral, his pet parrot was kicked out for cursing.

2619. As a Halloween prank, a Burger King franchise in Queens, New York, covered their building with a huge, white drape, turning itself into a ghost version of a McDonald's. The marquis on the front read: "Boo! Just kidding, we still flame grill our burgers. Happy Halloween!"

2620. In order to prevent your flatulence from smelling, it's possible to buy flatulence deodorizer pads. They are worn in your underwear.

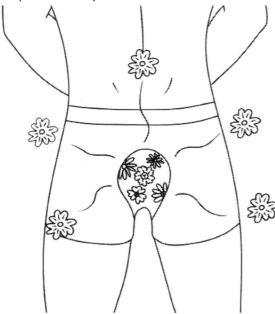

2621. One of Jennifer Lopez's nicknames in China translates to "Lord of Butt."

2622. Since the 1970's, Petaluma in California has been holding a world's ugliest dog contest. It's actually extremely competitive and the title is a fiercely desired one.

2623. At Super Smash Bros, poor personal hygiene and body odor were such big problems that they started to disqualify tournament participants if they stank. They went so far as to distribute deodorant to the contestants.

2624. "Goat Song" is the classical Greek term for the word "tragedy." Scholars believe that the main prize in competitions of dancing or singing during that time was a goat.

2625. There's an island called "Just Enough Room" on the Saint Lawrence River between Canada and the US, where there's literally just enough room for

a tree and a house.

2626. A woman named Alice Pick once attempted to use a million dollar bill for a purchase that came to $1,600 in Walmart. She expected to receive all of the change too.

2627. Anthony Victor has the longest ear hair ever, according to Guinness World Records, measuring over seven inches (seventeen centimeters) at its longest point.

2628. On January 1, 1976, a law that relaxed the use of marijuana came into effect in California. Art student Danny Finegood and some of his classmates from Cal State Northridge took $50 worth of fabric to the Hollywood sign and changed it to read Hollyweed. They used the joke as a school project, earning them an A.

2629. There is a photo series created by photographer Chompoo Baritone that exposes the truth of pictures. He mocks Instagram users who prop and filter their lives to make them seem more amazing than they really are.

History & Culture

2630. Vice President Andrew Johnson took his vice presidential oath while completely drunk. During the previous weeks, he had been suffering from typhoid fever, so he took three glasses of medicinal whiskey as a way to prepare himself. He rambled on in a drunken stupor for seventeen minutes.

2631. In 1896, a British man named Walter Arnold was given the world's first speeding ticket for driving four times the speeding limit. Arnold was going eight miles (twelve kilometers) per hour in a two mile (three kilometer) per hour zone; he was caught by a policeman on a bicycle, and was fined one shilling, which was about eight US cents.

2632. Different cultures across the world used to practice cranial deformation, and the practice is older than written history. The earliest record of a cranial deformation process was written by Greek physician Hippocrates, who is regarded as the father of medicine.

2633. Many people were baptizing their children using beer in place of water during the thirteenth century, and it became such a problem that Pope Gregory IX had to issue a decree stating that baptisms that were conducted this way were invalid.

2634. A number of European governments looked into plans to drain the Mediterranean Sea and construct several dams in the 1920's. This would have created important farmland and it would have resulted in a new continent called Atlantropa. The plan was set aside, even though it had become quite popular.

2635. Louis Antoine ascended to the French throne as king during the French Revolution in 1830, after King Charles X, his father, abdicated. But after being king for a mere twenty minutes, Antoine renounced the throne too.

2636. Twenty seven commoners occasionally evacuated the whole city in ancient Rome, leaving the elites to care for themselves, in what was called the "Cessation of the Plebs."

2637. Adolph Hitler tried to seize power in Munich, but he failed and, in 1924, he was imprisoned in Bavaria, Germany, at Landsberg Fortress. While there, the future dictator was so broke, that he once wrote a letter to a Mercedes-Benz dealership owner called Jakob Werlin, begging for a loan so he could purchase a limousine that he desired.

2638. When Harry S. Truman, the President of America, went to Disneyland in 1957, he humbly declined a ride on Dumbo the Flying Elephant that was offered to him. Truman was a democrat his entire life, so he didn't want to be seen riding an elephant, which is the Republican Party symbol.

2639. Next to the statue of liberty, there is a broken chain and shackle hidden by the statue's robes, and it symbolizes the abolition of slavery.

2640. During a White House dinner party in 1933, Amelia Earhart and First Lady Eleanor Roosevelt snuck out right after the main course, and they spontaneously flew a plane over Washington D.C., before coming back for dessert.

2641. In the 1950's, the American Federal Government asked the Greenbrier Hotel in West Virginia to construct a top secret underground bunker where congress would meet in the event of a nuclear war. It was code named "Project Green Island," and it was built between 1959 and 1962. It remained secret for years, until 1992, when the Washington Post learned of it and reported about it. It was in White Sulphur Springs, West Virginia.

2642. The first Roman fire brigade consisted of 500 men and it was created by Marcus Licinius Crassus. The brigade would show up at a burning building and start haggling with the property owner over the price of their services. If Crassus didn't get a high enough payment offer, he would literally let the building burn to the ground, then he would ask the owner to let him buy it for a fraction of its original value.

2643. In 1989, an old painting was bought at a flea market in Adamstown, Pennsylvania, by a Philadelphia financial analyst; he bought it for four dollars just because he liked the frame. However, an original Declaration of Independence was found hidden behind, which went on to sell at auction for $2.42 million.

2644. The only president who did not reside in the White House was George Washington, despite being the one who actually chose the site for the presidential residence.

2645. In ancient Egypt, men used to take breaks from work to take care of their menstruating daughters and wives.

2646. On January 21, 1977, in his first day at duty, President Jimmy Carter fulfilled a campaign promise by granting unconditional pardons to several men who had evaded the draft during the Vietnam War by fleeing the country or failing to register.

2647. In 1962, Crayola voluntarily changed the name of the flesh-colored crayon to peach, partially as a result of the US Civil Rights Movement.

2648. Archaeologists found a ring inside a viking grave in the 1800's in Sweden that had "For Allah" engraved on it, showing there was linked trade between the Islamic world and the Swedish Vikings from over a thousand years ago.

2649. In ancient Egypt, people used to be paid for their services in bread and beer, as well as in grain, meat and cloth rations, which were considered the necessities of life. Bread and beer, however, were the most basic items of the Egyptian diet.

2650. The stop sign actually started in Detroit, Michigan, back in 1915. It was originally black lettering on a white background. It then changed to black lettering on a yellow background before it was finally red and white.

2651. The very last time that someone was executed by a guillotine was on September 10, 1977.

2652. Thomas Edison used Morse code to propose to his second wife Mina Miller Edison.

2653. Theodore Roosevelt was an avid reader. He was known to read on average a book a day while he was president. He habitually read several books at a time, rotating between them depending on his mood.

2654. On March 17, 1762, the first Saint Patrick's Day parade was held in New York.

2655. Before President Lincoln became a politician or even a lawyer, he partly owned a tavern in New Salem, Illinois. This makes him the only American president who was a licensed bartender.

2656. The 1865 version of America's twenty dollar bill featured an artistic impression of famous Native American woman Pocahontas, during her baptism. She was depicted kneeling before a priest, as settlers and Native Americans looked on at opposite sides.

2657. University of Arizona researchers have discovered subtle alterations in Ronald Regan's manner of speaking that indicated that his mental state was in decline years before his Alzheimer's diagnosis.

2658. Early humans used hunting techniques that were similar to those used by hyenas, wolves, and spiders. It involved tracking fast-moving prey over long distances, and it's known as persistence hunting. Humans were partly protected from heat because they could sweat, and this enabled them to endure long runs. That way, they wore down the prey before catching and killing it.

2659. Minnesota joined the union and became a state in 1858, but the University of Minnesota was established in 1851, meaning that the University was established long before the state.

2660. When the young George Washington ran for the Virginia House of Burgesses in 1758, he used his whole campaign budget to purchase 160 gallons (605 liters) of alcohol, which he served to the 391 guests who showed up.

2661. Nelson Mandela was actually an amateur boxer. He used to train at the Donaldson Orlando Community Center gym in Johannesburg. More than the violence of the sport, he enjoyed the science behind it.

2662. The former Soveit leader Mikhail Gorbachev's wife created a recipe book on how to cook potatoes. It was gifted to Britain and now sits in the British foreign office.

2663. In ancient China, small feet represented the height of female refinement. As a result, there used to be a practice where girls would have their toes and arches broken, tied, and bound underneath their feet before the arch of the foot could develop. This way their feet could fit into tiny little shoes.

2664. On Valentine's Day of 1884, Theodore Roosevelt's mother and first wife both died. His mother died of typhoid fever and, twelve hours later, his wife died from Bright's disease and complications from giving birth to the couple's first child two days before.

2665. The sister ship of the Titanic, the Olympic, offered to take in the survivors when the Titanic sank. The Captain of the Titanic rejected the offer however, as he was afraid that this would cause a panic among the survivors seeing a virtual mirror image of the ship that had just sank, asking them to come on board.

2666. At the National Museum of Health and Medicine in Silver Spring, Maryland, there are fragments of President Lincoln's skull that can be seen today on display next to the bullet that killed him.

2667. From the 16th century up until the 1960's, Egyptian mummies were actually ground up and used to produce a brown paint color called Mummy Brown. The powder was mixed with white pitch and myrrh to make a rich brown pigment.

2668. The first housewarming parties were literally held to warm houses and send the spirits away. All guests would bring over pieces of wood and they would light fires in every fireplace in the new home. There was a belief that empty houses would attract spirits and ghosts, so when people would move in, they would warm the house to send the spirits away.

2669. In the past, the main purpose of marriage was to procreate, so Romans used to shower the new bride with fertility symbols like wheat grain. This wheat used to be baked into small cakes to be eaten in a tradition known as con-fer-ee-a-tee-o, meaning eating together. The guests of the ceremony used to throw handfuls of honey-eyed nuts and dried fruits called confetto, which gave birth to the tradition of throwing confetti at weddings.

2670.	Wrongful Conviction Day is celebrated every year on October 2. The day was actually launched by the Association of Defense of the Wrongfully Convicted to bring awareness to people who have been convicted of crimes that they didn't commit.

2671.	When Genghis Khan died, his successors killed anyone who witnessed his funeral procession in order to keep his burial place a secret. About 800 soldiers were massacred as well as 2,000 other people. The location of his tomb is still unknown to this day.

2672.	Back in 1938, when minimum wage first became mandatory in the US, it was twenty five cents an hour. If adjusted for inflation, it would be $4.31 cents an hour today.

2673.	Mahatma Gandhi never won the Nobel Peace Prize. He was nominated five times between 1937 and 1948 and was one of the most powerful symbols for nonviolence in the world as well as one of the most respected.

2674.	The Russian communist revolutionary Vladmir Lenin was put on display in the Red Square of Moscow after his death against his wishes, which were to be buried next to his wife.

2675.	There was a calendar made during the French Revolution known as the "French Republican Calendar" that had 100 seconds in a minute, ten hours in a day, ten weeks in a month, and twelve months in a year.

2676.	In a village in Groningen, the Netherlands, there is a large fort in the shape of a star. It was built in 1593 with the intention to control the only road between Germany and the city of Groningen, which was controlled by the Spaniards during the time of the Eighty Years War.

2677.	The first ever decree about human rights was issued by Persian King Cyrus the Great in 539 B.C. The decree established to free the slaves, declared that all people had the right to choose their own religion, and established racial equality.

2678.	The expression "paying through the nose" comes from Vikings times. It used to be a Viking punishment for those who refused to pay taxes which consisted of slitting the nose from tip to eyebrow.

2679.	On June 1, 1923, Canada approved the Chinese Exclusion Act, which lasted until 1947. The law stopped Chinese immigration to Canada for almost a quarter of a century.

2680.	Mushrooms were considered the plant of immortality by ancient Egyptians. In fact, mushrooms were decreed food for royalty by the Pharaohs of Egypt, so no commoner could even touch them.

2681.	The best man has that name because historically they were the best with their sword. This was so he would be in close proximity if the bride tried to escape or if the family attempted to stop the wedding.

2682.	People used to use moist bread to erase pencil marks before the invention of rubber erasers by Edward Nairne, in 1770. In fact, the invention was discovered by accident by Edward thinking that he had grabbed bread.

2683.	The swastika symbol was actually used by many other cultures throughout the past 3,000 years before the Nazis used it. It has represented life, Sun, power, strength, and good luck.

2684.	15th century Romanian Vlad the Impaler, the cruel warlord who helped inspire Bram Stoker's 1897 vampire novel "Dracula," is actually one of Prince Charles' ancestors.

2685.	People with dwarfism in ancient Egypt were regarded to have special powers, were treated like Gods, and given the highest social positions.

2686.	In ancient Rome, women used to dye their hair blonde with pigeon dung. In Renaissance Venice, they used to dye it with horse urine.

2687.	Since 720 B.C., the Chinese have recorded solar eclipse sightings.

2688.   In ancient times, Egyptians would treat toothaches by putting dead mice into the mouths of people. They also used to mash up dead mouse paste with other ingredients to treat patients with pain.

2689.   Bending trees intentionally used to be a way to mark trails by Native American people. Some trees still remain today as hidden monuments.

2690.   Back in 1976, pinball machines were actually banned in New York City.

2691.   About 35,000 year ago, the first ever sewing needles were made of bone by early humans. It's thought that bone needles were preferred over metal as a sewing tool because metal tended to rust and stain the fabric that it was used on.

2692.   Cinnamon was an ingredient used in embalming in ancient Egypt, as it preserved the dead.

2693.   Ancient warriors used to use the monkshood plant to poison the water of their enemies. In addition, it was used as a popular werewolf detection tool; the flower was held under the alleged werewolf's chin, and if a yellow-tinged shadow appeared, that meant that that person was a werewolf.

2694.   Gobekli Tepe is thought to be the world's oldest temple. Located in Turkey, it was built 6,000 years before Stonehenge, even before the invention of the wheel.

2695.   In ancient China, seeing a spider dropping down from its web was a sign of good luck, even luckier if it was a white spider. People believed that they would be blessed with gifts and good luck from heaven.

2696.   For thousands of years the Mayans have cultivated Central American stingless bees, even keeping them as pets around their home. Some of the hives have been recorded to last over eighty years, being passed down from generation to generation.

2697.   The children's ring game known as "Ring around the Rosie" makes reference to the Great Plague of London, back in 1665. It refers to the rosy red rash in the shape of a ring that someone with the plague would develop. The pocket full of posie refers to the fact that people filled their pockets and pouches with sweet-smelling herbs or posies, as it was believed that the disease was transmitted via bad smells. And the ashes refer to the cremation of the dead bodies.

2698.   In honor of Roman dictator Julius Caesar, the month of July was named after him. He actually helped develop the Julian calendar, which is the precursor to the Gregorian calendar that we use today.

2699.   The largest prehistoric man-made mound in Europe is found in Silbury Hill, near Avebury in Wiltshire, England. It stands 130 feet (thirty nine meters) high and its purpose is still unknown.

2700.   In ancient Egypt, if a cat would pass away, the members of the family would shave their eyebrows off in mourning.

2701.   The oldest acting parliament in the world is the parliament of Iceland, which was founded back in 930 AD. Political gatherings typically lasted for two weeks, during the month of June, which was a period of continuous daylight and nice weather.

2702.   In the Satere-Mawe Indian culture, there is an initiation ritual for thirteen year old boys that consists of making them wear gloves made of bullet ants for ten minutes. Although they are repeatedly bitten, which is incredibly painful, they must not cry out if they want to be declared a man.

2703. Cobwebs actually have antifungal and antiseptic properties that keep bacteria away and minimize the chance of infection. In fact, the Greeks and Romans would use cobwebs to treat cuts in ancient times. Soldiers also used them to heal wounds, combining honey and vinegar to clean the lesions, and then covering them with balled-up spider webs.

2704. During the mummification process, ancient Egyptians sometimes used lichen and onions to fill the body's cavities and often reused that as fake eyes.

2705. The game hopscotch has its origin in ancient Britain, during the Roman Empire. The original courts were ninety eight feet (thirty meters) long and were used for military exercising. Soldiers used to run in full armor and field packs to improve their footwork. Later on, Roman children drew their own, smaller courts and added a scoring system; and thus, hopscotch was born and spread throughout Europe.

2706. In 2010, the University of Tubingen in Germany discovered that King Tut the Pharaoh was actually very frail and had bone disease and malaria. They believe this might have been due to incest.

2707. When the Great Pyramid of Cheops was under construction in ancient Egypt around 1580 B.C., the first ever documented workers strike occured when the workers did not get their daily ration of garlic. They were given garlic to improve their health and increase their stamina, and when their rations weren't distributed, they stopped working.

2708. Oxford University is such an old institution that it existed 200 years before the Aztec Empire was formed. The school was operational in 1096 A.D., while it wasn't until 1325 A.D. that the Aztec civilization began.

2709. A seal discovered in a Sumerian tomb that dates back to 3000 B.C. depicts the earliest evidence of the use of drinking straws. It has an image of two guys drinking beer through what looks like primitive straws.

2710. Lots of Buddhist monks practiced self-mummification for centuries. They'd only consume nuts, seeds or fruits they'd gathered from nearby mountains and forests, along with water, and they'd lock themselves in small tombs that had breathing tubes and bells. If a day passed without the monk ringing the bell, the others assumed he was dead, then they'd take out the breathing tube and seal the tomb for 1,000 days so the body could mummify.

2711. The US received a birthday card from Poland in 1926, and more than five million people had signed it.

2712. The Great Fire of London left more than 70,000 people homeless after destroying more than 13,300 buildings in 1666. Despite all the destruction, only six deaths were verified in official records.

2713. Roman emperor Gallienus discovered that a jewel dealer had sold fake gems to his wife, so he had him arrested and thrown into an empty arena. He let the man stay there nervously listening to the roaring sounds of hungry lions, waiting to be torn to pieces. When the cage doors finally opened, instead of a vicious lion, a little chicken walked out. A herald then declared that the man had practiced deceit, and in turn he had had deceit practiced on him.

2714.   Having bridesmaids in a wedding was originally intended to confuse evil spirits or those who wished harm on the bride.

2715.   As far back as 200 B.C., the Han Dynasty of China drilled for natural gas, transported it in pipelines and gas containers, and burned it on stoves, even though natural gas only became commonly used in the 1800's.

2716.   In the past, the toga was only allowed to be worn by free Roman citizens. Foreigners and exiled citizens could not appear in public wearing one.

2717.   There was a medieval belief that crocodiles shed tears of sadness while they killed and consumed their prey. From this myth, which dates back as far as the 14th century, the term "crocodile tears" actually derived. The belief started from a book called "The Travels of Sir John Mandeville" and later on, it was found in the works of Shakespeare. From there, crocodile tears became an idiom as early as the 16th century.

2718.   Napoleon Bonaparte, the Emperor of the French in 1804, was buried without his penis as it was cut off during autopsy and given to a priest.

2719.   Before Saladin, the first Sultan of Egypt, died in 1193, he had given all of his fortune to the poor, so by the time he died, his final wealth consisted only of a single piece of gold and forty pieces of silver, not even enough to pay for the funeral.

2720.   "Enbrotherment" was a legal classification in the Middle Ages where two men were allowed to pool their resources, move in together, and basically live like a real married couple.

2721.   In the eleventh century, Vikings sailed to North America and settled there. They fished for salmon, built canoes using animal hides, and even planted wild grapes.

2722.   The Orkney Viking ruler, Jarl Sigurd the Mighty, died in 892 A.D. after he was bitten by a man he had decapitated in battle. Sigurd beheaded the man, and then mounted his head on his horse, and as he was riding off, the teeth in the head scratched his leg. It created a wound that became septic, and eventually caused his death.

2723.   In a Spanish cave in 2013, scientists discovered fossilized remains of a fractured human skull. To their astonishment, the skull belonged to a murdered young adult that lived there 43,000 years before. They think it might be the first ever murder case.

2724.   The first street in the world to be lit by gas lights was Pall Mall, in 1807, in London. The street still exists today, but modern lamp posts are used in place of gas lights.

2725.   Back in the eighteenth century, they used to charge three half-pence to admit visitors into the London Zoo. However, those who didn't have the money could be let in if they brought a dog or a cat as food for the lions.

2726.   During the 1500's and 1600's, women who were seen gossiping, riotous, or troublesome were made to wear the scold's bridle, also known as branks, as punishment. It was made of an iron frame that encased the head, and at the front was a bridle or bit, like a horse, that extended into the mouth and held down the tongue with a spiked plate. It literally made it impossible to speak, and was basically a muzzle for a woman.

2727.   Even though we associate Cleopatra with the Egyptian Great Pyramid, the fact is that she lived during times that were closer to the invention of smartphones than the construction of those gigantic ancient wonders of the world. Wooly mammoths were still walking around at the time when the Great Pyramid was finished.

2728.   Archeologists found what they think are the oldest pieces of chewing gum, at Orust Island in Sweden, in 1993. They dated back more than 9,000 years, and they were three bits of chewed birch resin.

2729.   Most gladiators were vegetarians. Their diets used to consist mainly of barley and vegetables.

2730.   During Roman times, salt used to be highly precious. It was worth its weight in gold and soldiers were sometimes paid in salt, hence the word salary.

2731. The Vikings used to find new lands by releasing ravens from their boats and following where they went. They became their favorite symbol and resulted in them using the bird on their flag.

2732. Breast bags were the name given to bras in medieval times.

2733. King Tutankhamun was not buried alone. Two miniature coffins that contained two fetuses were also found in the chamber. Recent DNA analyses suggest that one of the mummies was his stillborn daughter and the other was likely his child also, although experts believe that he left no living heirs.

2734. The longest standing alliance in the world is held between the United Kingdom and Portugal, which started in 1386.

2735. In the 1850's, to avoid people racing in their horse carriages, the pathways of the roads in Central Park were designed to be curved.

2736. The barber's pole colors of red, white, and blue are a legacy of an era when people went to barbers not just to have a haircut or shave, but also for bloodletting and other medical procedures. At that time, barbers used to cut hair, do some bloodletting, pull teeth, and even set broken bones.

2737. During the Victorian era and the early 20th century, people used to send vinegar Valentines as well as the usual Valentine's cards on Valentine's Day. Sold in the United States and Britain, the cards featured an illustration and a short verse of insults instead of love. It was a way for people to insult someone without actually doing it to their face.

2738. Russian ice slides from the 17th century were actually the inspiration for the modern rollercoaster. They were tall, wooden structures with ice frozen over a long, sloping ramp; they used to rise up over seventy nine feet (twenty-four meters) with ramps that stretched for hundreds of meters; the ice sleds were simply a block of ice with a straw mat.

2739. Notorious Roman Emperor Caligula loved his horse so much that he had a marble stall in an ivory manger. In fact, he wanted to appoint the horse to the High Office of Consul, as an expression of his absolute power, but he was killed before he could do it.

2740. Women in the Victorian era would wear hats decorated with dead birds treated with arsenic. Today, some of these hats are on display in museums and still have traces of arsenic on them.

2741. During the 18th century, British wealthy landowners would hire hermits to live on their land for aesthetic purposes. These hermits would only live on their estate and think about their existence while providing wisdom with visitors. One ad that was looking for a hermit, however, demanded that they could not talk to anyone, cut their hair, or even leave the estate.

2742. According to historian Andrew Mahain Sutherland, there was a mountain man in the 1800's named John Johnson who went by the nickname "Liver-Eating Johnson" because he ate the livers of about 300 Crow Indians. The reason he did this was to avenge the murder of his wife, who was from the Flathead

American Indian tribe. The consumption of their livers was considered an insult to the Crow because they believe that they were important for the afterlife. After making peace with the tribe eventually, John died at the age of seventy five in Santa Monica, California in 1900.

2743. March 1 was designated as the New Year in the early Roman calendar. It had ten months, which is still reflected in some of the names of the months. For example, September through to December, our ninth through to twelfth months, were originally positioned as the seventh through tenth months. Septum is Latin for seven, Octo is eight, Novem is nine, and Decem is ten.

2744. Victor Lustig, a maverick con man, sold the Eiffel Tower for scrap in 1925 to a metal buyer who gave him a large bribe in cash, thinking that he was a corrupt French government official. The buyer discovered he was scammed when he went to claim the Paris landmark, but by then, Lustig had run away to Austria.

2745. There were so many lobsters when the first European settlers reached North America that they washed ashore in piles up to twenty four inches (sixty one centimeters high).

2746. According to scientists, Ramses II, the ancient Egyptian Pharaoh, lived to be either ninety two or ninety six years old, outliving many of his older sons. Through CT scans, scientists also found that Ramses II had red hair, as well as arthritis in his hip, and gum disease.

2747. The popular saying "bless you" after a sneeze originated from the 14th century, when Pope Gregory the VII asked for it to be said after every time he sneezed so he could be protected against the plague.

2748. In the 1700's, coins were actually made of real gold and silver, so often criminals would shave down the sides of the coins and sell the shavings. Consequently, the US Mint began adding ridges to the coins, a process called reeding, to make it impossible to shave down without being detected, while also making counterfeiting more difficult. Today, no coins are made from precious metals, but the tradition has continued on coins of higher value. The reeding also helps the visually impaired to tell the difference between coins.

2749. In ancient Sparta, there was a training program called "Agoge" that was mandatory for all male citizens, except for the firstborns of the ruling houses. Some of the training consisted of being underfed to encourage stealing; if the students were caught however, they would be punished. The reason behind this was that their master wanted them to become fit soldiers, not fat ones.

2750. There is a sealed wine bottle that dates back to between 325 and 350 A.D., during the ancient Roman period, called the "Speyer." It was found when archeologists were excavating a fourth-century nobleman's tomb. It is considered the oldest-known bottle of wine in the world.

2751. In 1620, the colonists aboard the Mayflower decided to settle at Plymouth after sixty four days at sea because they ran out of beer on the ship. Their beer was a relatively low alcoholic formula and was drunk because it was boiled purer than regular water.

2752. In the 1800's, one of the first ever iron maidens was found in a castle in Nuremberg, Germany. It is a device of torture where the person is put inside a sarcophagus with spikes on the inner surface. When the doors were closed, the spikes would puncture several organs, including their eyes, but not deep enough to kill them, just deep enough that they would bleed to death over several hours.

2753. In 1974, when transporting the mummified remains of Ramses II, an Egyptian passport was issued, which listed his occupation as "king deceased."

2754. Dog saliva was considered to be medicinal by the ancient Mesopotamians. They documented that when a dog licked their wounds, the recovery process was faster.

2755. In order to ward off evil spirits, ancient Egyptians would rim their eyes with kohl, a mixture of lead, copper, burned almonds, and soot.

2756. Around 300 B.C., turkeys were a symbol of power to the ancient Mayans, so they used to worship them like gods. They believed that they had supernatural abilities; as a result, they were exclusively owned by the most rich and powerful people.

2757. In 2014, the earliest evidence of human footprints was discovered by scientists outside of Africa, on the Norfolk coast in the east of England. The footprints were found on the shores of Happisburgh and were more than 800,000 years old.

2758. In Bolivia, there is a limestone wall that has over 5,000 dinosaur footprints, some of them dating back nearly sixty eight million years.

2759. The Incas used to measure their units of time based on the time a potato would take to be cooked.

2760. Between 1347 and 1350, approximately twenty million people were killed in Europe by the Bubonic Plague, also known as the Black Death. That was close to the 30% of the continent's population at the time.

2761. The Maya and other ancient peoples of southern North America used to go to dentists to decorate their teeth with notches, grooves, and semi-precious stones like jade.

2762. To cool wine down, ancient Egyptian pharaohs used to make slaves fan it all night.

2763. In Medieval England, before the Black Death, women were the ones who originally brewed the majority of the ale. Women in brewing are also found to date back to ancient Mesopotamia. Some of the titles given to them were alewife and brewster.

2764. Discovered in the 1920's, the Nazca Lines are ancient geoglyphs found in southern Peru that span over 321.6 square miles (518 square kilometers). They have more than 800 straight lines, 300 geometric figures, and seventy animal and plant designs, which are only appreciated in full from air.

2765. In ancient Greece, a truce was called during the Olympics so that athletes and spectators could travel safely. No wars were permitted and no arms could be carried. Initially, the truce would last one month; but in later centuries, it was extended to three.

2766. In 2016, the oldest human fingerprint was discovered by a team of archeologists in northern Kuwait. The 7,300-year-old human fingerprint was found on a piece of broken clay pot, dating to the Stone Age, that is, 8,700 B.C. to 2,000 B.C.

2767. The first century A.D. Greek tune Seikilos Epitaph is the oldest musical composition to have survived in its entirety. The song was found in Turkey engraved on an ancient marble column, and it was used to mark women's grave sites.

2768. Bagpipes are commonly identified with Scotland, however, they were actually introduced to the British Isles by the Romans.

2769. Scipio Africanus was a Roman soldier who survived battles at Ticinus, Cannae, and Trasimene, all of which his country lost. He, however, ended up leading the Roman army as a general, and he defeated Hannibal, one of history's greatest military commanders.

2770. The oldest continuously used national flag, according to the Guinness World Records, is the Dannebrog or Danish cloth, the flag for Denmark, which has been in use since the 1370's.

2771. The earliest case of hearing loss documented in writing is thought to be from ancient Egypt in 1550 B.C. In that era, people injected red lead, goat urine, olive oil, bat wings and ant eggs in the ear canal in an attempt to cure bad hearing.

2772. The New Year was celebrated between March 25 and April 1 by the French. In 1564, after the introduction of the new Gregorian calendar, the festivity was moved to January 1. Some people however resisted the change and became victims of pranks, including invitations to non-existent New Year's parties on April 1. This is why we celebrate April Fools Day on April 1st.

2773. The pyramids of Giza were more ancient to the ancient Romans than Rome is ancient to us.

Human Body & Human Behavior

2774.   There is a condition called argyria that turns a person's skin a bright blue in color and it's caused by chronic exposure to silver. A man named Paul Karason from California developed this by using a special silver-based preparation to treat a skin condition and drinking colloidal silver, a product that consists of silver particles suspended in liquid.

2775.   The most common eye color in the world is brown. More than 55% of people worldwide have brown eyes and almost all people from Africa and Asia have brown eyes.

2776.   Laron syndrome is a genetic disease that causes short stature growing, long life expectancy, and near immunity to cancer and diabetes, among others.

2777.   The experiences that you have throughout your life leave chemical markers on your DNA; these markers basically ingraine superficial experiences into your offspring.

2778.   There is a health condition called geographic tongue, which is actually a map-like feature across your tongue and, in some cases, the entire mouth.

2779.   One effect of alcohol abuse is alcohol myopia, a condition where drunk people for the most part only respond to their immediate environment, and they lack the ability to consider the future repercussions of their actions.

2780.   Even though it can be infuriating to listen to someone who's always sarcastic, research shows that when we hear such witty and sly comments, they can really improve our creative and analytical thinking.

2781.   Babies already have a great sense of taste when they are born, and it might be better than the one adults have, but they are unable to taste salt until they are roughly four months old.

2782.   Millions around the world claim to have photographic memories, but in reality, there's no scientific proof that it even exists in adult human beings.

2783.   The irrational fear of colors is called chromophobia. In serious cases, the condition can affect one's daily activities and limit their lives.

2784.   Hair can grow on any surface on the human body, with the exceptions of the lips, mucus membranes, soles of the feet, and palms of the hand.

2785. The red appearance of blood is the result of how iron interacts with oxygen. Each hemoglobin blood protein has subunits called hemes which bind with iron molecules that in turn bind with oxygen. Oxygenated iron turns red, and deoxygenated iron turns dark red.

2786. When you get goosebumps and start to shiver, that sensation is an emotional response that's known as frisson.

2787. Men tend to suffer the most when having a breakup. In a study that involved 5,705 participants from ninety six countries, it was found that while women experience intense pain immediately after a breakup, they can get over it quickly. On the contrary, men move on quickly, but they remain damaged for longer.

2788. A "gut feeling" can be actually interpreted as a chemical signal that your stomach creates to warn your brain of danger.

2789. People who are afraid to sleep or fall asleep have a disorder called somniphobia. Somniphobia is closely linked to fear of the unknown because such people are mostly afraid of what might happen should they fall asleep.

2790. It's not 100% true that blind people see nothing at all. According to studies, only about 10-15% of blind people see nothing at all.

2791. Based on a study performed by Andreas Keller at Rockefeller University, the average person can tell the difference between 1.7 trillion different smells, with combinations of thirty ingredients.

2792. Human eyeballs are always the same size from the moment of birth, but our nose and ears never stop growing.

2793. Studies have shown that the exposure to stress for long periods can permanently destroy neurons in the brain, which affects learning, impulse control, reasoning, and memory. In other words, stress literally kills your brain.

2794. Humans are most sensitive to the color green, and can differentiate between more shades of green than any other color. This is the reason why you see green in night vision goggles.

2795. Eyebrows renew themselves every sixty four days.

2796. A study published in the Journal of Hand Therapy revealed that millennials, particularly boys, have weaker muscles in their hands from all the texting, snapping, scrolling, and gaming that they do. The advantage, however, is that they have stronger thumbs.

2797. There are many benefits to having a beard such as preventing asthma attack, protection from the sun and even slowing the aging process.

2798. It takes forty three muscles to frown but only seventeen to smile.

2799. The clavicle, also known as the collarbone, is the most commonly broken bone.

2800. Around 10% of the world population has outie belly buttons.

2801. Boanthropy is a real psychological disorder that affects individuals who believe that they are cows, or other types of bovines.

2802. People with multiple personality disorder, technically known as dissociative identity disorder, can change from one consciousness to another with drastically different physiological tendencies. They can experience changes in pulse rate, blood pressure, and the amount of blood pumped to the brain. There are cases where the alternate personality sees quite well, even though the main personality needs prescription glasses.

2803. Newborns are able to see almost immediately, although their vision is fuzzy and blurry. They also have excess folded skin at the inner corners of their eyes, which makes most of them cross-eyed. The excess skin disappears within the first three months.

2804. Humans weigh 154 pounds (seventy kilos) on average, and more than 0.000007 ounces (0.2 milligrams) of that is pure gold.

2805. Research has shown that men who take a lot of selfies are more likely to show higher levels of narcissism.

2806. Your respiratory and cardiovascular systems can sync to musical tempos according to research conducted in 2009 at University of Pavia, Italy. In theory, this means music can be a potential therapy for people with stroke and other conditions.

2807. Researchers in Canada have learned that dopamine is released into our system when we listen to music and we feel a strong emotional connection with a particular song. That explains why we might get goosebumps when we hear a song that we really love.

2808. Several studies have shown that being called "baby" has a positive effect on the female brain. The theoretical explanation is that, on a subconscious level, it feels nice to know that if you choose to act like a baby, you have someone who's willing to support you.

2809. The Moken people can see clearly underwater because they have adapted to control pupil dilation in places with inadequate light. They develop this special ability in childhood.

2810. Distichiasis is a very rare condition where sufferers have two layers of eyelashes. They can actually be painful and should be removed. Unfortunately, even via electrolysis, they will likely grow back.

2811. There was a skeleton body found in 2015 in a Chilean ghost town that was only fifteen centimeters long. Scientists classified it as an actual human body that had the development of a child who was six to eight years old.

2812. A study done between October, 2013, and February, 2014, by UBC researchers concluded that people who are narcissistic, psychopathic, or have machiavellian tendencies are less convincing online than they are in person. That's because once the non-verbal cues are removed, it's much easier to spot someone with these characteristics.

2813. The Journal of Neuroscience found in 2014 that brain patterns synchronize together when people have conversations. This is because our brains are constantly trying to predict what the person is going to say next.

2814. Kissing someone for the first time causes a spike in dopamine making you crave more, while at the same time, endorphins are released making you feel a wave of euphoria.

2815. People can actually develop tonsil stones. When debris such as dead cells, mucus, or bacteria, gets trapped in the nooks and crannies of the tonsils, it can harden or calcify into stones. Those people who suffer from chronic inflammation in their tonsils or repeated bouts of tonsillitis are more likely to develop the stones.

2816. The purlicue is the term given to the space between your thumb and your extended forefinger.

2817. On average, a person yawns approximately 250,000 times over the course of their life. Even babies in the womb do it as early as twelve to fourteen weeks.

2818. Based on research done at King's College, London, teenagers who have acne will also have a longer young-look than those who have clear skin.

2819. Synesthesia is a neurological condition in which two or more senses are attached. Among the different types of synesthesia, there is one that is called mirror touch where people with it feel exactly what others feel as pain and pleasure.

2820. More nerve receptors are found in women than in men, causing them to feel pain in a more intense way. However, they also have a higher tolerance for it.

2821. According to different studies from the University of Chicago, lonely people spend more time in their beds regardless of whether they're tired or not. Chronic loneliness can cause insomnia, as well as the need to get in bed without feeling tired.

2822. When you are hungry, the growling noises that your stomach makes are caused by the muscular activity in the walls of your stomach and small intestines. There are contractions in the stomach that break down ingested foods and move gas, causing vibrations that end as the growling sound.

2823. Studies have shown that Alzheimer's disease does not affect emotional memory as strongly as informational memory. If bad news is given to Alzheimer's patients, they will quickly forget the news, but will remain sad without knowing why.

2824. Earwax isn't actually wax. It is mostly shedded layers of skin consisting of about 60% keratin, 12% to 20% saturated and unsaturated long chain fatty acids, squalene, alcohols, and between 6% to 9% cholesterol. The technical term for earwax is cerumen.

2825. Intergluteal cleft is the medical term for your butt crack. It's also known as the natal cleft and the vertical gluteal crease.

2826. In 2014, a study was conducted that found that there is a correlation between shrinkage of the brain and sleep deprivation. It's unknown which causes which however.

2827. In 2015, the life expectancy of Americans declined for the first time since 1993 by 0.1 years to 78.8. Life expectancy in the United States is actually lower than other developed countries like Canada, France, and Germany.

2828. In the morning you are up to 0.8 inches (two centimeters) taller than at night; this is because throughout the day of walking and standing, the cartilage in your spine gets compressed.

2829. Pandiculation is the act of stretching or stiffening your arms and legs when waking or from when you are tired.

2830. Eyelashes' growth cycle is only three months, which is why they don't grow very long. About one to five fall out daily.

2831. Based on studies done by Dr. Norman Harden, a headache expert at the North Western University, from 5% to 10% of people never experience headaches or face pain in their entire lifetime.

2832. There is an extremely rare genetic disorder called adermatoglyphia in which people are born without fingerprints. People with this condition have entirely flat finger pads and they don't have the arching or looping ridges of fingerprints as other humans do.

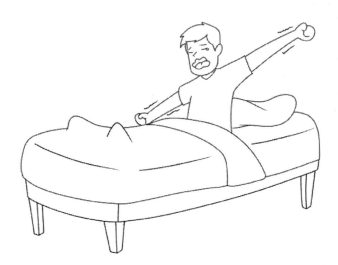

2833. Up to 0.3 gallons (1.5 liters) of liquid can be held by the human stomach at any given time. When it's fully distended, it can also hold up to 16.91 cups of food, which is about fifty times the normal volume of the stomach.

2834. While breastfeeding, the baby gives germs to the mother so her immune system can respond and synthesize antibodies that are given back to the baby.

2835. The University of Bristol conducted a study in 2013 that showed that 75% of people who have the gene ABCC11 don't produce any underarm odor.

2836. The feeling of not finding joy in things that usually bring you joy is called anhedonia.

2837. The fear of developing a phobia or anxiety about showing symptoms of a phobia is called phobophobia.

2838. Human brains are very similar to nuclear reactors in some ways. For example, they can cool down and heat up, and if your brain does overheat, you can experience a meltdown.

2839. The act of "fubbing" or "phone snubbing" is becoming a very real epidemic among Americans according to new research published in the Journal of Computers and Human Behavior. Fubbing is the act of snubbing someone in a social situation by looking down at the phone instead of paying attention to them; this behavior can affect and damage relationships, even leading to severe depression and lower rates of life satisfaction.

2840. Tears of joy are your body's way of balancing out your emotions helping equalize your body.

2841. Given that the left lung shares the same space in our chest as the heart, it is slightly smaller than the right lung.

2842. According to a study conducted by National Geographic, the urge to travel in humans is caused by the same gene responsible for ADHD and thrill-seeking behavior.

2843. Cold urticaria is the name given to a type of allergy produced by cold temperatures. It triggers hives,

swelling, and itching. When being too severe, it can actually result in fainting, shock, or even death. It has no cure.

2844. Your body paralyzes itself when you fall asleep to stop you from acting out your dreams. Sometimes, however, this doesn't happen and is known as sleep paralysis.

2845. The fish odor syndrome is a genetic disease where a person excretes an excess of a chemical called TMA in their urine, sweat, and breath, causing them to smell like rotting fish. People who suffer from this have on average two million sweat glands.

2846. When farting, the chemical compounds that we emit may vary depending on what we have eaten, and also varies from one person to another. Essentially, the typical breakdown of a fart is about 20-90% nitrogen, 0-50% hydrogen, 10-30% carbon dioxide, 0-10% oxygen, and 0-10% methane.

2847. If you have an injury to your hand or fingers resulting in nerve damage, your fingers won't wrinkle when submerged in water.

2848. Brooklyn College conducted a study which found that males are better at tracking quick moving objects while females excel at discriminating between different colors. This is due to evolutionary adaptation from our caveman days.

2849. According to the Program Coordinator of the National Institute of Health's Human Microbiome Project, our bodies have enough bacteria to fill a large soup can. That is nearly five pounds (two kilograms) of bacteria.

2850. Eating a late night snack before going to bed can cause you to have nightmares. When you eat, your metabolism is increased, so it signals the brain to become more active, which can result in scary dreams.

2851. At about nine meters underwater, your blood actually looks green because there is no red light under water, therefore, there is no red light that can bounce off of your blood into your eyes.

2852. Blowing your nose too hard, vomiting, or coughing excessively can actually cause your eyeball to pop out of its socket. It is known as exophthalmos and, if you are brave enough, you can just pop it back in.

2853. In 2013, the Stockholm University Stress Research Institute in Sweden conducted a study that tested sensitivity to sounds immediately after a few minutes of artificially induced stress. It was found that stress makes exhausted women oversensitive to sounds. Even the normal decibel levels of a conversation can sometimes seem painfully loud to them.

2854. Due to the lack of a liver enzyme, about 50% of Asians have trouble metabolizing alcohol, and as a result, they end up with a red face when they drink, sometimes known as "Asian flush."

2855. Based on studies performed at the New York University School of Medicine, the higher up you are in altitude, the higher your risk of getting sunburned, with an increase of 60%.

2856. The largest artery in the human body is the aorta. It's about the size of a garden hose.

2857. The reason why the hairs on your arms are short is because the cells that make them are programmed to stop growing every couple of months. The hair follicles on your head, on the contrary, are programmed to let your hair grow for years at a time.

2858. Based on a study conducted by a company called "Enigma" in February 2017, key brain regions are smaller in people with ADHD. These brain regions include the parts responsible for emotions, goal-directed action, learning, responding to stimuli, rewards, motivation, as well as memory.

2859. Borborygmi is the name given to the grumbling you get in your stomach. It's the result of the movement of gas within the intestines.

2860. A study done at the University of Edinburgh found out that those who smoke large amounts of cannabis in their lifetime have reduced bone density and are more prone to fractures.

2861. Feeling chills while listening to music is the result of your brain releasing dopamine, a chemical that motivates you and makes you feel good while you anticipate the peak moment in that song.

2862. Based on a study published in the Journal of Chemosensory Perception in 2012, people who scored high on a test for psychopathy had more issues for telling and identifying different smells. In other words, if you have impaired smell, there are chances you could be a psychopath.

2863. People on average blink about twelve times per minute. That's about 10,000 blinks on average per day.

2864. Every two to four weeks, our entire outer layer of skin sheds. We actually shed at a rate of about 500 million cells a day. This is the major contributor to house dust.

2865. On the average adult scalp, 115 feet (thirty five meters) of hair fiber is produced every day. On average, 90% of scalp hairs are growing while 10% are resting.

2866. Research found in a study in 2015 showed that people use more of the DNA that's passed on from their fathers than their mothers.

2867. The average lifespan of a human taste bud is seven to ten days. Human taste bud cells undergo continual turnover, even into adulthood.

2868. Rhinorrhea is the medical term for a runny nose.

2869. Humans have a gene called the "Sonic Hedgehog gene." It was first discovered in the fruit fly and is named for the spiky appearance of fruit fly larvae that have mutated versions of the gene. The name Sonic was given by British student Robert Riddle who took it from a British comic book of his daughters.

2870. Sphenopalatine ganglioneuralgia is the scientific term for brain freeze. It happens because the cold dilates arteries causing a sudden rush of blood to the brain, which raises the pressure and causes pain.

2871. There has been an increase in the life expectancy of people with Down syndrome from twenty five years in 1983 to sixty years today.

2872. Paper cuts often bleed very little or not at all and leave the skin's pain receptors open to the air, which is the reason why they hurt so much.

2873. Congenital amusia is a type of disorder where people can't recognize common songs from their culture, can't differentiate when notes are out of tune, and sometimes say that music sounds like banging to them.

2874. Aphantasia is a condition where sufferers are unable to create visualizations in their minds.

2875. The average umbilical cord measures about twenty inches (fifty centimeters).

2876. Aquagenic urticaria is a rare condition that causes sufferers to break out in hives when their skin comes in contact with water no matter its temperature. Doctors are still in doubt as to what causes it.

2877. Based on a study done by Aric Prather, assistant professor of psychiatry at the University of California, people are four times more likely to get a cold if they get less than six hours of sleep per night.

2878. Approximately one in 200 people are born with an extra rib called a cervical rib. At the back, it connects to the seven cervical vertebrae in your neck. At the front, in some people, the rib can be floating and have no connection. Similarly, it can be connected to your first rib by a band of tough fibrous tissue, or there may be a joint to connect it to your first rib. It can also be just on the right side, just on the left side, or even both sides.

2879. Approximately 80% of Americans have siblings. Older siblings tend to be less extroverted than younger siblings. Although the siblings tend to resemble each other in looks and intelligence, they have quite different personalities.

2880. Witzelsucht, a German term that means joke addiction, is a type of condition that some people with brain disorders may suffer. Those afflicted have a compulsion to constantly tell jokes.

2881. The University of Warsaw found that the average human can track up to four moving things at one time; however, a gamer is able to track up to seven.

2882. The reason we can't see our own eyes in the mirror is because of something called saccadic masking. Our brain purposely blocks our vision in instances; otherwise our view would be like watching a video that's being shot with a shaky hand.

2883. A dead person can also get goosebumps; however, they aren't triggered the same way as a living person. It can occur when "rigor mortis" sets in, which is when muscles contract and causes the body to stiffen up. There are tiny muscles beneath our hair follicles which also contract, causing the hair to stand on end and make it look to have goosebumps.

2884. Drinking too much water can be just as harmful to your health as not drinking enough water. It is known as overhydration and it can cause nausea and vomiting, headaches, and changes in your mental state, such as confusion or disorientation.

2885. If we had the same vision as an eagle, we would be able to see an ant walking on the ground from the top of a ten story building.

2886. In 2015, a study published in the Journal of Analytical Chemistry by a university in Albany demonstrated that gender can be determined from the concentration of amino acids that are found in a fingerprint. As it turns out, women have more amino acids than men.

2887. When someone gets pregnant while already pregnant, that's referred to as superfetation. The second conception may happen within a few days or weeks after the first conception.

2888. The University of Montreal did a study and found that anyone can become a good singer. It's a skill that you can develop and becomes better with practice and worsens by lack of use.

2889. There was a study conducted in 2014 that linked sleep patterns with people's behavior and character traits. Those who stayed up later tended to be greater risk takers than those who woke up early.

2890. According to research, about 40% of all twins have created their own language that only they can understand when using it.

2891. A Stanford study revealed that there is a high correlation between walking and creative thought output in comparison to sitting. Results showed that those who walked demonstrated a 60% increase in creative thought output.

2892. Our urge to breathe mainly comes from our bodies wanting to get rid of carbon dioxide, not because of our need for oxygen.

2893. Smells can influence our dreams according to a study done in 2008. Subjects of the study were exposed to the scent of roses while sleeping, giving nearly all of them pleasant dreams. However, when the air around those subjects was infused with the smell of rotten eggs while sleeping, they had negative dreams.

2894. An ultracrepidarian is a person who always gives their opinion and thoughts on topics they have little expertise in.

2895. According to a 2011 report in the Journal of Evolutionary Psychology, women's voices increase in pitch when they talk to a man they find attractive.

2896. The tongue is the part of the human body that heals the quickest. Due to the rich supply of blood that the tongue receives, any injury there is able to heal twice as fast than any other part of the body.

2897. Each human eye can only hold 0.00024 ounces (seven microliters) of liquid, meaning that when you cry, the drainage ducts around the eye are flooded. That's why tears roll down your face and you get a runny nose when you cry.

2898. The complete loss of your sense of smell is called anosmia. Without your sense of smell, food doesn't taste the same, you can't smell perfume or the scent of a flower, and you can find yourself in a dangerous situation unknowingly.

2899. A study done by the University of New South Wales found that having good manners makes people see you as a person with greater interpersonal warmth. It also makes you a happier person.

2900. Phytophotodermatitis, also known as margarita dermatitis or lime disease (not to be confused with Lyme disease with a Y), is a toxic reaction that results from citric acid mixed with sunlight. It can cause second degree burns and is very painful.

2901. According to different studies, people who stay up late, known also as night owls, tend to be more extravagant, impulsive, and novelty seeking. They are also more likely to develop addictive behaviors, mental disorders, and antisocial tendencies.

2902. Based on research done at Norway's University of Bergen, there is a link between being addicted to work and anxiety. They studied more than 16,000 workers across the country and found that almost 8% of workaholics were more likely to suffer from ADHD, OCD, depression, and anxiety. The study also revealed that people who work more than fifty five hours per week were at a higher risk of heart attacks and strokes.

2903. Based on a study performed by the sociologist Nick Wolfinger at the University of Utah, people have a better chance of not getting divorced if they get married between the ages of twenty eight and thirty two.

2904. It's estimated that 350 million people worldwide suffer from depression according to the World Health Organization. This disorder is also a primary cause of disability in the world and is a major contributor to the overall global burden of disease.

2905. The brain does not have any pain receptors, so if you were having brain surgery, you wouldn't feel any pain.

2906. About 25% to 40% of people have motion sickness, a sensation of dizziness that occurs when you are on a car, boat, plane, or train. According to the University of Maryland Medical Center, women are more susceptible than men and Asians are more susceptible than white or black people.

2907. We can train our brain to slow down time by observing and paying attention to things more closely. This is due to the fact that when memories are created with more detail, moments seem to last longer and the brain takes longer to note down this information, making time seem like it's moving slower.

2908. Every time an event is recalled by your brain, it distorts it just a little bit. In fact, when you remember something that happened in the past, you're actually remembering the last time that you remembered it, and so on.

2909. According to research conducted by scientists, self-discipline is a better indicator of success than your IQ score.

2910. It was discovered that people are most likely to discover a good idea when they're doing a monotonous task such as showering, driving, or exercising. This is due to the fact that the body is in a more relaxed and less distracted state, allowing dopamine to flow through the body, triggering thoughts.

2911. There are more neurons lining your stomach than there are in your spinal cord, so basically the digestive system can work without depending on the brain. That is why when you are flooded with emotion, the neurons react and you get a gut feeling.

2912. When you sit for longer than three hours per day, your life expectancy can be reduced by up to two years. It can be reduced by an additional 1.4 years if you are watching TV as you sit down.

2913. According to neuroscientists at the University of Geneva, when you nap in a hammock, you get a deeper sleep than you do when you sleep at night in your bed.

2914. Humans yawn approximately 240,000 times throughout their lives, and a yawn lasts six seconds on average, meaning that we all spend about 400 hours of our lives yawning.

2915. When in loud surroundings, people will more likely try to hear something that's whispered into their right ear over their left one, according to a 2009 study. Also, it was found that people were more likely to do what you wanted if you delivered the request into their right ear.

2916. Pronoia is a real phenomenon and it's often considered to be the opposite of paranoia. Pronoia is a condition where people believe that others are conspiring without their knowledge, to do positive things for them.

2917. Teenagers who are stressed are almost immediately soothed when they hear their mother's voice, according to a 2010 study. This happens because the oxytocin, the bond-forming hormone, is released when a person recognizes that someone they love is nearby.

2918. Drinking beer can actually make a person smarter, according to an Oregon State University study. Hops contain a chemical that has positive effects on your intellectual function. The caveat is that you would need to drink 3,530 pints of beer per day to notice the results.

2919. Our eyes can detect a candle flame from as far as 1.7 miles (2.75 kilometers).

2920. Humans are the only creatures whose brains tend to shrink. The brains of chimpanzees and other animals stay the same.

2921. A compound called acetaminophen, which is a common ingredient in pain relievers such as Tylenol, has been found to make people less empathetic towards others, according to research conducted in 2016 at Ohio State University. This means it reduces the users' ability to understand other people's pain.

2922. Up to twelve ounces (300 milliliters) of liquid can be held by the average human bladder.

2923. According to a study published in the Journal of Neuroscience, anxiety disengages the prefrontal cortex, which is a region of the brain that plays an important role in flexible decision making.

2924. Research has shown that when men text more in a relationship, both partners are less happy and the woman wants to end the relationship. However, when the woman texts more often, both parties are more fulfilled and happier in the relationship.

2925. Lycanthrope is a condition where sufferers have delusions where they think they are a wolf or another wild animal.

2926. The reason why bruises turn colors is because the body is breaking down and reabsorbing the hemoglobin that leaked from the broken blood vessels.

2927. After death, rigor mortis (postmortem rigidity) sets in within two to six hours from the hour of the death, starting with the eyelids, neck, and then jaw.

2928. The reason your eyes are red in some photos is because the flash of the camera passes into the eye, through the pupil, reflects the fundus at the back of the eye and appears red because of the blood in the eye.

2929. In 2010, a study done by the Department of Experimental Psychology at the University of Bristol revealed that, under stress, caffeine makes men less, but women more effective as partners.

2930. The most weight of all the toes on your foot is carried by your big toe, bearing nearly 40% of your body's total weight.

2931. In one ounce of blood there are approximately 150 billion red blood cells, while in one pint of blood there are 2.4 trillion red blood cells. In fact, under stress, the human body can produce 119 million red blood cells per second.

2932. Stanford University has conducted clinical studies that show that people who experience auditory hallucinations, like schizophrenia, hear voices that are shaped by cultural influences. In Africa and India, voices are described to belong to family members or spirits, while in America, people describe voices as violent, torturous, and hateful yelling from strangers.

2933. More than 95% of humans have a natural immunity to leprosy.

2934. Sometimes non-threatening lumps may form in the armpits of breastfeeding women. It happens when the breast glands are so full with milk that some of it overflows to the surrounding areas.

2935. Your kidneys receive approximately 25% of all the blood in your heart.

2936. Writer's cramp is the term for when you get muscular spasms in your forefingers and thumb, but the medical term for the phenomenon is called graphospasm.

2937. You have a magnetic bone within your head right now. It's located above your nose where some think your third eye is situated, and it's called the ethmoid bone. Because it's magnetic, it aids your sense of direction.

2938.   Your cheeks turn red when you blush and the exact same thing happens to your stomach. Blushing causes capillaries all over the body to widen for higher blood flow, and because capillaries are near the surface, it causes red coloration. Blushing is just more noticeable on the cheeks than the stomach.

2939.   Individuals who literally hate everything and everyone are known as miso maniacs. The hate comes from the fear that everyone already hates them, so they are merely reciprocating.

2940.   Satoshi Kanazawa, a research psychologist, studied over twenty thousand students for five years, and he established that night owls – those who preferred to sleep and wake up late – tend to be smarter than early risers. A different study showed that despite what early risers believe, night owls actually use their time in a productive manner. They stay mentally sharp for longer than early risers.

2941.   When people get kidney transplants, surgeons don't usually take out the defective organ. They just add the third one into the body.

2942.   If by some tragedy you lose a thumb or finger and a doctor isn't there to save it on time, you can actually replace it by transplanting a toe in its place, in a procedure known as toe-to-hand transplant.

2943.   Stomach acid has a pH range of one to three, which means it's extremely strong. It has a similar approximate strength to battery acid. A single drop of stomach acid can corrode through a piece of wood.

2944.   There's a condition called white coat syndrome that affects 20% of patients, and it involves the dramatic rise in their blood pressure when they are in a doctor's office.

2945.   With your eyes closed, you can still touch your nose because of proprioception, a sense beyond the basic five ones that you know about. It's an extra meta-sense that enables you to feel the positions of your body parts relative to each other.

2946.   People who are born with lighter-colored eyes, such as green, blue, or grey, are more likely to become addicted to alcohol, according to researchers who studied the phenomenon at the University of Vermont. Those with blue eyes developed alcohol dependence at the highest rate.

2947.   The loud gurgling sounds produced by your stomach on occasion have a name. It's known as borborygmus, and although people think it's your body's way of telling you that you are getting hungry, it's really just your intestines shifting gases around the place.

2948.   A small number of people are born with total immunity, or some level of resistance, to the AIDS causing virus HIV. Unfortunately they only make up an estimated 1% of the population.

2949.   The fear of snakes is called ophidiophobia, and it affects one in three adults.

2950.   Graphologist Cathy McKnight claims that experts could discover more than 5,000 personality traits of an individual just by studying his or her handwriting. She says that individuals who write in large letters are typically outgoing and desire to be noticed, while those who prefer small letters tend to be more introverted, but have a stronger ability to focus or concentrate.

2951.   UCLA scientists used MRI scanners to determine that when people felt heartbroken, e.g. at the end of a relationship, the parts of their brains that lit up were the same ones that did when they felt physical pain.

2952.   Both your mood and your manner of thinking can be influenced by the kind of music you listen to. Research indicates that various genres of music affect you differently, with some making you more patient, others making you more confident, and some that even make it possible for you to overcome emotional trauma a lot faster.

2953.   12% of humans dream in black and white as per the US National Library of Medicine. Those aged twenty five or less only dream in color, and those aged fifty five or higher say they only dream in color 75% of the time.

2954.   Your heart will beat roughly three billion times if you are fortunate enough to live the average length of a human life.

2955. When a woman reaches her early thirties, her fertility starts to decline, and it speeds up when she gets to thirty five. She only has a 5% chance of getting pregnant during any particular month from the age of forty. This happens because women are born with all the eggs they are ever going to have throughout their lives, so as they age, the eggs age too, and they reduce both in number and quality.

2956. When a human adult is bitten by a Russell's pit viper, they can go through what seems like reverse puberty. The snake is native to Southeast Asia, and its venom can destroy someone's pituitary gland, to the extent that it stops secreting hormones. As a result, the person may lose their fertility, sex drive, and body hair. That's if the snake bite doesn't actually kill the person.

2957. You can distinguish between identical twins by looking at their belly buttons. Navels aren't genetic, they are scars that are left behind when the umbilical cord is removed.

FIND THE DIFFERENCE

2958. The average person produces two swimming pools worth of saliva in their mouth in a lifetime.

2959. Studies have actually proven that opposites do attract. A couple having too much in common is more likely not to last as long together. On the contrary, having different opinions while still respecting your partners is healthier in relationships.

2960. A study done by psychologist Adrian Furnham found that perfectionism can lead to depression. Often, perfectionists have unrealistic views of failure and are overly critical of themselves, leading to them having a negative impact on their day to day lives.

2961. According to the American College of Allergy, Asthma, and Immunology, if you get bitten by a lone star tick, you are vulnerable to develop an allergy to red meat, including beef and pork. The allergy symptoms may include a stuffy and running nose, nausea, and skin rash after eating meat.

2962. According to recent scientific findings, the five tastes or senses that your tongue can recognize are sweet, sour, salty, bitter, and umami. Parmesan cheese is an example of umami.

2963. There are three different types of tears: basal tears keep your eyes lubricated; irritant or reflex tears are produced when you get something in your eye; and emotional tears, produced during moments of intense feeling.

2964. The University College of London found that teenagers are less likely to be empathetic than adults due to the continual development of their brains. Their neural area that is associated with empathy and guilt when they're making decisions is not being used to full capacity.

2965. People who wake up late at night are more likely to display antisocial personality traits, such as machiavellianism and narcissism, as well as to have more psychopathic tendencies. This was evidenced during a study done by Doctor Peter Jonassen from the University of Western Sydney in 2013.

2966. Limbal dermoids are a type of tumor that can grow on the eyeball. They are made of connective tissue, skin, fat, hair, teeth, cartilage, and even bone.

2967. The toughest and hardest substance in the human body is tooth enamel, not our bones as we may think. Dental enamel has to withstand heat and cold, as well as biting into hard materials. It is the most mineralized substance in our bodies and it protects the inner portions of the teeth from damage and decay.

2968. When horror movies make us jump of fright, our bodies react by going into flight or fight mode because of the connections our brains make between the fake events on the screen and the real events we have actually experienced or even just been told about.

2969. Loving someone and being loved in return makes wounds heal faster, as different research conducted at the University of North Carolina have shown. This is due to the release of oxytocin in the blood.

2970. Dyslexic people actually see numbers and letters backwards. It's basically a reading disorder, not a vision or seeing disorder. This means that Braille readers can also be dyslexic.

2971. If a person sleeps too much, sits too much, and has an overall sedentary life, they are four times more likely to die early.

2972. The jawbone or mandible is the hardest bone in the human body. It's also the largest and strongest bone in the human face.

2973. According to a scientific study conducted in 2008, owning a cat can help reduce a human being's risk of a heart attack or stroke by over 33%.

2974. In 2015, a study published in BMC Evolutionary Biology found that after analyzing the spine shapes of modern humans who suffer from lower back pain, they have spines that are similar to chimpanzees; therefore, they are less well-adapted for walking upright.

2975. A study published in the Journal of Behavior Therapy and Experimental Psychiatry revealed that our mood can affect how we walk and vice versa. If we are sad, we walk slumped-shouldered; if we are happy, we walk bouncing. Additionally, if we imitate a happy walk, it makes us feel happier, and sadder if we imitate a sad way of walking.

2976. The average human head weighs ten pounds (4.5 kilograms).

2977. It has been scientifically proven that taking a warm bath before bed helps you sleep better. When our bodies cool before rest, melatonin is released, which is the hormone that induces sleep. So heating yourself up before bed will speed up the cooling process and you will feel tired quicker.

2978. Psychopaths don't have the ability to see the negative consequences of their actions, only the positive ones.

2979. 40% of pregnant women develop gingivitis at some point during their pregnancy as a result of varying hormone levels. This condition is called "pregnancy gingivitis."

2980. Based on two different studies performed by researchers, it was concluded that people who drink their coffee black or bitter are more associated with antisocial personality traits and sadism.

2981. The human scalp has on average 100,000 hair follicles.

2982. In 2014, in the Cappadocia region of Turkey, a massive underground city was discovered. It had everything from churches, waterways, fountains, kitchens, and even wineries and oil presses. The city is the size of sixty-five football fields and housed about 20,000 people at the time.

2983. Due to genetics, if your parents or grandparents have a history of multiple cavities or dentures at an early age, you have a higher risk from suffering the same outcome.

2984. Washing your hands with soap is more effective to kill bacteria and prevent disease than any vaccine out there according to the World Health Organization.

2985. The Kleine-Levin syndrome or Sleeping Beauty syndrome is a very unusual disorder where those affected sleep for up to twenty hours per day for days, weeks, or even months at a time; they only wake to use the restroom or to eat.

2986. Your organs and tissues aren't the only ones made of water. Your skeletal system contains water, and 31% of your bone mass is water.

2987. If you clamp your nostrils and mouth shut during a sneeze, your eardrums or sinuses could be damaged or it can cause an ear infection. Sneezes are actually quite powerful; the sudden expulsion of air can propel mucus droplets at rates of up to one hundred miles (160 kilometers) per hour.

2988. According to the Center for Disease Control, people with weak immune systems are more at risk for contracting bacteria.

2989. Brain maturity is not fully reached by most people until they are about twenty five years old. Until then they go through puberty.

2990. Approximately one liter of saliva is secreted by our mouths per day.

2991. On average, the human small intestine is twenty feet long (six meters) and about one inch (2.54 centimeters) in diameter.

2992. Goosebumps serve an evolutionary purpose. They appear when the muscles beneath the body rise up to enable the hair to stand straight. The purpose is to get the whole outer coat to puff out to increase insulation and keep you warm.

2993. The human tongue has between 2,000 and 4,000 taste buds. They contain sensory cells that renew themselves every seven days.

2994. There is a syndrome where people sneeze when they look at the sun. It's called a photic sneeze reflex, also known as autosomal dominant compelling helio-ophthalmic outburst syndrome. The abbreviation is "ADCHOO."

2995. According to different studies conducted by the Global Commission on Aging at the Transamerica Center for Retirement Studies, traveling brings great benefits to your mind and body, as it promotes brain health and decreases your risk of heart attack and depression.

2996. Walking corpse syndrome or Cotard syndrome is a mental disorder where patients experience delusions that they are dead, don't exist, are putrefying, or have lost their vital organs.

2997. Taller people have more cells in their bodies than shorter people; in consequence, they are at a greater risk to be diagnosed with cancer as more mutations in the cells can occur.

2998. When staring at a bright light such as the sun or a strong light bulb, 7% of the people will experience a sneeze reflex. Of that 7%, 94% of them will be Caucasian.

2999. There is a condition called "situs inversus" where one in about every 8,500 people is born with their organs in their chest and abdomen in perfect mirror image reversal of their normal positioning. These people have their hearts on the right and liver and spleen on the left.

3000. To go into hypovolemic shock, it only takes the loss of 20% of your blood. The condition leads to major organ failure because the heart loses the pressure it needs to circulate blood.

3001. The Dunning-Kruger Effect is a cognitive bias where smart people underestimate themselves while ignorant people think they are brilliant. In other words, the highly-skilled assume that things that they find easy are also easy for others, while the unskilled are so incompetent that they can't even recognize their own stupidity.

3002. Shy people are more likely to experience anxiety when they're hungover than their extroverted counterparts. The term is called "hangxiety." Professor Celia Morgan of the University of Exeter remarked that shy people should accept the fact that they're introverted and that should help the transition from heavy alcohol consumption.

3003. The metallic smell you get from smelling money coins is the result of your body's oils breaking down in the presence of iron or copper. If you use a paper towel to pick up a penny, however, you can tell there is no odor.

3004. Heteropaternal superfecundation is a very rare phenomenon that occurs when two twins have two different fathers. Only a few cases have been documented worldwide.

3005. There are thousands of microscopic mites living on your face right now. There are actually two species: demodex folliculorum that live in your pores and hair follicles; and D. brevis that settle deeper in the oily sebaceous glands in your face.

3006. It takes fifty hours of socializing to go from an acquaintance to a casual friend, according to a recent study by the University of Kansas. To become a real friend, it takes another forty hours, and a total of 200 hours to become a close friend.

3007. All human embryos start off as females in the womb, and the reason why men have nipples.

3008. Exercising is not only good for you but increases your productivity. Regularly exercising makes you smarter, happier, and more energetic, making you last longer throughout the day.

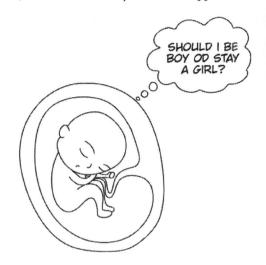

3009. There is a neuropathic disorder called trigeminal neuralgia that causes episodes of intense pain in the face that comes from the trigeminal nerve. The pain is so intense and excruciating that the disorder is referred to as suicide disease.

3010. Paradoxical undressing occurs when people are experiencing hypothermia and, suddenly, they feel irrationally hot and want to take off their clothes.

3011. There are no muscles in our fingers to facilitate movement. Flexing and curling our fingers, for example, is actually made possible by specific actions of the tendons, bones, and muscles that are found in the palm of our hands.

3012. About fifty ounces (1.5 liters) of clear and thin phlegm are created by a healthy person's sinuses a day, and most of it is swallowed.

3013. In a seven year study, researchers from Alberta, Canada, discovered that human urine contains at least 3,079 different chemical compounds.

3014. According to BMC Medicine, the frequent use of saunas is related to a lower risk of death from cardiovascular disease in men and women who are more than fifty years old. The study also showed that saunas lower blood pressure.

3015. There is no way to hum if your nose is completely plugged.

3016. Every twenty seven days, your human skin regenerates itself. The skin replaces itself 900 times on average in one lifetime. Tattoos are however not replaced when the skin regenerates because the ink is infused deep inside the dermis layer, so it doesn't fall away or get exfoliated, and may only come off if you are injured.

3017. The belief that balding comes from the mother's side of the family is actually a myth according to Men's Journal. In fact, it comes from the genes from both sides of the family. It's also a myth that wearing hats will make you go bald.

3018. Some women have a rare trait which gives them four color receptor cells in their eyes letting them see up to one hundred million colors. The average human only has three color receptors which let them see about a million colors.

3019. The print of our tongues is different for every individual, just like fingerprints.

Beep!!

3020. Research conducted in 1978 followed over five hundred people who were prevented from attempting suicide found that, thirty years later, 90% were still alive or had died from natural causes. The study concluded that suicidal behaviors are impulsive and spur of the moment that can be prevented.

3021. Sweat is actually odorless. But when bacteria on the skin and hair metabolize the proteins and fatty acids in sweat, the unpleasant odor is then produced.

3022. By communicating with the brain, gut microbiota can make changes in one's mood or personality.

3023. It's possible for tonsils and adenoids to grow back after surgery, although it's not very common. If even a small amount of tissue is left behind, the whole thing can grow back.

3024. On average, women have longer legs and shorter torsos in comparison to men. Additionally, they often have shorter arms than their male counterparts.

3025. Maladaptive daydreaming is a mental disorder that causes people to daydream repeatedly to escape reality. It is a defense mechanism usually caused by trauma and abuse.

3026. On average, a human will produce seventy two million red blood cells, shed 174,000 skin cells, and have twenty five thoughts every thirty seconds.

3027. According to a study conducted by Cristel Antonia Russell and Sidney J. Levy in 2012, watching your favorite movie repeatedly can be good for you, as the repetition can calm you down. Knowing the outcome of a story helps you feel safe in an unpredictable world, as well as helps comfort you by recapturing lost feelings.

3028. It's estimated that in 21% of identical twin pairs, one is right-handed while the other is either left-handed or ambidextrous.

3029. When exposed to certain ingredients such as sandalwood oil, our skin has the ability to smell and is even able to heal itself.

3030. "Cute aggression" is the term used to refer when thinking that something such as a puppy or kitten is so cute that you could crush it. This happens when the neurons in the brain fire and create electrical activity, which makes you more aggressive.

3031. The measles virus deletes the immune system's whole memory, leaving a patient susceptible to other infections for the next three years, according to a study conducted in 2015 by a team of Princeton researchers.

3032. In France, there was a man named Tarrare with a weird medical condition that caused him to be always hungry and attempt to eat anything and everything that he sees.

3033. The average person will grow nearly 600 miles (965 kilometers) of hair in their lifetime, according to The Express. Presumably, this is cumulative of each hair on your body laid end to end. Nose hairs alone contribute 6.5 feet (1.98 meters) of the total.

Interesting

3034. As of 2015, according to the American Kennel Club, the Labrador Retriever has been the most popular dog in the United States for the last twenty five years.

3035. There is a tribe in South America known as the "Tukano tribe" where the men must marry outside of their language group so that the children will be born into a multilingual household.

3036. The 911 system in New York City handles more than eleven million calls per year, making it the largest of its kind in the whole country.

3037. Scrooge McDuck is the richest fictional character, according to a study done by Forbes Magazine, and he was theoretically worth $65.4 billion as of 2013. The dragon from The Hobbit, Smaug, is the second richest fictional character. It's estimated that he has hoarded gold and other kinds of treasure worth $54.1 billion by estimates.

3038. Car oil cans have numbers such as 10W-40, where the "W" stands for winter. When the "W" number is lower, it means the oil works better in cold temperatures.

3039. Mount Everest got its name in 1856 from George Everest, a British surveyor. Before that, the Nepalese called it Sagarmatha and the Tibetans called it Chomolungma. The Brits renamed it in honor of Colonel George Everest who was in charge of the survey that verified that the summit was indeed the highest one in the whole world.

3040. Forty is the only number whose letters are already in alphabetical order when spelled correctly. The only number whose letters are in reverse alphabetical order is one.

3041. A study done over the span of twenty years shows that it's better to spend money on experiences rather than material possessions. The joy we associate with possessions tends to fade fast, but good experiences become parts of our very identities.

3042. In an open field in Georgia, five large granite slabs, each weighing twenty tons, showed up mysteriously, with carvings of guidelines on what should be done in the event of an apocalypse. It had ten new commandments, like a rule about keeping the population below 500 million, getting rid of petty laws and useless officials, and uniting people with a new language.

3043. The theory that you swallow eight spiders every year in your sleep is a myth and it's more likely that spiders have never come anywhere close to your mouth.

3044.   In Q-tips, the "Q" means quality. At first they were called Q-tips Baby Gays, but the latter part of the name was dropped.

3045.   Irish sheep farmer Paul Brennan is a drone enthusiast who uses his RC QuadCopter to look after his sheep. The sheep get scared and run in the opposite direction when they hear the approaching buzzing drone. Brennan uses this to direct his herd from one field to the next, or wherever he wants the sheep to go.

3046.   The word "laser" is actually an acronym. It stands for Light Amplification by Stimulated Emission of Radiation.

3047.   Soap operas, or soaps, are called such because the shows were mostly sponsored by soap companies in the past. They were mainly shown during the day and advertisers wanted to reach their main demographic: the housewife.

3048.   In the United States, there are more than 4.6 million twenty six year old people. That is more than any other age group.

3049.   The world's shortest street is Ebenezer Place in Wick, Scotland, at only 6.7 feet (2.05 meters) long.

3050.   Quicksand isn't able to suck you under because humans aren't dense enough, however, if you move around, the sand liquifies and you will begin to sink; so as long as you don't panic, you will only sink half way.

3051.   Flipping a coin is actually 51/49, and not 50/50, biased for the face that is showing when the coin is flipped.

3052.   There are no reptiles in Antarctica because they need heat to keep their bodies functioning, and cannot survive under severe, extended cold temperatures. They would literally freeze solid.

3053.   A study led by researcher Colin Wright at the University of California demonstrated that paper wasp queens pass their personality onto the colony. The team of researchers found out that it was possible to predict paper wasp behavior six weeks before they even hatched just by watching the queen.

3054.   There is a 70% chance that your last name is Patel if you are an Indian American and own a motel.

3055.   The world's smallest fully functioning revolver is the Swiss mini-gun C1ST. It's only 2.2 inches (5.5 centimeters) long and weighs 0.7 of an ounce (nineteen grams).

3056.   In 2007, the Bayer College of Medicine concluded in a study that magnesium is the key to healthy bones, not calcium.

3057.   In February, 2017, soft tissue collagen and iron rich proteins were discovered inside a 195 million year old dinosaur bone by researchers at the University of Toronto. The elements were found within a rib of a Lufengosaurus dinosaur, a long-necked herbivore that roamed across what is now southwestern China during the early Jurassic period.

3058.   A study done by an economics professor at Emory University discovered that couples who spend less than average on their weddings have lower divorce rates.

3059.   Studies show that you see yourself 20% less attractive than you actually are. This is because you only see your looks reflected in the mirror and not your personality.

3060.   The fear of ventriloquist dummies, animatronic creatures, wax statues, or anything that resembles a being that seems to have feelings or perceptions is called automatonophobia.

3061.   The Brain Structure and Function journal published a study that shows the effects of both silence and different types of noise on mice. They found that two hours of silence per day promoted cell growth in the part of the brain that controls memory, emotion, and learning.

3062.   Chinese checkers wasn't actually invented in China, nor has a connection to any Asian country. The star-shaped marble game originated in Germany in 1892. When the game reached the United States, it started to be known as Chinese checkers, as American companies wanted to take advantage of the popularity of oriental imports.

3063. If you could dig a hole through the Earth and jump through it without dying, you would not come out the other side. You would fall down for twenty minutes until you reached the center; then, technically, you would be considered falling up until you made it to the opposite surface. However, if no one was there to catch you, you would fall down again over and over forever.

3064. There is a mushroom species called the Spongiforma squarepantsii. It was named by researchers at San Francisco State University after SpongeBob SquarePants because it reminded them of the cartoon character. It's shaped like a sea sponge, has large holes in it, and has an orange color.

3065. When the first woman becomes president of America, the husband will be known as the first gentleman.

3066. Pliny the Elder, a philosopher from the first century AD, accurately identified amber as fossilized resin from a pine tree. He also had a very deep appreciation of all sorts of minerals, including diamonds, rock crystals, and sapphires.

3067. Villagers in Central China were, for decades, digging up dinosaur bones in the area, and making traditional medicines and soups because they believed the bones belonged to ancient magical dragons.

3068. According to legend, Canada got its name after Jacques Cartier, a French explorer, who confused the word Kanata which was used by St. Lawrence Iroquoian to mean "village," for the name of the entire land that he was standing in. Before Canada was named after Cartier's mistake, several other names for the land had been proposed. They included New Albion, Cabotia, Transatlantica, Laurentia, Ursalia, and Superior.

3069. Being friendless might be as deadly as smoking, according to a 2016 study done at Harvard. Researchers found a connection between being lonely and having high levels of proteins that cause blood clotting and lead to strokes and heart attacks.

3070. When a dual involves three opponents instead of the usual two, it's called a truel. Each person tries to kill the other two, just as you'd expect.

3071. The traditional white hat worn by chefs is called the "toque blanche," and it has one hundred folds in it. The number of folds is believed to represent the one hundred different ways to cook eggs.

3072. Hurricanes, cyclones, and typhoons are technically the same weather phenomenon. They are just classified differently based on where they form. Those that form in the Northern Pacific and the Atlantic Ocean are named hurricanes, the ones in the Northwestern Pacific are typhoons, and the ones forming in the Southeastern Indian Ocean are referred to as severe tropical cyclones.

3073. Orange is the worst possible color that you can wear to a job interview, according to a survey that involved 2,099 hiring managers. Blue and black are considered the best colors.

3074. The largest maker and exporter of fireworks in the world is China. The country makes 90% of all fireworks on earth.

3075. Cars were believed to be healthier and cleaner transportation alternatives in the early 1900's because they didn't leave horse manure on the roads. Due to the pollution caused by the horses, and the high cost of running stables and feeding horses, horse-drawn carriages were no longer used in the streets of New York after 1917.

3076. The first use of the term "trick or treat" was recorded in Blackie, Alberta, in 1927. A local paper reported that some pranksters had been going from door to door, demanding that the homeowners either give them a treat, or they'd pull a trick on them.

3077. The Global Tiger Summit of 2010 was the first ever gathering of world leaders that was specifically meant to discuss the fate of any other species besides human beings.

3078. James Comey, the former FBI director, insisted that as part of their training, new intelligence analysts and special agents must tour the United States Holocaust Memorial Museum.

3079. The Swedish army tried to create a moose cavalry back in the 1700's because they thought it would instill fear in the enemy. They turned out to be really hard to domesticate because the soldiers couldn't feed them properly, and they were also quite vulnerable to various kinds of livestock diseases.

3080. Back in the day, when rabbit ears were put behind a man's head, it meant that his wife was cheating on him. The two fingers held up symbolized the horns of a stag, which had apparently lost its mate to a rival stag.

3081. A compass doesn't actually point towards the geographical North Pole, it points to the planet's magnetic north pole by using the earth's magnetic field to find it. The magnetic north pole shifts in loops of forty nine miles (eighty kilometers) per day.

3082. In Centralia, Pennsylvania, there is an underground fire in the coal mines that has been burning since 1962. Although it is unknown how the fire really started, it's believed that burning trash from a nearby landfill accidentally burned coal beneath the old entrance to the mine; later, the fire spread wildly through all the mines.

3083. On October 21, 2016, Wonder Woman was officially appointed as the new honorary ambassador for women and girls by the United Nations.

3084. According to researchers at Ohio State University, some people are more vulnerable to what they call experience talking. It occurs when, while reading a book or story, people change their behavior or thoughts to match those of a fictional character in a book or story that they can identify with, so subconsciously they become that character.

3085. A software designer once conducted a study and found there was a correlation between students' SAT scores and what music genre they listened to. From highest to lowest SAT scores, the genre goes techno, classic rock, country, rock, rap, R&B, classical, alternative, reggae, oldies, pop, hip-hop, jazz, and lastly gospel.

3086. Studies conducted by the University of Queensland and the University of New South Wales have found that people with dark eyes are more pleasant, while people with blue eyes tend to be more competitive.

3087. The green patches on potatoes indicate the presence of chlorophyll which means there is also a concentration of solanine, a harmful toxin. So when you see these green patches, you should remove them completely and discard them.

3088. Political participation and collective governance were greatly valued by ancient Greeks. The word "idiot" was used in ancient Greece to describe someone who did not contribute to politics or the community.

3089. A sample of 160,000 Facebook users was analyzed by research scientists working alongside Facebook. They discovered that people who prefer dogs instead of cats had more online connections on average, and were more likely to be in a relationship than those users who prefer cats.

3090. The first active president of the United States to visit the Japanese city of Hiroshima since the bombing during World War II was President Barack Obama, in May of 2016.

3091. Back in Gregorian times, a mixture called fard used to be applied on sunburned faces and acne breakouts. It was a combination of sweet almond oil, honey, and spermaceti, which is a waxy substance found in the head of a sperm whale. The ingredients were dissolved over heat and once it had cooled, it was applied to the affected areas and left on overnight.

3092. Phosphines is the name given to those little flashes of light you see when you close or rub your eyes. Because atoms in the eye emit and absorb particles of light, the light flashes inside your eyes. The optic nerve sends light signals to the brain making the phosphines visible.

3093. In the Viking tradition, when important Vikings died, they were put into a burial ship along with their clothes and jewelry. Then they were either buried or set on fire and pushed out to sea.

3094. After his death in 1790, Benjamin Franklin willed the cities of Boston and Philadelphia $4,400 each; the clause stipulated that the money could not be spent for 200 years. By 1990, Boston's trust was worth over $5 million.

3095. An example of an apex predator is the great white shark. This means that as an adult, it has no natural predators in its ecosystem.

3096. To the Aztec people, the act of giving birth was considered equal to a man in battle. If a woman passed away during childbirth, she became a "Companion of the Sun," rising to one of the highest Heavens, the same as a male warrior who died in battle.

3097. Vexillologist is the term used to refer to someone who studies and collects information about flags.

3098. The heart of a shrimp is located in its head.

3099. Google found that test scores and college degrees don't give an accurate representation of a person and 14% of their employees haven't ever been to college.

3100. In Iowa and Montana, if someone can't pay back their student loans, their driver's license will be revoked.

3101. Several studies carried out by the University of North Carolina concluded that good looking people are less likely to be hired for a job when being interviewed by someone of the same sex. These people often also feel very lonely as they are viewed as unapproachable and intimidating by others and even doctors give less care to them when being treated for pain.

3102. According to a survey conducted by Buy T-Shirts Online, those who wear black are seen as serious and reliable. Almost 50% of women and 64% of men agree that black projects confidence.

3103. The freezing brain feeling you get when having cold foods like ice cream is caused by a sudden surge of blood to the brain.

3104. The country that consumes the most Coca-Cola per capita in the world is Iceland.

3105. Howard Lutnick donated over sixty million dollars to Haverford College, the place he went to study when he was younger. When he was there, he lost both his parents to cancer, however the college let him go there tuition-free for his whole degree, and he wanted to pay them back for it.

3106. The fear of Halloween is called samhainophobia.

3107. There is an ancient belief about swans being silent for their entire life until they sing one beautiful song just before dying. From this belief the term swansong was derived.

3108. An octothorpe is the name of the symbol commonly called a number sign, a pound symbol, or most recently the hashtag symbol. The name was given by technicians in a lab that created Bell telephones in the 1960's.

3109. As a way to prevent hunched backs, Dutch designer Jeffrey Heiligers has created posture garments. After working with a physiotherapist to identify positions that cause back, neck, and shoulder pain, he created clothes that tighten slightly and become uncomfortable when the wearer slumps their shoulders.

3110. John Tyler, Millard Fillmore, Andrew Johnson, and Chester A. Arthur served their entire terms as presidents of the United States without a vice president.

3111. Ferrule is the name given to the metal band that joins the eraser to a pencil. It is also the name of the metal band at the end of a cane.

3112. In the days following September 11, around 36,000 units of blood were donated to the New York Blood Center by New Yorkers willing to help. However, blood cannot be used more than a few weeks after donation, so unfortunately many units had to be discarded.

3113. "Left Handers Day" is celebrated every year on August 13.

3114. In 1948, farmer Cecil George Harris of Rosetown, Saskatchewan, wrote one of the most unique wills ever written. He scratched his will into the fender of a tractor that he was trapped under for ten hours during a heavy storm. His will read: "In case I die in this mess, I leave all to my wife." He died that night from his injuries. A judge ordered that portion of the tractor to be cut off and it is now displayed under a piece of glass in the University of Saskatchewan Law library.

3115. The first son of a former president who became president himself was John Quincy Adams. George H.W. Bush and George W. Bush are the only other father-son presidents.

3116. The designer brand store Kate Spade was co-founded by David Spade's brother Andy, along with his wife Kate in New York.

3117. If you put a tube of regular water and a tube of morphine water in a rat enclosure, the rat will always drink the drugged water until it dies. However, if you give the rat ample space, games, and friends, the rat won't touch the drugged water, even if you try to trick it by swapping the water tubes.

3118. In 1992, a 100-tree swastika was found by locals from Zernikow, Germany, during an aerial survey. It was made up of a group of large trees only visible from the air and was almost 200 square feet (nineteen square meters). In autumn, the yellowing trees stand out against the surrounding evergreens. It's not known exactly who planted these trees, but apparently it was created during Hitler's peak in the 1930's.

3119. According to a study of surgical residents who participated in the Rosser Top Gun Laparoscopic Skills and Suturing Program, surgeons who played video games made 37% fewer errors than those who did not, and even completed the surgery 27% faster.

3120. Another name for hiccups is singultus.

3121. The fear of seeing, hearing, or writing poetry is called metrophobia.

3122. The sackbut was the name originally given to the trombone.

3123. A study showed that female servers who drew a little smiley face on the bill increased their tips by up to 20%.

3124. Saddam Hussein had the Quran transcribed by an Islamic calligrapher in his own blood during the 1990's. Over a two year period, he had over seven gallons (twenty eight liters) of blood drawn.

3125. Barbara Millicent Roberts is actually Barbie's full name. Her inventor, Ruth Handler, created her back in 1959 and named her after her daughter Barbara. Ken also has a full name too, which is Ken Carson.

3126. The Mickey Mouse brand has recognition of 97%, higher than that of Santa Claus.

3127. The designer of the international biohazard symbol, Charles Baldwin, stated: "we wanted to create something that was memorable but meaningless, so that we could educate people as to what it means."

3128. Friggatriskaidekaphobia is the fear of Friday the 13th.

3129. The only president of the United States to remain a lifelong bachelor was James Buchanan, the 15th president.

3130. The "Pigg-O-Stat" is a device that came out in the 1960's. It's used when radiologists need to safely immobilize babies and young children who can't or don't want to sit during an x-ray.

3131. In 1928, the founder of the Kodak Company was so upset by the different numbers of days in each month that he suggested that the company operated on a thirteen month year, where each month had exactly four weeks. They actually implemented it all the way up to 1989.

3132. Hippophobia is not the fear of hippos as it sounds but horses.

3133. During the 1930's, the US was in short supply of fabric so the women started using flour sacks to make dresses. Flour mills began printing patterns and different colors onto them in response for more variety.

3134. Former American President Richard Nixon gave up his Secret Service bodyguards in order to save money for the government, saving an estimated three million dollars.

3135. In 1850, American Express was founded as a freight and valuables delivery service. Because the US Postal Service was unreliable at the time, and it only allowed shipment of letter-sized envelopes, the company saw a business opportunity to ship larger parcels. Later on, the company took a turn when it began to realize more profit from a sector of its customer base that included banks and other financial institutions.

3136. The number twenty three is used by Nissan in car racing. In Japanese, the number two translates to "ni" and the number three translates to "san," so twenty three translates into Nissan.

3137. Based on a survey done by Boston University researchers, young people who consume Jell-O shots are more likely to get into fights after consuming alcohol. Researchers, however, do admit that more investigation needs to be done on this subject.

3138. The average claw machine is only programmed to give the claw full strength every twenty tries.

3139. "The ultimate" is the name given to the last thing on a list; "the penultimate" is the second last; and "the antepenultimate" is the third last.

3140. The fear of ferns is called pteridophobia.

3141. The Wieliczka Salt Mine in Poland is located more than 1,000 feet (305 meters) underground. It's one of the world's oldest salt mines still in operation, although the production of table salts was actually stopped in 2007. Over the course of the years, sculptures and even four chapels have been carved by miners, all made of salt. As salt mining slowed and then stopped, the chambers have been transformed into an incredible underground amusement park with grand halls, health spas, museum worthy art, and record setting spectacles.

3142. The only king in a pack of cards without a mustache is the King of Hearts. It's believed that the kings were all based on historical figures, such as Charlemagne and Alexander the Great. The King of Hearts is supposed to have been Charlemagne, despite the fact that he is often portrayed as having a full beard and mustache.

3143. A Yale University study once found that one of the most recognizable scents to adults is the aroma of Crayola crayons. In fact, it ranked 18th, just ahead of coffee and peanut butter.

3144. A lawyer from Kenya named Felix Kiprono offered Barack and Michelle Obama seventy sheep, fifty cows, and thirty goats as a dowry for their daughter, Malia.

3145. Thomas Jefferson argued that the constitution should expire every nineteen years as one generation shouldn't have the power or right to bind the generation after.

3146. The chewed end of a cigar smoked by Sir Winston Churchill sold at auction for £2,000. It was taken from his ashtray by a nurse who was looking after him while he was recuperating from a broken hip in Middlesex Hospital in 1962.

3147. There are no official duties concerning the role as the first lady, a position that is also unpaid. Despite this, many of them work hard to accomplish projects that they are passionate about and are notoriously targeted for appearance based criticism.

3148. The original game of billiards was played on lawns outside. Then the game moved indoors to a wooden table with green cloth to simulate grass. That is why most pool tables are still covered with green felt.

3149. The average millennial is only worth roughly $17,600, and the main reason for this is high student loan debts.

3150. In late February, 2017, Adolph Hitler's telephone was sold at auction in the United States for $243,000. It was recovered from the Fuhrer bunker and kept in a box at an English country house since 1945.

3151. In 2014, "CareerBuilder" did a study that showed that only 48% of Americans would quit their jobs if they won the lottery. Of those who said they would keep working, 77% stated that they would do it because they would be bored if they didn't work. Of them, 76% said work gives them a sense of purpose and accomplishment. Of them, 42% said that they would want financial security alongside the lottery win. Finally, 23% said that they would just miss their coworkers.

3152. The US Department of Treasury Law forbids the use of portraits of living persons from appearing on government securities like money. Moreover, the portraits have to be of deceased people whose places in history are well-known by the American people.

3153. Research in the UK for car accidents showed that short female drivers who sit close to the steering wheel are more likely to be injured and even killed if an airbag goes off.

3154. In 2010, after the BP oil spill, Stephen Colbert stated that every time he said the word "bing," the Microsoft search engine would donate $2,500 to oil spill cleanup efforts. He managed to say "bing" forty times, raising $100,000 for the Colbert Nation Gulf of America fund.

3155. There was no one who was awarded the Nobel Peace Prize in 1948 as there wasn't a suitable candidate, but also as a tribute to Mahatma Gandhi who was assassinated that year.

3156. According to the joint-secretary of Nepal's Ministry of Tourism, novice climbers are not allowed to climb Mount Everest. In fact, climbers are required to have reached the peak of at least one 21,000 foot (6,500 meter) mountain in their lifetime in order to qualify to climb the mountain.

3157. Szechuan peppers contain a molecule that makes your cells' touch receptors feel like they're being rapidly vibrated, giving you that numb, tingly feeling.

3158. It is physically impossible for raindrops to form from pure water alone. At the very center of every single raindrop there is a mineral dust particle.

3159. In the United States, 2016's Black Friday was a record breaking day for gun background checks. A total of 185,713 background checks were processed by the FBI, 400 more than the previous year. Black Friday is often the biggest day of the year for gun sales because of the huge discounts offered.

3160. Based on population estimates released by the US Census Bureau in 2015, millennials aged eighteen to thirty four had surpassed baby boomers aged fifty one to sixty nine as the country's largest living generation, with 75.4 million millennials and 74.9 million baby boomers. Generation X, of ages thirty five to fifty, is projected to pass the boomers in population by 2028.

3161. The smallest adult of all time according to the Guinness World Records is Chandra Bahadur Dangi from Nepal. He was only 1.79 feet (0.54 meters) tall.

3162. Usain Bolt, known for being the fastest man on Earth, has a condition called scoliosis, which creates a curvature of the spine and gets worse as the body ages and grows.

3163. The Titanic used to have its own newspaper called "The Atlantic Daily Bulletin." It was printed daily on board and it had news, ads, stock prices, horse racing results, gossip, and the day's menu.

3164. The jump in Mexican jumping beans originates from a moth larva inside the pod that twitches when abruptly warmed.

3165. The first atomic bomb ever made was "the Gadget." It was successfully tested at Trinity Site, New Mexico, on July 16, 1945. The test code was named Trinity and it unleashed an explosion with the energy of about twenty kilotons of TNT.

3166. One barrel of wine contains around twenty five cases, or 300 twenty five ounces (750 millimeter), bottles of wine.

3167. The lampposts in New York City's Central Park have numbers on them to help people navigate in case they get lost. The first two or three numbers indicate the closest cross street, while the last number shows what side of town you are closest to. Additionally, an odd number means you are on the west side, while an even number means you are on the east.

3168. In the last thirty five years, the FedEx logo has won over forty design awards and was ranked as one of the eight best logos. The white arrow in the logo is crafted by blending two different fonts together and it was an intentional design choice.

3169. Contrary to most people's belief, there is no lead in a pencil. Its core is made of a non-toxic mineral called graphite.

3170. The biggest tire graveyard in the world is located in Sulaibiya, Kuwait. Every year, enormous holes are dug into the desert and filled with old tires. There are more than seven million tires there already. In fact, the dump is so large that it's actually visible from space.

3171. Every six years hurricane names are recycled, except for those hurricanes that have been so deadly and costly whose names are no longer reused.

3172.   If there was a way to just harness .1% of the energy of the oceans tides, we would have enough energy for the current demand of the globe five times over.

3173.   Technically, the eyewear industry is monopolized by one Italian company: Luxottica Spa, which owns brands such as Ray-Ban, Persol, and Oakley. They also make glasses for Chanel, Prada, Armani, Burberry, Versace, Dolce Gabanna, and a lot more. They also own retail brands like LensCrafters and Sears Optical.

3174.   Soviet dictator Joseph Stalin had an accident involving a horse-drawn carriage when he was only twelve years old, which caused his left arm to be distinctly shorter than his right arm. His arm had to be reconstructed by surgery, leaving it shorter and stiffened at the elbow.

3175.   In 1952, President Harry Truman started the tradition of top secret intelligence briefings, a tradition still practiced to this day. He wanted to make sure that his successor was better prepared than he was, so he offered classified briefings to each of the nominees.

3176.   In Washington, the American capitol subway system is a transit system exclusively used by members of the Congress and Capitol Hill staff members.

3177.   Cocoa beans were often used by the Aztec natives as currency.

3178.   A study done in 2013 showed that fans of Harry Potter were more politically tolerant, open to diversity, less authoritarian and less likely to support the use of torture or deadly force.

3179.   Based on a report provided by the Center for Disease Control and Prevention's National Center for Health Statistics, today American men weigh on average 196 pounds (eighty nine kilograms), which is fifteen pounds (6.8 kilograms) more than twenty years ago. Additionally, women weigh 168 pounds (seventy six kilograms) on average, which is sixteen pounds (7.2 kilograms) more than twenty years ago.

3180.   Before 1970, the exclamation mark was not part of the keyboard. Before it was added that year, you would have to type a full stop, then hit the backspace key to move back before adding an apostrophe over the full stop.

3181.   The "Highway HiFi" was a record player offered by Chrysler in its new cars from 1956 to 1958. However, because they had a tendency to break, the device was later removed.

3182.   A senator named Larry Pressler refused a bribe offered to him from the FBI in the 1970's. He was called a hero for his act, but he didn't think that refusing the bribe should be considered a heroic act.

3183.   The patron saint of Ireland, Saint Patrick, wasn't actually Irish. Although the exact birth place and date is unknown, it is believed that he was born around 375 A.D. in Scotland, and his real name is believed to be Maewyn Succat, taking the name Patrick upon becoming a priest.

3184.   The real name of Ulysses S. Grant, the 18th president of the United States, was actually Hiram Ulysses Grant. The middle initial "S" meant nothing and it was the result of an error from Ohio Congressman Thomas Hammer; he accidentally wrote his name as Ulysses S. Grant when he was nominated to attend West Point.

3185.   The Church of Scientology has been in the country of Germany since the 1970's, however, the German government doesn't recognize it as a religion and only as an abusive business that's masquerading as religion.

3186.   If you drop a steel ball and a rubber ball, both of the same size, from the same height, the steel ball will actually bounce higher as it snaps back to its original shape faster than the rubber ball.

3187.   In 2015, selfie sticks were banned in Disney parks for safety reasons, as the long arms could collide with a ride's mechanism or stick another guest.

3188.   Andrew Johnson and Bill Clinton are the only two US presidents who have been impeached so far. However, neither of them was convicted of charges filed against them.

3189. In the past, in order to cure head lice, gasoline, kerosene, benzene, and turpentine were all used as treating substances. References to it appear in medical journals as far back as 1917.

3190. Having more stainless steel in your kitchen reduces the amount of odor from garlic or onion.

3191. On July 16, 1935, the "Park-O-Meter" was the world's first parking meter to be installed. It was set up on the southeast corner of what was then First Street and Robinson Avenue, in Oklahoma City.

3192. The blackest black material which is able to absorb 99.96% of visual light is called Vantablack. People who have seen this say it's like looking into an abyss.

3193. More than seventy separate pieces of wood are contained in a violin.

3194. A German psychology study in the 1980's found that husbands who kiss their partner before leaving for work lived longer, earned more, and had fewer car accidents.

3195. On the Titanic, there were twelve confirmed dogs onboard, but only three of them survived.

3196. In the United States, it's estimated that nearly 14.5 million people have survived cancer.

3197. On August 20, 1977, Voyager II was launched; while on September 5, Voyager I was launched. They were sent on different trajectories and Voyager I was put on a path to reach Jupiter and Saturn ahead of Voyager II.

3198. Since the first nuclear test explosion on July 16, 1945, at least 2,054 nuclear test explosions have been performed by eight nations at dozens of test sites around the world.

3199. The three most common mental illnesses in the United States are depression, alcohol dependency, and social anxiety disorder.

3200. Former American Presidents Thomas Jefferson and Jimmy Carter both used to be peanut farmers.

3201. At the Nuremberg trials, genius level IQ test scores were achieved by several Nazi leaders.

3202. Engineers in Canada receive an iron ring to remind them to have humility upon graduation. The ring is given in memory of a bridge that collapsed twice due to incorrect calculations involving iron.

3203. "Beano" was originally the name for bingo. It was called this because players used beans to cover the numbered squares.

3204. It's estimated that every three days, the equivalent of the world's population use Otis elevators, escalators, and walkways.

3205. Before Martin Luther King Jr. went up to do his famous speech in Washington in 1963, he added the "I have a dream" line minutes before he started.

3206. Harry Truman, the 33rd president of the United States, and Gerald Ford, the 38th president, both died on the same date, December 26.

3207. The US penny used to be composed of 95% copper and 5% zinc before World War II. But because those metals were unavailable during the war, they were then made of zinc coated steel. The final change was made in 1982, after several revisions to the composition, to 97.6% zinc and 2.4% copper, and is still used today.

3208. Naturally blonde people represent only 2% of the entire world's population.

3209. In the early days of the Indie 500, having an onboard mechanic was mandatory. Cars then used to have two seats, one for the driver and one for the onboard mechanic. The mechanic monitored the gauges, made repairs, and sometimes would even massage the driver's arms and neck. The onboard mechanic was mandatory from 1912 to 1922, and then again from 1930 to 1937.

3210. According to a study conducted by Psychological Science, only 1% of friendships made in the 7th grade remain intact by the 12th grade.

3211. Arcuate is the name given to the orange stitching on the back pockets of Levi jeans. It has literally no function and during World War II, it was painted on as rationing.

3212. The reason why there are holes at the top of pen caps is to prevent you from choking if swallowed.

3213. According to research done by the University of Toronto, people who trust more are better at spotting liars.

3214. Instead of floating to the top, the bubbles in Guinness beer actually sink to the bottom.

3215. The odds of an average golfer getting a hole in one on a par three are approximately 12,500 to one.

3216. In 2013, in order to help tackle the problem of alcoholism in the country, scientists from the University of Chile developed a new vaccine that will give anyone who drinks even a small amount of alcohol an immediate, very bad hangover.

3217. Zambia is a country with very fertile lands, however, not much agriculture grows there. This is because when there is any greenery, the hippos come out and eat everything.

3218. Traditionally, sailors whose wives deliver children when they are at sea are supposed to be the first to get off the ship when it docks.

3219. When doctors in Fortaleza ran out of human and pig tissue used to treat burns, they started using the skin of tilapia, which is a popular kind of fish in the area. They got incredible results because tilapia have more collagen than human tissue, and collagen is needed to form scars. There are ongoing clinical trials, and the treatment could be used in other countries in the future.

3220. The Corn Flakes rooster pictured on the cereal box is named Cornelius Rooster. The Leo Burnett Ad Agency, also called the Critter Agency, made Cornelius after successfully making mascots such as Frosted Flakes' Tony the Tiger, and Rice Krispies' Snap, Crackle, and Pop.

3221. The first US president, George Washington, was the only one to ever get 100% of Electoral College votes.

3222. Mel Carnahan died in a plane crash in 2000, and three weeks later, he won the Missouri US Senate election. The post was given to his wife Jean Carnahan by Governor Roger B. Wilson, and she served a two year term.

3223. There are exactly ten people who have been named honorary Harlem Globetrotters, and they include two popes, Francis and John Paul II.

3224. The CUNY Economics PhD program did a study that found that since 2011, when Uber was introduced in New York City, accidents related to drunk driving were reduced by 35%.

3225. The Ninetieth Indianapolis 500 took place on May 28, 2006, and it was the first such event to only have Honda engines in the field, because Toyota and Chevrolet had pulled out of the event. For the first time ever, no engine issues were reported for an entire month.

3226. To treat eczema outbreaks, you can apply Vaseline and then wrap the affected area with plastic wrap.

3227. In the 1800's, the first Tuesday in November was made election day by congress in the United States to accommodate farmers and rural workers. November was the month that suited farmers best because the fall harvest was over by then, spring was planting time, and summer was when they worked the fields. Additionally, the weather in November in most of the country was still mild enough for traveling. As far as Tuesday, it was picked because most residents of rural America had to travel far to reach the voting center, so Tuesday gave them enough time to start traveling on Monday instead of Sunday, which would have interfered with church services.

3228. Sphygmomanometer is the device that measures blood pressure.

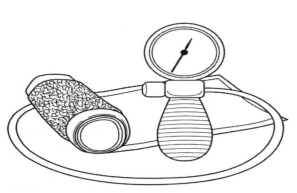

3229. American federal agents used sleep deprivation among other tactics to end the standoff during the fifty one day siege in Texas at the Branch Davidian Compound in Waco, in 1993. They broadcasted loud noises all night long, using speakers that were pointed towards the building. The noises included chanting, jet engine sounds, screams of rabbits being slaughtered, and popular music.

3230. Around a billion cigarette lighters are sold in America every year, and of those, roughly 700 million are imported with 400 million of them coming from China alone.

3231. The National Park Service claims that George Washington ended up with a biracial family after Parke Custis, his adopted son, had children with their slaves.

3232. A survey conducted in the US workforce showed that over 30% of workers would give up a raise in exchange for seeing their immediate supervisor fired.

3233. In some hospitals there exists a device that detects exactly where the patients' vein is and projects it on their skin.

3234. A study published in the Journal of Addiction in 2008 indicated that roughly 76% of adults experience some form of hangover after drinking.

3235. In the Judaism religion, there are eight different levels of charity. The highest level being supporting someone into finding them a job which allows them to be self-sufficient.

3236. In 2013, a research conducted by the Oxford University showed that guys need to have at least two "boys' nights" a week to stay healthy.

3237. The ten documented people who have lived the longest are all women, ranging from 116 years old to 122 years old.

3238. In 2012, after research was done for packaging tobacco products by the Australian government, it was determined that the color Pantone 448 C, also known as opaque couche, is the most offensive color to put beside the health warnings related to smoking. The color is used to make the cigarette packages look as unappealing as possible to discourage people from smoking.

3239. Based on New England Journal of Medicine reports, there is a thirty year old man from India who developed an unusual flower-shaped cataract with ten petals after sustaining a concussion from a bike accident.

3240. Coal mine fires can burn for decades or even centuries. There are actually thousands of these fires across the world.

3241. Britain used to have a half penny coin, until it was decommissioned in 1984.

3242. A professor of nutrition at Kansas State University acted as a human guinea pig for his students to prove that counting calories is the only thing that matters when losing weight. He ate junk food such as

Oreos, Doritos, Twinkies, and other unhealthy snacks for two months straight and still lost twenty seven pounds.

3243. Prior to getting married, Amish men are actually clean shaven, however, they are required to grow their beards after marriage. All other aspects of Amish life are determined by a list of written and oral rules known as Ordnung, which outlines the essentials of the Amish faith and helps to define what it means to be Amish.

3244. Mary Josephine Fitzgerald was the grandmother of John F. Kennedy who not only outlived John, but was never told about his assassination.

3245. The letter "J" is the only letter of the alphabet that doesn't appear on the Periodic Table.

3246. A bowl of dry corn flakes contains about 25,000 more genes than the whole human body. At the same time, humans have over 1,700 more genes than earthworms.

3247. Studies show that people notice your shoes or whatever you are wearing on your feet on a subconscious level before they notice anything else about you.

3248. 17,000 people from twenty eight developed western nations participated in a survey that found that live-in boyfriends on average did more housework than married men. It also found that married women did more chores than live-in girlfriends.

3249. In the 1960's, Columbia University researchers conducted an experiment called the "Smoke-Filled Room," in which students were put in rooms and asked to fill forms while smoke was pumped inside through vents. Students who were alone almost invariably left the room to report the smoke. Strangely, when the students were joined in the room by actors who pretended not to notice the smoke, only one out of ten of them went to report the smoke. Most of the others kept trying to fill their forms, as they occasionally waved the smoke away.

3250. John and Frances Canning invited Queen Elizabeth to their wedding in Manchester in 2012 as a joke. They were surprised and astonished when she actually showed up.

3251. Cannabinoids are a group of chemicals usually found in cannabis plants, but they are only present in two other places: in chocolate and in the human brain.

3252. Sir Hugh Beaver, managing director of Guinness Brewery, unsuccessfully shot at a golden plover in 1951, and subsequently got into a debate on whether the bird was the fastest of all European game birds. He realized that there was no resource he could reference to settle the argument, so he made his own resource, and the Guinness Book of World Records was born.

3253. The laser doesn't actually take the ink away when it's used to remove tattoos. It merely breaks down the ink so that your body can flush it out. So your tattoo technically leaves your body when you go to the toilet.

3254. In an effort to prove that the Earth was hollow, John Quincy Adams, during his tenure as US president, began an expedition to the center of the Earth.

3255. Have you ever heard a catchy song, and then, after that, it got stuck in your head, replaying itself over and over again? There's an actual name for such songs. They are called "earworms."

3256. Thomas Jefferson purchased a new thermometer several days before he signed the Declaration of Independence on July 4, 1776. He used it to record the temperature in Philadelphia, Pennsylvania, on the historical day, and it was seventy six degrees Fahrenheit (or twenty four degrees Celsius) when the document was signed.

3257. "Ingvar Kamprad Elmtaryd Agunnaryd" is the full name from which the popular name of the Swedish furniture chain IKEA is derived. It's actually the name of the company's founder, the name of the farm in which he grew up, and the name of his hometown.

3258. Dog collars that have studs and spikes are used for decorative purposes these days, but originally, these dog collars were used by shepherds who put them around dogs' necks in Turkey years ago, to protect the dogs from wolves.

3259. Robert Heft submitted a design of the American flag in 1958, and then President Dwight D. Eisenhower accepted it as the official design. Heft, who was seventeen at the time, had gotten a B minus for his flag design, but his teacher changed his grade to an A after the flag was chosen by the president.

3260. Although the cities of Nagasaki and Hiroshima were the sites of nuclear bombings, those places are no longer radioactive today because the explosion happened fairly high up in the air, and the resultant radioactive fireball never touched the land which reduced the nuclear fallout.

3261. Every day at five in the morning, John Quincy Adams, the sixth president of America, would swim naked in the Potomac River.

3262. The Federal Emergency Management Agency (FEMA) informally uses a scale called the Waffle House index to state the severity of an incoming storm. Waffle House is known for leaving its restaurants open despite bad weather, so, when they label a storm as "the restaurant is closed," it implies that there's imminent severe damage.

3263. In 2000, during the prime of Blockbuster Video stores, the company made about $800 million from collecting late fees, which accounted for 16% of their revenue.

3264. MIT mails out acceptance notices each year on March 14, which is called "Pi Day," at 6.28pm, which is known as "Tau Time."

3265. 80% of the press coverage of Donald Trump during his first one hundred days as president were negative according to a Harvard study.

3266. People who hold the belief that human life can be sustained without water and food but merely by prana are known as breatharians. Prana is what's known as life force, and it's the light and air around a person. Many breatharians claim that they have lived for extended periods of time without water and food, but unfortunately, some people have died trying to replicate their example.

3267. Limes sink in most cases when placed in a pool of water, but lemons float. Orange fruits will float when they are whole, but they'll sink when they are in slices.

3268. A small town in Iowa called Riverside declared in 1985 that it was the future birthplace of original Star Trek series character James Tiberius Kirk, who was the captain of the USS Enterprise.

3269. Although gothic architecture is often linked with vampires, one of its core design principles is to let in as much natural light as possible.

3270. In 1972, Shirley Chisholm became the first black woman to run for the presidency in the US. Although she never expected to win, she ran only to prove that Americans could vote for a black woman.

3271. When Paris' sewers get clogged, officials often use large wood and iron rolling balls to clean them out, the same technique used over a hundred years ago.

3272.   A nurdle is the name given to that blob of toothpaste in the shape of a wave on your toothpaste box.

3273.   A man named Daryl Davis befriended some members of the KKK in the 1980's which caused them to leave the group as they slowly learned all the misconceptions of the black community.

3274.   The first woman to vie for the presidency was Victoria Woodhull, in 1872, running as an equal rights party nominee against Ulysses S. Grant. This happened fifty years before the 19th amendment that gave women the right to vote.

3275.   Robert F. Kennedy (a former attorney general) actually failed third grade and attended almost a dozen schools. He was smaller than his siblings and was often considered the runt of the family.

3276.   Cigarettes used to be sold in vending machines that only accepted quarters and cost twenty three cents. Instead of cigarette companies increasing the price, they included two pennies inside of each box.

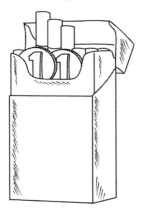

3277.   Major league baseballs are actually stitched by hand. In total, 108 stitches cover a single ball.

3278.   There is a pee repellent paint used to protect public walls from bodily fluids, as it causes urine to splash back at the offender. In fact, San Francisco is using this paint inspired by Hamburg, Germany, who painted all their city walls with this repellent and saw public urination drop significantly.

3279.   There is an uninhibited granite islet named Rockall in the Atlantic Ocean where less than twenty people have been to. That means that more people have stepped foot on the moon than have been to Rockall.

3280.   Thanks to his role in mediating the Treaty of Portsmouth, which ended the Russo-Japanese War, Theodore Roosevelt won the Nobel Peace Prize in 1906, becoming the first American to get the award. He later used the prize money to fund a trust to promote industrial peace.

3281.   The seventh largest human gathering in the history of the world occurred in the city of Chicago, where it was estimated that five million people gathered at Grant Park for a rally to celebrate the Cubs World Series win.

3282.   Rhinestones got their name from the Rhine River. In fact, the Austrian factory that produced them used energy that was driven by the Rhine River.

3283.   In 1862, fractional currency comprising ten, twenty-five and fifty cent denominations were issued by the US government in the form of notes. They were printed between August 21, 1862, and May 29, 1863. Today, they are extremely rare and valuable.

3284.   Martin Luther King Jr. was originally named Michael. When his father traveled to Germany, he became deeply inspired by the protestant reformation leader Martin Luther. In consequence, he changed his own name as well as the name of his five year old son.

3285.   There is a doll created for Nivea that is made of UV-sensitive material. The doll turns into a painful-looking bright red if left out in the sun, so applying sunscreen to it turns it white again. It was made with the purpose of teaching children the importance of wearing sunscreen.

3286.   The LG in "LG Corporation" stands for Lucky Goldstar, which is its former name and it is also the acronym of the company's tagline: "Life's Good."

3287.   Back in 1919, if you bought a single share of Coca-Cola stock, it would be $40. If you kept it till today, it would be worth $9.8 million.

3288.   The world's biggest online shopping day is on Single's Day in China; it's when uncoupled folks celebrate by buying themselves gifts.

3289. There is only one ventriloquist museum in the world. Located in Fort Mitchell, Kentucky, the museum houses 750 ventriloquist dummies from over twenty different countries.

3290. A wine for cats was created by a company called Apollo Peak, in Colorado. It contains no alcohol and is made of catnip with beets to give it the typical red wine color. It comes in flavors like pinot meow and moscato. Single serving bottles cost $5 while eight-ounce bottles cost $12.

3291. Only 10% of the world's population lives in the southern hemisphere. That means there's only eight hundred million in the south compared to the six billion in the north.

3292. The youngest president in US history was Theodore Roosevelt at just forty two years old. He took office in 1901, after the assassination of William McKinley, for whom he served as vice president.

3293. To make change for a dollar in the US, there are 293 different combinations.

3294. Li Ka-shing is the richest man in Hong Kong. He dropped out of school before he turned sixteen and now has an estimated net worth of $20.1 billion.

3295. In 1945, Harold Matson and Elliot Handler started Mattel Toy Company in a garage. The name Mattel is a combination of their names. They actually started out by producing picture frames, but when Elliot started making dollhouse furniture from the picture frames scraps, they were so successful that they switched over to making only toys.

3296. In 2013, a study conducted by researchers at the Harvard School of Public Health revealed that drinking several cups of coffee a day could reduce the risk of suicide in men and women by about 50%.

3297. Gun silencers don't actually silence a gun. The hot gases released after a gun is shot expand quickly and create shock waves when they leave the chamber of the gun. Silencers contain a series of expansion chambers that cool and dissipate the gases before they leave the barrel of the gun. They work similarly to the muffler on your car.

3298. The university that has produced the greatest number of billionaires in the world is the University of Pennsylvania with twenty five billionaires.

3299. According to a study published in the Journal of Current Biology, people who exercise four hours after learning something new retained the information better two days later than those who exercise immediately or not at all.

3300. According to a study published by the Journal of Transportation, people who are bicycling are in the best mood compared to any other means of transportation.

3301. Before his assassination in 1968, Robert Kennedy had eleven children with his wife Ethel. They also had thirty five grandchildren.

3302. Throwing a penny from the top of the Empire State Building would not be lethal to anyone on the ground as it's too small and flat. According to physicist Louis Bloomfield from the University of Virginia, if a penny landed on someone from that height, then it would feel more like getting flicked and not even that hard.

3303. In Cleveland, there is a system where college students get to live for free at retirement houses as it's mutually beneficial for both parties. The retirees get contact with younger people where studies have shown helps beat dementia and the students save on housing costs.

3304. The most googled person in 2016 was President Donald Trump, not only in the United States, but also in more than eighty eight countries, from India to Mexico to Belgium.

3305. On average, people who smoke can die ten years earlier than non-smokers according to the Centers for Disease Control and Prevention. Additionally, for every person who dies because of smoking, at least thirty people suffer from a severe smoking related illness.

3306. In 1990, disabled activists left their wheelchairs behind and crawled up the steps of the Capitol. The protest aimed to encourage a vote on the Americans with Disabilities Act.

3307. Lightning usually strikes the same place repeatedly, particularly if it's a tall, pointy, isolated object. The Empire State building, for example, is hit on average twenty three times a year by lightning.

3308. The world's first hot air balloon trip occurred in September, 1783, in Versailles, France. The passengers however were a rooster, a duck and a sheep, not human beings.

3309. Caucasians tend to get gray hair first, followed by Asians, then African-Americans. Scientists still don't know why.

3310. To keep with the continuity, naturalist Sir David Attenborough always wears a blue shirt and khaki pants in his specials, as they can sometimes film thousands of miles and months apart.

3311. "Globe Chase Tag" is actually a competitive international league for the popular game "Tag You're It."

3312. In February 2016, a license plate was auctioned off in Hong Kong for $2.3 million. It has the lucky number 28 which sounds like the words "easy" and "to prosper" in Cantonese. For this reason, the number is thought to bring good fortune to the owner.

3313. Tesla doesn't have a marketing budget and instead puts all its money into making their product as good as possible.

3314. The oldest person to ever visit the South Pole was famous astronaut and adventurer Buzz Aldrin, in 2016, at the age of eighty six. However, after he began to experience altitude sickness and was short of breath, he had to evacuate.

3315. The first American president to be given a secret service code name was former President Harry S. Truman, who served from 1945 to 1953. His code name was General.

3316. According to a study published in the Journal of Neurobiology of Aging, the more flights of stairs a person climbs or the more years of school a person completes, the younger the brain physically looks. Jason Steffener, a scientist and researcher at Concordia's Center, found that the brain age decreases by 0.95 years for each year of education, and it decreases 0.58 years for every daily flight of stairs climbed.

3317. The most recent test of a nuclear bomb goes to North Korea, according to the Guinness World Record, which happened on May 25, 2009.

3318. Some studies suggest that gifted people tend to have bad handwriting because their brains are normally working faster than their hands.

3319. The second non US born First Lady is Melania Trump. The first one was Louisa Catherine Adams, wife of John Adams, the sixth president of the United States.

3320. Coconuts can be classified as fruits, nuts, or seeds. Many people consider them to be the tree of life as every part of a coconut can be used as food, fiber, drink, utensils, fuel, and even instruments.

3321. The best time to spray perfume onto yourself is right after a bath or shower. The scent lasts longer when it's applied to hydrated skin.

3322. By just spinning an egg you can tell the difference of a hard-cooked one from a raw one. If it spins easily, it's hard-cooked. If it wobbles, it's raw.

3323. Frankenstein's monster was never actually given a name, but he tells his creator, Victor Frankenstein, that he should be called Adam (based on Adam in the Bible). Victor, however, does not refer to the monster as Adam, but he uses instead various insulting names like devil, the demon, specter, thing, being, and ogre.

3324. Forty eight hours after quitting smoking, your sense of smell and taste begin to improve dramatically.

3325. The news about the assassination of President Abraham Lincoln reached London eleven days after the fatal event happened.

3326. Researchers at the University of Helsinki have found that running in shoes that are highly cushioned make your legs stiffer and increase impact loading. Research proved that extra cushioned shoes actually alter the spring-like mechanisms of running.

3327. Some Maltese churches have two clocks. The one placed on the right side reads the correct time, and is used by the faithful to know when to go to mass. The one on the left is set to read the wrong time, supposedly to confuse the devil so he can't disrupt the church services.

3328. According to a memo from a top franchisee, only one out of every five millennials has ever tried a Big Mac.

3329. The fear of baldness is called peladophobia.

3330. Certain studies carried out by the Indiana University Media School showed that watching cat videos seems to boost viewers' energy and positive emotions.

3331. American presidents who've served from January 1, 1997, onwards are to be given life-long secret service protection along with their spouses, according to a law passed in December, 2012. The protection extends to any of their children aged sixteen or under.

3332. Before the Grand Prix featured sponsor decorated vehicles, the cars had the colors of the countries they were from. Germany's team used to have a white car, but in 1934, it came in overweight,

so they peeled off all the lead paint, leaving a silver shining car. As a result, Germany changed its color to silver, and Mercedes Benz was inspired to make the famous race cars.

3333. "Froggyland" is a museum in Croatia that exhibits 507 stuffed frogs. The frogs are actually the work of 20th century Hungarian taxidermist Ferenc Mere, who spent ten years stuffing and meticulously organizing the frogs.

3334. It was actually perfectly legal to possess and consume alcohol privately during America's Prohibition Era. Only the production, importation, transportation and sale of alcohol was outlawed.

3335. After the assassination of Abraham Lincoln, his body was taken on a two-week, 1,600-mile (2,574 kilometer) tour by train. Also the body of his son, William Wallace Lincoln, who had died of typhoid fever at the age of eleven, and buried in the DC area in 1862, was taken along with it. The tour involved 400 train stations and viewings were arranged where his body was on display for mourners.

3336. The only two animals in the world who engage in tongue kissing are humans and bonobo chimpanzees.

3337. Originally, the traffic and train light for go was white while caution was green. However, the white light for go caused several accidents. In 1914 for example, one of the red lenses fell out of its holder leaving a white light behind; this ended up with a train running a stop signal and crashing into another train. As a result, the railroad changed it so that the green light means go and yellow was chosen for caution, mainly because it's the most distinct color from the other two.

3338. The procedure of transferring stool from a healthy donor into a gastrointestinal tract of a patient is called fecal transplant. The procedure is done when antibiotics kill off too many of the good bacteria in the digestive system.

3339. Research conducted by scientists from Psychology Today concluded that if a person's body odor smells good to you, it means that their immunity genes are opposite to yours. This allows higher chances for people with opposite immunity genes to mate, which results in descendants with stronger immune systems.

3340. After his death in 1506, Christopher Columbus actually kept on traveling. After he died, he was buried in Valladolid, Spain. However, three years later, his remains were taken to his family in a mausoleum in Sevilla. In 1542, his remains were moved to Santo Domingo, Hispañola, in accordance with his son's will. Then, in 1795, his bones were moved to Havana. Finally, more than a hundred years later, his remains were sent back to Sevilla, in 1898.

3341. Shigeki Tanaka watched Hiroshima get destroyed by the atomic bomb as he grew up in a neighboring town in Japan. Six years later he went to America, the country responsible for the bombing, participated in the Boston City marathon, and won the race on April 19, 1951.

3342. According to the Down Syndrome Program at Boston Children's Hospital, a twenty five year old woman has a one in 1,200 chance of giving birth to a baby with Down syndrome. The chances in a thirty five year-old mother are one in 350. The chances in a forty year old mother are one in 100. And a mother who's forty nine years old has a one in 10 chance.

3343. Amish consider that formal school learning only provides limited value; that is why Amish kids only go to school until the eighth grade. They prefer to emphasize on agriculture as well as manual trades.

3344. According to the Dead Sea Scrolls and other various ancient manuscripts, Goliath stood at 6.75 inches (2.06 meters) tall. In contrast, the Masoretic Texts describe him to be 9.74 inches (2.97 meters) tall. Most scholars believe, however, that the shorter height was the accurate one.

3345. The one ounce gold American Eagle coin is legal tender; they are worth $1,295 US dollars each. The one ounce silver American Eagle coin is the only silver bullion coin that is approved as legal tender and is worth about $17.50 US each.

3346. Based on reports done by the US Bureau of Labor Statistics, a $100,000 year salary in 1950 is equivalent to more than $1 million salary in 2019 when adjusted for inflation.

3347. The political opponents of Andrew Jackson used to refer to him as a jackass, so he decided to adopt the name and use it as his campaign symbol. Eventually, it became the symbol of the entire Democratic Party in America.

3348. To produce a USD $100 bill, it only costs 14.3 cents. However, it costs over 1.43 cents to make every penny. This is the reason why other major countries have already eliminated pennies altogether.

3349. When Barack Obama visited Cuba in March, 2016, he became the first US president to do so in eighty eight years. Calvin Coolidge was the last president to make the trip in 1928.

3350. People in North America take less time for vacation, work more, and retire later than other industrialized countries.

3351. Sushi is actually meant to be eaten with your hands and sashimi with chopsticks.

3352. In 2014, a study done by St. Michael's Hospital on homeless men revealed that almost half of them have suffered from at least one traumatic brain injury in their life. In 87% of the cases, those injuries occurred before they lost their homes.

3353. In Devon, UK, there is a nightclub that gave out free lollipops to its clubbers to reduce late-night rowdiness. They hoped that drunken clubbers would be busy sucking the lollipops, hence they wouldn't shout or cause any trouble. It worked.

3354. The only American president with a PhD. was President Woodrow Wilson.

3355. A type of tumor known as "teratoma" can grow hair, teeth, organs, and limbs. Scientists are still uncertain why they form.

3356. According to the University of Southern Queensland, facial hair can block up to 95% of the sun's harmful UV rays, protecting you from cancer.

3357. According to a study conducted at the University of Central Florida, people who have had bad or abusive bosses in the past will make themselves into a better boss when the time comes.

3358. When photosynthesis occurs in oceans, as when algae turn sunlight into energy, it makes a ping sound. Scientists believe that these sounds could act as a sort of stethoscope when checking for health of a coral reef.

3359. In 2016, a report from the US News & World Report showed that only 18% of American drivers know how to operate a stick shift, and only about 5% of cars sold in the United States today come with a stick shift.

3360. French fries were partly made popular in America by Thomas Jefferson. He came back from France with instructions for making "pommes de terre frites a cru en petites tranches," which means raw potatoes that are cut into small pieces and deep-fried. Although French fries didn't become popular until the twentieth century, the recipe he wrote down is fifty years older than early French-fry entries on cookbooks.

3361. Mother Teresa was canonized on September 4, 2016, by Pope Francis, officially making her Saint Teresa. Her canonization happened almost twenty years after her death, in 1997.

3362. In 2010, a study revealed that men who wear red appear more attractive to women. Red appeared to signify higher status and power which lead to increased attraction.

3363. Richard Nixon appeared on the cover of Time Magazine fifty five times, more than any other individual.

3364. We are now living at a time that's closer to when the Jetsons was set (2062), than when it originally aired (1962).

3365. "Gitumo" is a form of meditation implemented by Tibetan nuns, which can actually change their core body temperatures. A team of researchers once recorded the internal temperature of the nuns in the freezing cold temperatures of the Himalayas, using special temperature measurements and, incredibly, the nuns were able to increase their core body temperature up to almost 101 degrees Fahrenheit (thirty eight degrees Celsius).

3366. Dr. Timothy Clarke Smith, of Vermont, was afraid of being buried alive, so he left precise instructions to build a window looking down into his coffin. He is currently buried in Evergreen Cemetery with a headstone that has a 1.18 foot (thirty centimeter) glass window that is still there today.

3367. The University of Washington Huskies have a live mascot, but it isn't a husky, it's really an Alaskan malamute they've named Dubs II.

3368. The land that served as the headquarters of the Ku Klux Klan in Atlanta, Georgia, was bought by the Catholic Church. They turned it into a church called the Cathedral of Christ the King.

3369. The University of Oregon's mascot, known as the Oregon duck, is based on Disney's Donald Duck. A special license agreement between the school and the company was signed.

3370. The largest known prime number ever discovered has 23.2 million digits. The Electronic Frontier Foundation offers prizes for anyone who finds record primes. Participants have the opportunity to win over $50,000.

3371. The creator of KFC, Colonel Sanders, was fired from a bunch of jobs, including being a lawyer, before he found himself broke at the age of sixty five, which is when he began his franchise.

3372. If you take a piece of fresh garlic, cut it in half, put it in a plastic bag, and then put your bare foot in it, you will be able to taste and smell the garlic after an hour. Garlic contains a molecule called "allicin" which can permeate through the skin of your foot and travel up your bloodstream to the mouth and nose.

3373. According Steve Levitt, an economist from the University of Chicago, for every mile (1.6 kilometers) that you walk drunk, you are eight times more likely to die than if you were to drive a mile drunk.

3374. Washing machines and chainsaws are very popular among Amish families. In fact, 97% of them use motorized washing machines while 75% of them use chainsaws. In contrast, only 6% of them use tractors for field work.

3375. People born in the month of May may have the lowest risk of illness and disease according to a study conducted at Columbia University.

3376. One of the worst and most unprofessional fonts is known to be Comic Sans, also known as typeface. However, it is frequently used by and for people with dyslexia because they are able to focus on the individual parts of the words thanks to the irregular shapes in the letters.

3377. Tobacco has natural sugar in it. Sometimes, however, sugar is added to tobacco manufacturing to create a sweeter smell and taste.

3378. Patients in hospitals who have a view of trees and natural scenery recover faster than those who do not, according to the American Association for the Advancement of Science. Experts gathered this information between the years of 1972 and 1981, by observing patients who stayed in a particular suburban Pennsylvania hospital.

3379. A biotech startup has succeeded in printing 3D rhino horns that are genetically similar to a real horn. The company plans to flood Chinese and Vietnamese markets, where demand is often high, and bring down the price, and hopefully the demand.

3380. The first official coin to go into circulation in the US was created by Benjamin Franklin. Instead of it saying "In God We Trust," it said "Mind Your Business."

3381. The most expensive liquid on Earth is scorpion venom valued at almost forty million dollars per gallon. You'd have to milk two and a half million scorpions to obtain a whole gallon of liquid.

3382. The "PT" in PT Cruiser stands for "personal transport."

3383. George Washington was promoted to history's only six star general in 1976.

3384. President Theodore Roosevelt didn't like the idea of putting "In God We Trust" on US currency.

He thought it would be unwise to cheapen such a motto by using it on coins, the same as using it on postage stamps or in advertisements.

3385.   The majority of car airbags can deploy at speeds of up to 200 miles (322 kilometers) per hour. At speeds that high, airbags can cause real harm to a car occupant, and it can break one's bones.

3386.   Bill Wilson, the co-founder of Alcoholics Anonymous, thought that using LSD could help treat alcoholism based on his own experiences with the drug. In fact, he suggested incorporating the drug into the program, but the other leading members refused.

3387.   When it comes to long-distance running, humans are the best on the planet. We can outrun every animal on the planet and run in conditions that no other animal can run in.

3388.   On December 12, 1925, the first motel ever opened in San Luis Obispo, California, and was called the "Milestone Inn." The purpose of the motel was to lodge automobile travelers, which is the main reason they are called motels.

3389.   Patients with Parkinson's were given placebos and, those who believed it was medicine worth $1,500, showed more positive results than patients who were told they were getting a drug worth $100, according to a study published in the Journal of Neurology. In both cases, the doctors only gave them saline shots.

3390.   "Vinculum" is the name given to the line that separates the top and bottom numbers of a fraction.

3391.   The piercing screeching sound that many, particularly in America, associate with the bald eagle, isn't from the eagle at all. Hollywood wanted to make the eagle, the symbol of America, sound more fierce, so they frequently dub the screech of the red-tailed hawk onto the bald eagle. The actual bald eagle doesn't sound like a tough predator swooping in from the sky, but more like a singing parakeet.

3392.   "Something Store" is an online shop that for $10, will randomly select an item and send it to you. You'll only know what you get once you receive the item.

3393.   Jens Stoltenberg, a former Norwegian Prime Minister, once drove a taxi around because he wanted to hear what real Norwegian voters had to say. He thought that taxis were actually one of the few places where people can freely share their opinions.

3394.   It's against the honor code to consume alcohol for Brigham Young University students. For that reason the university holds a Milktober Fest, as an alternative to Oktoberfest, where they promote drinking milk and doing homework before the midterm season.

3395.   Endling is the name given to the last individual of a single species. When it dies, the species is extinct for good.

3396.   1% of static on your television comes from the light of the Big Bang.

3397.   In 1881, in Tombstone, Arizona, the famous gunfight that took place at the OK Corral between the Earp Brothers along with Doc Holiday against the cowboys lasted only thirty seconds.

3398.   According to William A. Hiscock from Montana State University, if you were in a spaceship that continually accelerated at 1G and traveled to the center of our galaxy and back, it would only take forty years. However, after coming back, 60,000 years will have passed on Earth although only forty years have passed for you. This means that you can technically go into the future.

3399. On June 7, 2017, in the Swedish city of Helsingborg, the Museum of Failure was opened for the first time. It was purposefully created by Samuel West who wanted people to think differently about failure by realizing that success wouldn't exist without it.

3400. American presidents are not allowed to go to the top of the Gateway Arch in St. Louis, Missouri, as the US Secret Service forbids it. The only one who was the exception to this rule was Dwight D. Eisenhower, when he visited the monument in 1967 at seventy seven years old. The Arch was actually closed to the public as he insisted on riding the tram to the top.

3401. Dementia Village, a small village in Holland, is inhabited by people with dementia. The village has been designed to be a normal environment with grocery stores, restaurants, cafes, and gardens, within a secure perimeter. Patients can safely roam around without feeling locked down or confused.

3402. Florida has a mythical creature called the "Skunk Ape," the same way that Northern States have the legend of BigFoot. It's said to be a 7.87 feet (2.4 meter) tall human-like primate, and it smells like cow manure or rotten eggs, according to stories that were very popular in the 1970's. There were so many reported sightings of this creature that state lawmakers even tried to make it a criminal misdemeanor to kidnap, possess, molest, or hurt humanoid or anthropoid animals.

3403. In 2016, the Journal of Evolutionary Biology published a study suggesting that when it comes to facial hair on men, more women prefer them to have five to ten days of growth instead of being clean-shaven.

3404. Someone who works with iron and steel is called a blacksmith, while someone who works with white metal such as tin and pewter is called a whitesmith. There is also a brownsmith who works with brass and copper.

3405. The generic term used for various small fish that are sealed in cans or other containers is sardine.

3406. In the presidential election of 1872, women's rights activist Susan B. Anthony voted illegally. She was tried, convicted, and sentenced to pay a $100 fine. Although she didn't pay it, she was released anyway.

3407. Ten years after the 9/11 events, the New York Times created a "Portraits of Grief" which was an archive of articles about all the victims of 9/11 and how the families are coping with the grief.

3408. According to studies, if you're feeling sad, drawing a picture of your favorite food can actually cheer you up. In 2013, a study by researchers at St. Bonaventure University in New York showed that people who drew pictures of pizza and cupcakes had up to a 28% increase in their moods.

3409. The most photographed person from the 1800's was American abolitionist Frederick Douglass.

3410. Sperm whale oil was often used by the automotive industry to lubricate new cars years ago. In fact, the substance was so good that huge mammals were actually hunted almost to extinction. As a result, the US declared sperm whales an endangered species and switched to the new whale-free automatic transmission fluid.

3411. A person who totally abstains from consuming alcohol is called a "teetotaler." To teetotal literally means to never consume alcohol.

3412. Dr. Rush's Bilious Pill was a type of remedy taken by the explorers of the Lewis and Clark when they felt constipated on their journey. The pill was made of ten grains of calomel which contains mercury. Experts were able to locate the exact spot where they camped in Montana by finding some signatures of mercury in their pit latrines. Before they set off on their journey, Lewis and Clark were informed by American President Thomas Jefferson that they would possibly encounter mountains of salt, Welsh speaking Indians, herds of wooly mammoths and giant ground sloths. Although they did not encounter any of these things, Lewis did find 178 species of plants that were unknown, as well as 122 new animals such as grizzly bears and coyotes.

3413. In 1973, a computer at MIT predicted that by the year 2040 our society would end as a result of overpopulation, pollution levels, or lack of natural resources on Earth.

3414. Napoleon Bonaparte, the French army leader, really hated losing games, particularly card games.

He frequently cheated, but most people never called him out, to avoid upsetting him. His mother, however, always called him out. He in turn would tell his mother that she was rich and could afford to lose, but he was poor and needed to win.

3415.   Eructation is the proper medical term for burping or belching.

3416.   There is actually a difference between terror and horror. Terror occurs in anticipation of the horrifying experience, while horror occurs after.

3417.   The reason why t-shirts are called that are because they are shaped like a "T" when laid down.

3418.   An analysis of hundreds of basketball halftime speeches from several high school and college games was performed by the Journal of Applied Psychology. The result showed that the more negative the coach was at halftime, the better the team played in the second half, even if a team was already up at half-time.

3419.   Artificial intelligence is capable of accurately guessing if someone is gay or straight, according to a study performed at Stanford University, in 2017. Researches created a computer algorithm that could distinguish between gay and straight men 81% of the time, while for women it was 74% of the time.

3420.   In the United States, 14.5% of men are over six feet tall. Despite this, 58% of CEOs at Fortune 500 Companies are more than six feet tall.

3421.   The White House, the Treasury building, and foreign diplomatic missions in Washington along with the first family are guarded by nearly 3,200 special agents and 1,300 uniformed officers. The team also provides security to other politically relevant individuals, such as the vice president, the president-elect, the vice president-elect, former presidents and their families, presidential candidates visiting heads of state, and representatives of the US performing special missions overseas.

3422.   A study conducted at the University of California Davis revealed that adding a small amount of seaweed to a cow's diet reduces their methane production by almost 60%. This finding could lessen the amount of greenhouse gasses that bovines emit.

3423.   It's possible to get music from the classic Sega games on Spotify. Tracks like "Outrun," "Sonic the Hedgehog," "Shinobi," "Golden Axe," and "Jet Set Radio" can be found. In fact, there are more than a dozen full albums to choose from.

3424.   When nuclear weapons are detonated over high altitudes, they can cause retinal burns in the eyes if looked at without safety goggles, and the sky can light up for up to thirty minutes.

3425.   Oyster spat is the name given to a baby oyster.

3426.   The first American president to have a Christmas tree in the public part of the White House was President William H. Taft. It was placed in the blue room and, in fact, the room still hosts the official Christmas tree today.

3427.   Mugen Puti Puti was created by the Japanese in 2008, a toy made from silicon that feels like popping bubble wrap, which you can do forever.

3428.   The cat is the only domestic animal not mentioned in the Bible.

3429.   In 2005, a Valentine bear called "Crazy for you Bear" was released by the Vermont Teddy Bear Company. The bear came wearing a straight jacket and commitment papers. Sales were actually good until advocates for the mentally ill protested it, and the company stopped making them.

3430. To help create an underwater reef for crustaceans and fish, more than 2,500 decommissioned subway cars in New York have been dropped into the Atlantic Ocean.

3431. When the ill-fated Donner Party set out from Springfield, Illinois, in 1846, a young lawyer named Abraham Lincoln considered joining the group on their journey. He eventually changed his mind and decided to not go given that he had a child at home and his wife Mary Todd was also pregnant.

3432. Sleeping under a weighted blanket seems to provide a better night's sleep to people with anxiety, depression, or insomnia. These blankets are filled with plastic pellets and add weight, and cost anywhere from $120 - $250.

3433. The first time that Julius Caesar saw giraffes, he named them camelopards since they looked to him like both camels and leopards.

3434. Minus forty degrees Fahrenheit and minus forty degrees Celsius are exactly the same temperatures. Fahrenheit devised his scale using the coldest temperature that he could produce using brine as the zero point, and the temperature of the body as 100. Celsius used the freezing and boiling points of water as his zero point and 100.

3435. If you want to temporarily get rid of the feeling of nausea, smelling rubbing alcohol can actually help. After three or four deep breaths, the isopropyl in the alcohol pads greatly reduces nausea and vomiting.

3436. At the University of Ohio's campus, there are utility tunnels lined with pipes that run under most of the buildings. They were created in the late 1800's as a way to access the pipes in case of an emergency without digging through the lawn, and they are still in use today.

3437. According to studies, psychopaths are immune to contagious yawning and are also less likely to be startled.

3438. On the evening of September 11, 2001, a candlelight vigil was carried out by hundreds of Iranian people who gathered in Madar Square, Tehran, to express sympathy and support for the American people.

3439. Lots of Mayflower pilgrims were running away from prosecution in England, and some others were actually leaving because they feared that the Dutch Republic was influencing their kids.

3440. Český Krumlov is a castle located in the Czech Republic that has a bear moat. The moat originally housed bears as protection, in 1707, and has been reconstructed in the 1990's, where bears were once again added to the moat.

3441. The North compounded the counterfeit problem experienced in the South during the American Civil War, when they printed large numbers of fake notes and distributed them in many southern communities. This resulted in serious inflation, which negatively impacted the economy of the confederacy.

3442. In the early 20th century, Sears published and distributed tombstone and monument catalogs among Americans.

3443. The study of bells and how they are cast, tuned, rung, and sound is called "campanology." It also comprises the history, methods, and traditions of bell-ringing as an art.

3444. The USS Sequoia was a presidential yacht used from the Herbert Hoover administration until Jimmy Carter sold it in 1977. It had an elevator for Franklin Roosevelt, but Lyndon Johnson replaced it with a Liquor Bar.

3445. The eagle used to be a fifth playing card suit. In the United States, those cards were green with an eagle on them instead of red or black. In England, they were blue with a royal symbol for a crown. They were originally created to be used in the game of bridge.

3446. In 1986, waterbeds were so popular that they took up 20% of the bed market that year. These days, they make up less than 5% of bed sales. They were originally used as a form of therapy for medical patients back in the 19th century.

3447. Nemanja Petrovic, a Serbian street beggar, realized that he was able to make more money by begging if he was not around while he did it. He made a sign that said "Invisible beggar" and tossed it on the ground with his hat and shoes, and left. When he came back, he found his hat full of money.

3448. The Journal of Positive Psychology showed that over half of all people have no clue at what their strengths are or what they're good at.

3449. On July 4, 1826, US former Presidents John Adams and Thomas Jefferson both died in different states from different illnesses. On that same day, the country was celebrating the 50th anniversary of their Declaration of Independence. President James Monroe also died on July 4, but in 1831. In other words, three of the five first US presidents died on Independence Day.

3450. Back in 2007, the Royal Canadian Mint issued the world's largest coin. It was twenty inches (fifty centimeters) in diameter and one inch (2.5 centimeters) thick. It was made of 99.99% gold bullion; it weighs 220 pounds (a hundred kilograms) and is worth an estimated $1 million.

3451. Since 2007, McDonald's has been taking advantage of the used cooking oil in the UK. The leftover oil has been used as fuel for more than half of their fleet of delivery trucks.

3452. An extra inch (2.54 centimeters) in height correlates with earning $800 more a year, according to anthropologist Thomas Gregor, from Vanderbilt University. If you roll this amount over a thirty year period, then it would equate to earning hundreds of thousands of dollars more than someone that's only an inch shorter.

3453. A Gallup poll from 1966 showed that 66% of Americans had an unfavorable opinion of civil rights activist Doctor Martin Luther King Junior. The percentage actually increased by 26% from the poll taken in 1963.

3454. Although Steve Irwin is known as an animal lover, there was one in particular that he didn't like very much. During an interview with Scientific American magazine, he said that: "For some reason, parrots have to bite me. That's their job; I don't know what it is." He also confessed that one almost ripped his nose off once.

3455. The Australian Center for Ancient DNA found out in a study that Neanderthals would self-medicate to deal with pain. When they had pain, they would eat poplar which contains a painkiller and salicylic acid, which is the active ingredient in aspirin.

3456. The first politician to ever use political TV ads was presidential candidate Dwight D. Eisenhower, during his 1952 campaign. He created forty twenty-second TV ads where he answered questions from the audience.

Inventions & Inventors

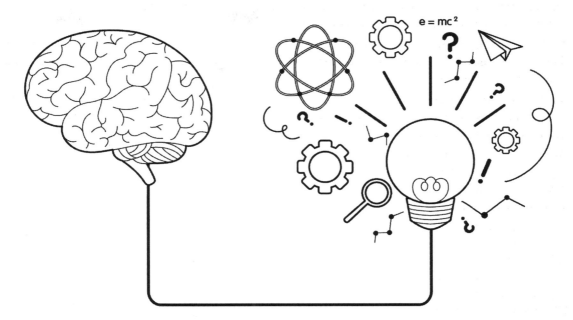

3457. A device that can communicate with fireflies was invented by Joey Stein, of Genius Ideas, in New York City. At the push of a button, it sends out a come hither message that attracts fireflies, letting users observe them up close.

3458. In 1924, Kleenex tissues were first introduced to the public. However, they were intended to be used with cold cream to remove makeup and clean the face. The "kleen" in the name represented the physical clean itself, and the "ex" was tied into the company's other popular and successful product at the time, the "Kotex."

3459. Uritonnoir is the name of a urinal designed by a French firm called Faltazi. It's made using a bale of straw, and it makes nutrient-rich compost out of urine.

3460. A five-story 3-D printed apartment building was created by a WinSun Decoration Design Engineering Chinese firm. It took twelve years to complete, and it remains the tallest 3-D printed building in the world.

3461. When cologne was first marketed in its early days, it was sold as protection. People would actually drink and wear "eau de cologne" thinking it would keep them from getting the plague.

3462. To publicly identify DUI offenders, the state of Ohio issues them with scarlet letter license plates. They are red-on-yellow plates that have been around since 1967, but became compulsory from January, 2014.

3463. Kevin Kumala, an entrepreneur, studied bioplastics with his school friends, and they created their own formula that utilized organic resins, vegetable oil, and starch from cassava. Their material was 100% organic-based, and it was compostable and biodegradable. It could break down immediately in hot water, or over thirty days at sea or on land. Kevin says the material can't leave traces of toxic matter, meaning it can be dissolved and ingested, and it could potentially eliminate pollution.

3464. In 2017, a German company created the first rope free elevator system that is able to go sideways as well as up and down using a new magnetic technology.

3465. A grown-up version of the red and yellow Little Tikes toy car was created by UK brothers Jeff and John Bitmead. It's legal for transit, fully functional, and can go up to seventy miles (113 kilometers) an hour.

3466.   Norwegians, in collaboration with Viking Garden Company, made the world's fastest lawnmower, which can travel as fast as 132 miles (214 kilometers) an hour. It has a 408 horsepower, a V8 engine and Formula 3 wheels.

3467.   The guy who first discovered and sold Vaseline was named Robert Chesebrough, and he believed in the jelly so much that every single day, he ate a spoonful of the substance until his death at age ninety six.

3468.   Kentucky Fried Chicken partnered with Huawei, the Chinese phone maker, to create a limited edition phone in commemoration of their thirtieth anniversary since entering the Chinese market.

3469.   A pacifier that contained a nipple with a magnet was invented in 1969. It was meant to remove pins, nails, or any other metallic objects from the baby's mouth.

3470.   In England, the ballpoint pen is called a biro, as it was invented by Hungarian newspaper journalist Laszlo Biro, and his chemist brother.

3471.   Naval engineer Richard James accidentally invented the Slinky. In 1943, while he was working with tension springs, he discovered that when one of the springs fell, it kept moving. He thought it would make a great toy and so the Slinky toy was born.

3472.   In 2006, the European Company Vestergaard Frandsen launched the "LifeStraw," a straw that makes contaminated water safe to drink. Users just suck up the contaminated water through it as any other regular straw. Its technology removes 99.9% of parasites, 99.9999% of viruses, and provides one person with an entire year's worth of drinking water without the use of batteries or chemicals. It costs only $20 per straw.

3473.   Bluetooth got its name from Ericsson's Viking Heritage, the Swedish communication company. It's named after Danish Viking King Harold Blatand. Blatand translates to Bluetooth in English and incredibly the Bluetooth symbol is actually Blatand's initials inscribed in runic symbols.

3474.   In Silicon Valley, there is a statue of Nikola Tesla (20th century inventor and engineer) that radiates out free Wi-Fi. There's also a time capsule inside that will be opened up in 2043.

3475.   Famous artist Leonardo da Vinci was dyslexic. Also peculiarly, not because of his dyslexia, he chose to write all of his notes to himself backwards in mirror writing, meaning that you can only read them in the reflection of a mirror. Notes that he wrote to other people, however, were written by him in a normal direction.

3476.   In 1927, architect John W. Hammes invented the first garbage disposal. He wanted to make cleaning up for the kitchen easier for his wife.

3477.   There is an airplane with a detachable cabin designed by Ukrainian engineer Vladimir Tatarenko. In case of an emergency, the cabin breaks off, deploys parachutes, and floats passengers safely to sea or ground.

3478.   FINDER, which stands for Finding Individuals for Disaster and Emergency Response, is a device developed by NASA that helps them find people who are still alive and buried after an earthquake or collapsed building. In previous tests, it was able to detect a heartbeat through thirty feet (nine meters) of rubble and twenty feet (six meters) of solid concrete. The device could also be used for finding people that are lost in the forest or trapped in a burning house.

3479.   All "Ford Model T" cars manufactured between 1914 to 1925 were painted black because it was the one color paint they could dry quickly, and the car maker wanted to do things faster to maintain its very high production volume.

3480. Back in the 1970's, in order to collect audio intelligence, the CIA created a spy drone the size of a dragonfly called the Insectothopter. It didn't work however, as it couldn't withstand any type of crosswind while it was flying.

3481. Finder.com is a personal finance website that has launched a programmable handbag designed to help you monitor and curb your impulsive spending, at a cost of $5,000 US. It uses GPS tracking and it can be programmed to lock if you enter any of your pre-programmed danger zones. The handbag will actually vibrate and flash lights to indicate how many times you have taken out your wallet. It will also flash yellow lights and vibrate every two hours to remind you to put on sunscreen.

3482. There was a knife the Russian Forces created that has the ability to shoot out a bullet. The way to properly shoot it is to hold the blade while shooting to absorb the recoil.

3483. In 1910, the Wright brothers (aeroplane pioneers) flew together for the only time. This is because their father was scared of losing them both in an accident. He gave them permission just once that year.

3484. In order to treat burn victims, scientists have created a 3-D printer that uses a patient's own skin cells to print skin grafts, including hair follicles and sweat glands.

3485. Leo Fender invented the telecaster, the first electric guitar in the world to be mass produced, and he owns Fender Electric Instrument Manufacturing, but strangely, he couldn't actually play any of the musical instruments that he created.

3486. In 1953, Norm Larsen invented the WD-40 oil. He was actually trying to conceive a formula to prevent corrosion, which is done by displacing water. So WD stands for "water displacement" and the number 40 is because he finally achieved success on his 40th attempt.

3487. "LifeGem" is a company that plans to create a certified high-quality diamond from the ashes of a loved one who has passed away, including pets.

3488. In 1945, engineer Percy Spencer invented the microwave by accident. One day while working in the lab testing magnetrons that produced microwaves, he noticed that a candy bar he had in his pocket was melting. He soon realized the effect that the microwaves had.

3489. In 2012, the first solar power ski lift in the world was built in the town of Tenna, Switzerland. It has around eighty solar panels and it can pull 800 skiers up the mountain per hour.

3490. In Victorian times, men with mustaches would use a mustache spoon or etiquette spoon to eat their soup. It had a special guard to help keep their neatly kept mustaches clean while they ate.

3491. In order to slow drivers down, optical illusion speed bumps are now being used. This was first introduced in Vancouver, and now other provinces and states in the United States are experimenting with it. One of them involves a three-dimensional little girl chasing a ball.

3492. A material that can turn heat from your body into an electrical current has been developed by scientists. The new material is called power felt.

3493. Since 1878, the headphone jack, like the one some smartphones have now, has remained relatively unchanged other than size.

3494. Someone has invented a type of knife for the sole purpose of being able to empty a Nutella jar clean.

3495. Doctor Henry Heimlich, the man credited for developing the Heimlich maneuver, actually used it himself for the first time in his life on May 26, 2016. He saved a woman that was choking at his senior center. He was ninety-six years old at the time.

3496. In the year 1900, a new alarm mechanism was developed by inventor Ludwig Ederer. When the alarm went off, the bed rose to a forty five degree angle and tipped you out of bed.

3497. Inventor Alexander Graham Bell was given his middle name, Graham, when he was ten years old.

3498.   A new material stronger than grapheme was created by researchers from MIT. It's ten times stronger than steel, with only 5% of its density.

3499.   There is a way to send secure passwords through the human body instead of the air. The idea was actually devised by computer scientists and electrical engineers from the University of Washington. They use benign low frequency transmissions generated by fingerprint sensors in touch pads on devices.

3500.   A robot that picks up dog poop was designed by the University of Pennsylvania's GRASP Lab. It was named "POOP SCOOP," which stands for Perception of Offensive Products and Sensorized Control of Object Pickup. The robot is able to find and remove 95% of offensive droppings at a rate of one a minute.

3501.   Samuel Morse began his career as an artist, however, he abandoned this after his wife became sick and died while he was away on an art assignment. He ended up inventing a method to communicate long distances known as Morse Code.

3502.   In 1937, Teflon was accidentally invented by twenty seven year old chemist Roy Plunkett, while he was trying to create a new type of Freon for use in fridges and air conditioners.

3503.   The popsicle was invented by accident by eleven year old Frank Epperson from the San Francisco Bay area, in 1905. He left his sugary soda powder that he mixed with water outside overnight, and the next morning, it was frozen. He originally named it the Eppsicle, but the name was eventually changed to popsicle.

3504.   On August 5, 1914, the first electric traffic light was installed on the corner of Euclid Avenue and East 105th street in Cleveland, Ohio. The design consisted of four pairs of red and green lights that served as stop and go indicators, each mounted on a corner post. It was created by James Hodge, who received a US patent for his municipal traffic control system.

3505.   Nikola Tesla, the Serbian physicist, engineer, and inventor, died penniless and living in a small hotel room in New York City. He had a terrible case of OCD and had some peculiar patterns. He became fixated on pigeons, he had to have eighteen napkins during every meal, and he would count his steps wherever he walked.

3506.   In 1893, the Chicago World's Fair by George W. Ferris invented the first Ferris Wheel. It was 260 feet (seventy nine meters) high, cost fifty cents per ride, and could carry sixty passengers in each of the thirty six cars. That's a total capacity of 2,160 passengers.

3507.   The man who invented the ATM, John Shepherd-Barron, wanted the machine to have a pin number of six digits originally. Since his wife could only remember four numbers at a time, that became the norm.

3508.   A type of transparent wood has been developed by scientists in Sweden. The wood can actually be used as windows.

3509.   Hedy Lamarr was a famous actress in the 1930's who was also a mathematician and inventor; she created a frequency hopping spectrum technology that's currently still used in Wi-Fi and Bluetooth today.

3510.   In 1948, the dispenser was invented to resemble a cigarette lighter. Its purpose was to encourage people to quit smoking.

3511.   In 1881, a man named Theophilus Van Kannel invented the revolving door because he hated the idea of chivalry and opening doors for women.

3512.   In 1874, a fifteen year old boy named Chester Greenwood from Maine invented the earmuffs. He shaped two pieces of wire into circles and then connected them with a wire headband. To keep out the wind, his grandmother sewed velvet and beaver fur to the circles. In 1877, when he was eighteen, he got the patent, and by 1883, his factory was producing 30,000 ear muffs a year. By the time of his death in 1937, he was producing nearly half a million a year.

3513.   The Skunklock is a bike lock developed by US entrepreneur Daniel Idzkowski and Swiss-born engineer Yves Perrenoud. When cut by a potential thief, the lock emits a noxious chemical that induces vomiting and makes it hard to see or breath.

3514. Dr. James Naismith from Almonte, Canada, is actually the inventor of the basketball game. Back in 1891, he cut out the bottom of a peach basket and hung it ten feet (three meters) in the air, and thus the game was born.

3515. When creating the light bulb, Thomas Edison had a thousand unsuccessful attempts. When a reporter asked him: How does it feel to fail 1,000 times? Edison replied: "the light bulb was an invention with 1,000 steps."

3516. In 1871, Mark Twain invented and received a patent for the elastic clasp bra strap under his original name, Samuel Clemens. His patent said: "The nature of my invention consists in an adjustable and detachable elastic trap for vests, pantaloons or other garments requiring straps as will hereinafter more fully set forth."

3517. In 1857, at McGill University in Montreal, Canada, Thomas Dairy Hunt invented the green ink used in American money.

3518. Microlattice is a new type of metal created by Boeing that is 99.99% air. It is so light that it can actually sit on top of a dandelion without crushing it.

3519. In the patent for toilet paper, inventor Seth Wheeler made a drawing showing that toilet paper should go over, not under.

3520. American company Cabot Guns has manufactured the first gun made almost entirely from a piece of Gibeon meteorite. The meteorite was originally found in Namibia in the 1830's and it crashed on Earth about 4.5 billion years ago.

3521. "Aquaman crystals" are a type of crystal created by scientists at the University of South Denmark that can absorb a roomful of oxygen and store it for later use. This invention could actually be the key to underwater breathing. A handful of crystals could pull oxygen from the water and provide divers with air.

3522. According to records, John Joseph Merlin is the first person credited with inventing roller skates in London in the 1760's. He, however, wasn't a good skater. He reportedly went to a masquerade party in London at Carlyle House while wearing new skates, and he got seriously injured after crashing into a big mirror at the party.

3523. There are biodegradable caskets known as "Capsula Mundi" – which is Latin for "World's Capsule" – that were designed by Italian inventors Anna Citelli and Raoul Bretzel. They are egg-shaped caskets that break down to form soil nutrients for a tree that can be planted on the grave.

3524. When Thomas Edison developed health issues that forced him to use a wheelchair, businessman Henry Ford, who was a close friend of his, bought a wheelchair so that the two could race them in his estate. As Edison lay dying, his son Charles captured his last breath in a glass test tube, which he sealed with paraffin wax. Charles gave the test tube to Ford because he knew how dear the two were to each other. The test tube is on display in Detroit, Michigan, at the Henry Ford Museum.

3525. The "equal" sign (=) was invented in 1557 by Robert Recorde, a mathematician from Wales, who was tired of constantly using the phrase "is equal to" in his work.

3526. When the menstrual pad was first invented, it was held up by a belt.

3527. "Cover," the Dutch apparel company, has included technology in the creation of jackets and bags that block every in and outgoing signal, making the wearer completely untraceable by modern tracking devices such as computer chips embedded in credit cards. It can even take you off the cell phone grid.

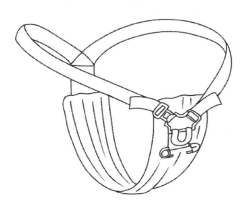

3528. A clock that runs for 10,000 years was built by the Long Now Foundation to be placed in a West Texas cave. The clock measures time in centuries and millennia, instead of minutes and seconds. It has a century hand and has a cuckoo that will sound every thousand years at each new millennium. It's also programmed to chime periodically, with each chime sound being unique and never repeated.

3529. Inventor Thomas Edison once tried to invent a "spirit phone" to contact the dead in the 1920's. Although most people thought he was joking, he genuinely wanted to create an ethereal device that would summon the living voices of the dead and record them for posterity.

3530. William Phelps Eno, the man who invented traffic circles, one-way streets, pedestrian safety islands, and taxi stands, never actually learned to drive because he thought that driving was a fad.

3531. A bio-battery powered by sugar with ten times the power storage capacity of lithium was made by Virginia Tech researchers. This implies that cellphones could potentially run on enzymes.

3532. Canadian optometrist Dr. Garth Webb invented a new contact lens that can improve human vision beyond 20/20. The bionic lens replaces the natural lens of the eye in an eight minute procedure which is also painless. It takes effect in only ten seconds and enhances eyesight for life.

3533. Einstein actually had an illegitimate daughter. She was born in 1902.

3534. Before dynamite got its name, the explosive was called "Nobel's safety powder," and was named after Alfred Nobel, who invented it.

3535. Oxbotica Company developed self-driving cars by teaching them to navigate using a series of software programs, including Grand Theft Auto Five. The company used GTA to simulate driving conditions because, as it claims, "there isn't enough time in a day to clock the real world miles that they needed."

3536. A professor of medicine at Harvard Medical School is working on a new device that measures sperm concentration using your phone's camera.

3537. One of the inventors of the taser, John H. Jack Cover, named it after his literary hero Tom Swift. The word is actually an acronym for Thomas A. Swift's Electric Rifle. Cover just added the "A" to Tom Swift's name.

3538. The Naviator is a drone that is not only able to fly but also swim. It was developed by Javier Diaz, a professor at the Department of Mechanical and Aerospace Engineering at Rutgers University.

3539. In 1824, while being only fifteen years old, Louis Braille developed the Braille system. He actually became blind at the age of three and was inspired to find a way for the blind to read and write.

3540. There is a type of HIV test that uses a USB stick developed by scientists at Imperial College London and US firm DNA Electronics. Using a drop of blood to detect HIV, it then creates an electrical signal that can be read by a computer, laptop, or handheld device.

3541. There is a special watch that keeps time with Martian solar days designed by watchmaker Garo Ansertian and used by NASA. The Martian day is a bit longer than Earth's, but this minimal variance can amount to physical and mental fatigue. Everyday team members are reporting to work thirty-nine minutes later than the previous day, so the watch is actually 24.65 hours.

3542.   A gigapixel art camera for preserving paintings has been created by the Google Cultural Institute. The device can scan a three foot by three foot (0.9 meter by 0.9 meter) painting in complete detail in thirty minutes, while other devices used to take a full day.

3543.   "Oleo sponge" is a reusable sponge developed by scientists that can absorb oil from the surface of water as well as below the surface. The sponge can help improve the ability to clean up large oil spills, as not all of the oil sits on the surface.

3544.   A man named Gay Balfour, from Cortez, Colorado, built the "Dog Gone Vacuum Truck." It's used to suck prairie dogs out of their burrows.

3545.   Nobel Laureate William Shockley, who's credited with inventing the transistor, once argued that individuals with IQs under a hundred should be paid and then willingly sterilized.

3546.   A philosopher named "Democritus" discovered the existence of atoms with spaces between them, way back in 400 B.C.

3547.   In 1881, dentist Alfred Southwick witnessed a weird accident when an intoxicated man died after he accidentally touched a live generator terminal. From there he got the idea for the electric chair.

3548.   Israeli company Tactical Robots built a drone ambulance called the AirMule that can take off and land vertically. It was designed for conditions where landing a helicopter is not viable, for example on a battlefield. It can carry up to 991 pounds (450 kilograms) for up to thirty one miles (fifty kilometers).

3549.   Alfred Binet invented the IQ test as a method to identify students who needed help. He actually disapproved of the use of the test as a ranking for unitary and linear intelligence.

3550.   In 2017, Tostitos, Uber, and Mothers Against Drunk Driving worked together to design an alcohol detecting chip bag for the Superbowl. The top of the bag had a sensor that could analyze a person's breath. If you had been drinking, a red steering wheel would appear on the bag along with a "Don't drink and drive" warning. If you were sober, green flashing lights would appear underneath the logo on the bag.

3551.   The first American woman to receive a patent was Mary Kies, from Connecticut, on May 15, 1809. Her innovation was to make a hat by weaving silk or thread into straw, creating a pleasing appearance that became a fashion fad.

3552.   "Radaranges" was the name originally given to microwave ovens. The invention is generally credited to American engineer Percy Spencer, who created it after World War II from radar technology developed during the war. It was first sold in 1946.

3553.   In Japan, a typhoon turbine has been developed by inventor Atsushi Shimizu. It can withstand typhoon-force winds and convert the energy into electricity. In fact, one typhoon could power all of Japan for fifty years.

3554.   The only American president to ever receive a patent was President Abraham Lincoln, on May 22, 1849. The patent was issued for a device that lifts boats over shoals; however, the invention was never manufactured.

3555.   Some of the world's oldest sunglasses were created by the Eskimo or Inuit of the Arctic on North Baffin Island, in northern Canada. Also referred to as snow goggles, they were made out of bone, leather, or wood, with small slits to see through; they were designed to protect the eyes from snow-blindness produced by the sun.

3556.   In Sicily, Italy, five high school students and their teacher created a prototype of a vending machine that turns plastic recyclables into phone cases. It grinds down the plastics into tiny pellets which are then melted and used to create 3D printed phone cases. The project was intended to encourage young people to recycle more.

3557.   Otto Fredrick Rohwedder was the first person to sell sliced bread, and he did it in America in 1928, in Davenport, Iowa. In 1912, Otto invented the single loaf bread slicing machine, which was the first in the world. He marketed his invention as the single greatest advancement in the baking industry, since they started wrapping bread, and he was right, because we term great ideas these days as "the greatest thing since sliced bread."

3558.   A device that can translate the vocalizations of animals into something that we can understand is being developed by scientists through the use of artificial intelligence. After studying and gathering data from prairie dogs for thirty years, scientists discovered that they have their own language system.

3559.   For just under $500, it's possible to buy a child-sized Tesla for your kids. The invention was actually an advertising strategy. Instead of spending money on ads, they make these cars; people buy them and advertise for them by sharing pictures on social media of how cool their kids are.

3560.   After many tests, a team of researchers at Michigan State University have created a transparent solar panel that can be used in buildings to potentially power the entire building. It can also be retrofitted to older glass buildings to harness power.

3561.   In the UK, a robotic rectum has been created by researchers for proctologists to practice their physical rectal exams. It allows medical professions to learn without the use of real life volunteers.

3562.   The Bios Incube is an invention created by Bios Urn. It's a type of incubator that monitors and cultivates trees from human ashes in people's homes. So instead of keeping your departed loved one in an urn on the fireplace mantle, now you can keep them in the form of a tree.

3563.   A scooter slash stroller hybrid was developed by Austrian inventor Valentin Vodev. By just clicking a button, the stroller transforms into a scooter and can travel as fast as ten miles (sixteen kilometers) per hour.

3564.   Russia has created a capsule that treats alcoholism. It's implanted under the skin and causes chemicals to release. This leads the user to feel nauseous, out of breath, and mental confusion when alcohol is consumed.

3565.   At the Dearborn Days Community Festival in Michigan, on August 13, 1941, Henry Ford presented a new car. It was called the soybean car because it was partly made of soybean, and it only weighed two thirds of what a standard steel car did.

3566.   The "Max Motor Dreams Cot" is a cot designed by Ford Motors that simulates night time driving conditions, including engine noises, street lighting, and car motion. It's programmed using a smartphone app that makes it possible to record and then recreate the comforting motion, sounds, and lights from an actual journey. You can use it to put your baby to sleep without needing to take him for a drive.

3567.   There is a life-sized robot that looks exactly like Scarlet Johansson, constructed by product and graphic designer Ricky Ma. It took him a year and a half and cost $50,000. He named her "Mark One" and she responds to a set of programmed verbal commands spoken into a microphone.

3568.   Since the death of Steve Jobs in 2011, he has won 141 patents as of January, 2016. Out of a total of 458 patents filed by Apple, mostly related to the design of Apple products, around one-third of them were filed by Steve Jobs himself.

3569.   A system that collects AC condensation and lets you drink the water from a tap on your dashboard was developed by Ford engineer Doug Martin. The water, however, needs to first be routed through a filter that removes any organic particulate contaminants.

Kids

3570. The Slumber Party Barbie was released by Mattel, in 1965. Apparently, one of her slumber party items was a pink scale that was permanently set to 110 pounds (fifty kilograms).

3571. According to a nationwide survey conducted by Visa in 2015, the average American family with teens in it spends roughly $324 on asking a date to the prom.

3572. San Diego schools had to ban the use of hypnotism after a fourteen year old girl had a hard time coming out of a trance-like state in one incident.

3573. Edwin Thomas Clint, who was named after actor Clint Eastwood, was an Indian child prodigy. He had made 25,000 works of art when he died of kidney failure just before turning seventeen, in 1983.

3574. One third of children learn how to use tablets and smartphones before they learn to speak, according to a 2013 report.

3575. According to a study done by Andrew Balmford in 2002, British kids aged eight could correctly identify 80% of all types of Pokémon, but they could only identify 50% of common types of wild animals.

3576. There is a CT scan room at the New York Presbyterian Morgan Stanley Children's Hospital that has been turned into a pirate themed island. Children enter the room by walking on a plank and then lay on a boat-shaped table.

3577. In South Korea, adopting children is seen as taboo. As a result, orphans there are rarely adopted unless a foreigner adopts one.

3578. Children under the age of seventeen in South Korea aren't allowed to play online games after midnight. This is monitored by KSSN: the Korean Social Security Number.

3579. When Mary, the Queen of Scots, became queen, she was only six days old. This was because her father died, and she was his successor.

3580. Based on studies performed by researchers at the Washington University School of Medicine in St. Louis, moms who are supportive and nurturing of their children during preschool years can actually boost the growth of their kids' brains. Researchers found that kids who were nurtured in their early years had a larger hippocampus, which is the part of the brain tied to learning, memory, and emotion control.

3581.   As of 2014, the Centers for Disease Control and Prevention, or the CDC, reported that one in sixty eight children, or more specifically, one in forty two boys and one in 189 girls has autism spectrum disorder, which includes a wide range of symptoms and skills in different levels of disability.

3582.   In Switzerland, there is a company that will name your baby for you. The cost for their service is $29,000 however.

3583.   The brain of children triples in weight during their first three years of life and they establish about 1,000 trillion nerve connections.

3584.   Some studies show that children will eat as much sugar as you give them because they're biologically wired to crave high-calorie foods during rapid growth. Until they are about sixteen, their bones stop growing, and that's when they start thinking of food as "too sweet."

3585.   "The Bikers Against Child Abuse," or "BACA," is a group of bikers who escort abused children to therapy sessions or school to help them feel safer and supported. They sometimes even attend the courtroom cases where victims testify against their abusers.

3586.   Elimination communication is a technique where, instead of using diapers, parents learn to use timing, signals, and cues to know when their baby needs to pee or poo.

3587.   In the past, many movie theaters used to have cry rooms where you could place your children if they were giving you trouble. This way you could still enjoy the movie while not disturbing others.

3588.   The first African American child to attend an all-white public elementary school in the American South was six year old Ruby Nell Bridges, in November of 1960. For her safety, she had to be escorted to school by federal marshals and spent the first year as the only student in her class.

3589.   In 2016, a study done by the laundry detergent brand Persil in the UK revealed that kids in the United Kingdom spend less time outside than prisoners. The survey of 2,000 British parents found that nearly three-quarters of children are spending less than one hour outside every day, and 20% don't go outside on a regular basis at all. However, British inmates receive at least one hour of suitable exercise outdoors every day.

3590.   "Natal teeth" is a term used to refer to babies who are born with teeth. According to the National Institution of Health, one out of every 2,000 to 3,000 babies is born with teeth.

3591.   Some babies are born with a condition called lidling, where the top part of the cartilage in the ear is basically folded so the top ridge is kind of rounded over. It's possible to reshape their ears however, by using a mold called "Ear Well" that can change their shape in about six weeks.

3592.   Before 1987, surgeries performed on infants were done without anaesthesia as they believed that kids weren't able to feel pain.

3593.   In Serbia, kindergarten kids usually strip down to their undergarments, go outside, and pour extremely cold water on themselves to strengthen their immune systems.

3594.   There is a Japanese tradition that dates back 400 years, where sumo wrestlers shake babies and make faces at them in an attempt to make them cry. It's claimed that crying brings good health, wards off evil spirits, and cures brain damaged babies.

3595.   A fifteen year old Pakistani school boy named Iksas Hassan confronted a suicide bomber who was about to enter his school on January 6, 2014. The bomber was forced to detonate before he entered the school that had 2,000 students, and although Hassan was killed, he saved the lives of hundreds of kids. He was considered a national hero in Pakistan, and was awarded a posthumous Star of Bravery.

3596.   In 2015, a French couple named their baby "Nutella." A judge ruled that it was contrary to the child's best interest to bear that name, as it was the name of a spread. The parents failed to appear in court, and they renamed the child Ella.

3597.   In 2013, a dog named Killian alerted their owners about the abusive behavior of a babysitter against their baby boy. Every time the babysitter was around, he would growl and stand between the baby and the sitter. The parents later recorded the abuse and the sitter was arrested.

3598.   Breast milk contains immunoglobulins, substances produced by the body's immune system, which work like a natural laxative. That is why breastfed babies poop more than formula fed babies.

3599.   Twenty four children ages seven to twelve were able to recognize their own mother's voice in under a second 97% of the time, even when the mom spoke in pure gibberish, according to a study done by the Stanford University School of Medicine.

3600.   The phenomenon of storm babies is real. During storms, barometric pressure can rise which causes some expectant women to spontaneously go into labor.

3601.   Newborn babies don't really shed any tears, even though they cry a lot. It's because their tear ducts aren't functional until they're between three and twelve weeks old.

3602.   India, like lots of other countries, has a yearly holiday to celebrate children. The unique thing is that their Children's Day is precisely nine months past Valentine's Day, on November 14.

3603.   There is a correlation between childhood defiance and success later on in life, as concluded by a forty year long study published in Developmental Psychology.

3604.   In Japan, there is a traditional pastime among children consisting of molding mud balls by hand into perfect spheres, which are later dried and polished into a shiny luster. The balls are called "hikaru dorodango."

3605.   A child prodigy named Ruth Lawrence was accepted into Oxford University at the age of ten when she passed the entrance exam and came first out of over five hundred students. She graduated two years later with a bachelor's degree and earned a doctorate's degree when she was only seventeen.

3606.   A study done by the University of Vienna found that the older a father is when he has a child, the less attractive the child will be.

3607.   Based on statistics provided by the World Health Organization, there are around 360 million people in the world with disabling hearing loss, which represents nearly 5% of the entire world's population. Thirty two million of them are children between the ages of zero and fourteen.

3608.   On January 13, 1996, nine year old Amber Hagerman was kidnapped and murdered, and the killer was never found. The Amber Alert that is put out when a child goes missing actually came about after this sad event. It alerts local broadcasters and law enforcement to come together to get information out quickly following a child's abduction. It's known nationwide as an Amber Alert, which stands for America's Missing Broadcast Emergency Response.

3609.   A diaper equipped with a waterproof baby wipe holding compartment was actually invented by actress Jamie Lee Curtis. Her experience and time spent at taking care of children made her think that the conventional diaper system could use some tweaking.

3610.   Dan and Caren Mahar, a New York couple, had their child diagnosed with xeroderma pigmentosum, a condition in which exposure to sunlight causes third-degree burns and cancer. The couple soon founded

Camp Sundown, a summer camp for kids suffering the genetic disorder where all camp activities are held after sundown.

3611.   Ester Okade is a ten year old girl who is already enrolled in university. She had the highest exam scores in her class and had mastered algebra when she was only four years old.

3612.   Back in the 1930's, mothers and nannies used to put babies inside newly invented baby cages, and then left them outside the window so they could get fresh air.

3613.   In London, researchers from St. George's University published a study in the Journal Archives of Disease in Childhood demonstrating that those children who spend more than three hours in front of a screen or using computers are at a greater risk of developing type II diabetes. These kids scored higher on various measures of body fat and had higher insulin levels.

3614.   In 2001, the State of Arizona passed a safe-haven law declaring that a parent is legally allowed to anonymously leave their newborn baby at a safe haven like a fire station, hospital, or church. The only requirement was that they did it in less than seventy two hours of the baby being born.

3615.   In comparison to adults, babies have sixty or more bones in their bodies.

Languages

3616. On March 23, 1839, the two abbreviated letters "OK" first appeared in print in the Boston Morning Post as a joke. It was intended to be a shortening of the words "orl korrekt," which was then the humorous misspelling of all correct. It continued to appear in newspapers and even in the presidential campaign of 1840, until it became commonly used.

3617. The translation of the word "tsunami" in Japanese is harbor wave.

3618. "Mayday" is a term used internationally as a distress signal. It comes from the French "venez m'aider," which translates to "come help me."

3619. Five is pronounced "haa" in Thai, so sometimes people in Thailand write 55555 when they mean haa-haa-haa-haa-haa.

3620. The English language has 3,000 words for being drunk, and two of them are osfusticated and ramsquaddled.

3621. When cats meow, they are using a language that they developed specifically to communicate with humans. Research shows that when felines communicate, it's very rare for them to meow at each other, but they always do it when they want something from their human masters.

3622. The nautical expression many assume to be "anchors away" is actually "anchors aweigh." The expression doesn't mean to go away in terms of distance. Instead, "anchors aweigh" refers to what happens when an anchor has just started to put weight onto the chain or rope that's hauling it up.

3623. Meteors were initially only referred to as comets. The word derives from the Latin word "comes," meaning hair, and referring to the flowing golden tail of hair that flashed through the sky.

3624. The name of the day Saturday comes from the planet Saturn, Sunday derives from the Sun, and Monday from the Moon.

3625. Nigel Richards from Malaysia once won the French Scrabble championship. Although he doesn't speak any French, he memorized the whole French dictionary to achieve this.

3626. "Shat mat" is an Arabic expression that means "the king is dead" and it's the origin of the term checkmate.

3627.   In Scotland, they have 400 words for snow, and three of them are spitters, snaws, and flindrikin.

3628.   The use of the letters Q, W and X was prohibited in Turkey for eighty five years. A law on the adoption and application of Turkish letters was established on November 1, 1928, making the letters illegal. The idea was to transition Turkey's system of writing from an Arabic-based one used by the Ottomans, to a Roman-based one.

3629.   "Ayotochtli" was the Aztec word for armadillo, and it translates to turtle-rabbit.

3630.   The Bolivian Constitution recognizes thirty seven national languages, although as of 2009, most of the population spoke Spanish.

3631.   The term barbarian originates from ancient Greece, and back then, it was used to refer to all people who didn't speak Greek. That included the Egyptians, the Meddeas, the Phoenicians, and the Persians. When ancient Romans adopted the term, they altered it to mean all foreigners who didn't share Greek and Roman cultural traditions.

3632.   In Toronto, Canada, over 180 languages and dialects are spoken as more than half of its population born outside the country.

3633.   Leontodon taraxacum is the original Latin name for the dandelion plant. In Greek, leontodon means lion's tooth, as the serrated leaves resemble the teeth of a lion.

3634.   The word "bae" translated to Danish comes out as the word "poop."

3635.   According to a study conducted by university professors across America, bi-cultural people may change their personality when they switch languages because language unconsciously affects people's interpretation of events. For example, women speaking Spanish were seen as more independent and assertive than women speaking English in similar situations.

3636.   The word "testify" derived from the Latin word for testicle. In ancient Rome, when two men took an oath of allegiance, they would hold each other's testicles; also men would hold their own testicles as a sign of truthfulness while bearing witness in a public forum.

3637.   The longest word in the English language, according to the Oxford English Dictionary, is pneumonoultramicroscopicsilicovolcanoconiosis. It refers to a type of lung disease and the word itself is forty five letters long.

3638.   In the 1960's, a new punctuation mark called the interrobang was made by the American Typers Association. It was a combination of a question mark and an exclamation mark, which was intended to be used at the end of an exclamatory rhetorical question, such as "what the heck."

3639.   The name salamander derives from the Greek word fire lizard. It came about when salamanders came running out of logs that had been thrown on a fire.

3640.   Navid Azodi and Thomas Pryor, both University of Washington undergraduates, have created gloves that can convert sign language into spoken word via Bluetooth. They are called "SignAloud."

3641.   According to a study done by researchers from the University de Montreal and published in the Journal of Neurolinguistics, bilingual brains are more efficient, and may be able to stave off symptoms of aging and dementia, in comparison to those people who aren't bilingual.

3642.   The word "schadenfreude" in German translates to "pleasure from seeing others fail or suffer misfortune."

3643.   The word Kia is derived from the Chinese language. The first syllable "Ki" means to arise or come out of. The second part of the word refers to Asia. So, basically, Kia means to rise up or come out of Asia.

3644.   The "your mother insult" is found in nearly all cultures and is as old as humanity itself; it can even be found in Shakespeare texts and the Bible.

3645.   There are twenty three official languages in India. Although Hindi is the official language of the Indian central government, and English is a provisional official sub language, all other individual state legislatures are free to adopt any regional language as the official language of that state.

3646. The only two English words that both begin and end in "und" are underground and underfund.

3647. The fear of your mother-in-law is called pentheraphobia. The origin of the word penthera is Greek, which means mother-in-law, and phobia meaning fear.

3648. The scientific word for picking your nose is rhinotillexomania. Rhino means nose, tillex means habitual picking, while mania means rage or fury.

3649. The only letter in the alphabet that doesn't appear in any US territory or state name is the letter "Q."

3650. "L'appel du vide," or the call to void, refers to the urge to jump, or the feeling of being pulled that you get when you are standing at a high place.

3651. More people around the planet learn English as a second language, compared to those who learn it as a first language.

3652. The expression "close but no cigar" is often used when someone fails to achieve something just by an inch. However, the phrase has its origins from the early twentieth century when people were awarded cigars for winning games at fairs, carnivals, and other recreational gatherings.

3653. There are only two fifteen letter words in the English language that do not repeat a letter: dermatoglyphics and uncopyrightable.

3654. In the English language, the only four words that end with "dous" are: tremendous, horrendous, stupendous, and hazardous.

3655. In an extinct Australian language called Mbabarom, the word for dog was dog, and it's pronounced just like we do in English. The strange thing about this is that the language was not related to English in any way.

3656. Twyndyllyngs is the longest English word that has no vowels, and it means twinlings, or twins.

3657. Certain words have been altered overtime due to metathesis, which refers to the swapping of sounds. For instance, bird used to be "brid," wasp was "waps" and horse was "hros."

3658. The term oxymoron is in itself an oxymoron. It was coined from two ancient Greek words; "oxy" meaning sharp, "moros" meaning dull or foolish.

3659. The word jaguar is adopted from "yaguar," a Native American term that means one who kills with a single leap.

3660. "Virgule" is the technical name for the forward slash.

3661. "Presidentress" was the official word used to refer to the president's wife, until 1849, in Dolly Madison's eulogy when Zachary Taylor referred to her as "our first lady."

3662. There are only two words in the English language that have all the vowels, including "y," in alphabetical order: facetiously and abstemiously.

3663. In Poland, they don't say "not my problem" and instead say "not my circus, not my monkey."

3664. The title "Mrs." has an "r" in it because the abbreviation comes from mistress, not missus.

3665. The word zip in "zip code" is actually an acronym for Zone Improvement Plan.

3666. An old slang term for moonshine is mountain dew.

3667. A study done by the University of Chicago discovered that people think more rationally and make better choices in their second language.

3668. The psychological act of repeating a word or phrase over and over again until it loses its meaning to the listener is called "semantic satiation."

3669. In the mountains of the Canary Islands, there is a language that consists of whistling and has been used for centuries. It's called Silbo Gomero and it's used by transferring Spanish into whistling sounds, which makes the messages travel further and louder than if you were to yell.

3670. The word emoji is the Japanese term for picture characters. They were created out of necessity back in 1999, when mobile carriers in Japan were struggling to support the messaging needs of eighty million users. Their hopes were that an emoji would reduce the need for multiple text messages or even picture messages.

3671. The word with the most meanings in the English language according to the Guinness World Records is the verb "set." The Second Edition of the Oxford English dictionary published in 1989 shows 430 senses listed in it. The word has the longest entry in the dictionary with 60,000 words, or 236,000 characters.

3672. There are four personal pronouns in the word USHER; he, she, her, and us.

3673. Every fourteen days, a different language dies, according to National Geographic. In addition, half of the roughly 7,000 languages spoken on earth will most likely disappear in the next century because more communities are starting to put aside their native tongues in favor of Mandarin, English, and Spanish.

3674. At the federal level, the United States does not have an official language. However, English is considered the official language in thirty two states.

3675. The word dinosaur was invented in 1842 by Sir Richard Owen who was biologist, comparative anatomist and paleontologist. It comes from the ancient Greek words "deinos," meaning fearfully-great, and "sauros," meaning lizard.

3676. Dysania is a term used to describe the difficulty of waking up and getting out of bed in the morning.

3677. The word "mortgage" comes from the French language meaning "death pledge," which refers to the death of a loan because you amortize a mortgage.

3678. The word "BASE" as in "base jumping" is an acronym for four categories of fixed objects from which you can jump. They are building, antenna, span, and Earth.

3679. The name LEGO comes from the abbreviation of the two Danish words "leg godt" which mean "play well."

3680. In 1912, HersheyPark in Hershey, Philadelphia, installed a new merry-go-round, and the guy hired to paint the amusement park signs wrote "CARROUSEL" instead of spelling it correctly without the additional "R." Rather than repainting the signs, the park chose to operate the ride using that name for the next thirty two years.

3681. The informal pronunciation of probably is "proly," which originated in the 1940's.

3682. The longest word that is typed with only the left hand on the keyboard is stewardesses.

3683. The term "freelancer" comes from the medieval era, when warriors were not under the oath of any lord, hence making them a freelancer.

3684. The Japanese term "tsundoku" refers to the act of getting reading materials or books and piling them up at home without ever reading them.

3685. Ukulele is the word for a music instrument, and in Hawaii where it originates, it loosely translates to "jumping flea." It's named that because the movements that a person's fingers make when playing the instrument resemble those of a quick hopping insect.

3686. In Italy, there are approximately 2,000 native Greek speakers today. They derive from the ancient Greek colonization on the Italian Peninsula.

3687. In Malay, "orang" means person and "hutan" means forest. In other words, orangutan means "person of the forest."

3688. The verb poop meant to produce a short blast of sound with a horn during the Middle Ages. This changed in the late 1600's according to the Oxford English Dictionary, and it meant to break wind.

Nature, Earth & The Universe

3689.　In Venus, one single day lasts longer than a whole year. It's because the planet rotates at a very slow rate, and is also very close to the Sun which means it has a shorter revolution around the Sun.

3690.　Astronomers in 2014 discovered a supernova which had been exploding continuously since the 1950's. It's an odd phenomenon because under normal circumstances, these explosions only last one hundred days.

3691.　There's a document called the "Outer Space Treaty" that outlines off Earth laws, and it was originally known as the "Treaty on Principles Governing the Activities of States in The Exploration and Use of Outer Space Including the Moon and Other Celestial Bodies." The treaty was signed by 107 countries.

3692.　The Mauna Loa volcano erupted in December, 1935, and created five rivers of lava that started flowing towards the town of Hilo in Hawaii, where 15,000 people resided. To save the town, the US Army Air Corps dropped twenty bombs onto the volcano in order to cut off the lava at the source. Although this hadn't been done before, it worked successfully.

3693.　The only planets in the solar system that rotate clockwise are Venus and Uranus. The other six planets rotate counterclockwise.

3694.　A volcano in Indonesia named Kawah Lijen burns blue lava as it has high amounts of sulfur gas inside of it.

3695.　In 1935, bush pilot Jimmy Angel accidentally discovered Angel Falls in Venezuela while searching for gold and diamonds. The fall was named after him.

3696.　Eighty eight Earth days make a year on the planet Mercury. The reason is because Mercury is tightly locked to the Sun and over the course of time, this has slowed the rotation of the planet to almost match its orbit around the Sun.

3697.　Six hundred and twenty million years ago, an Earth day was only 21.9 hours, meaning that earth's day-night cycle is growing longer year by year.

3698.　Venus and Earth have a number of things in common, which is why it's referred to as Earth's sister planet. It's a terrestrial planet and also orbits within our Sun's habitable zone.

3699. The diameter of the Sun is 864,000 miles (1,391,000 kilometers), which represents about 109 times the diameter of Earth.

3700. The largest island in the world is Greenland with an area of 822,000 square miles (1,300,000 square kilometers).

3701. The most polluted place on Earth is Lake Karachay, in Russia. It was used as a nuclear dumping site in the past by the Soviet Union. The radiation levels are so high that just one hour of exposure represents a lethal dose of radiation.

3702. After a meteorite fell on earth in 2007 in Peru's Puno Region, some locals started experiencing a mysterious illness. Some thought that an alien virus had descended upon the region, but it was soon discovered that because of the heat from the meteorite impact, arsenic in the ground had evaporated, and it had contaminated groundwater in the area.

3703. The oldest star in the universe was discovered by astronomers recently, and it's located right here in the Milky Way galaxy, just 2,000 light years from our planet. The Astrophysical Journal reported that it's a small red dwarf star, and it's roughly 13.5 billion years old.

3704. It's said that 40% of all meteorites that hit earth come from the same place, an asteroid within the main belt that's called Six Hebe, which was identified on July 1, 1947.

3705. The ice sheet over Antarctica is thicker than forty nine miles (seventy nine kilometers) in some areas. Ocean levels around the world would rise by about 197 feet (sixty meters) if the entire ice sheet melts.

3706. The Mammoth Cave is the longest cave system on Earth. It's in Kentucky State, has more than 398 miles (640 kilometers) of passageways, and is about double the length of the second longest cave, "the Sac Actun underwater cave," located in Mexico.

3707. Nearly five million people visit the Grand Canyon National Park in Arizona every year. The park is over 270 miles (434 kilometers) long, up to eighteen miles (thirty kilometers) wide and a mile (1.6 kilometers) deep. It also has artifacts from human inhabitants dating all the way back to 12,000 years ago.

3708. The sixth closest moon of Jupiter is Europa. One day on Europa is 3.55 Earth days and it takes Europa 3.55 Earth days to orbit Jupiter.

3709. A rare image that shows the death of a star was captured by NASA and the European Space Agency's Hubble space telescope, in February, 2017. The image showed the dying star transforming from a red giant to a planetary nebula called the Calabash Nebula. It's also known as the rotten egg nebula because it contains so much sulphur that it would smell like rotten eggs.

3710. The largest resource of uranium in the world is found in Australia with 31%. They are the world's third largest producer behind Kazakhstan and Canada, at around 12% of the world's annual production.

3711. According to NASA scientists, about 4.3 billion years ago, Mars may have had enough water to cover its entire surface in a liquid layer about 449 feet (137 meters) deep. This ocean could have contained more water than the Arctic Ocean, but it's lost about 87% of that water into space over time.

3712. Victoria Falls is considered to be the largest waterfall in the world. Even though it's not the widest waterfall or the highest waterfall, if all dimensions are taken into account, including the flow rate, then it's considered to be the biggest curtain of falling water in the world. The falls cascade into a deep gorge on the border between Zambia and Zimbabwe. During the rainy season, approximately 150,284,545 gallons (568 million liters) of water per minute falls over the falls.

3713.   Pluto has a large bright shaped heart on it known as the Tombaugh Regio that is made of ice, huge glaciers made of nitrogen, methane, and carbon dioxide.

3714.   The popular saying "the dog days of summer" refers to when Sirius, the Dog Star, rises in conjunction with the Sun, which happens from July 3 to August 11.

3715.   The Sun contains 74% hydrogen and 24% helium. The remaining 2% includes trace amounts of iron, nickel, oxygen, and all the other elements that we have in our solar system.

3716.   The Aurora Borealis in Fairbanks, Alaska, can be seen an average of 240 nights a year. On those nights, the phenomenon lights up the sky with colors ranging from yellow and greens to reds, purples, and blues.

3717.   The 2011 Japan earthquake was so powerful that it actually changed the Earth's rotation on its axis, shortening the twenty four hour day by 1.8 milliseconds.

3718.   The record for the volcano with the coolest lava is held by the Oldoinyo Lengai, in Tanzania. It is the only volcano in the world known to have erupted carbonatite lava, which is the coolest lava on Earth, erupting at 500 to 600 degrees centigrade. The lava is either black or brown and looks like runny mud.

3719.   The strongest hurricane recorded in the Western Hemisphere was hurricane Patricia, back in 2015. It had strong winds that reached 200 miles (321 kilometers) per hour.

3720.   The rings of the planet Saturn span 180,000 miles (290,000 kilometers). In some places, they are only thirty one feet (ten meters) thick while in others they can be 3,100 feet (966 meters) thick.

3721.   The lowest point in North America is located in the Death Valley National Park, in California. It's called the Badwater Basin and it is 282 feet (eighty six meters) below sea level.

3722.   Beetlejuice is a red supergiant in the constellation Orion that is getting close to the end of its life. It's the ninth brightest star visible in the Earth's sky. The star is so far away that it could have already gone supernova hundreds of years ago and we wouldn't know it yet, as it's around 642 light years away, meaning it would take 642 years for that light to reach us. In addition, it's a very large star measuring 860 million miles (1.4 billion kilometers) across, which is about 2,000 times the diameter of our own Sun.

3723.   In March 2017, remnant minerals of the Earth's original crust were discovered in northern Quebec, Canada, by geologists Johnathan O'Neill and Richard Carlson. It's estimated that it was first formed over 4.2 billion years ago.

3724.   In November of 2016, a strong earthquake with a 7.8 magnitude tore through New Zealand. It was so powerful that it actually dragged the sea floor 6.6 feet (two meters) above ground. In fact, it was still crawling in sea life when it was discovered.

3725.   The only continent without at least one desert region is Europe. In order for an area to qualify as a desert, it must get less than ten inches (twenty five centimeters) of rain per year.

3726.   The hottest year ever recorded was 2016. Overall temperatures over the continents and oceans were thirty three degrees Fahrenheit (0.55 degrees Celsius) above the pre-industrial average.

3727.   A mega-asteroid of around thirty miles (forty eight kilometers) across hit the Earth in Australia 3.5 billion years ago, causing tsunamis and craters bigger than many US states.

3728.   There is an asteroid named after actor Tom Hanks, as the "12818 Tom Hanks."

3729.   The largest living structure on Earth is the Great Barrier Reef, located between the Queensland coast and the western edge of the Pacific Ocean. It spans more than 1,243 miles (2,000 kilometers) of islands and submerged reefs.

3730.   29% of the total Earth's surface is occupied by land, 33% by desert, and 71% by oceans.

3731.   Ganymede is Jupiter's largest moon; it has a saltwater ocean buried under ninety five miles (152 kilometers) of ice. Scientists believe that it's sixty miles (ninety six kilometers) thick, which is near ten times deeper than our oceans.

3732.   For Pluto to orbit the Sun, it takes 241 years due to its orbit at an average distance of 3.7 billion miles (5.95 billion kilometers) from the Sun, while Earth only orbits at 93 million miles (149 million kilometers).

3733.   A galactic year or cosmic year is the duration of a complete rotation of the Milky Way, which is about 200 million terrestrial years.

3734.   The Milky Way is named the way it is due to the milky band on its edge that is made of millions of stars that shine incredibly brightly. The ancient Romans called it Via Lactea, translating to "a milky way."

3735.   To date, a total of sixty three moons have been discovered that belong to planet Jupiter.

3736.   There are between 100 and 400 billion stars within the Milky Way. However, because our solar system is located roughly 27,000 light years away from the galactic center, we can only see about 2,500 of them at any point from Earth.

3737.   The part of lightning that we can actually see, according to the National Severe Storms Laboratory, comes from the ground up, not the sky down.

3738.   From the closest point, Mars is 128,437,425 miles (206,655,816 kilometers) from the Sun and at its furthest, it's 154,845,701 miles (249,146,732 kilometers) away.

3739.   Besides the Earth spinning on its axis, it also moves at a speed of about 66,900 miles (107,000 kilometers) an hour around the Sun.

3740.   The fourth brightest object in our solar system after the Sun, Moon, and Venus, is Jupiter. It is one of the five planets that you can see from Earth with the naked eye.

3741.   In our universe, there are 173 known moons. However, if we include dwarf planets that have objects orbiting them, the number increases to 182.

3742.   The reason why the Sun and all the planets of the solar system are round is because the gravitational force of the planet's mass pulls all of its material towards the center, smoothing out any non-roundness.

3743.   The Atlantic Ocean is significantly saltier than the Pacific Ocean.

3744.   The longest solar eclipse in the 21st century lasted six minutes and thirty nine seconds. The next time another solar eclipse surpasses it in duration will be on June 13, 2132.

3745.   Just as we have leap years in our calendar, we also have leap seconds that are added every few years to adjust for Earth's speed of rotation.

3746.   The largest desert on Earth is the Antarctic Polar Desert, which covers the continent of Antarctica and is the size of about 5.5 million square miles (8.8 square kilometers).

3747.   Due to a huge earthquake in Nepal in 2015, Mount Everest shrank by an inch.

3748.   Proxima Centauri is the closest star to Earth, which is 4.24 light-years away. A single light-year is 5.86 trillion miles (9.44 trillion kilometers).

3749.   In December of 2016, and for the first time since 1979, it snowed in the Sahara Desert. The snow fell in the Atlas Mountains, in the northern edge of the Sahara Desert, and stayed for about a day.

3750.   "Alexander's band" or "Alexander's dark band" is the name of the dark band that you can see between the primary and secondary bows of a rainbow. It was named after Alexander of Aphrodisias who first described it in 200 AD.

3751.   When orbiting, Mercury gets so close to the Sun that its surface temperature can get as hot as 800 degrees Fahrenheit (427 degrees Celsius). However, given that there isn't much of an atmosphere there to keep all that heat trapped, when the night comes, temperatures substantially decrease, falling as low as -279 degrees Fahrenheit (-173 degrees Celsius).

3752. On the planet Uranus, summer lasts forty two years long and winter another forty two years. It's Earth's tilt that gives us our seasons, but Uranus is significantly more on its side in relation to its poles, hence the length of its seasons.

3753. All snowflakes being identical is actually a myth. There are only thirty five different shapes a snowflake falls.

3754. The planet Uranus has twenty seven moons, five of them large and the rest much smaller. The five larger moons are Miranda, Ariel, Umbriel, Titania, and Oberon.

3755. There are thousands of rogue planets in the universe and it's plausible that many of these could actually hold life.

3756. The strongest winds in our solar system occur on the planet Neptune, with winds up to 1,304 miles (2,100 kilometers) an hour. To put that into perspective, hurricane winds on Earth run at speeds of up to only 191 miles (119 kilometers) an hour.

3757. While digging in a mine two miles (3.2 kilometers) below the Earth's surface, researchers have discovered the oldest known pool of water on the planet in Ontario, Canada. It's estimated that the water has been there for almost two billion years.

3758. With more than 250,000 lakes, Ontario, Canada, contains about one-fifth of the whole world's fresh water.

3759. According to a study published by the Journal of Science, between 10 and 30% of the water on planet Earth predates the Sun, and our bodies contain some of that water.

3760. The trees on Earth outnumber the stars in the Milky Way. Even though exact figures aren't known, it's estimated that there are three trillion trees on Earth, which is way more than the estimated 100 billion stars in our galaxy.

3761. There's an estimated $771 trillion worth of gold in oceans across the world, but much of it is dissolved into the salty water, so it can't be extracted.

3762. The Hoba meteorite is the largest meteorite and also the largest piece of iron ever found. It was discovered in Namibia by a farmer who was plowing his field, in 1920. According to estimations, the meteorite weighed sixty six tons and measured 8.9 feet (2.7 meters) long, 8.9 feet (2.7 meters) wide, and about three feet (0.9 meters) thick. Experts guess that it fell to Earth approximately 80,000 years ago.

3763. In New Zealand, there is a group of caves known as the "Waitomo Caves" that were created over thousands of years by underground streams. Millions of glowworms illuminate the caves and there is a central glowworm grotto where most of the luminescent worms live.

3764. Atmospheric rivers, or rivers in the sky, are weather systems that move high concentrations of water vapor outside the tropics and can bring strong winds and floods.

3765. The distance between the surface and the center of the Earth is about 3,960 miles (6,378 kilometers) according to Universe Today.

3766. According to Tom Grazulis, a tornado specialist, about 75% of all tornadoes happen within the United States.

3767. The largest volcano and mountain in the solar system is actually Olympus Mons, located on Mars. It's over sixteen miles (twenty five kilometers) high, making it three times the height of Mount Everest.

3768. The only planet that rotates on its side is Uranus. Its spin axis lies ninety eight degrees off its orbital plane with the Sun. If compared to other planets, no other is tilted more than thirty degrees off its axis.

3769. The longest natural rock span in the world is found in the landscape arch in Arches National Park, Utah. It has a span of 290 feet (eighty eight meters).

3770. In Dominica, there is a boiling lake that is so hot that the center's temperature has never been determined.

3771. The tallest mountain on the African continent is Mount Kilimanjaro. It is also the highest free-standing mountain in the world.

3772. Most meteors are the size of a grain of sand and disintegrate in the air. The larger ones that actually reach the Earth are called meteorites and they are very rare.

3773. The most abundant star in the universe is the red dwarf star, which is much smaller than the Sun, but has a much longer lifetime. Their surface temperatures can reach 5,846 degrees Fahrenheit (3,230 degrees Celsius).

3774. The North American continent shares the same tectonic plate with half of Japan.

3775. It's estimated that the asteroid that impacted the Earth and killed the dinosaurs about sixty six million years ago would have hit thirteen on the Richter scale that's used to rate earthquakes. Anything that hits fifteen on that scale would totally destroy the planet.

3776. Electric blue fire streams down from the peak of Indonesia's Kawah Ijen Volcano during the night. Sulphur-based gases burn at the volcano, causing the glow.

3777. The highest temperature officially recorded on Earth was 134 degrees Fahrenheit (56.7 degrees Celsius). It happened July 10, 1913, in Death Valley, California, at the Greenland Ranch. The coldest recorded temperature was negative 135.8 degrees Fahrenheit (negative 94.7 degrees Celsius), according to data from NASA satellites. It occurred in Antarctica in August, 2010.

3778. The rings around planet Saturn have a circumference of roughly 500,000 miles (805,000 kilometers), but they are only about one foot (thirty centimeters) thick.

3779. The lengthiest mountain range in the world is really located under the sea. It's called the Mid Ocean ridge, and it's a volcanic ridge that stretches over 49,000 miles (80,000 kilometers).

3780. The Amazon River used to flow from east to west in prehistoric times, and not from west to east as it does today, according to studies done in 2006. In fact, for a brief period, it used to flow in both directions.

3781. The average distance from Earth to the Moon is long enough to fit in all the planets of the solar system.

3782.   If you look into the sky at night, you'll be able to see five times as many meteors past midnight than before midnight.

3783.   Lake Superior, which is located on American's northern border with Canada, is the third largest freshwater lake in the world. It contains enough water to cover both North America and South America to a depth of about one foot (thirty centimeters).

3784.   Situated on an island close to Sicily in Italy, Mount Stromboli is a volcano that's called "the Lighthouse of the Mediterranean." It has been erupting constantly for more than 2,000 years.

3785.   "The Bergie Seltzer" is the name of the fizzing sound produced by icebergs when they melt. The sound is produced when air bubbles that have been trapped under pressure in the ice for centuries finally pop.

3786.   Vulcan Point Island is located in the Philippines, within a lake, that's within an active volcano, that's within a bigger lake, that's within a much bigger island.

3787.   The Maldives would be the first country to vanish if oceans rise because of global warming. It's an island country that's also the flattest on Earth, and none of its land is more than nine feet (three meters) above sea level.

3788.   The largest known diamond in the universe discovered by astronomers is a star named Lucy, shaped by ten trillion billion karats. This white dwarf has a carbon interior that crystallized as it cooled, forming a giant diamond in the sky. The star was named by scientists after The Beatles' song "Lucy in the Sky with Diamonds."

3789.   In Chile, some parts of the Atacama Desert have not seen a drop of water since record keeping began.

3790.   A moonbow or lunar rainbow is a type of rainbow that can be seen at night and happens very rarely. In order for this to happen, a full moon is needed, it must be raining opposite to the moon, the sky must be dark, and the moon must be less than forty two degrees high.

3791.   Clouds in the sky look light and fluffy, however, the water in a medium-sized cumulus cloud could weigh about 1,100,000 pounds (500,000 kilograms).

3792.   The rings of planet Saturn are made up of dust, rock, and ice accumulated from passing comets and meteorite impacts on Saturn's moons.

3793.   Based on reports by the National Oceanic and Atmospheric Administration and NASA, the hottest month in 136 years of record keeping was July 2016.

3794.   In 1930, eleven year old Venetia Burney gave the name to the planet Pluto. She suggested the name Pluto to her grandfather, who in turn suggested it to a friend who happened to be an astronomy professor at Oxford University.

3795.   Studies performed by astronomers and geologists led by J. Alexis Rodriguez, at the Planetary Science Institute at Tucson, Arizona, revealed the occurrence of two massive tsunamis on Mars billions of years ago. They were both triggered by meteor impacts, creating waves as high as 150 feet (forty five meters).

3796.   Some scientists believe that our planet used to have two moons orbiting it. The little moon crashed into the bigger moon, creating the one moon that we know and love. They believe this because the far side of the moon is very different from the near side, which might indicate that the far side was changed by the collision that scarred it.

3797.   In 2010, the UN Environment Programme released a report stating that from 150 to 200 species of plants, insects, birds, and mammals go extinct every twenty four hours, which is about 1,000 times faster than the natural rate. According to biologists, the world has not seen a mass extinction like this since the end of the dinosaurs, which was about sixty five million years ago.

3798.   The foggiest place in the world is the Grand Banks, in Newfoundland, Canada, with 206 foggy days every year.

3799. According to Dr. Jeffery Kuhn from the University of Hawaii, the Sun is the most perfect sphere ever observed in nature.

3800. On January 22, 1943, the world record for the fastest temperature change was registered in Spearfish, South Dakota. The temperature rose from negative four degrees Fahrenheit (negative twenty degrees Celsius) to forty four degrees Fahrenheit (seven degrees Celsius) in the span of two minutes when the Chinook winds passed through. After the wind passed, the temperature dropped back down to negative four degrees Fahrenheit (negative twenty degrees Celsius) in just twenty seven minutes. The phenomenon caused glass windows to crack.

3801. In the Orion constellation's sword portion, the middle star isn't an actual start. That's the Orion Nebula, and it's the only nebula that can be seen with naked eyes from our planet.

3802. At the moment, there are about 1,400 asteroids in space that have the potential for creating a hazard, and they would result in serious devastation if they collided with Earth.

3803. Out of all the natural lakes in the world, over half of them can be found in Canada.

3804. The volcanic explosion of Mount St. Helens on May 18, 1980, remains as the fastest recorded avalanche in history, reaching a speed of 250 miles (400 kilometers) per hour.

3805. On February 10, 2017, there was a full moon, a lunar eclipse, and a comet that passed by. All three of them could be seen in the same night.

3806. The longest terrestrial mountain range is the Andes Mountains in South America, at 4,797 miles (7,725 kilometers) long. They cover a surface of more than 1,242,000 square miles (3,216,780 square kilometers), with an average mountain height of about 12,995 feet (3,962 meters).

3807. According to Neil Degrasse Tyson, the galaxy called M87 is so gigantic that it contains around one trillion stars.

3808. The "Georgium Sidus" was the name originally given to planet Uranus, after King George, the third of England. The name Uranus was proposed by German astronomer Johann Elert Bode and it did not become the common name until 1850.

3809. The winter was so cold in 2015 that it caused some parts of Niagara Falls to freeze, something that hasn't happened in decades.

3810. Due to the heavy dust particles that block out most of the Sun's light, sunsets on Mars are blue instead of red. However, the blue light pushes through the atmosphere better than the red or yellow colors, and is much more visible.

3811. The giant red spot on Jupiter is actually a storm. It has been going on for around 150 years and is twice as wide as Earth. On Earth, the largest and most powerful hurricanes ever recorded spanned over 1,000 miles (1,600 kilometers) across with wind speeds of up to 200 miles (322 kilometers) per hour. The giant red spot, however, has wind speeds twice as fast.

3812. Over 2,500 species of fish are found in the Amazon basin. That is more than the ones found in the entire Atlantic Ocean.

3813. Most planets have been named after Greek mythology characters. Uranus' moons on the contrary have been named after characters in Shakespeare's plays, such as Umbriel, Cordelia, and Ariel.

3814. The Indian Ocean earthquake and tsunami of 2004 was so powerful that it caused the entire planet to vibrate as much as 0.39 inches (one centimeter). It also distantly triggered earthquakes on the other side of Earth, as far as in Alaska. Additionally, it was the longest lasting earthquake ever recorded with a duration between eight and ten minutes.

3815. The speed of light travels at 186,000 miles (300,000 kilometers) a second. To put that into perspective, if you were traveling at the speed of light, you would be able to travel around Earth 7.5 times per second.

3816. The Amazon and the Rio Negro rivers are two of the largest rivers in the world. At some point they meet, but do not mix; although they are visually distinct, they both occupy the same body of water. This is due to their different speeds, density, and temperatures.

3817. Located in the McMurdo Dry Valleys of Antarctica, Don Juan Pond is the saltiest body of water in the world, with a salinity level of over 40%. It's an ankle-deep pond in the lowest part of Upper Wright Valley and it's so salty that its waters rarely freeze.

3818. According to records, the last time that all the planets in the solar system were aligned was 561 BC. The next alignment will take place in 2854.

3819. Scientists found out in March, 2018, that all galaxies rotate at the rate of a billion years for a single spin, and it's the same irrespective of the size of the individual galaxy.

3820. The Galapagos Islands are a chain of islands created by volcanic activity. The islands house a great variety of fauna species, although no animals are actually native to the Galapagos. Every species of animal there came from floating on ocean or air currents.

3821. Crescent Lake is an oasis located in the middle of the Gobi Desert, 3.7 miles (5.9 kilometers) from the outskirts of the city of Dunhuang, in western China. It is believed to have been there for over 2,000 years.

3822. There is a lake in Victoria, Australia, that can glow in the dark. The light is created when microorganisms in the water are disturbed which creates a chemical reaction called bioluminescence.

3823. Lake Baikal in Siberia is the deepest lake in the world at over 5,382 feet (1,641 meters) deep. It's also the most voluminous freshwater lake on Earth, containing nearly 20% of the world's unfrozen fresh water.

3824. Similarly to our earthquakes, there are moonquakes on the moon, with the difference that they are weaker and less common. In fact, there are four known types: deep moonquakes, shallow moonquakes, thermal moonquakes, and meteorite moonquakes.

3825. Fifteen days before or after a solar eclipse, there is always a lunar eclipse.

3826. The only river in the world that crosses the Equator twice is the Congo River by flowing north and south of it. It's also the only major river in the world that crosses the Equator even once.

3827. Putting aside the Earth's 18.6 miles (thirty kilometers) per second revolution around the Sun, all things located along the equator are moving at about 990 miles (1,600 kilometers) per hour, while all things located at the north and south poles are basically stationary, only spinning in its position.

3828. The planet Saturn is mostly made up of gas. If it was put in a really large bathtub, it would float.

3829. The Andromeda galaxy is so gigantic that if it were brighter and we could see it, it would look bigger than the Moon to us. To put it into perspective, the Moon is at a distance of 248,400 miles (400,000 kilometers) from Earth, but the Andromeda galaxy is fifteen quintillion miles (twenty five quintillion kilometers), or 2.5 million light years away from us.

3830. According to astronomers' calculations, it takes the Sun 226 million years to completely orbit around the center of the Milky Way Galaxy. Since the Sun was formed 4.6 billion years ago, it has completed this orbit only 20.4 times. The last time it did it, dinosaurs roamed the Earth.

3831. Forty to fifty million years ago, Antarctica's climate was very similar to the current weather in California.

3832. The loudest sound ever recorded on the planet was caused by the eruption of the Krakatoa volcano in Indonesia, in 1883. It could be heard thousands of miles away in Australia and the Island of Rodriguez.

3833. In 2008, a rare event was seen over the sky where a conjunction of the Moon, Venus, and Jupiter formed a smiley face. The event was visible from all parts of the world, even in cities with light pollution like New York City.

3834. 90% of all the ice on the planet is found in Antarctica, in an area that is just under one and a half times the size of the United States. In some parts like east Antarctica, ice averages 1.2 miles (two kilometers) thick.

3835. Only when a funnel cloud touches the ground, is it considered a tornado.

3836. At the upper atmosphere, the Earth receives 174 pedo watts of solar radiation. About 30% of that is reflected back to space and the rest is absorbed by clouds, oceans, and land masses.

3837. The only gemstone that doesn't literally belong to this world is the peridot gem. They have been spotted on comets, in large formations on Mars, and inside certain meteorites that have hit the Earth from deep space.

3838. Approximately six million tons of mass are lost in the Sun every second due to nuclear fission and solar winds. However, over the last 4.5 billion years, it has only lost about 0.05% of its original mass.

3839. The planet Uranus has a diameter of 31,700 miles (51,100 kilometers) across, which is four times bigger than Earth.

3840. On July 10, 1958, a 7.7 magnitude earthquake struck the region of Alaska, resulting in a tsunami that caused the largest waves ever recorded in Lituya Bay. One of the waves measured a maximum height of 1,718 feet (524 meters).

3841. The only place in the world where you can see the sunrise on the Pacific Ocean and setting on the Atlantic is Panama.

3842. Phong Nha-Ke Bang National Park in Vietnam is home to the largest cave in the world. The cave is big enough to fit a whole Manhattan city block on the inside, or fly an entire Boeing 747 aircraft through it. It is 21.1 miles (thirty four kilometers) long.

3843. "The Terminator" is the name of the line on Earth that separates day from night. Other names to refer to it include "the gray line" and "the twilight zone." Our atmosphere also bends sunlight by half of a degree, which is 37.2 miles (sixty kilometers). For this reason, the land covered by sunlight is greater than the land that is covered by darkness.

3844. Research done by the Australian National University found that there are more than ten times as many stars in the night sky than there are grains of sand in all the beaches and deserts in the world.

3845. One megawatt of wind energy represents 2,600 fewer tons of carbon dioxide.

Plants, Flowers & Trees

3846.   The cobra lily is a rare plant that grows in Oregon and Northern California that lures insects into themselves with a sweet smell so they can eat them. They even have several see-through false exits that exhaust their victims as they try to escape.

3847.   Around 700,000 leaves are shed by a fully mature oak tree each autumn.

3848.   Crown shyness is a weird phenomenon found in some tree species, where their crowns don't touch each other even when they're fully grown. The tree canopy ends up with channel-like gaps. Today there is still no scientific explanation why it happens.

3849.   "The Senator" was a cypress tree located in Longwood, Florida, and it was 3,500 years old, which made it the fifth oldest in the world. Regrettably, a woman burned down the tree in 2012 by accident when she went into its hollowed out trunk to hide as she abused drugs. The woman later regretted her actions, saying she could not believe she destroyed a tree that was older than Jesus.

3850.   The dandelion plant, or weed, is actually edible. The flowers are sweet and crunchy and can be eaten breaded, fried or raw, while the leaves can be eaten in a salad or steamed. The plant can be also used to make wine and the roots can be dried and roasted and used as a substitution for coffee.

3851.   In the Namib Desert, there is a plant known as the Welwitschia that can live for 1,000 years. In fact, there are some species that exist right now that, through carbon dating, are shown to be 1,500 years old.

3852.   In 1723, a single coffee seedling was carried by French Naval Officer Gabriel de Clieu all the way from France to the Caribbean island Martinique. There it spread and birthed eighteen million trees over a period of fifty years. Eventually, those trees made it to South and Central America.

3853.   There is a plant that imitates the anus of a dead animal so it can attract flies for pollination.

3854.   When plants convert sunlight and nutrients into energy through photosynthesis, they emit a type of light called fluorescence. This light can't be seen by the naked human eye, but it's often picked up by satellites orbiting the earth.

3855.   One of the classical gardens of Suzhou, located in China, holds the title of the world's oldest consistently tended garden. It is over 973 years old.

3856. Cashew trees develop "false fruits" that resemble red apples, upon which the actual cashews grow. The apple-like false fruit is edible and it's used to create jams and beverages in India and Brazil where most cashews come from. However, the cashew itself is the real fruit of the tree.

3857. Older redwood trees have thick barks and deep grooves which create a protective barrier around the trunk, and they ultimately make the tree fireproof.

3858. One of the hardest plants to grow in the world is wasabi. In order to be cultivated well, it needs cold pure running water. In addition to that, it takes over a year for it to mature. If there is too much humidity or the wrong nutrient composition, the entire crop will be completely wiped out.

I'M SORRY, BUT THIS POT IS TOO HUMID FOR ME

3859. The tapioca plant can be highly toxic if not prepared properly, according to the American Cancer Society. The plant naturally produces cyanide, which is poisonous to humans. However, the substance is removed during processing, so anyone can enjoy a tapioca pudding without worrying about it.

3860. In Peru, fried or roasted guinea pig, known also as cuy, is considered a delicacy. In fact, it has been part of the Peruvian diet for around 5,000 years.

3861. The Svalbard Global Seed Vault holds over 850,000 copies of seeds from across the planet just in case of a global disaster. It is located inside a mountain on the Norwegian island of Spitsbergen.

3862. The Raffia palm is the tree with the longest leaves in the world. Each leaf can be up to eighty feet (twenty four meters) long and up to ten feet (three meters) wide. It is native to some African countries.

3863. According to scientists, a single ragweed plant can release one-billion grains of pollen over the course of a single season and can travel hundreds of miles on a gentle breeze.

3864. The world's tallest tree is located in California's Redwood National Park. It's a redwood tree named "Hyperion" and it's 379 feet (115 meters) tall.

3865. The Double Tree of Casorzo is a unique tree found near Piemonte, Italy. It's actually two trees in one, a cherry tree growing on top of a mulberry tree.

3866. In 2009, a new species of pitcher plant was found by scientists in the Philippines jungle, becoming the largest carnivorous plant ever discovered. It's called the Nepenthes attenboroughii, named after Sir David Attenborough. Carnivorous plants usually eat things like insects and spiders, but this one is so big that it actually eats rats.

3867. Jia Haixia, a double amputee, and Jim Wenqi, a blind man, with combined efforts, have planted over ten thousand trees in Northern China and plan on planting another ten thousand.

3868. Sunflowers are actually a cluster of dozens of little flowers as each petal is a single-petaled flower.

3869. The "Old Man of the Lake" is a floating tree trunk located in Crater Lake, in Central Oregon. The tree has been bobbing completely vertically in the lake for over a hundred years. It has even been referenced in writing as far back as 1896.

3870. The petals of skeleton flowers are so delicate that they become transparent when it rains.

3871. In the village of Al Walaja, within the Bethlehem district of Palestine, there is an olive tree that is over 4,000 years old. It was named Al Badawi, after a wise villager who lived in Al Walaja over 200 years ago. The tree is thirty nine feet (eleven meters) tall and eighty two feet (twenty five meters) in diameter, and is compared to that of ten average sized olive trees put together.

3872. In 2008, the first known coffee plant that contains no caffeine was discovered. It was named Coffea charrieriana.

3873. The tropical cycads known as Lepidozamia and Encephalartos create the world's largest African pine cones, measuring almost 3.28 feet (one meter) in length and weighing up to ninety nine pounds (forty five kilograms).

3874. In Japan, a tiny drone has been used by researchers to pollinate a real flower. They achieved this by attaching horsehair bristles from a paintbrush to the bottom of the drone to imitate the fuzzy torso of a bee. Then they covered the hairs with a sticky gel, which captures the pollen when it touches the flower.

3875. The scent of freshly-mowed grass is actually the lawn's response to injury. Green leaf volatiles are volatile organic compounds released by plants. When they are injured, these emissions increase exponentially.

3876. In Brazil, there are mushrooms that can glow in the dark. They are part of the genius mycena, a group that includes about 500 species worldwide, although only thirty three are known to be bioluminescent.

3877. There is an algae that tastes like bacon when fried which has nearly twice the nutritional value as kale. The algae was developed by scientists at Oregon State University.

3878. Banana plants are not actual trees. They are herbs or hibiscus plants. Their trunks aren't made of any woody material, and instead, they consist of tightened leaves.

3879. Australians grow poppies in farms and it supplies 50% of all the legal opium used around the world to manufacture morphine and other painkillers. Poppy farmers have a hard time keeping out the wallabies which love to eat the poppies, get high, and then run around in circles.

3880. A sort of floating forest is being built in Rotterdam, in the Netherlands. A number of trees had to be removed for development, so they are placing them in boats throughout the waterfront.

3881. Susan McLeary, a floral designer based in Michigan, makes jewelry out of plants that you can wear for two to four weeks, and then you can transfer them to containers and keep them as plants.

3882. Thompson & Morgan, a UK-based horticulture company, has developed a plant that grows both cherry tomatoes and potatoes. It was developed in Canada and it's called the ketchup and fries plant; it can be bought in Canadian Costco retailers and even in some independent garden centers.

3883. Around Christmas time, some cities spray their trees with fox urine as a way to punish tree thieves who cut down trees illegally. The urine freezes on them and is completely odorless outdoors, but if brought indoors, would stink up your whole house.

3884. The oldest tree known to have been planted by humans is 2,300 years old according to the Guinness World Records. It's known as the sacred fig, or Bow Tree, and was planted in Sri Lanka in 288 B.C.

3885. There is a white oak tree in Athens, Georgia, that legally owns itself, and eight feet (2.4 meters) of land surrounding it. According to newspapers, a deed written by Colonel William Jackson was written to the tree, giving ownership of the land to itself in the 1800's.

3886. The tumbleweed is seen as a symbol of desolation in the American West, but it doesn't actually originate from America. It's a flowering plant called "kali tragus" that's native to Russia, and it first grew in South Dakota in 1879 after its seeds were accidentally mixed with imported flax seeds.

3887. People all over India worked together on July 11, 2013, to plant more trees in twenty four hours than any other group before. As part of the effort to fight climate change, they broke the world record when 800,000 volunteers showed up to take part in the activity, and they managed to plant approximately fifty million trees.

3888. There is a species of orchid that looks pretty much like a monkey. It only grows at high elevations, in certain mountainous areas of Ecuador, Colombia, and Peru.

3889. There are ambulances that are called to come and help when trees are infected with fungi, insects or pests in India. The ambulance is stocked with fungicides, pesticides and insecticides.

3890. When feeling threatened, the mimosa pudica plant, native to Central and South America, also known as touch-me-not plant, plays dead. If it's touched by a predator, its stems release a chemical that causes leaves to shrivel up. Once the danger is gone, it comes back to life.

3891. The Crooked Forest, in Northwest Poland, is a forest of about 400 pine trees that grow with a ninety degree bend at the base of their trunks before rising vertically again.

3892. Back in the 1600's, tulips used to be the most expensive flower. They were even more valuable than most people's homes and cost nearly ten times what the average working man would earn in a whole year.

3893. In the small town of El Valle de Anton, Panama, there are trees growing that have square trunks, a strange phenomenon of nature that it's believed doesn't occur anywhere else in the world. In fact, experts from the University of Florida took a few tree seedlings and planted them in other locations. The trees didn't retain their rectangular shape and had normal, circular trunks.

3894. The largest individually produced flower in the world is the Rafflesia arnoldii plant. It grows more than 35.8 inches (ninety one centimeters) across and weighs almost 24.2 pounds (eleven kilograms).

3895. In 1925, a huge Sequoia tree found in California's Kings Canyon National Park was named the country's national Christmas tree. It measured 298.4 feet (ninety one meters).

3896. There is a six thousand year old baobab tree in South Africa that is so big that it could fit a small building inside of it.

3897. The holiday favorite, mistletoe, is actually a parasite that lives by sucking the nutrients from trees. When it spreads to the branches, the tree dies. Despite this, the parasite feeds birds, may treat cancer, and inspires kissing.

3898. In New York City's Central Park, there are about 18,000 different kinds of trees.

3899. In ancient Rome, Belladonna plants were used as ingredients in drops to make women's eyes larger. These plants are also known as "Deadly Nightshade" due to being quite lethal even in small quantities. Nowadays, it is still used by doctors to dilate patients' eyes.

3900. Most fruits grow on trees. Pineapples, however, grow on shrubs; and each pineapple plant only grows one pineapple.

3901. The giant hogweed is federally listed as a dangerous and noxious plant. Contact with its sap can cause the skin to be extremely sensitive to sunlight.

3902. The corpse flower is a type of flower that only blooms every seven to ten years. The flower actually smells like putrefying and decaying flesh.

3903. The Australian Bull Oak is known to be the hardest wood in the world; it requires 5,060 pounds (2,295 kilograms) of force to embed a steel ball into it. On the contrary, the softest wood in the world is the

Cuipo, which only requires around twenty two pounds (ten kilograms) of force to embed a steel ball inside of it.

3904.   A professor from the University of Syracuse invented a multi-colored tree that produces over forty types of different fruits. The name of the tree is the "Tree of Forty Fruit."

3905.   In 1964, Australian scientists Isabel Joy Bear and RG Thomas conducted a study to determine the reason behind that powerful, wonderful scent of fresh rain. They concluded that it's a mixture of plant oils that are secreted by some plants after an arid period, bacterial spores, and the ozone.

3906.   Indonesia has created a male contraceptive from a plant called the gendarussa which is 99% effective.

3907.   The scents produced by flowers decrease as global temperatures increase.

3908.   Have you ever walked through the woods after a rain stormed and smelled a sweet lingering scent? That scent is really a bacteria called actinomycetes, and its spores are usually formed in the dry soil, until they are splashed into the air when it rains.

3909.   Plants of the genus Dieffenbachia are commonly referred to as "mother-in-law's tongue" because when someone comes in contact with their poison, they can be rendered temporarily speechless.

3910.   Bamboo flowering occurs very rarely. Some species can develop flowers after 65-120 years. The weirdest thing is that when they do flower, all plants of that one bamboo species develop flowers at the same time no matter where they are located in the world.

3911.   Jill Hubley, a web designer based in Brooklyn, New York, created a detailed map identifying every single tree in New York City, based on the last tree census data back in 2005.

3912.   On a genetic level, fungus are more closely related to animals than they are to plants.

Really?

3913.　Following the breakdown of his marriage in 2008, a man named Ian Usher from Perth, Australia, sold his entire life on eBay for $399,000. The sale price not only included his home, car, and motorcycle, but also a two week trial in his job and an introduction to his friends.

3914.　According to a study published in the Journal of Environmental Science Processes and Impacts, all snow, including yellow snow, can be harmful if eaten because it attracts particles from car exhaust fumes like a magnet.

3915.　In 2012, more than 30% of all deaths in Russia were caused by alcohol.

3916.　Joy Milne, a lady from Perth, has the ability to smell Parkinson's disease. She noticed her husband had an odor when he was diagnosed with Parkinson's. Upon mentioning it to Dr. Tilo Kunath of the Edinburgh University School of Biological Sciences, the doctor tested her, and she accurately detected the disease 100% of the time.

3917.　Studies done in 2011 show that judges are more lenient in their court decisions at the start of the day, and immediately after lunch break.

3918.　In a letter to a magazine, Albert Einstein stated that if he was young again, he would become a plumber instead of a scientist. The Chicago plumber's union made him an honorary member in response.

3919.　Wenseslao Moguel was a twenty five year old Mexican Revolution suspect who became known as El Fusilado or "The Executed One," after he was caught on March 18, 1915, and shot nine times by a firing squad. He somehow survived, and lived another sixty years.

3920.　If Japanese police come across someone who is acting violently or is drunk, they place the person on a futon, and then roll him into a burrito.

3921.　"Mountain Peaks Therapy Llamas and Alpacas" is a real faith-based non-profit whose goal is to spread God's love through the use of animal-aided therapy. They hire out decorated alpacas and llamas to act as guests during themed events.

3922.　There was a raffle in 1912 that was conducted on behalf of a Parisian orphanage in France, which needed money to keep operating. The people who won the raffle were given babies as prizes.

3923.   The Madison City Council in Wisconsin voted on September 1, 2009, fifteen to four, in favor of naming the plastic pink flamingo the official bird of the city, and that decision remains in place today. Plastic pink flamingos are so common in America, that there are more of them in people's yards than there are real ones living out in nature.

3924.   When a virtually invisible amount of the element tellurium is ingested, it makes one's sweat and breath smell like garlic. Eating one fifteen thousandth of a gram, about the same volume as a few sugar crystals, can make you smell for eight whole months.

3925.   Researchers from John Hopkins and three other universities discovered in 2000 that when snowflakes land on water, they create noises that are extremely loud for marine animals.

3926.   A Netherlands IKEA had to cancel its one Euro Sunday breakfast offering because demand for it got so high, that it started to cause road closures and traffic jams.

3927.   A British MP named John Stonehouse tried to fake his own death, but was later discovered hiding out in Australia after someone mistook him for a different famous missing person.

3928.   The CEO and owner of Aldi Nord supermarket, Theo Albrecht, was kidnapped in 1971, and held for ransom for seventeen days. He bargained with his captors, and had seven million German Marks paid to them. Later, he succeeded in claiming the money as a business expense on his taxes.

3929.   Catnip is more effective in repelling mosquitoes than DEET, a popular component of bug repellant, according to the American Chemical Society.

3930.   The Mermaid Parade is an annual event in Coney Island, New York, where participants dress in hand-crafted mermaid costumes and other eye-catching outfits.

3931.   For the last 460 years, the students at Christ's Hospital School in England have worn the same uniform.

3932.   The cost of a tourist visa to travel to China is $140 for Americans and $30 for the rest of the world.

3933.   It is not possible to swallow and breathe simultaneously.

3934.   Mohammad Mastafa, a New York City hot dog vendor, pays around $289,000 a year for his eatery location.

3935.   Kechari mudra is a yoga practice where you roll your tongue up in your nasal cavity. It's believed to help you overcome thirst, hunger, decay, and death.

3936.   Initially it was turnips, potatoes, and beets that were carved to make jack-o'-lanterns, not pumpkins.

3937.   For anyone seriously interested in surfing, it's actually possible to get a university degree in it.

3938.   There is a kitchen exclusively for pastry at the White House.

3939.   Peanuts can be used to produce dynamite. When peanut oil is processed, it can produce glycerol, which can later be used to make nitroglycerin. And nitroglycerin is the main element used in dynamite.

3940.   One of the scientists who discovered the DNA's double helix once quoted: "Wouldn't it be great if we can make all girls pretty by engineering genes that would influence beauty?"

3941.   Allodoxaphobia is the fear of people's opinions. People suffering from this live in constant fear and anxiety of hearing other people's opinions about them.

3942.   If you were a student in 1978 working a job paying minimum wage, you could easily afford a full year's tuition at any four year college.

3943.   Given the extreme weather conditions where camels live (places with little water), their digestive systems wring their food dry of almost all of its moisture. In fact, their poop is so dry that it's even possible to use it to start a fire.

3944.   A flea is able to jump one hundred times its own height by pushing off from the ground or pet using their toes. They take off at speeds of three miles (five kilometers) per hour and reach speeds as fast as four miles (seven kilometers) per hour.

3945. In 1839, there was a story published by a writer named Edgar Poe about four sailors who were stranded out in sea with no food, and had to kill one of the members, Richard Parker, for food. Forty five years later, a yacht that was going to Australia from England sank, and the four crew didn't have enough food to survive. One of the members was sacrificed to save the other three. His name was Richard Parker.

3946. Coulrophobia is the fear of clowns. Over the last twenty years, it has increased considerably due to their portrayal in popular culture, and the more common scary clown phenomenon where people have been dressing up as clowns to scare others.

3947. As a result of tourists throwing good luck coins since the 1950's, a blue-crystal hot spring located in Yellowstone National Park is now turning green.

3948. The remains of an eighteenth century ship were found buried about twenty feet (six meters) beneath the site of the World Trade Center. The thirty two foot (nine meter) ship remnant was discovered as bulldozers were excavating a parking structure.

3949. Every year in America, there are about 40,000 toilet-related injuries, and some of them even result in death.

3950. Almost all witch windows in existence are found in Vermont State, and they look like ordinary windows except that they are opened at a forty five degree angle. Legend has it that when windows are turned to such an angle, it makes it hard for witches to fly into the home on their broomsticks.

3951. It's against the law for anyone to possess golden and bald eagles or parts of their bodies, as per the National Eagle Repository. The repository has a specific site where they distribute golden and bald eagles that are found dead to Native Alaskans and Native Americans, who have been using these birds for cultural and religious rituals for centuries.

3952. According to the North American Association of State and Provincial Lotteries, Americans spent over seventy billion dollars buying lottery tickets in 2015.

3953. Researchers interviewed parents from 384 families with multiple children in a 2005 study, and they discovered that 70% of fathers had a favorite child and 74% of mothers did as well.

3954. Taking baths was very uncommon in the Tudor Era. People believed that the plague was airborne and that they would contract it if their pores opened up.

3955. When Andrew Jackson was first inaugurated as president, he held a White House reception that was open to the public. About 1,200 people came, got really drunk, and trashed the executive building. In fact, the party got so crazy, that the president jumped out of the window, and spent his first night as president sleeping next door.

3956. It's illegal to sell cats and dogs in Beverly Hills pet stores if they are not rescued or from pet shelters.

3957. Citizens in Canada can sign up to get a free flag that's retired from the top of Parliament Hill.

3958. Blasphemy is still a crime in Ireland according to the Defamation Act of 2009. Those found guilty could be fined up to €25,000.

3959. In Piedmont, Italy, there is a huge stuffed pink bunny over 200 feet (sixty meters) long on top of a hill, simply for the entertainment of hikers to enjoy. It is fully biodegradable and will be gone by 2025.

3960. More than one ton of hair is extracted from waste water at treatment plants around the world each month. In most places, the hair is taken to landfills and buried, but some companies use the hair for other things.

3961. The richest cat in the world belonged to a UK man named Ben Rea. Rea left a seven million pound inheritance to his cat Blackie upon his death in May, 1998. Rea originally had fifteen cats, but they all passed away except for Blackie.

3962. A couple of Princeton University researchers turned a cat into an actual working phone in 1929. The cat survived somehow, but it later died when the two decided to re-do their experiment.

3963. In Germany, there is a time honored tradition called Der Sternewirth, where employees working at breweries are allowed to consume as much free beer as they want to during work hours.

3964. 23,000 people were surveyed in twenty two countries, and it was revealed that 20% of people in the world believe that there are aliens that look like us, and are walking among us. That belief is held by as high as 40% of people in India and China.

3965. Chicago is nicknamed the Windy City, but not because of its weather. It originally got the name from people who were critical of the politicians there, referring to them as windbags.

3966. In some places in Europe, and particularly in Slovakia, there is a Christmas tradition where before they kill a carp and prepare it for Christmas Eve dinner, they let it swim around in the family's bathtub for one to two days.

3967. Before Saddam Hussein, the Iraqi president, was captured and killed, he wrote four novels, and a number of poems. Most of his works were blocked from mass production. He chose to use the pen name "He Who Wrote It" for the first two novels he wrote.

3968. Laura Buxton, a ten year old girl released a balloon full of helium in 2001, along with a note asking for it to be returned to her home address in Midlands, England. Another girl found it 140 miles (225 kilometers) away; her name was Laura Buxton too. Adding to the coincidence, the two girls were only a few months apart in age, they were of the same height although they were a bit tall for their age, and they each had similar pets, including a three year old black Labrador retriever, a guinea pig, and a bunny.

3969. If you accidentally run over an animal in West Virginia State, the law gives you the right to claim it as your property, bring it home, and eat the roadkill for dinner.

3970. In four of the five largest cities in America, namely New York, Los Angeles, Washington D.C., and Chicago, it's more cost effective to rely on an Uber than a personal car, as per a 2018 report. Dallas is the odd one out, and you can actually save $116 by using a personal car there.

3971. Panhandlers who begged for money outside the Walmart in Coos Bay, Oregon, made way more money than the majority of the employees at the store, according to a 2008 survey. In some instances, they made more money per day than employees did the entire week.

3972. Carhenge is a popular recreation of the Stonehenge that's made using old cars, and is located right outside Alliance, Nebraska, in America. It includes thirty nine different trucks and cars, all models from the

1950's to the 1970's, that are carefully arranged to resemble the mysterious landmark as precisely as possible.

3973. Before being picked up by Netflix, the show Stranger Things was rejected twenty times by other networks.

3974. The oldest US president in history was Donald Trump, at more than seventy years old.

3975. Hoover-Ball was a game invented by White House physician, Admiral Joel Boone, for President Hoover. It was a combination of tennis, volleyball, and medicine ball, created to help keep President Hoover physically fit.

3976. In an effort to prevent wrinkles, a British woman named Tess Christian has not smiled or laughed in forty years.

3977. Baby koalas eat something known as pap, which is a liquefied form of their mother's feces. The substance actually gives them the necessary microbes to digest the toxins in the eucalyptus that they later need to eat to survive.

3978. Accents change approximately every twenty five miles (forty kilometers) in the UK.

3979. In Saudi Arabia, the Muppet Show was actually banned because of Miss Piggy, in 1979. As Prophet Mohammed declared the flesh of swine an abomination, all merchandise bearing her likeness was removed from shops and destroyed.

3980. The Romans considered women with unibrows attractive and desirable from 753 to 476 AD. Lots of women who didn't naturally have unibrows used paint to join their eyebrows to look prettier.

3981. At the Mutter Museum in Philadelphia, it's possible to see pieces of Albert Einstein's brain.

3982. In warm climates, oranges can be green and are perfectly ripe. In fact, they are on their way to being rotten when they are turning orange.

3983. Giraffes can actually hum. The hum however is a low frequency sound at about ninety two hertz.

3984. The only two divorced men to ever be elected president of the United States are Ronald Reagan and Donald Trump, in over two centuries worth of presidential elections.

3985. A gallon of barbecue sauce was discovered twenty years ago for the McJordan Burger promotion which was sold for almost ten thousand dollars in 2012.

3986. The only marsupial in North America is the opossum.

3987. A father in China once hired a pro gamer to kill his son in a video game so he would become discouraged to continue playing and go look for a job.

3988. On the isolated island of Surtsey that hadn't been visited in forty years, a tomato plant was found on the coast of the island. It was discovered that it came from a previous scientist who went to the toilet in the bush.

3989. The term "sandwich" is thought to come from John Montagu, fourth Earl of Sandwich, a town in the county of Kent in southeast England. While gambling, he would ask his servants to bring him slices of meat between two slices of bread so that he wouldn't have to leave the game.

3990.   George Pullman was a railroad tycoon who was buried during the night under eight feet (2.5 meters) of layered steel, reinforced concrete because the family was scared his former employees would desecrate his corpse.

3991.   As much as thirty-two people used to die in hot car deaths every year in Miami. Since 2016, Florida Governor Rick Scott has approved a law that makes it legal to break into any locked vehicle in order to rescue a vulnerable person or pet that they believe to be in danger of suffocation.

3992.   Hugo Chavez, a former Venezuelan president, stated once that Muammar Gaddafi was welcomed in the country, but that Charlie Sheen was not.

3993.   Studies from the London School of Economics in 2010 showed that men who are unfaithful tend to have lower IQs.

3994.   In March of 2017, the world's first fluorescent frog was discovered in Argentina. Under regular light, the polka dot tree frog appears to have a dull, browny-green skin with red dots. However, under UV light, it glows a bright fluorescent green.

3995.   In 2002, Australian friends Hoss Siegel, Josh Spiegel, and Ross Koger wanted to bring some creativeness and fun into their lives, so they got a bunch of friends together, built cardboard suits of armor, weapons, and vehicles, and held a brave heart-style battle. Since then, the game has grown into a large, annual event held on Boxing Day, and it's called Box Wars.

3996.   Although naked mole rats are rodents, they live like many insects. For example, they live in colonies that are led by a queen or dominant rat; and the queen is the only female to breed and bear young.

3997.   In 1858, London experienced something that is historically referred to as "the Great Stink." As a result of so many people dumping sewage into the Thames River, the smell resulting was overwhelming. In fact, in an attempt to suppress the smell for the MPs, the curtains of the commons were soaked in chloride and lime. Later, a bill was rushed through Parliament in eighteen days to provide more money to build a new sewer system for London.

3998.   If jellyfish wash up to shore, they will eventually evaporate in the sun as they're 98% water.

3999.   It's possible to get slivers or splinters just like wood ones from hair. In fact, they're very common with dog groomers and hair stylists.

4000.   President Reagan raised tariffs to 45% on Japanese bikes that entered the country, saving Harley Davidson Motorcycles.

4001.   It is known that the word "dude" was first used in the 1800's. It was used as an insult towards young men who were too worried about keeping up with the latest fashions.

4002.   A man from Oklahoma named Paul Phillips loves fishing so much that he actually dug up his own pond and then built a house over it. The living room has a trap door from where he can fish whenever he wants.

4003.   The Great British Duck Race is an event held every year in London where people purchase rubber ducks to help support various charities. The ducks are then raced more than half a mile (0.8 kilometers) down the River Thames. The first one over the finish line wins a cash prize. In 2009 a world record for the largest plastic duck race was set with over 205,000 ducks.

4004.   In India, scientists at Junagadh University have extracted gold from the urine of rare indigenous breeds of cattle. They analyzed 400 Gir cows and found traces of ionized gold salts in their urine. Scientists were able to isolate, precipitate, extract, solidify and melt between three to ten milligrams of gold per liter of urine.

4005.   In 2016, the Turkish Ed Rolf family got poisoned from eating food that was prepared to celebrate getting out of the hospital for food poisoning.

4006.   During his lifetime, David "The Bullet" Smith has been shot from a cannon more than 5,000 times.

He is the highest flying human cannonball in the world today with his world record breaking in human cannonball shots. He appeared on season seven of America's Got Talent.

4007.   Paul Erdos, a fast and clever mathematician, could calculate in his head how many seconds a person had lived after knowing the person's age.

4008.   The shortest president the United States has ever had was James Madison, the fourth president. He was only 5.3 feet (1.6 meters) tall and weighed about one hundred pounds (forty-five kilograms).

4009.   You can actually purchase cyberbullying insurance in the United Kingdom and Ireland. The insurance company Chub will pay out as much as $74,600 to help with court costs and relocation fees.

4010.   In the late 1970's, President Jimmy Carter installed thirty-two solar panels on the White House roof. In 1981, when Ronald Reagan took office, he had them removed because he thought it was a joke. Then when President Obama moved in, he had all the solar panels reinstalled.

4011.   In 1938, Adolph Hitler was named Man of the Year by Time Magazine.

4012.   In 2016, a fried chicken scented candle was released by KFC.

4013.   Doctors have a checklist with nineteen questions before they see a patient that has reduced deaths by more than 40%. Some of the questions include "do we have the right patient" and "what operation are we performing."

4014.   In 2015, a military Disneyland park called "Patriot Park" was opened in Russia. All visitors, including children, can ride in tanks, shoot guns, and buy and sell military gear.

4015.   Isaac Newton predicted that the world would end in 2060.

4016.   In 2008, the Coral Spring beach in Jamaica was actually stolen and the thieves were never caught. Massive amounts of sand were stolen until it basically wasn't a beach any more.

4017.   In the late 1900's, Howard Hughes, an American business mogul, bought an entire casino named "Silver Slipper" so that he could get rid of the neon sign. Apparently the sign was visible from Hughes' bedroom and it was keeping him up at night.

4018.   There is now a complete new industry around the globe where students have their university papers and other work done by unemployed graduates and professors. The students don't get in trouble as the work isn't copied and done from scratch.

4019.   156 people have been exonerated and freed from death row since 1973, according to the Death Penalty Information Center.

4020.   In 2007, a curry dish was delivered from Wales in the UK to New York in the US at a price of $3,900. The dinner order was placed by Kanye West. The dish itself only cost nineteen pounds and the rest was the delivery fee.

4021.   90% of US media, including TV, radio, and news, is owned by only six corporations: Disney, CBS, Viacom, Newscorp, GE, and Time Warner.

4022.   Thomas Edison, the man who is credited with inventing the light bulb, was afraid of darkness.

4023.   According to a soldier who was guarding Saddam Hussein after his capture in 2003, the only time he ever looked defeated was when someone brought him the wrong cereal.

4024.   More people die from sand castles than they do from sharks, as people fall into holes that are dug up for building those sand castles than they are from being attacked by sharks.

4025.   The light on your microwave uses more electricity than it does to heat up your food.

4026.   At CIA headquarters in Langley, Virginia, there's a Starbucks where employees undergo an intense background check before they are hired. They're also not allowed to put customers' names on any of the cups. In fact, it's one of the busiest Starbucks in the country.

4027.   Almost 5% of New Yorkers have a net worth of over a million dollars, which means one in twenty people in New York is a millionaire.

4028. In 2015, nearly 12,000 gallstones were removed from a patient by Dr. Makhan Lala Saha, a gastrointestinal endosurgeon in India. They ranged up to five millimeters in size and it took his assistant four hours to count them.

4029. Buildings in Hong Kong have gaping holes in them. The reason why is to allow dragons to roam freely from their mountain homes to the sea.

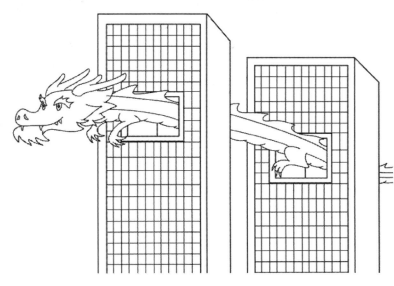

4030. In Los Angeles, there is a Santa Claus University that teaches professional Santa Claus skills such as toy knowledge, poses, and how to avoid a lawsuit. A great Santa Clause can make up to $100,000 a year.

4031. Up until 1966, LSD or acid was legal in California.

4032. According to the Farmer's Almanac, counting the chirps made by crickets can determine the temperature outside. So to convert cricket chirps to Celsius, you count the number of chirps in twenty five seconds, divide by three, and then add four to get the temperature.

4033. Magician and escape artist Harry Houdini used to sell war bonds at the beginning of World War I, as well as teach American soldiers how to free themselves from German restraints.

4034. Being sarcastic is believed to enhance creativity in all parties involved in the conversation.

4035. The widest human mouth according to the Guinness World Records measures 6.7 inches (seventeen centimeters); it belongs to a man named Francisco Domingo Joaquim Chiquinho from Angola.

4036. The prison's executioner in the state of Florida is an anonymous, private citizen, who is paid $150 per execution.

4037. In 1975, a seventeen year old boy was killed by a taxi while riding his Moped. The accident occurred exactly one year after his seventeen year old brother was killed while riding the same Moped, in the same street, by the same taxi and driver who, by the way, was carrying the same passenger.

4038. In Texas, possessing a pair of pliers is against the law.

4039. Taco Bell's flagship restaurant in Las Vegas began allowing people in 2017 to get married inside the restaurant. They even installed a wedding chapel on the second floor for nuptials.

4040. USS Yorktown was the original name of the USS Enterprise. It was named after a World War II aircraft carrier.

4041. George Washington asked his staff to wait two days after his death to bury him because he was so afraid of being buried alive.

4042. Approximately 50.6 pounds (twenty three kilograms) of manure are produced by a 1,000 pound (454 kilogram) horse per day, which equals to 19,900 pounds (9,000 kilograms) of manure per year.

4043. To cut down on their delivery time for products, Apple flies their stock first class instead of shipping it.

4044. Surprisingly, Abraham Lincoln was in the National Wrestling Hall of Fame. He had a remarkable physical size at six foot four (1.95 meters) and he was widely known for his wrestling skills; in twelve years, he had only one reported defeat.

4045. During exams, Internet black-outs have been imposed by governments in Iraq and India as a way to prevent students from cheating.

4046. If the entire globe's human population all came together into the Grand Canyon, we wouldn't be anywhere near close to filling it up.

4047. The Empire State Building makes more money as an observation spot than it does from renting office space.

4048. In 1859, English settler Thomas Austin released twenty four rabbits onto his property in Australia; he thought that the introduction of a few rabbits could provide a touch of home in addition to a spot of hunting. By 1920, the rabbit population had reached ten billion.

4049. Nodding your head in Albania means "no" and shaking your head means "yes."

4050. Fourteen year old Xiao Yun, from China, ran away from home and was missing for ten years, even thought to be dead. She was found at the age of twenty four living in an Internet cafe. As she was good at the game Crossfire, other gamers paid to watch her play it. She slept at Internet cafes and public bath houses for a complete decade.

4051. The first police force in Australia was actually formed from the best-behaved convicts.

4052. In Finland, mobile phone throwing is an actual sport.

4053. McDonald's has its own university in Shanghai, China, called the Hamburger University. It trains students in restaurant management skills and has over 275,000 graduates. With a selection rate of 1% at its campus, this intense week-long training program is more exclusive than Harvard.

4054. Wu Hsia, from China, had an ex-girlfriend and current girlfriend jump off a bridge into a river; they wanted to see who he would rescue. He rescued his current girlfriend.

4055. According to a study conducted at Harvard and published in the New York Times, if you were born on September 16, you share a birthday with more people than anyone who was born on a different date.

4056. In Ribeauville, France, bees started producing honey in different shades of blue and green. Further studies by beekeepers later revealed that instead of collecting nectar from flowers, the bees were feeding on remnants of colored M&M candy shells that were being processed by a plant located 2.5 miles (four kilometers) away.

4057. A man named Seth Horvits accidentally received a military assault rifle when he ordered a TV from Amazon in 2012.

4058. The original design for Mount Rushmore was to carve the four presidents from the waist up, but the lack of funding made the carver stop after the faces were completed.

4059. William Mckinley won the US election in 1896 by campaigning only on his front porch while his opponent spoke at over 600 events.

4060. J. Paul Getty, one of the richest men of all time from the oil and gas industry, had a pay phone installed in his house after visitors racked up his phone bill.

4061. A study conducted by TDG Research revealed that the average Netflix subscriber spends more than 550 hours every year using the service.

4062. The skull that Russians kept as proof of Hitler's death actually belongs to a woman.

4063. You could hear a hyena's laugh if you were sitting eight miles (thirteen kilometers) away.

4064. In Zhengzhou, China, there is a Korean restaurant where people don't have to pay for their meal if they're the five most attractive customers of that day.

4065. "Som Biotech Research Foundation" is a dog cloning service in South Korea that will actually clone your beloved pooch for around $100,000.

4066. Conflict Kitchen is a restaurant located in Pittsburgh that only serves cuisine from countries that the US is in conflict with. When they started serving Palestinian food, they received death threats.

4067. Originally, the word outlaw meant "outside the protection of the law." In other words, you could rob or kill without having legal consequences.

4068. If you immerse a pearl in vinegar, it will actually dissolve as it is mostly calcium carbonate, which is susceptible to even the weakest acid solution.

4069. A third grade girl was expelled from school for a year for carrying a dangerous weapon. Her grandmother made a birthday cake for her and sent her to school along with the cake and a knife to cut it. The teacher used the knife to cut the cake and then reported the girl to the school authorities.

4070. Approximately 2.3 million people around the world are employed by Walmart.

4071. Disney Parks can actually deny people access to their parks if they find that they have a questionable tattoo.

4072. The world record for the largest ball of chewing gum is held by Barry Chapelle from Los Angeles. Over a six year period, he chewed 95,200 pieces of Nicorette gum, forming it into a giant gumball that weighs more than 174 pounds (seventy nine kilograms) and measures over 4.9 feet (1.5 meters) in circumference.

4073. As of 2019, the total amount for US student loans hit a trillion dollars. This is bigger than some countries' whole economies.

4074. In 2014, a parking space in London sold for 400,000 pounds. That's two and a half times the cost of the average UK home.

4075. Bob Marley suffered from racism when growing up as he was seen as a white man due to having a British father.

4076. Declaring and paying state tax on goods that have been bought online from out of state is supposedly a voluntary duty for all Americans. However, accountants and tax lawyers are some of the only people who actually pay it.

4077. Japanese Company Dentsu requests all new employees and recently promoted executives to climb Mount Fuji. The event has occurred every July, since 1925.

4078. It's estimated that people throw away nearly $4.5 million into fountains and wishing wells every single year.

4079. In Japan, gun laws are so severe that after a police officer once killed himself with a gun, he was posthumously charged with breaking the law.

4080. The city of Moscow ran out of vodka at the end of World War 2 because the Russians partied so hard.

4081. Duke, a nine year old Great Pyrenees dog, is the honorary mayor of Cormorant Township, in Minnesota. He is actually in his third term.

4082. Abraham Lincoln, the 16th president of the United States, never actually slept in the Lincoln bedroom. He would rather use it as his personal office.

4083.   In the United States, when someone reports their company for tax evasion, the person receives anywhere from 15-30% of the amount collected. A man named Bradley Birkenfeld was a whistleblower on the USB AG Swiss Bank tax evasion scheme and received $104 million as a reward.

4084.   China celebrates over ten million weddings every year. With couples spending an average of $12,000 on each wedding, that's a total of $120 billion.

4085.   A student in 1979 could pay off their college tuition by working 385 hours, however, a student now would have to work over 7,000 hours to do the same.

4086.   Steve Jobs, the creator of Apple, didn't want his own kids to have iPads and even limited their use of technology to a minimum.

4087.   In 1989, three daycare centers were forced to remove their murals of Mickey, Donald, and Goofy, under threat of legal action by Disney.

4088.   The first US president to be born in a hospital was President Jimmy Carter.

4089.   In 1890, when the Ouija Board was asked what it should be called, it spelled out "Ouija." After it was asked what it meant, it said "Good Luck."

4090.   If you have to start a fire, you can use Dorito chips as kindling. The seasonings on spicier varieties and the oils enable the fire to keep burning longer. Cheetohs and Fritos also work quite well as kindling.

4091.   Although there was plenty of evidence to prove otherwise, the CEOs of the seven largest tobacco companies went before congress in 1994 and testified that nicotine was not addictive.

4092.   An art student at Syracuse University stole a real skull from a mausoleum in 1988 to use it in a sculpting class. He was caught by the police, who later found out that the skull belonged to John J. Crouse, who served as the Syracuse mayor between 1876 and 1880.

4093.   A Swedish member of parliament named Erik Brandt nominated German dictator Adolf Hitler for the Nobel Prize in 1939. Ultimately, the nomination was cancelled, and a peace prize was not awarded to anyone that year.

4094.   The creditors who issue the most elite and exclusive credit cards make them using solid gold, and they occasionally decorate them using diamonds.

4095.   Skatole is a potent smelling chemical compound that is a component of many perfumes, and ironically, is naturally present in human feces.

4096.   Roger Fisher, director of the Harvard Negotiation Project and a law professor at the same school, published a thought experiment in 1981 on the Bulletin of the Atomic Science. He postulated that the nuclear launch codes should be implanted inside the chest of a willing young person, and the president would have to cut them out of the person's body before launching the nuclear weapons.

4097.   When trains were first invented, some believed that women shouldn't travel at speeds of fifty miles (eighty kilometers) per hour or higher because it would cause their uteruses to fly out of the body.

4098.   On May 19, 2004, a boa constrictor got itself trapped between two huge generation units, causing a fifteen-minute nationwide blackout in Honduras. When the boa was electrocuted, it triggered a short circuit that caused the emergency system to shut down the entire power plant.

4099.   Jack Ryan, the original creator of the Barbie Doll, used to previously design military grade missiles.

4100.   One of the most needed items at homeless shelters are socks, however, they are often the least donated.

4101.   According to vet doctor Joyce Armen, given the huge mass that horses have, they can safely drink alcohol.

4102.   If adjusted for inflation, George Washington was worth a staggering $525 million.

4103. By licking a US stamp, you consume 1/10 of a calorie. However, by licking a British stamp, you get 5.9 calories per lick, and the adhesive on a larger commemorative or special British stamp contains 14.5 calories.

4104. In 2002, a Hooters in Panama City, Florida, offered employees a chance to win a Toyota. Jodee Berry, the winning waitress, was given a toy Yoda action figure as a prank, so she sued the company and won enough to buy any type of Toyota she wanted.

4105. If you chew gum for eighteen hours, apply lip balm 1,500 times, or sing a song twenty three times, you would burn off 200 calories.

4106. There are therapists known as wealth therapists who help super wealthy individuals who are mentally unable to cope with their wealth.

4107. Master builder at LEGO, Steve Gerling, had never touched a single LEGO before he started his job.

4108. Hitler actually had a pet alligator named Saturn that the Russians were gifted by the British government.

4109. In 1784, Thomas Jefferson proposed to end slavery in all the territories, but his bill was lost in Congress by a single vote.

4110. In 1958, a man named Robert Lane from New York City named his son Winner and, later, another son Loser. Winner ended up as a criminal with a long prison record. Loser on the contrary, went on to prep school on a scholarship, graduated from college, and joined the New York Police Department.

4111. "NineBot" is a Chinese Segway rip-off company that used the money that it got from selling rip-off Segways to buy the original Segway Company.

4112. Steve Jobs' GPA was 2.65 when in high school.

4113. The UK based company Gumdrop recycles gum into bins and they're made out of entirely recycled gum.

4114. A sixteen year old student in Ohio won an essay contest for the question "what to do with Hitler after the war" with one sentence which was: "Put him in black skin and let him live the rest of his life in America."

4115. According to the Guinness World Records, on March 30, 2003, a 2.3 feet (seventy centimeter) round, ten pound (4.5 kilograms) coconut was husked by Siddaraju Raju, from Bangalore, India, using only his teeth.

4116. In the 1980's, it was actually possible to call 1-900-909-FRED to have Freddy Kruger of Nightmare on Elm Street tell you scary stories.

4117. Doctor Roswell Park was called on as he performed surgery on September 6, 1901. He said he couldn't leave, not even for the president of the United States himself. Strangely, it was President William McKinley who needed his help because he had been shot, but Doctor Park still wouldn't leave surgery. President McKinley died, and a couple of weeks later, Dr. Park saved a woman who came in with injuries similar to the president's.

4118. Research done in London shows that over a million lives could be saved each year if everyone in the world washed their hands properly.

4119. Ambrosia is a startup based in Monterey, California, that infuses clients with blood plasma from young adults or teenagers to slow down aging.

4120. A bird dropped a baguette on the large Hadron Collider in 2009, and it was blamed for causing a technical fault.

4121. On average, every motorists spends more than two days per year in traffic, just waiting for the light to turn from red to green.

4122. California's wildfire firefighting personnel consist of 50-80% inmates, and they are paid less than two dollars an hour.

4123. It's alleged that Alexander the Great, Napoleon, Hitler, and Mussolini suffered from ailurophobia, which is the fear of cats.

4124. A vat in London holding 161,000 gallons (610,000 liters) of beer burst on October 17, 1814, and that caused other nearby vats of beer to rupture as well. As a result, more than 388,000 gallons (1,470,000 liters) of beer flooded the streets, and eight people drowned.

4125. More Americans voted during the fifth season finale of American Idol than during the 1984 election in which Ronald Reagan won the presidency. There were 54.5 million votes cast during the election, compared to sixty three million for the TV show.

4126. In order to understand and cure diseases more effectively, scientists in Japan successfully designed and bred fluorescent monkeys. The researchers however received a lot of backlash from various ethical groups who didn't approve their experiments.

4127. The United States nuclear weapons system is very much out of date and it still runs on floppy disks, which were last popular in the 1980's, according to a Government Accountability Office report.

4128. Times Square had a waterfall back in 1948 that was known as the Bond Waterfall. It had a height of twenty six feet (eight meters), a length of 131 feet (forty meters) and was designed to flow at a rate of 8,350 gallons (38,000 liters) per minute.

4129. Artist Bart Jansen together with Arjen Beltman, a radio control helicopter expert, turned Bart's dead beloved pet cat, Orville, into a remote-controlled helicopter. They named him the Orville Copter.

4130. Several people who hiked in the Tomoka Riverside woods close to Daytona, Florida, between 1955 and 1966 reported seeing a strange pink-colored fog that seemed to stay near the ground. Lots of these people believe the fog was carnivorous, and they blame it for the disappearances of about twelve different people. To date, no one knows what the fog was, or where it originated from.

4131. A six acre island in Maine was purchased by the makers of Cards against Humanity, a popular game, and they renamed it "Hawaii II" because it is in the mainland.

4132. When you are deep in sleep, you burn more calories than you do when you are sitting on a sofa and watching TV.

4133. If you take the total number of people bitten by sharks in the whole world in a year, and then multiply it by ten, you'll end up with the approximate number of people who are bitten by other people, just in New York alone.

4134. If you started out with one cent and you doubled your money every single day, you'd be a millionaire just twenty seven days later. You would have $1,342,177 on day twenty seven.

4135.   If you take a close look at the Liberty Bell in Philadelphia, you'll notice that Pennsylvania is wrongly spelled, and it's missing one "N."

4136.   Daniel Boria, a twenty six year old business owner from Calgary, Canada, was arrested after he tied 120 helium balloons to his chair on July 5, 2015, and used it to float over the city. Daniel said he was trying to advertise his cleaning business. He was fined $25,000 for his stunt.

4137.   The number of possible piece placement iterations on a chess board outnumber the number of atoms in the known universe.

4138.   According to a study, mass murderers and serial killers are born in higher numbers in November than in any other month.

4139.   President Charles King of Liberia ran for re-election in 1927, and he got 234,000 votes, although Liberia had only 15,000 registered voters at the time. King's election holds the Guinness World Record for being the most fraudulent one in history.

4140.   The Nazi party actually pioneered the first ever public anti-tobacco and anti-smoking movement in history, after German doctors found links between lung cancer and cigarette smoking.

4141.   Bruce Buffer, the UFC announcer, and Michael Buffer, the boxing announcer, were actually long-lost half-brothers, and they had never met until they realized that they have the same biological father when they were grownups.

4142.   Ludger Sylbaris got into a bar brawl and was placed in solitary confinement, just before a major volcanic eruption destroyed the city of Saint-Pierre. Ludger was one of just three survivors of the eruption because his cell was heavily sheltered. That prison cell still exists today.

4143.   "Vortex I" was an event hosted from August 27 to September 3, 1970, in Clackamas County, Oregon, and was attended by tens of thousands of people. It was a free biodegradable festival of life, and to date, is still the only large scale rock event in America that was facilitated by a republican governor. However, it turned out that the entire event was an elaborate plan to keep the youth away from a Portland convention that then President Richard Nixon attended, and the plan actually worked.

4144.   A two-lane road could be constructed between the cities of New York and San Francisco, just by using the same amount of cement that went into constructing the Hoover Dam.

4145.   Hurricane Harvey caused so much rainfall in the American South on August 28, 2017, it forced the National Weather Service to add two new colors, light purple and dark purple, to their graphical reports because the flood water had more than doubled the fifteen inch maximum represented by a dark red indicator.

4146.   Scholars believe that the symbol "@" dates back hundreds of years ago and that it was invented by monks.

4147.   The Federal Government of the United States owns one marijuana farm, which is located at the University of Mississippi campus.

4148.   In 1997, a survey done in America showed that 12% of people thought that Noah, the biblical character who built an arc, was the husband of Joan of Arc. Although both figures did receive messages from God, that's as far as their similarities go, because they didn't even live in the same era in history.

4149.   Every forty six seconds in the United States, a truck, car, or other type of vehicle is stolen, according to a report by the National Highway Traffic Safety Administration. The 1994 Honda Accord was the most stolen vehicle in 2011, as per the National Insurance Crime Bureau, and it held the same position in 2008, 2009, and 2010.

4150.   Mikhail Gorbachev, former leader of the Soviet Union, appeared in a 1997 Pizza Hut advert with Anastasia, his ten year old granddaughter. The ad used footage of the two in a Pizza Hut to argue that capitalism is preferable to communism because it made luxuries, such as the restaurant, available to people.

4151. President John F. Kennedy had such a privileged childhood and upbringing that he said that he only found out about the Great Depression by reading books about it at Harvard.

4152. A new exhibit that showcases the world's largest collection of fossilized poop was opened on August 3, 2015, at the South Florida Museum. The largest of all the fossils was excrement from a prehistoric crocodile. It is as big as a puppy. It was nicknamed "Precious."

4153. The metal lubricant WD-40 has many other uses. For instance, it can kill insects and cockroaches, and you can spray it over your doors, windows, and screens to keep insects out.

4154. Nerf, the toy company, first started its slogan as "Nerf, throw it indoors, you can't damage lamps, or break windows, you can't hurt babies, or old people."

4155. On average, people spend over three months of their lives on toilets, with men spending four minutes longer than women on toilets every day.

4156. If your eyes were as good as the Hubble Space Telescopes' Wide Field and Planetary Camera, you'd be able to read standard fine print newspaper pages from more than one mile (1.6 kilometers) away.

4157. Based on statistics, more people have died from selfies than shark attacks.

4158. In 2003, when a Coca-Cola employee was caught drinking Pepsi on the job, he was immediately fired.

4159. There has only been a total of 260 years of peace since the beginning of recorded history.

4160. During World War I, a flock of forty-eight sheep were kept by Woodrow Wilson on the White House lawn to save money on groundskeepers. The sheep also collected over fifty thousand dollars for the Red Cross through the auction of their wool.

4161. In 2013, PayPal put over $92 quadrillion into executive Chris Reynolds' account by mistake. They soon admitted their error and offered to donate money to a cause of Reynolds' choice.

4162. McDonald's was nicknamed "Macca's" in Australia. In 2013, this name became so popular that it was changed officially, including on signs.

4163. After saving someone for drowning, lifeguard Thomas Lopez from South Florida was actually fired. The reason why was because the man he saved wasn't technically in his assigned lifeguard area.

4164. In 2010, a computer programmer bought two large pizzas and paid ten thousand Bitcoins. If he'd kept those a little longer, they'd be worth one hundred million dollars today.

4165. In Brisbane, Australia, there's a golf course with full grown bull sharks living in the water hazards.

4166. In 2002, an entire family was saved by actor Vin Diesel from a burning car accident.

4167. White supremacist and racist Craig Cobb agreed to take a genetic test and received the results live on television. Surprisingly for him, he was found to be 14% Sub-Saharan African.

4168. Michael Buffer, a ring announcer, has trademarked the term "Let's get ready to…" which has netted him over four hundred million dollars.

4169. There are more trade regulations imposed upon bananas than upon AK-47s.

4170. In 2016, a survey done by Pew Research concluded that of 1,520 adults living in all fifty American states and the District of Columbia, over one in four people didn't read a single book within the last twelve months.

4171. If you want to climb Mount Everest, you have to save between $60,000 and $120,000. This price includes sherpas, supplies, and permits.

4172. American scientists blew up a hydrogen bomb that was a hundred times as powerful as the one used in Hiroshima right outside the atmosphere in the summer of 1962, just to find out what would happen.

4173. Based on information provided by the Center of Disease Control and Prevention, one in six US adults binge drinks about four times a month.

4174. A man named Forest Fenn hid a treasure worth between one and three million dollars in the Rocky Mountains. To find it you have to solve his riddle, which no one has yet done.

4175. Mark Zuckerberg initially claimed publically that there would never be a dislike button as it would be "bad for the world."

4176. Crystal meth used to be prescribed as a diet aid after the Second World War; it actually remained legal right up until the 1970's.

4177. A survey released by Travelzoo revealed that 64% of Americans confess to peeing in the pool or ocean while on vacation.

4178. Based on reports issued by the Literacy Project Foundation, forty five million Americans are functionally illiterate and cannot read above a fifth grade level. Moreover, 50% of adults cannot read a book written at an eighth grade level.

4179. New Zealand doesn't issue residency visas to people with high BMI; there have even been cases of people rejected just because of their weight.

4180. On January 19, 1977, it snowed in South Florida for the first time in recorded history. Jim Lushine, a retired meteorologist, thought that cocaine was falling from the sky after perhaps a bad drug drop had gone bad.

4181. Even though slavery was abolished in the United States in 1865, there was a family of slaves working in rural Louisiana until 1961.

4182. About half of Australia's koalas have chlamydia, which can also infect humans.

4183. Donald Trump describes himself as a philanthropist, however, he ranks as one of the least charitable billionaires in the entire world.

4184. If you want to be an actor in a zombie movie, you actually have to go to zombie school where you're marked on whether you're a convincing zombie or not.

4185. According to Oxfam, 70% of all clothes that are donated worldwide go to the African continent.

4186. Based on research conducted at the University of California, in Berkeley, girls who are exposed to chemicals in toothpaste, make up, soap, and other personal care products, may reach puberty earlier than boys, as the chemicals contained in these products speed up the process.

4187. When playing Monopoly with his kids, Pablo Escobar used to cheat, hiding extra money ahead of time near where he planned to sit.

4188. After a successful career as a heavyweight champion, George Foreman became the pastor of North Houston's "Church of the Lord Jesus Christ." The sixty eight year old reverend was inspired to join the church as he himself grew up in poverty and wanted to help others.

4189. Nagasaki was destroyed by a nuclear bomb, and just a few weeks later, members of the team that dropped the bomb toured the devastated city. They all kept their real identities secret for the trip, but they managed to talk to some Japanese locals.

4190. Queen Elizabeth conferred Bill Gates with an honorary knighthood, but because he's American, he cannot use the title Sir.

4191. Inspired by KFC fried chicken scented sunscreen, Edmonton's La Poutine Restaurant and Food Truck collaborated with the Wild Prairie Soap Company to create a poutine-flavored lip balm, which has been sold out almost everywhere since its release.

4192. When Bill Gates was worth over thirty billion dollars in 1997, he was still seen catching economy class in the air.

4193. Kyu-Shirataki is the name of a defunct train station located on the island of Hokkaido, Japan. The station operates just for one girl, so that she can attend school every day. The train only makes two trips: one when the high school student leaves for school and the other when she returns.

4194. When Wolfgang Amadeus Mozart was only seven years old, he proposed marriage to Marie Antoinette, who was also the same age.

4195. Billionaire David Tepper once paid $43.5 million for a beachfront mansion just to later demolish it. The previous owner of the mansion was actually Tepper's former boss, who denied him a promotion when both worked together.

4196. There are approximately 40,000 unclaimed bodies in morgues across the United States according to sixwise.com. Some of them have no family or the family members aren't able to afford the cost of burials or cremation.

4197. In Shanghai, if you don't send greetings or visit your elderly parents, your credit score can get lowered.

4198. There is a bank in Italy known as the Credem Bank that accepts cheese from local producers in exchange for cheap loans. The bank currently holds over four hundred thousand wheels of Parmesan cheese which is worth almost two hundred million euros.

4199. Up until the late 1960's, Disneyland used to ban long-haired male visitors to their park with the excuse that they didn't meet the unwritten dress code.

4200. In 2016, thirty two year old Joey Jaws Chestnut from California reclaimed his title by winning the Annual Nathan's Hot Dog Eating Contest, held at Coney Island. He had seventy hot dogs in just ten minutes, which is one hot dog every 8.6 seconds.

4201. Urea, the main ingredient in urine, actually has properties to unboil an eggwhite in just a matter of a few minutes.

4202. A small LED light bulb can actually be powered by the electricity that is made from the human brain.

4203. Back in the 1800's, the teeth from dead soldiers were removed and used to make dentures for the rich whose teeth were rotten.

4204. In many different instances, nuclear reactors in various countries have been powered down because of overheating. Strangely, jellyfish has been the cause of the problems in these cases. The creature clogs up water intakes in the reactor cooling systems, and it has to be taken out before the reactor can work properly again.

4205. "The Spirit of Ecstasy" is actually what the hood ornament on a Rolls Royce car is called.

4206. There is only one stop sign in all of Paris.

4207. Elon Musk didn't like the school that his kids were going to so he made his own called "Ad Astra" which means "to the stars."

4208.   Originally, the chainsaw was developed to assist with giving birth by cesarean section and not for cutting wood.

4209.   In 1991, a man named Steve Feltam gave up everything he had to look for the Loch Ness Monster full time. He quit his job, sold his house, left his girlfriend, bought a 1970 camper van, and has been living in it by Lake Loch Ness ever since. He also holds the current Guinness World Record for the longest time spent looking for the Loch Ness Monster.

4210.   In 1996, the commencement address to 245 graduates at Southampton College was delivered by Kermit the Frog.

4211.   A gun that could shoot darts causing heart attacks was once created by the CIA and revealed during a congressional testimony in 1975. The dart only left a tiny red dot upon penetration of the skin, but the poison itself worked rapidly and then denatured quickly afterwards.

4212.   Ralph Lauren, the iconic designer, was named Ralph Lifshitz until he was sixteen. He and his brother Jerry were made fun of in school, so they both changed their surname to Lauren.

4213.   Riding a roller coaster is one of the most effective ways to dislodge a kidney stone, according to a 2018 Michigan State University study. Of all roller coasters tested, it was found that Disneyland's Big Thunder Mountain was the most effective of all.

4214.   China has a law that makes it illegal not to visit your parents regularly if they are over sixty.

4215.   People with bumper stickers are more likely to have road rage and be involved in accidents according to research conducted at Colorado State University.

4216.   Actor Tommy Lee Jones and Vice President Al Gore were freshmen roommates while at Harvard.

4217.   There is a love motel for dogs in Sao Paulo, Brazil, with rooms decorated with satin sheets, romantic music, and heart-shaped ceiling mirrors. Renting a room for your dog for two hours costs about $50.

4218.   In England, there is a statute that prohibits anyone from entering the Houses of Parliament wearing a suit of armor. This has been enforced since King Edward II decreed the law in 1313. It stated that "Every man shall come without force and armor."

4219.   If Adidas finds any player having anything to do with Scientology, they will cancel any sponsorship deal they have.

4220.   In 2012, a chicken McNugget was sold on eBay by a woman named Rebecca Spiggot, from Dakota City. She sold it for eight thousand dollars, simply because it looked like George Washington.

4221.   A live alligator was once thrown into a Wendy's drive-thru window by a man in Jupiter, Florida, after the server handed over his drink. The man confessed to picking up the 3.5 feet (1.07 meter) long gator from the side of the road; he was charged with aggravated assault, unlawful possession, and transportation of an alligator.

4222.   In 2013, a man in Michigan whose house was set to be demolished, switched his house numbers with his neighbor. The company in charge of the operation ended up demolishing the wrong house.

4223.   Even though it is very unusual, it is possible to get heart cancer. At the Mayo Clinic, one case of heart cancer is treated every year.

4224. Between 2006 and 2012, fishing was the activity that accounted for the most lightning strikes and deaths, with a total of twenty six deaths.

4225. In Italy, it's forbidden to leave towels, chairs, or sun umbrellas overnight to save a spot on a busy beach. Officers will take what you left behind and fine you about $220 to get your property back.

4226. The average family household loses up to sixty socks every year.

4227. According to the Guinness World Records, on June 17, 1998, a man from the United Kingdom named John Evan set a world record in Los Angeles by balancing eighteen empty beer kegs on his head for ten seconds.

4228. A hundred cats were unleashed into an IKEA in England in 2010, just so they could see what would happen.

4229. US former President John Quincy Adams had an alligator as a pet. He used to keep it in the bathtub in the East Room of the White House.

4230. When senior crayon maker at Crayola Emerson Moser retired after working for thirty seven years at the company, he made an announcement that he was in fact colorblind.

4231. A man named Seth Putnam once wrote a song about how stupid being in a coma was. Shortly after he wrote it, he went into a coma. When he woke up afterwards and was asked how it felt, he responded: "Being in a coma was just as stupid as I wrote it was."

4232. Saudi Arabia's Grand Mufti, Abdul Aziz Al Sheikh, has banned chess in Islam, as it's believed to be a form of gambling and a waste of time and money. He also claimed that it causes hatred and enmity between the players.

4233. A Chinese man bought and raised two puppies, taking care of them despite their frequent killing and eating of chickens. He later realized that they were bears.

4234. A man named Roger Tullgren from Sweden was given benefits for his disability when his obsession with heavy metal music was officially declared as an addiction.

4235. In China, there are some restaurants that lace their foods with opiates to keep customers coming back.

4236. Bill Gates got married on the Hawaiian island of Lanai. To ensure his privacy, he rented every room at the hotel he was staying at (up to 250 rooms), and chartered every helicopter close-by.

4237. Close to $1 billion worth of gift cards are unused every year according to the advisory company CEB TowerGroup.

4238. In 1952, the presidency of Israel was actually offered to Albert Einstein, but he politely turned down the offer.

4239. There was an island called "Sandy Island" that was located between New Caledonia and Australia, according to maps, for over a hundred years. That was until a team of scientists went to look at it in 2012 only to find out it didn't exist.

4240. Men have a tendency of being more emotionally affected than women with regard to relationship issues, it's just that they are better at hiding it.

4241. If you earn just $32,000 per year, that puts you in the top 1% of income earners in the world.

4242. In the 19th century, Americans intentionally filled their parks with squirrels for entertainment purposes. Before that, squirrels were hardly found outside of forests.

4243. In some China subway stations, there are people who are employed to shove passengers into crowded trains so the doors can shut as quickly as possible avoiding delays.

4244. It's against the law to wrestle a bear in Alabama.

4245. Millionaire Steve Jobs used to pay only $500 a month in child support to his daughter Lisa.

4246. There have been seven divorce settlements involving more than one billion dollars. The most recent one was between Jeff Bezos, the Amazon founder, and his wife Mackenzie, which was thirty five billion dollars.

4247. In 2008, Steve Kreuscher, a fifty seven year old school bus driver and amateur artist from Chicago, changed his name to "In God We Trust." The reason why is because it symbolizes the help that God gave him during difficult times.

4248. President Abraham Lincoln suffered from heavy depression. He refused to carry a knife, as most men used to do, because he was afraid that he would harm himself. In the summer of 1835 and in the winter of 1840, he went through major depressing episodes.

4249. In order to avoid euthanization, about fifty cats and dogs are transported from Houston to Colorado every week.

4250. From 1986 to 1988, Clint Eastwood was the Mayor of Carmel, California. His salary was $200 a month.

4251. There is a dog named Body that makes almost two hundred thousand dollars a year by modeling clothes on Instagram.

4252. A man who was morbidly obese took part in an experimental fast in 1965. He was only given potassium tablets and multivitamins. He lost 273.4 pounds (124 kilograms) as a result.

4253. Samsung, the huge manufacturer of TVs, cell phones, and home appliances, began as a grocery store.

4254. Gypsum or white mineral spar used to be extracted from the bed of Niagara River and some traders sold it to tourists who were led to believe that they were bits of petrified mist that came from the Niagara Falls.

4255. Soviet geologists discovered a family in the middle of Serbia in 1978 that hadn't seen another human in over forty two years.

4256. In order to accommodate racial segregation laws, the Pentagon was built with extra bathrooms.

4257. It's harder to get into the new Apple store in New York than it is to get into Harvard. Only 7% of applicants get accepted into Harvard while Apple's acceptance rate is only 2%.

4258. One hookah session delivers about twenty five times the tar, two and a half times the nicotine, and ten times the carbon monoxide if compared to one cigarette.

4259. Treating a heroin addiction in the United States has a five year cost of $318,500, while an oxycodone addiction is $132,405.

4260. Bradley Corporation, an international manufacturer of commercial hand washing products, conducted a Healthy Hand Washing Survey that revealed that only 66% of Americans wash their hands after using a public washroom, while almost 70% of them admitted to skip the soap.

4261. Three months after Charlie Chaplin died, his corpse was stolen by two auto mechanics who intended to extort money from his family. The thieves were later caught and Chaplin's body was found eleven weeks later. To avoid similar attempts later on, his body was reburied under concrete.

4262. Rosa Abbott was the only female passenger that went down with the Titanic who survived. She was a third class passenger.

4263. Boiling water in a paper cup is actually possible, by holding it over a stove at a proper distance from the flame.

4264. When the secretary of Steve Jobs was once late to work, Steve handed her the keys to his Jaguar and said "don't be late again."

4265. There is a perfume that is Play-Doh-scented.

4266. Due to an unintended acceleration in Toyota vehicles, once the company had to recall over nine million of their cars and had to pay more than $3 billion in fines and settlements.

4267. Back in 1903, a man named John Thurman started a horse-drawn vacuum system offering a door-to-door service. It cost $4 per home.

4268. In 2017, a rule against putting the number 69 on drivers' license plates was issued by the California Department of Motor Vehicles, except if the year model of the vehicle is 1969.

4269. Theoretically, it's possible to get addicted to cuddling. Couples that tend to cuddle a lot can experience oxytocin withdrawal when they are not together.

4270. Up to five million people worldwide are bitten by snakes every year according to the World Health Organization. The majority of these events occur in Africa and Southeast Asia.

4271. Armand Hammer, a businessman, coincidentally served as a director for the company Arm and Hammer.

4272. It is illegal to commit suicide in Japan by jumping in front of a train or killing yourself in your apartment building. The building or train company can sue the family for clean-up fees, income loss, and any negative publicity that might be brought upon by the suicide.

4273. In 1936, the founder of Adidas drove to the Olympics, persuaded and convinced US sprinter Jesse Owens to wear his shoes. Later, Owens successfully won four medals and letters came in from other national teams interested in buying their shoes. By World War II, they were selling 200,000 pairs a year.

4274. Originally Play-Doh was manufactured as a product to clean coal residue from wallpaper.

4275. Blowing smoke in someone's face can be considered a case of assault and battery in the US.

4276. Alex Stone, an American high school student from South Carolina, was arrested and suspended from school due to a creative writing assignment where he mentioned buying a gun to shoot his neighbor's pet dinosaur.

4277. In 1948, the Chicago Daily Tribune mistakenly announced that Thomas Dewey had won the US presidential election race when it was actually Harry S. Truman who won.

4278. The domain name VacationRentals.com was bought for a whopping $35 million.

4279. Cat owners have been known to compare their cat's head to the smell of sunshine or freshly baked bread. After spending four months sniffing cats, a company in Japan actually made a spray that makes everything smell like a cat's head.

4280.   Igor Vorozhbitsyn, a forty two year old Russian fisherman, was violently being attacked by a bear when suddenly Justin Bieber's Baby ringtone went off from his phone, scaring the bear away into the woods. The ringtone had been installed by his granddaughter on his phone and it literally saved his life.

4281.   Giovanni Giacomo Cassanova, or better known as just Cassanova, was actually preparing to become a priest when he discovered his vocation as a lover and libertine.

4282.   Winston Churchill drinking habits were a bit questionable. He used to have three to four weak whiskey sodas, a bottle of wine or champagne with lunch, and another with dinner, and finished off with either cognac or brandy.

4283.   Students in North Korea have textbooks that claim their leader Kim Jong-Un learned to drive when he was only three years old.

4284.   The creator of Doritos, Arch West, was buried with his creation sprinkled over his body.

4285.   In 2004, in Chicago, a bus that was transporting the Dave Matthews Band dumped 797 pounds (362 kilograms) of waste off a bridge into a river, splashing onto a boat full of tourists. The driver was sentenced to eighteen months of probation, 150 hours of community service, and $10,000 in fines.

4286.   The St. Malo castle walls in France are notorious for being a safe haven for pirates.

4287.   Donald Trump once attempted to have the phrase "You're Fired" trademarked, but he was denied.

4288.   The International Potato Center, or CIP, located in Lima, Peru, proved once that it was possible to grow potatoes on Mars, by simulating a Martian environment on Earth.

4289.   James Fallon, a renowned neuroscientist, studied the brains of psychopathic killers. During his studies, he scanned his own brain as a control, finding that he himself was a psychopath.

4290.   John Antioco, the CEO of Blockbuster, in the 1990's laughed in Reed Hastings' face when he offered to form a partnership with him. That company was Netflix.

4291.   The company "12 South" released a candle that smells like an Apple Macbook that has just been removed from the box. The company actually specializes in selling Mac accessories. The candle is made up of soy wax that is scented with mint, peach, sage, lavender, basil, and mandarin; it costs $24.

4292.   A study showed that HIV testing kits saw a 95% increase in sales after actor Charlie Sheen revealed that he was HIV positive. The study was called "the Charlie Sheen Effect."

4293.   According to a study conducted in Fullerton by Iris Blandon-Gitlin, from California State University, a lie will be more convincing if peeing while telling it. There is a phenomenon called the inhibitory spillover effect where focusing on controlling your bladder also allows you to focus on hiding any signs you might have when lying.

4294.   The entire village of Sodeto in Spain won the lottery in 2012, except for one man who was never asked if he wanted to buy a ticket because the people selling forgot to ask him.

4295.   Due to an infection, Pope Francis had one of his lungs removed when he was a teenager.

4296.   FIAT workers in Sodertalje, Sweden, found out that the Google Street View car was going to be in town, so they sent a FIAT to drive next to the car when it was going around the Volkswagen headquarters for forty five minutes.

4297.   The DNA of the chicken that's served at Subway was once tested by researchers at Trent University in Ontario, Canada. The tested sample was only about 50% chicken, and the rest was soy filler.

4298.   UPS drivers must follow a specific route that includes never turning left. Even though it can sometimes take longer to get to their destination, it reduces the chance of an accident and actually saves fuel.

4299.   Sitting on a sea turtle is considered a third degree felony in the United States.

4300.   Before being elected as president, Barack Obama had won two Grammy Awards. Both were for best spoken word album: one for an audio recording of his 1995 Memoir "Dreams from My Father," and the second was for "The Audacity of Hope."

4301. In Germany, there are elevators with no doors; they are called paternoster elevators. They go floor to floor on a loop and you can just hop out when you get to your floor.

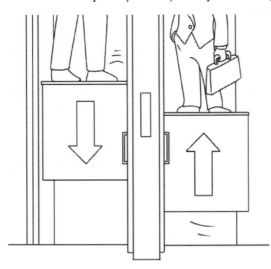

4302. The first selfie photograph was taken in 1839.

4303. Hydrogen peroxide is not recommended for cuts and wounds, as it slows healing by killing healthy skin cells as well as bad ones.

4304. In America, citizens can mail a request to the FBI asking for the file that the bureau has on them.

4305. As a result of mismanagement, the social news site Digg was sold for $500,000. The company was once valued at $200 million.

4306. There is a village in France known as "Sarpourenx," where it's illegal to die because of space restrictions.

4307. Before it was popular to watch Netflix and to pause live television, EastEnders, a British television show, would cause major spikes in the country's power grid, forcing backup power stations to come on. This happened because when it was time for a commercial break, millions of viewers would put on tea kettles at the same time, and that would draw all the electricity at once.

4308. It's possible to buy toothpaste infused with caffeine that gives you a boost with your morning brush. It's found on the market as "Power Energy Toothpaste" and, unlike coffee, it takes effect almost immediately, making you more alert before you are even finished brushing.

4309. In 1967, Florida issued a law allowing Disney World to build a nuclear power plant. Although they had never built one and have no intention to do it, the law still stands.

4310. In 1946, The United States attempted to buy Greenland for one hundred million dollars.

4311. There is a gold plated Sony Walkman that costs around $3,680. It was created as the Japanese electronics giant focuses on higher end products in its audio division.

4312. Famous designer Hugo Boss used to make Nazi uniforms. In fact, he was part of the Nazi party.

4313. Chewing gum causes you to produce more saliva, which increases swallowing, which increases the amount of air that you swallow, which makes you fart more.

4314. Steve Jobs used to often eat at his biological father's Mediterranean restaurant in San Jose, California, without ever knowing that the owner was his father. They even met a few times.

4315. Renegade was President Obama's Secret Service code name.

4316. There was a violinist in the early 1800's named Niccolo Paganini that was so good that people thought he sold his soul to the devil for his talent. He was forced to publicly show his mother's letters to prove that he was human.

4317. In 2008, a geocache was placed on the International Space Station. Since then, it has been visited four times by other astronauts.

4318. Music used to be released on a Tuesday due to shipping before the pre-digital era. After July 10, 2015, new music is now mostly released on Fridays.

4319. In 1939, a rally of 20,000 Nazi supporters was held at Madison Square Garden, in New York City, by the German American Bund.

4320. In Sydney, Australia, there is a hangover clinic. An hour treatment can cost $200 and it includes a half gallon of hydration drip, oxygen therapy, and vitamins to help you recover from a night of excessive alcohol.

4321. In 1980, Saddam Hussein was given Detroit's key to the city.

4322. To count to the number one trillion, it would take you approximately 31,709 years.

4323. Thousands of plastic, yellow ducks fell out of a cargo ship in the Pacific Ocean in 1992, many of which have been turning up in random locations around the world for the past twenty eight years.

4324. According to the International Society for Photogrammetry and Remote Sensing, the largest irrigated crop in the United States is lawn grass. Every year lawns are given so much water that it's almost enough to fill the Chesapeake Bay.

4325. Getting red eyes from swimming is not actually caused by the contact with too much chlorine. According to health experts, it's the result of being exposed to bodily fluids in the water, like urine, feces, and sweat.

4326. In a 2014 study conducted by JAMA Dermatology, it was found that tanning caused more cases of skin cancer than the number of instances of lung cancer that were caused by smoking.

4327. It's possible to be prosecuted criminally for making death threats written in emojis.

4328. Researcher James Gilpin has developed a new way to make whiskey by taking the sugar from the urine of elderly people with diabetes. He then bottles the whiskey with the name and age of the person who donated the urine.

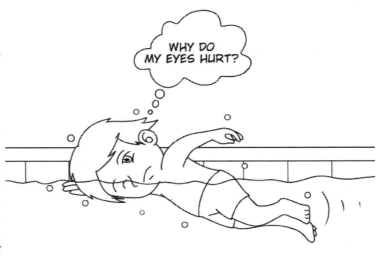

4329. If you were to double a penny every day, after thirty days you'd have five million dollars.

4330. Taiwanese comedian named Wu Zhaonan, who is recognized by Taiwan as a national treasure, created the popular Mongolian barbecue dish. He invented it when he was running a food stall in Taipei before he was famous. He was also a recipient of the lifetime achievement award from the Lincoln Center.

4331. There is a 137+ year-old secret and exclusive camp known as the Bohemian Grove that is only open to the rich and powerful men of the world. Richard Nixon was once a member, but referred to it as: "the most faggy goddamn thing you'll ever imagine."

4332. The world's best-selling musical instrument is the harmonica.

4333. Dentistry is one of the oldest professions in the world. Humans have been performing it since 7000 BC.

4334. J. Fred Muggs was a chimpanzee that co-host NBC's Today Show from 1953 to 1957. According to estimations, he brought in the network around $100 million.

4335. Humans are not able to walk in a straight line without a visual point. In fact, we will gradually walk in a circle when blindfolded.

4336. The first planet to be found through mathematical predictions instead of telescopic location was Neptune.

Royalty

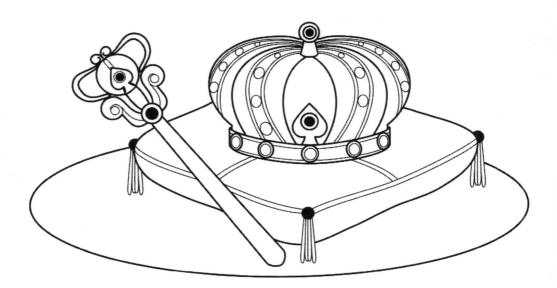

4337. The longest serving British monarch in history is Queen Elizabeth II. She is also the longest serving living monarch.

4338. Queen Alfreda, the wife of King Edgar the Peaceable, was the first woman of England to be crowned as a queen with a coronation ceremony in the 10th century.

4339. King Edmund Ironside had only served as King of England for seven months, when on November 30, 1016, he was assassinated while on another throne. It's alleged that he was on the privy, and an assassin who was hiding beneath it, stabbed him a number of times from below.

4340. In 1140, when King Conrad III of Germany invaded a castle, the women of the castle were granted free departure and were also allowed to take what they could carry on their backs. After thinking quickly, the women took the men on their backs and walked out. The king kept his word, allowing the men to leave that way.

4341. When he watched the gladiator fights, then Roman Emperor Nero used to wear sunglasses made of emerald.

4342. Members of the British royal family had no surname before 1917, but only the name of the house or dynasty to which they belonged. In fact, kings and princes were known by the names of their countries that their families ruled.

4343. The day after the terrorist attacks of 9/11, the British Queen broke tradition during the changing of the guard by having the guards play the Star-Spangled Banner. It was a way to show the UK's sympathy for the tragedy the US had to go through and for all those who lost their lives.

4344. Queen Elizabeth and her husband, Prince Phillip, are actually relatives (they are third cousins).

4345. Queen Elizabeth is considered the first head of state to have used electronic mail. She sent her first email on March 26, 1976; the message was transmitted over ARPANET, the forerunner for the modern Internet.

4346. Over the reign of Queen Elizabeth II, she has owned more than thirty Corgis.

4347. The only country that doesn't feature its name on its stamps is the United Kingdom. However, all

UK stamps do have a picture of the monarch's head.

4348.   The color purple was known as a royal color in history due to the fact that they relied on dyes back then and it was so hard to obtain that only the royals could afford it. It was only found from the sea and took twelve thousand snails to produce only one and a half grams of purple dye.

4349.   In England, all swans are legal property of the Queen.

4350.   "The Licktators," a London based ice cream company, teamed up with breast-feeding campaigner Victoria Hilly to celebrate the birth of royal baby number two by relaunching their breast milk flavored ice cream. Called the Royal Baby Gaga, the ice cream is made of donated breast milk that has been screened with hospital standards, and Madagascan vanilla.

4351.   The water used to baptize all royal babies is brought from the river Jordan, as it is where it is said that Jesus was baptized by John the Baptist.

4352.   The youngest king in British history to ascend to the British throne was Henry VI, the only child of King Henry V. He was only eight months and twenty five days old by then.

4353.   In the 1500's, King Francis the first of France bought the Mona Lisa from Renaissance artist Leonardo de Vinci.

4354.   The King of Yugoslavia, Alexander the first, refused to go to any events on a Tuesday since three of his family members had died on this day of the week. When he was finally convinced that nothing would happen, he made an appearance on a Tuesday in October of 1934, and was assassinated.

4355.   In 1252, the King of Norway gave a polar bear to King Henry III. It was kept in the Tower of London chained up with a collar around its neck. Despite this, the animal was allowed to swim and hunt for fish in the River Thames.

4356.   12th-century King Henry II of England had a personal entertainer named Roland the Farter. Every Christmas, he would perform a dance for the king that always ended with a jump, a fart, and a whistle at the same time. Thanks to these annual performances, he was given a manor house and over 100 acres of land.

4357.   It came out in 2017 that Willem-Alexander, the Dutch King, had been moonlighting as a pilot for the past twenty one years, and that he secretly co-piloted passenger flights two times every month. After his coronation as king in 2013, he chose to keep co-piloting passenger flights because he really enjoyed flying.

4358.   For thirty years, Ella Slack has been the body double for Queen Elizabeth. She actually takes the place of the queen during practices for large events.

4359.   To protect the royal lineage in the event of a plane crash, two heirs to the throne aren't supposed to travel together on the same plane. This tradition was broken by Prince William, who took his son Prince George to Australia on the same flight when the little prince was nine months old.

Science

4360. Scientists examined 125 million year old dinosaur remains, and found that they had dandruff. Nature Communications published a study explaining that just like birds do today, dinosaurs used to shed their skin in tiny flakes.

4361. A ten year old fifth grader from Kansas City, Missouri, named Clara Lazen, was the first to theorize the existence of a hypothetical molecule called tetranitratoxycarbon, in 2012. She was studying a molecular model in science class, and she discovered a configuration that had never been documented before. She, along with her science teacher, were credited as co-authors of a published scientific paper.

4362. In the 1930's, a baby chimp was adopted by two psychologists who tried to raise her as their own child, together with their infant son. They wanted to see if the chimp would learn human behavior. They stopped the experiment nine months later because their son began behaving more like the chimp.

4363. The world's smallest periodic table according to the Guinness World Records was written by scientists at the University of Nottingham. By using a beam of accelerated gallium ions and imaging, they engraved the periodic table onto a strand of hair that belonged to green chemist-professor Martyn Poliakoff.

4364. In Russia, scientists at the Institute of Cytology and Genetics had a local artist named Andrew Kharkevich make a sculpture to honor lab mice, as a way to create a tribute to all mice used in studies. The artist sculpted a monument featuring a bespectacled mouse knitting a strand of DNA.

4365. Scientist Marie Curie, who discovered radium in 1898, was the first woman to receive a PhD from a French university. She was also the first woman ever to be hired as a professor at the University of Paris. In addition, she became the first woman to win a Nobel Prize and also the first person ever to win the award twice for two separate scientific fields.

4366. Several studies were conducted by James Reyniers, an American scientist, in which he created clean-rooms and put in different animals to see if they would survive without bacteria. He discovered that it was a technical possibility for animals to survive without it, but many of them would die because they needed certain bacteria in their digestive systems to help break food down and extract some nutrients.

4367. Chinese scientists collected stem cells from human urine, and in July, 2013, they successfully used them to grow teeth.

4368. Scientists from Tufts University have created worms with the heads and brains of other species of worms. They achieved this by manipulating proteins that control conversations between cells, instead of altering the worm's DNA.

4369. Carbon black is a chemical used to make car tires, which gives them the black color. It's added to protect tires against ozone and UV damage. It significantly prolongs the life of any tire, and for this reason all tire manufacturers use it.

4370. There is a protein found in the vampire bat's saliva that acts as an anticoagulant; it helps to keep their victim's blood flowing while they feed. Researchers have actually been studying the protein to see if it can help dissolve blood clots and help with stroke victims.

4371. Tear gas isn't actually gas, but a solid or liquid that gets turned into an aerosol. Today, the most commonly used tear gas is made of chilli pepper oil.

4372. "Penguin One" is a chemical compound that received its name because of the fact that its molecular structure looks like a penguin.

4373. German scientist Dan Frost has literally made a diamond out of peanut butter. While trying to create crystalline structures like those in Earth's lower mantle, he actually discovered how to form diamonds out of substances high in carbon.

4374. In order to reduce cases of dengue fever and other diseases, Scientists from Florida State in the US are planning to release genetically modified mosquitoes into the wild. The males still mate with females, but the hatchlings die before adulthood due to the presence of new genes.

4375. In 2014, a study done by the Stanford School of Medicine showed that the blood of young mice has the ability to restore the mental capacities in old mice. When given infusions of blood plasmas from young mice to old mice, old mice actually outperformed on spatial memory tests, compared to those old mice that were given plasma from other old mice.

4376. The "Super STEM 3" is a super powered electron microscope that can examine objects a million times smaller than a human hair.

4377. Atoms at room temperature never actually touch each other in the regular sense of the word. It means that you aren't touching that seat you are on, or the floor you are standing on, you are merely floating just a little bit over those surfaces.

4378. In 2014, "Condiment Junkie," a UK-based sensory branding company, performed an experiment where they played recordings of cold and hot water being poured into glasses, and people were asked to identify if the water was cold or hot. Amazingly, 96% of participants could identify hot and cold water from the sounds. It's because hot and cold water have differences in viscosity, which affect how the water pours, and by extension how it sounds.

4379. Botulinum is the most lethal of all toxins known to man, but it's also the active ingredient in Botox injections and, additionally, it's used for muscle spasm treatment.

4380. Simcardia is an artificial heart device that allows people to live provisionally without a heart. The device is frequently used by those who are waiting for a heart donor.

4381. Scientists are developing flexible electronic skin for prosthetic limbs that can help replicate the sensory capabilities of real skin, including feeling temperature changes.

4382. Water doesn't conduct electricity very well. In fact, it's really an insulator. Water only conducts electricity because of the impurities in it, and not the water molecules themselves.

4383. Several researchers have come to the conclusion that Maurice Hilleman, an American doctor, saved more lives in the twentieth century than any other scientist. The reason is because he's created about nine of the fourteen vaccines that are usually given to children, including the chicken pox, measles, and mumps vaccines.

4384.   Infertile mice were able to give birth after they were implanted with ovaries that were artificially created with three-dimensional printers, on May 17, 2017. Ultimately, the hope is that the ovarian bioprosthesis procedure could work on humans.

4385.   The speed of light in a vacuum can travel 186,282 miles (299,727 kilometers) per second.

4386.   Dr. Wuzong Zhou, of Saint Andrews University, discovered that every second that a candle flame burns, approximately 1.5 million diamond nanoparticles are created, which unfortunately are burned away during the process. His findings, however, could lead to research into how diamonds could be created in a less expensive way.

4387.   In Japan, a team of biologists at the Osaka University discovered a new way to grow parts of the human eye (retina, cornea, lens, etc.) simply by using a small sample of adult skin.

4388.   A whole genus of ferns was named after Lady Gaga. A DNA sequence spells out Gaga and the ferns have Gaga-like qualities. Some of them resemble her extravagant stage costumes and one of them is even called the Gaga monstraparva.

4389.   On August 3, 2016, a neuron out of germanium antimony telluride was created by IBM scientists in Zurich, Switzerland, which replicates a biological neuron. This could actually be the first step for developing an artificial brain.

4390.   300 dairy cows were genetically engineered by Chinese scientists to produce milk that contains nutrients found in human breast milk. This could actually represent a viable alternative to regular infant formula in the future.

4391.   The weight of all the electrons in motion that make up the Internet at any given time is equal to fifty grams according to BSOS. In other words, the Internet is estimated to weigh about the same as a medium sized egg or a strawberry.

4392.   Scientists have trained some African giant pouched rats to detect tuberculosis using their sense of smell, and they've been found to be more accurate than most lab tests.

4393.   A yoctosecond is one-trillionth of a trillionth of a second. It is comparable to the time that it takes light to cross an atomic nucleus.

4394.   Twenty years ago, scientists found the bones of a Scandinavian woman that date back 5,000 years ago. When her bones and teeth were deeply examined, an ancient strain of bacteria that caused the plague was found. Scientists believe that an early form of the plague developed in Europe between 6,100 and 5,400 years ago.

4395.   Besides Neanderthals, humans interbred with another ancient species called Denisovans. Scientists once found a 90,000-year-old skeleton of a girl who was a hybrid between the two species.

4396.   Jukusui-Kun, meaning deep sleep, is a kind of stop snoring pillow bot developed by Akiyoshi Kabe of Waseda University, in Japan. The polar bear shaped pillow can gauge snoring levels and will touch the snorer to get them to roll their heads to help them stop snoring. It monitors snoring with a built-in mic and a device worn around the wrist that measures blood oxygen levels, which happen to drop when the person starts snoring.

4397.   A method to use the vascular network in spinach leaves to deliver blood, oxygen, and nutrients to grow human tissue is being developed by researchers at the Worcester Polytechnic Institute. In the future, they hope to be able to use this to filter blood better to damaged tissue in the human heart.

4398.   On January 27, 1888, the National Geographic Society was founded with thirty-three members that included geographers, explorers, teachers, lawyers, cartographers, military officers, and financiers. All supporters had an interest in scientific and geographical knowledge and wanted to share it with everyone.

4399.   Homeopathy treatments in America must be labeled as "not effective" unless they are scientifically proven to work.

4400. Two neuroscientists were successful in implanting a fake memory in a mouse's brain in 2012. The mouse was aghast as it remembered something that never really happened to it.

4401. According to a study led by researchers from The University of Queensland and Monash University, the protein found in funnel-web spider venom may protect the human brain from damage after suffering a stroke. The venom was recreated in a lab and it was found that the protein blocked acid-sensing ion channels in the brain, which is one of the key things that cause brain damage after a stroke.

4402. Scientists from Georgia State University have found that monkeys are susceptible to optical illusions, just like humans. To test this, capuchin and rhesus monkeys looked at a visual illusion where two dots were surrounded by rings, but were actually the same size, and they were tricked much like many people were.

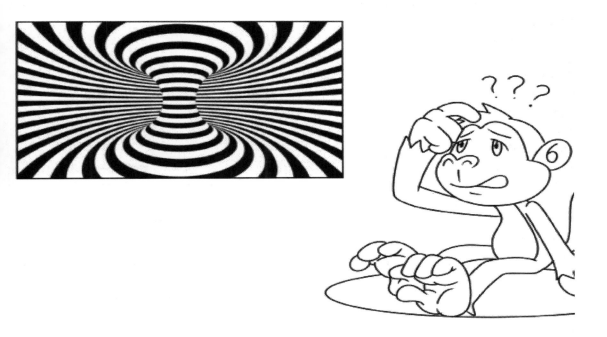

Shocking

4403. Kristoffer Koch, a Norwegian student once spent twenty seven dollars on Bitcoin and forgot about them. Years later he remembered, and found out they were worth $886,000.

4404. In 1998, about 700,000 video cameras that were sold by Sony had the ability to see through clothes. When the infrared lens was used in daylight, it was actually possible to see details like tattoos, underwear, and body parts through certain types of clothing.

4405. Xenophyophores are one of the largest living single-celled organisms of the world. Some of them live in the deepest part of Marianas Trench, 6.2 miles (ten kilometers) deep.

4406. Truth in Advertising, also known as TINA, is an advertising watchdog group who allegedly found that over a hundred Walmart products were labeled made in the USA, when in fact, they were made elsewhere.

4407. The biggest tapeworm to ever be removed from a person during an operation was a whopping 108 feet (thirty three meters) long.

4408. The tongue-eating louse is an actual parasite that swims its way through a fish's gills, then starts eating its tongue. After eating the tongue, it latches onto the stub that remains, and literally becomes the fish's new tongue. The parasite doesn't attack humans, but if you pick it up, it will bite you.

4409. A Burundi woman named Noela Rukundo escaped death after the hit-man sent to kill her family let her go because he didn't believe in killing women. Five years later, her husband was shocked when she showed up at her own funeral.

4410. Pablo Escobar made so much money from his drug empire that, at one point, he wrote off 10% of the money because rats ate it in storage.

4411. The majority of dinosaurs depicted in Jurassic Park, the successful 1993 Steven Spielberg film, aren't actually from the Jurassic period, but are from the Cretaceous period, so the title is misleading. Velociraptors are shown as slippery-skinned lizards in the movie, but quill knobs found on some fossils indicate that they had feathers.

4412. Mathematicians estimate that each glass of water you drink contains at least a single molecule of water that was drunk by Cleopatra. What's more, for every sip you take, there's one molecule that was drunk by a dinosaur.

4413. A carbon dioxide eruption occurred in Lake Nyos, Cameroon, in 1986. The gas shot up 328 feet (a hundred meters) in the air, and created a cloud, which later settled close to the ground, killing more than 1,000 people, along with 3,000 cattle.

4414. On December 26, 2004, Tilly Smith, an eleven year old girl from Oxshott, Surrey, saved a hundred tourists' lives from the tsunami that hit Thailand. She spotted key signs of an oncoming tsunami, which she had learned in geography class a couple of weeks earlier.

4415. The number of tigers in captivity in the US is higher than the number of tigers living out in the wild.

4416. It takes longer to train as an Itamae or sushi chef in Japan than it does to train as a doctor. Some people work for up to twenty years before they receive such a noble position.

4417. On May 17, 2016, the Richmond Times published the obituary of a woman named Mary Anne Noland. There she stated that faced with the prospect of voting for either Donald Trump or Hillary Clinton, she literally chose to die.

4418. One of the deadliest spider bites in the world is from the Australian funnel web spider. A bite to a person's torso could actually kill them in around fifteen minutes.

4419. In England and the United States, in the late 18th and early 19th century, parents of crying and colicky children would give them something called Godfrey's Cordial, also known as "mother's friend." It was a combination of opium, treacle, water, and spices that helped quiet them down.

4420. In 2009, Bill Gates gave a speech about malaria education and eradication. He actually released mosquitoes into the audience to make them be more aware about the illness. Malaria is transmitted from person to person via mosquito bites.

4421. Dermatologists agree that people should only be taking showers every two or three days with lukewarm water, as daily showers can cause dry skin and irritation.

4422. In 1986, pilot Alexander Kliuyev from the former Soviet Union made a bet with his copilot while flying the plane that he could land an airplane blind. He then curtained the cockpit windows and crashed the plane into the landing strip, killing seventy out of eighty seven passengers.

4423. In the United States, approximately 2.7 million animals are euthanized every year.

4424. The country with the highest murder rate in the world is Honduras. The city of East St. Louis, in Illinois, however, has a higher murder rate than Honduras.

4425. In 1986, 1.5 million balloons were released in Cleveland by the United Way as a publicity stunt. The event, however, clogged the land and waterways in northeast Ohio, causing major airport runways to shut down, and forcing the Coast Guard to suspend search and rescue for two men who ended up drowning.

4426. On average, two out of every five girls in Tanzania get married before they turn eighteen. That is close to fifteen million girls a year.

4427. More than sixty lives have been claimed by the Indianapolis 500 race, one of them being an innocent bystander.

4428. About 30% of the world's waste is produced by the United States alone. In fact, nearly 46% of the lakes in America are very polluted and hence risky for swimming, fishing, and aquatic life. In addition, it is estimated that 25% of the world's natural resources are used by the nation.

4429. A report by the Smithsonian shows that sharks were swimming in oceans long before trees sprouted from the ground. The Archaeopteris is the oldest known tree and it's about 350 million years old, but sharks have existed for more than 400 million years.

4430. Statistically, you are more likely to drown in freshwater than seawater. 90% of all drownings happen in freshwater, mostly in swimming pools, rivers, and bathtubs.

4431. Muhammad Ali, the world champion boxer, went to Iraq in November, 1990, to meet the dictator Saddam Hussein. Somehow, he managed to negotiate for the freedom of fifteen American prisoners, and he flew back home with them. He did this despite the disapproval of then President George W. Bush.

4432. It may sound disgusting, but when you were in the womb, you swam around in your own urine, and you drank it regularly.

4433. In 2006, an extremely old clam was found by a group of researchers in Iceland. In order to find out its age, researchers didn't count the rings on the outside of the clam, but instead they opened it and counted the rings on the inside, causing the clam to die. The clam turned out to be 507 years old, the world's oldest animal.

4434. 725,000 people are killed by mosquitoes every year.

4435. A report from 2006 indicated that in the US alone, 7,000 people had died because of doctors' sloppy handwriting, and 1.5 million people had been injured because of the same reason.

4436. Psychopaths make up about 1% of the population, and apparently, they are good in business. A study done in Australia showed that out of five CEOs, one or more of them is a psychopath. This number rivals the percentage of psychopaths who are in prison.

4437. Some people in Hammersmith, London, reported seeing a ghost in the area near the end of 1803. On January 3, 1804, Thomas Millwood, a bricklayer, was strolling through the area while wearing his all white work attire, when he encountered an armed patrol. One member thought he was the ghost, so he shot him in the head and killed him instantly.

4438. In Zimbabwe's Nkayi District, on January 28, 1962, Johannes Reliker was working at Kamativi, a tin mine in the area, when he was attacked by a massive swarm of bees. He was stung more than 2,443 times. After his ordeal, the stingers were removed and counted, and he set the world record for being the person who survived after the highest number of bee stings.

4439. David Merrill, a high school student at the time, performed an experiment where he made rats listen to heavy metal rock for twenty four hours a day, so he could test its negative effects on their ability to get around a maze. He was sort of correct in his hypothesis because, instead of the rats becoming smarter, they killed each other.

4440. United Airlines has a worse track record than any other airline when it comes to pet deaths during flights, according to the Air Travel Consumer Report.

4441. Across the world, cheating on final exams is frowned upon. However, in Bangladesh, students who are older than fifteen can actually go to jail if they are caught cheating.

4442. Three guys from Sweden made an attempt in 1897 to be the first people to go to the North Pole by riding there in a hot air balloon, but sixty five hours after taking off, the balloon crashed. Their bodies were found by a ship thirty three years later in a camp, and it appeared that they had survived for several weeks by hunting polar bears.

4443. Thousands of people were infected with HIV by the drug manufacturer Bayer, after the company sold them blood-clotting medicine that was contaminated.

4444.   Punt guns is a type of gun that was first used in the 1800's, usually in commercial waterfowl hunting. The guns could fire almost one pound shots that could kill fifty to a hundred birds in a single shot. The barrels had an opening upwards of two inches (five centimeters) in diameter, weighed over ninety nine pounds (fifty kilograms), and measured almost ten feet (three meters) long.

4445.   Oxana Malaya from the Ukraine lived with dogs for five years, surviving on raw meat and scraps, after being abandoned by her alcoholic parents. At some point, she began to walk on all fours, pant with her tongue hanging out, whined and even barked. She was actually raised by a pack of dogs on a run-down farm in the village of Novaya until she was finally discovered in 1991. She had almost forgotten how to speak.

4446.   ISIS' fortune is bigger than several countries. The group makes about $1 million to $5 million a day.

4447.   Bagel head was a body modification trend in China. By injecting saline solution into the skin, people created a bagel-shaped knot on their foreheads, causing it to swell. After it reached maximum puffiness, the injector used his thumb to create an indentation in the head, making it look like a bagel that lasted up to twenty-four hours.

4448.   The venom of the Bruno's casque-headed frog is so strong that a single gram is enough to kill eighty people.

4449.   According to the National Retail Federation, cigarettes, energy drinks, high-end liquor, and infant formula are the four most common grocery items shoplifted by people.

4450.   A discarded fishing line takes about 600 years to degrade in the ocean.

4451.   The very first attempt to assassinate a president of the United States was made at Andrew Jackson. Richard Lawrence, an unemployed house painter, tried to shoot him but his gun misfired.

4452.   Killer bees, also known as Africanized bees, are hybrid breeds that escaped from quarantine and spread throughout the Americas.

4453.   From 2014 to 2016, the UN Food and Agriculture Organization estimated that almost 800 million people in the world suffered from undernourishment, with most of the people living in developed countries.

4454.   On January 15, 1919, a storage tank burst on Boston's waterfront, releasing almost two million gallons of molasses. The fifteen foot (4.5 meter) high, 160 foot (forty eight meter) wide wave ran through the city's north end at thirty five miles (fifty six kilometers) per hour, killing a ten year old boy and injuring many people. It was so powerful that it even swept a train off its tracks and toppled electrical poles.

4455.   The world's largest snake ever captured was a reticulated python found at a Malaysian construction site. It measured twenty-six-feet (eight meters) long and weighed approximately 550 pounds (250 kilograms). It ended up dying just three days later after its discovery while laying an egg.

4456.   In just three strides, a cheetah can reach thirty nine miles (sixty-four kilometers) per hour. In just three seconds, it can reach sixty miles (ninety-seven kilometers) per hour.

4457.   If Henry Ford were still alive, his estimated net worth would have been around $200 billion today.

4458.   A blue whale's heart is so big that it can reach the size of a small car and can weigh almost one ton.

4459.   Up to 150 gallons (560 liters) of milk a day can be consumed by baby blue whales from their mothers.

4460. In the United States, there are more jails and prisons (approximately 5,000 more) than degree-granting colleges and universities. In fact, there are more people living in prisons than on college campuses in the south part of the country.

4461. President Taft recommended in 1910 that everyone should receive three months of vacation per year.

4462. There are some large insects unique to New Zealand known as the giant wetapunga. When they are fully grown, they can weigh more than a mouse.

4463. Nestle used to use slave labor in the production of its Fancy Feast cat food brand in Thailand and admitted it in November of 2015.

4464. Charles Osborne got a severe case of hiccups that started in 1922 and ended in 1990. He was hiccuping forty times a minute for sixty eight years. The oddest thing is that when the hiccup stopped, it stopped for unknown reasons.

4465. Bruce Lee, the legendary martial artist, was also a champion ballroom dancer. In 1958, he entered the Hong Kong Cha-Cha Dance Contest and won. He used to trade dance lessons for martial arts lessons.

4466. On average, Americans work 137 more hours per year than Japanese workers, 260 more hours a year than British workers, and 499 hours more a year than French workers.

4467. Family members of officials in China are taken on tours to prisons to show them what awaits if they choose to engage in corruption.

4468. The longest burp ever recorded according to the Guinness World Records was one minute, 13 seconds, and 57 milliseconds. It was achieved by Italian woman Michele Forgione, on June 16, 2009, at the 13th annual Rock Beer Festival.

4469. Approximately 10% of boneless and skinless breast meat has what is called "woody breast." It is when the meat is laced with hard or woody fibers, which makes it tough and chewy. The reason that causes it is still unknown.

4470. In 1942, a frozen lake full of skeletons was discovered by a British forest guard in India. The alarming discovery was found about 160,000 feet (4,800 meters) above sea level, at the bottom of a small valley.

4471. As of 2019, the cheapest gas prices in the world belong to Venezuela at just over a penny a liter.

4472. According to Guinness World Records, the place with the greatest temperature range is Verkhoyansk, in Russia, which ranges from -90.4 degrees Fahrenheit to 98.6 degrees Fahrenheit (-68 degrees Celsius to 37 degrees Celsius).

4473. In Orlando, there is a statue of a homeless Jesus sleeping on a bench. It was installed in a place where the homeless were banned from sleeping on benches.

4474. On average, five to seven adults are reported missing every day in Las Vegas.

4475. Children as young as five years old were used as chimney sweeps back in Victorian times. They were sent up the chimney to clean out soot and debris. Some chimneys were as narrow as twelve inches (30.4 centimeters), so if they got stuck, the master chimney sweeper would light a fire to encourage them to continue working. Shockingly, some of them couldn't make their way out and died of suffocation.

4476. The leading cause of death among children aged ten to nineteen is road traffic crashes.

4477. Donald Trump's star on the Hollywood Walk of Fame has been vandalized several times in the past. The greatest one occurred in October of 2016, when a man named James Otis dressed up as a construction worker, set up construction cones and signs around Donald Trump's star, and took a sledgehammer to the star, destroying it completely.

4478. Ethan Couch, an American teenager, killed four pedestrians while driving drunk. Surprisingly, he was given no prison time after claiming affluenza, a mental illness for being too wealthy.

4479. Thirty nine members of the Heaven's Gate cult committed mass suicide on March 26, 1997. They believed that their souls would be transported to a space ship that was following the Hale Bob Comet.

4480. Based on the World Health Organization statistics, there were around 108 million people suffering from diabetes in the world in 1980. This number rose to 422 million in 2014.

4481. In the 1970's, people in Cambodia were murdered for being academics or for simply wearing glasses.

4482. In the Philippines, there's a restaurant called the "Tacsiyapo Isdaan Floating Restaurant" where customers are allowed to throw plates against a wall to release any anger they might have.

4483. Confidential data that leaked from the maritime industry revealed that a big container ship can emit the same amount of cancer and asthma-causing chemicals as fifty million cars. Based on this, the top fifteen largest container ships in the world may be emitting as much pollution as 760 million cars on Earth all together.

4484. A woman in Florida spent six years of her life sitting on a couch. She died during surgery, when doctors tried to remove her skin grafted to the couch fabric.

4485. The National Suicide Prevention Lifeline fielded the greatest number of calls in its history the day after Robin Williams committed suicide.

4486. Professor Charles Gerba of the University of Arizona's Department of Soil, Water, and Environmental Science states that about 20% of office coffee mugs carry fecal bacteria.

4487. In April of 2016, a seventeen year old girl in India had a 2.2 pound (one kilogram) hairball removed from her stomach after she had been regularly chewing on her hair for five years.

4488. At an anti-helmet rally event, motorcyclist Philip A. Contos died after he flipped over his handlebars and hit his head on the pavement.

4489. In 2015, the National Fire Protection Association reported 1,345,500 fires in the United States alone. In fact, the number grows by almost 4% every year.

4490. Jerome Rodale was a longevity expert and the father of organic farming. During an interview at the age of seventy one, he announced that he had decided to live to be 100, declaring that he had never felt better in life. Minutes later he died of a heart attack while still filming.

4491. Robert Emmet Odlum, a professional high-diver, was the first person to jump off of the Brooklyn Bridge. He wanted to prove that people did not die by simply falling through the air, so he jumped off the bridge falling 130 feet (41 meters) safely through the air. Unfortunately, he died when he hit the water.

4492. The leading cause for accidental deaths in 2014 wasn't the usual car crashes but accidental drug overdoses.

4493. In January of 1966, Spain was accidentally bombed by the US. Four nuclear weapons were carried by an Air Force bomber when it collided with its refueling tanker over the Spanish town of Palomares, sending the bombs screaming towards the ground.

4494. In the 13th century, Frederick II, emperor of Germany, wanted to find out which language humans would speak naturally, so he gave the care of fifty newborns to nurses who would only feed and bathe the babies, but were not allowed to speak or hold them. The emperor got no answer because all children eventually died.

4495. In 2014, a fan waving a flare at a Polish soccer game burst into flames when a security guard used pepper spray on him, without knowing that the substances were combustible.

4496. The World Health Organization estimates that around 50% of all medications are prescribed, dispensed, or sold inappropriately. Even more, half of the patients don't even take their medication correctly.

4497. In August, 2016, a single lightning strike killed 323 reindeer in the Hardangervidda National Park, in Norway. Due to a heavy storm, they were huddled together and were killed because of ground current that had stopped all of their hearts.

4498. The world record for the most bones broken in a lifetime is held by Evel Knievel, the pioneer of motorcycle long jumping exhibitions, who has suffered 433 fractured bones.

4499. A man named Julien Barreaux from France spent several months finding the online character who stabbed him in an online game. He found the person living just a few miles away, and when he saw him in real life, he stabbed him in the chest.

4500. The killer clown was the nickname given to serial killer John Wayne Gacy, who killed thirty three boys and young men in the 1970's. He used to perform as someone called "Pogo the Clown" at children's events. In fact, while being in prison, he painted several self-portraits of himself as a clown, and although most were destroyed, some still exist and are highly prized.

4501. In 1990, a man named Jesse Sharp paddled over the Niagara Falls in a kayak. His plan was to paddle on after the fall to a restaurant downstream where he had made restaurant reservations. Jesse didn't wear a life jacket and his body was never found.

4502. A kitchen chopping board has about 200% more fecal bacteria on average compared to a toilet seat.

4503. A report by the independent Berkeley Earth Science Research Group indicates that in Delhi, India, the quality of air was so poor at one point, that merely breathing the air in the city was as harmful as smoking forty four cigarettes every day. On one specific day, the US Embassy Air Quality Index recorded an air quality reading of 1,000 marks. To put that into perspective, anything more than twenty five marks is unsafe according to the World Health Organization.

4504. According to the Mayo Clinic, 30-35% of people over the age of sixty five who crack their ribs end up contracting pneumonia.

4505. Because of the high number of suicides committed at Mapo Bridge in Seoul, South Korea, in 2012, the local authorities partnered with ad and insurance companies to start a campaign where paintings, sculptures, motion activated lights, and messages were put there. This was meant to show people that they weren't alone. Sadly, the next year, the rate of suicides increased six fold.

4506.   Dodge City, Kansas, was such a dangerous place between 1876 and 1885, that any adult living there had a one in sixty one chance of getting murdered.

4507.   While playing Pokémon GO, nineteen year old Shayla Wiggins from Riverton, Wyoming, found a dead body floating in a river. She was trying to find a Pokémon from a natural water resource, but shockingly stumbled across something else.

4508.   Approximately a quarter of all Russian males die before the age of fifty five, mostly due to alcoholism.

4509.   Over twenty people die each year using elevators in the US alone. Over a thousand die from taking the stairs however.

4510.   In 2000, the cigarette company Phillip Morris introduced fire-safe cigarettes, which actually had a higher risk of starting fires when left unattended.

4511.   Weather in the United States is actually affected by pollution in China. Once the pollution gets into the atmosphere over the US, it stops clouds from producing rain and snow. It also takes just five days for the jet stream to carry heavy air pollution from China to the United States.

4512.   Criminal Billy Milligan had a mind so disturbed that it fractured into twenty four different personalities. For each personality, his speech pattern and accents were different, and he even sat in different ways in chairs.

4513.   While building the Hoover Dam, ninety six people in total died from industrial fatalities which included drowning, blasting, falling rocks or rockslides, falls from the canyon wall, and truck accidents.

4514.   The last state in the United States to lift the ban on interracial marriages was Alabama, in 2000, over thirty years after the Supreme Court ruled that such a ban was unconstitutional.

4515.   From 1946 to 1958, America blew up at least twenty three nuclear bombs at seven different test sites in the vicinity of Bikini Atoll, one of the Marshall Islands. As a result, Bikini Atoll took up a new flag in 1987, one that looked like the American flag but with five black stars in place of the white stripes. Three stars symbolized the islands destroyed by the bombs, and the other two represent the two islands currently occupied by Bikini natives, Ejit and Kili islands. The flag signifies a great debt, which Bikini maintains that it's still owed by America.

4516.   Data from the American Veterans Affairs Department shows that out of one hundred people, about seven or eight of them will suffer from post-traumatic stress disorder at least once in their lives. Currently, eight million grownups have PTSD.

4517.   The god of smallpox is named Sopona, and was worshipped in Nigeria, until it was outlawed after media reports indicated that a cult was intentionally spreading the disease to make the god more powerful.

4518.   After it's used for ten years, the average mattress will double in weight because it accumulates dead skin, dust mites, and sweat.

4519.   The Center for Disease Control and Prevention estimates that, in 2014, smokeless tobacco and cigarette companies pumped nine billion dollars into advertising and promoting their products just in the United States alone.

4520.   The US government put poisonous chemicals in industrial alcohol in the Prohibition Era, hoping that it would deter people from stealing, distilling, and selling it, and that resulted in more than 10,000 deaths because the plan didn't work.

4521.   Regina Rhode had the tragic misfortune of being a student at Columbine High School during the mass shooting, and then again at Virginia Tech during a similar shooting. Luckily, she managed to avoid the shooter in both instances.

4522.   As a bomber flew over North Carolina in 1961 with a crew of eight, it crashed and dropped two very powerful hydrogen bomb payloads, and it killed three crew members. The two bombs dropped before the bomber hit the ground, and they didn't go off. The cleanup crew located all the remnants of the first bomb, but they weren't able to find parts of the second one.

4523.   In five coordinated attacks in 1985, the Aum Shinrikyo cult, in Japan, released sarin gas on three metro lines in Tokyo during rush hour. Twelve people died as a result, and fifty others were seriously injured with some dying later. More than 200 cult members were arrested and thirteen senior leaders were executed after receiving death sentences.

4524.   If you are a man in America, you are five times more likely to be killed by lightning than your female counterparts, according to America's National Health Protection Agency. Data from 1968 to 2010 showed that 85% of the 3,389 people killed by lightning strikes were male.

4525.   According to the penal code of the US state of South Carolina, first time domestic abuse offenders can be jailed for a maximum of thirty days, while those arrested for abusing dogs can be jailed for a maximum of five years.

4526.   500 million people were infected by the global influenza pandemic that took place from 1918 to 1919. That was about a third of Earth's population at the time, and between twenty and fifty million people died as a result of the disease.

4527.   Because he was delusional and obsessed with Jodie Foster, John Hinckley Junior tried to assassinate President Ronald Reagan in 1981. He was released from a psychiatric institution on September 10, 2016, and he now lives with his mom.

4528.   During the anti-Sikh riots that occurred between October 31 and November 3, 1984, more than 2,800 Sikhs were killed. Some reports indicate that the numbers were much higher, closer to 8,000 in total, and roughly 3,000 within Delhi alone.

4529.   A thirty seven year old Scottish man from Glasgow set the world record for suffering the longest hangover. He consumed more than sixty pints (thirty five liters) of beer in a span of four days, and he ended up having serious hydration symptoms for the next four weeks. He had to see a specialist who put him on blood thinning treatments for six whole months, and after that, his headaches and blurred visions eventually subsided.

4530.   Based on reports issued by the World Health Organization, about 265,000 people die every year from burns that occur mostly at home or the workplace.

4531.   In Vicenza, Italy, a grandmother accidentally sent five people to hospital, two adults and three children. She made them cocoa without knowing that the packets had expired back in 1990.

4532.   On the night of January 27, 1993, Andre the Giant died in a hotel room in Paris. Coincidentally, he was in Paris to attend his father's funeral.

4533.   In 2015, a Russian suicide bomber had the intention of killing hundreds in Moscow on New Year's Eve. The plan failed as she received a text message from the wireless carrier wishing her a Happy New Year, which triggered the belt bomb and killed her alone.

4534.   Based on reports done by the World Health Organization, in the last forty five years, suicide rates have increased by 60% worldwide. In fact, the approximate mortality rate is sixteen per 100,000 people, or one death every forty seconds.

4535.   On September 13, 1916, an elephant nicknamed Murderous Mary was hanged in the town of Erwin, Tennessee, because she mauled one of her keepers to death. To do so, a huge crane was required. At the time, hanging and lynching were both a popular form of justice.

4536.   Scaphism was a horrifying ancient type of torturous execution. People killed using this method were made to drink very high amounts of honey and milk, and were then stripped naked, and placed between two hollow trunks, or rowboats. Some more honey would be put on the person's body, and that would attract all sorts of vermin and insects, which would burrow into the person's body and eat him from the inside out, leaving them to die a horrible death.

4537.   Throughout Walter Summerford's life, until his death in 1912, he was struck by lightning three different times. Four years after his death, his tombstone too was struck by lightning.

4538.   The reason why all cruise ships contain morgues is because about 200 people die while at sea every year, hence they need somewhere on the ship to be stored.

4539.   The Great Pacific Garbage Patch, or the Pacific Trash Vortex, is a collection of garbage found in the north part of the Pacific Ocean, made of tiny particles of plastic that never degrade. It spans waters from the west coast of North America all the way to Japan.

4540.   President James A. Garfield was assassinated less than four months after becoming president. The shot he received in the back was not fatal as it did not hit any of his vital organs, and the bullet lodged behind his pancreas. Later, it was found that it was the doctors who actually killed him.

4541.   Felix Batista was a hostage negotiator who, in 2008, was kidnapped in Mexico after presenting on how to survive when kidnapped. He has not been found to this day.

4542.   In 1931, an eleven year old named Wilbur Brink was playing in his front yard when he was suddenly hit by a stray tire flying out that instantly killed him. The tire came from a wreck involving race driver Billy Arnold who was racing at a spot across the street.

4543.   As per the Center for Disease Control and Prevention, 30,700 Americans lost their lives to alcohol related causes in 2014, a number that's higher than the combined total deaths that resulted from heroin and prescription pain medication overdoses.

4544.   Under Hitler, Nazi Germany guillotined about as many people as those who were executed using the same method during the French Revolution.

4545.   The only IRS revenue officer to ever be killed while in duty was Michael Dillon. In 1983, he went to collect a sum of $500 from a former service employee on behalf of the IRS. Unfortunately, he was shot three times by the resident with an M-1 rifle and was killed instantly.

4546.   On January 23, 1556, a deadly earthquake occurred in Shaanxi, China, killing an estimated 830,000 people. The magnitude of the quake was approximately 8-8.3. Although it wasn't the strongest tremor on record, it struck in the middle of a densely populated area with poorly constructed buildings and homes, resulting in horrific death tolls.

4547.   Based on the State Health Department records, Hawaii's visitor drowning rate is thirteen times higher than the national average over the past decade, and ten times the rate of the number of its own inhabitants.

4548.   After cardiovascular disease, cancer is the second leading cause of death in the world. Every sixth death in the world is caused by cancer.

4549. Takuya Nagaya, a twenty three year old man from Japan, started to slither on the floor saying that he had become a snake. His parents thought that he had been possessed by a snake, so his father Katsumi spent the next two days head butting and biting his son to "drive out the snake," causing his death in the process.

4550. On August 21, 1986, a volcanic lake known as Lake Nyos in Cameroon, Africa, released 1.2 cubic kilometers of CO_2 in approximately twenty seconds, suffocating over 1,746 people. This massive wave of deadly gas swept over the countryside, killing people as far away as fifteen miles (twenty five kilometers).

4551. In the 1700's, you could come into the Zoo of London for free if you brought a dog or cat to feed the lions.

4552. In China, a puppy was taught to smoke cigarettes by his owner, a twenty three year old chef named Zeng Ziguang. The man would blow smoke in his face to get him used to the smell and used treats to get him to hold the cigarette in his mouth. After a month, the puppy was smoking a pack a day.

4553. In the United States, around 795,000 people have a stroke every year with about three in four being first time strokes. In fact, every forty seconds, someone in the United States has a stroke.

4554. Studies show that most missing children are actually abducted by parents or relatives.

4555. On the Titanic, there were over thirteen couples celebrating their honeymoon. Unfortunately, none of them survived upon impact and the subsequent sinking of the boat.

4556. There were so many murders between the 1970's and 1980's in Miami that the medical examiners had to rent refrigerated trailers from Burger King to fit all the extra corpses they had coming in.

4557. In 2015, a study done by Common Sense Media and CEO James Steyer revealed that the average teen spends up to nine hours a day on social media.

4558. On April 14, 1986, the biggest hailstones ever recorded hit Bangladesh. They weighed over two pounds (one kilogram) each and killed ninety two people.

4559. In 2014, an entire family died from the fumes of rotting potatoes in their cellar, except for an eight year old girl. Each family member checked on the other by walking into the cellar, but died instantly as soon as they entered the room.

4560. A Russian man named Alexei Roskov drank three bottles of vodka, jumped out of a building five stories high, walked back up, and then jumped out of it again, all because his wife was nagging at him. He survived the second time as well.

4561. The sister ship of the Titanic, Britannic, was sunk during World War I. Although the ship was greatly improved after the Titanic sank, it still sank in only fifty five minutes.

4562. On October 6, 1909, Vancouver unveiled its first ambulance. When they first took it for a test drive around town, it ended running over and instantly killing a wealthy man from Austin, Texas, becoming the first person the ambulance picked up.

4563. Teddy bears have caused quite a lot of deaths in the last ninety years. This is because parts of teddy bears such as the eyes and nose can become choking hazards as well as being a tripping hazard for young toddlers.

4564. In the US alone, 8,179 toothpick related accidental injuries were reported from 1979 to 1982. Additionally, three people died as a result of swallowing small bits of wood. Currently, about 9,000 people a year, most of them children ages five to fourteen, end up in American hospitals after choking on toothpicks.

4565. In 1518, in Strasbourg, there was an outbreak of manic dancing known as the "Dancing Plague" that consisted of 400 people, mostly women. Over the course of one month, fifteen people a day died from heart attacks and exhaustion.

4566. On January 25, 1979, Robert Williams became the first known human to be killed by a robot. While he was working for the Flat Rock Assembly Plant in Detroit, Michigan, he was tragically killed by an industrial robot arm.

4567. According to studies, using a hands-free device to talk on the phone while driving is equally or more dangerous than driving drunk.

4568. In the Olympic Stadium of Athens, in Greece, women are forbidden to wear high heels or tall hats.

4569. Barbara Soaper, from Michigan, gave birth to her three children on 08/08/08, 09/09/09, and 10/10/10 respectively. The odds of this happening are fifty million to one.

Space & NASA

4570.   Peggy Whitson is the first female astronaut to become a two time commander of the International Space Station, and she has logged more spacewalking time than all other female NASA astronauts. She also went to space at age fifty six, making her the oldest female astronaut to accomplish that feat.

4571.   Three men attempted to sue NASA for trespassing on Mars in 1997. The men from Yemen stated that they inherited the red planet from their ancestors three thousand years ago. They didn't win as there's an international treaty that mentions everything that's in the solar system, except the Earth, is the property of everybody on the globe.

4572.   The NASA logo meatball design consists of a sphere that denotes a planet, stars that symbolize space, a red wing-like chevron that represents aeronautics, and a spacecraft flying around it.

4573.   NASA held the Space Poop Challenge in October 2016. It consisted of creating a system inside of a spacesuit that collects human waste for up to 144 hours and roots it away from the body without the use of hands.

4574.   NASA's Skylab IV mission was manned by a crew of three, when on December 28, 1973, they held a one day mutiny, where they switched off all communication channels with ground control for twenty four hours. They spent that day taking in the view of the Earth, and just relaxing.

4575.   Based on a study done by NASA, the heart of an astronaut becomes more spherical and loses muscle mass while in space. However, once they are back on Earth, the shape returns back to normal.

4576.   George Alrdich is the official smeller for NASA. He has worked there for over forty years and his job is to smell things to make sure there aren't any nasty smells for the International Space Station or the space shuttles.

4577.   In the past, astronaut food was packed in tubes similar to toothpaste tubes. Astronaut John Glen, the first American to orbit Earth, had to endure bite size cubes, freeze dried powders, and semi liquids stuffed into aluminum tubes. According to him, the foods were very unappetizing and hard to rehydrate, and creating crumbs had to be prevented from ruining instruments.

4578.   Salt and pepper are carried in liquid form into space. If astronauts tried to sprinkle regular salt and pepper, they would just float around.

4579. The astronauts of Apollo 11 went to space without life insurance because they couldn't afford the rates. Instead they signed dozens of autographs and gave them to their loved ones to sell if anything did happen.

4580. An astronaut's heart literally starts to shrink when it's exposed to microgravity in space for long periods of time.

4581. Given Iceland's lack of vegetation and volcanic geology, it's the place that looks the most like the moon. Because of this, in 1965, Apollo astronauts traveled there as field training.

4582. Playtex, the women's bra manufacturer, actually designed Neil Armstrong's lunar astronaut outfit.

4583. Thanks to the live transmissions from space from the crew of the Apollo 7, a special Emmy Award from the National Academy of Television, Arts, and Sciences was given to them in 1968.

4584. Astronomers thought that they discovered a new asteroid, but it turned out to be the third stage of the Apollo Twelve Spacecraft, which had been orbiting the Sun for thirty years. The object now known as J002E3, wandered close to Earth in the early 2000's, and it was pulled into the hill sphere, the second strongest nearby source of gravitational force after the Sun.

4585. Planet Uranus was discovered by astronomer William Herschel on March 13, 1781. It was the first discovery to be made using a telescope and the first discovery of modern times.

4586. As part of the management training program, NASA often shows the Hollywood movie Armageddon and then asks its new staff to identify as many scientific inaccuracies as they can. There are at least 168 of them.

4587. Coincidentally, astronaut Buzz Aldrin's middle name was Moon.

4588. Apollo 16 astronaut Charles Duke was the youngest man in history to walk on the moon at the age of thirty six. He left a photo of his family on the moon with the inscription: "This is the family of astronaut Charlie Duke, from the planet Earth, who landed on the moon on April 20, 1972." The picture still remains on the moon's surface.

4589. On the fortieth anniversary of his moon walk, Buzz Aldrin, the veteran astronaut, recorded a song entitled "Rocket Experience," both to commemorate his historic feat, and to raise money for organizations that are committed to exploring space.

4590. Moon dust smells like spent gunpowder according to astronauts that have been to the moon.

4591. As part of the training program, all US astronauts are required to learn Russian. This is because they have to be able to run the International Space Station using Russian language training manuals if necessary.

4592. The flag erected on the moon after Apollo 11 landed on its surface was purchased at a local Sears store for $5.50.

4593. Florida-based company "Moon Express" has been given permission by the United States government for lunar landing, the first of several missions to visit the moon and harvest resources from it. It is the first time ever that the American government has approved a private company to land on the moon.

4594. Most Americans did not support the idea of a moon landing before it actually happened, as they thought the government was spending way too much money on space.

4595. In the Pacific Ocean, off the coast of New Zealand, there is a 2,484 mile (4,000 kilometer) spacecraft cemetery where satellites and other spacecraft plunge back to Earth. The spot was selected because of how isolated it is from humans and shipping traffic. There are over 150 crafts in this cemetery.

4596. As of July 2011, more than one million observations have been made by the Hubble Space Telescope over the course of twenty one years, which have generated almost fifty terabytes of data. In fact, it produces over eighty gigabytes of data every month.

4597. If you could drive in a straight line to outer space, it would only take an hour to get there if you were going sixty miles (ninety kilometers) an hour.

4598. The Hubble Space Telescope travels around the Earth taking pictures of the stars, planets, and galaxies at about 24,928 feet (7,600 meters) per second.

4599. There are more than 3,200 confirmed new planets that have been discovered by telescope.

4600. India had a successful mission to Mars in 2014 that cost less than the movie "Gravity," that starred George Clooney and Sandra Bullock. The Mars mission cost fifty eight million dollars (USD) while the movie cost seventy five million dollars (USD).

4601. The NASA-operated Cassini Spacecraft returned to Earth on April 26, 2017, after becoming the first spacecraft to travel through the narrow space between Saturn and its rings. It came around 200 miles (320 kilometers) close to the innermost visible edge of Saturn's rings, and within 1,900 miles (3,060 kilometers) of the planet's cloud tops.

4602. The four largest doors on Earth are found on NASA's Vehicle Assembly Building, and they are all 456 feet (139 meters) high. It takes forty five whole minutes to open or shut the doors completely.

4603. At the Kennedy Space Center Titusville, Florida, NASA has a vehicle assembly building that is so gigantic that it has its own weather. Because of the humidity in the building, rain clouds usually form inside it.

4604. When people die in long-term space missions or in space settlements, NASA has a plan for disposing their bodies. The body is frozen in an airlock, and then a robotic arm shakes it vigorously, until it crumbles into small pieces and becomes space dust.

4605. During space shuttle missions, NASA makes morning wake up calls to astronauts. The call recordings are selected by friends and family of each crew member, or by the flight controllers.

4606. Eugene Shoemaker, a planetary scientist who died in 1997, is the only human that's buried on the moon. NASA's Lunar Prospector went to the moon's South Pole on a mission to find water on January 6, 1998, and it carried an urn with Shoemaker's ashes. On July 1, 1999, the same spacecraft was deliberately crashed into the surface of the moon, thus making Shoemaker the first person to be buried off-world.

4607. When renowned astronaut Neil Armstrong, the first man to walk on the moon, sent his job application to NASA, it arrived a week late. Fortunately, his friend Dick Day, who also worked for NASA, managed to sneak his application in with the ones that came in on time. Were it not for his good friend Day, Armstrong would never have walked on the moon.

4608. Some metal pieces of the fallen World Trade Center were used to build both of NASA's Mars Rovers. The metal was made into shields to protect drilling mechanisms.

4609. To honor fallen astronauts, Apollo 15 crew placed a small aluminum sculpture on the moon as well as a plaque bearing their names. In 1971, that number was fourteen.

4610. Before the Apollo 11's team was set to launch, astronauts Buzz Aldrin, Neil Armstrong, and Michael Collins signed a significant number of envelopes as a form of life insurance for their families. All envelopes were given to a friend who, on important days such as the day they landed on the moon, would give an envelope to their families. In case they did not return from the moon, their families could sell them.

4611. If you cry in outer space, your tears never fall; they just stay under your eye, like a blob.

4612. If the Apollo 11 moon landing was indeed faked by the US government as conspiracy theorists claim, it means 400,000 people would have had to participate in the cover-up.

4613. On December 7, 1972, the crew of the Apollo 17 space shuttle took the famous picture of the Earth known as "The Blue Marble," the only whole Earth photo taken by human hands. Since then, nobody has been able to be far enough from Earth to take a similar photo.

4614. In South Africa, a group of high school girls from Cape Town have designed and built the first private satellite of the continent. It was launched into space in May of 2017 and it collects information on agriculture and food security within the continent.

4615. November 2, 2000, was the last date when all living human beings were on Earth at the same time. After that day, the International Space Station has been occupied continuously.

4616. Pre 2006, all cosmonauts in Russia carried machetes, pistols, and shotguns into space so when they returned, they were able to defend themselves in the Siberian wilderness against bears, wolves, and other animals.

4617. On February 6, 1971, astronaut Alan Shepard became the first and only person to play golf anywhere other than Earth. He used a makeshift six iron he had smuggled on board Apollo 14 to hit two golf balls on the Moon's surface.

4618. In 2015, a gigantic cloud of methyl alcohol, also called methanol, surrounding a stellar nursery was discovered by astronomers; it measured over 310 billion miles (500 million kilometers) across. In the future, it could help astronomers understand how some of the most massive stars in the universe are formed.

4619. Eugene Cernan was the last astronaut to walk on the moon. In December, 1972, before he got back into the lander, he used his foot to write the initials TDC over the dusty moon surface. They represented the names of his daughter Tracy, and in theory, they are still written on the moon today.

4620. Over the course of years, thousands of satellites have been launched into space amongst meteors, but only one has been hit and destroyed: the European Space Agency Communications Satellite Olympus.

4621. If swimming on the moon were possible, you could walk on the water's surface and jump out of the water like a dolphin.

4622. The Apollo 11 moon landing took less computing power than a Google search query takes today.

4623. Many astronauts after returning home from trips to space report letting go of objects in midair, still expecting them to float.

4624. A total distance of 1.74 billion miles (2.7 billion kilometers) has to be traveled by NASA's robotic spacecraft Juno to arrive on the planet Jupiter. It launched from Cape Canaveral on August 5, 2011, and arrived on Jupiter on July 4, 2016.

4625. In February 2017, 104 satellites on a single mission were successfully launched by India from the Sriharikota Space Center in South India, beating the previous record of only thirty-seven satellites launched by Russia in 2014.

4626. Over 500,000 pieces of debris orbit Earth, traveling at speeds up to 17,489 miles (28,163 kilometers) per hour. From these intense speeds, even the tiniest chip of paint can cause damage to space crafts.

4627. Tornadoes can occur on the surface of the Sun. In September of 2015, NASA captured on film a giant swirling plume of superheated plasma churned above the surface of the Sun for about forty hours. It was five million degrees Fahrenheit (2.7 million degrees Celsius).

4628. Tetris was the first videogame ever to be played in space. Aleksandr A. Serobrov, a Russian cosmonaut, brought a Game Boy along during a 1993 space mission, and he played Tetris on it.

4629. Twenty of the twenty four men who traveled to the moon on Apollo 8 and Apollo 10 through seventeen missions were Boy Scouts. This includes eleven of the twelve moonwalkers and all three members of the Apollo 13 crew.

4630. In order to avoid being hit by lethal-sized space debris, the International Space Station had to be moved three separate times in 2014.

4631. NASA astronaut Scott Kelly spent almost a year living aboard the International Space Station. When he came back home, he found out he was two inches (five centimeters) taller than his identical twin brother Mark. Due to gravity, the disks of the spinal column get compressed on Earth. So in space, as there is no gravity, the disks actually expand and the spine lengthens, making astronauts taller.

4632. Astronaut ice cream has always been a myth, as it has never been eaten in space. In fact, it was used as a marketing ploy to influence the young and impressionable ones.

4633. The moons of the moon are called "sub moons," according to astronomers Una Cormaya of the Carnegie Institute for Science and Shawn Raymond of the Laboratory du Astophysice du Bordeaux. Other scientists, however, are using the term "moon moons." There are no known moon moons in our solar system.

4634. Some of the Apollo 11 astronauts are on the Hollywood walk of fame such as Neil Armstrong, Edwin E. Buzz Aldrin Jr., and Michael Collins. Their marker isn't in the shape of a star, but round like the Moon.

4635. Between 1969 and 1972, 841 pounds (382 kilograms) of lunar rocks, core samples, pebbles, sand, and dust from the lunar surface were brought back to Earth by six Apollo missions. The six space flights returned 2,200 separate samples from six different exploration sites on the moon.

4636. NASA purchased a nineteen million dollar toilet from the Space Public Corporation and SP Korolev Rocket, a Russia-based aerospace firm in 2007. The price may seem high but this toilet makes drinking water out of urine.

4637. Humans put a man on the moon before they put wheels on luggage.

4638. Thirty six seconds after launch, on November 14, 1969, the Apollo 12 was struck by lightning and moments later, it was struck again. The second strike tore through the ship and wiped out many of its electrical systems. One of the flight controllers actually switched the spacecraft's signaling conditioning equipment to auxiliary. Fortunately, the Apollo 12 was able to continue on to successfully land on the moon.

4639. According to NASA, a trip to Mars would take about two-and-a-half years to complete. To begin with, six months are needed to travel to Mars and another six months to return. On top of that, astronauts that go would have to stay eighteen to twenty months on the planet before the planets realign for a return trip. The whole trip could cost up to $40 billion.

4640. Our pollution has actually reached Mars. In 2012, NASA discovered a bright object on the surface of the red planet, and became intrigued as to what it could be. Later they discovered that it was a piece of plastic from the Curiosity Rover.

4641. John Glenn, the first astronaut to orbit the Earth, made history again by becoming the oldest man to fly in space at the age of seventy seven, on October 29, 1998. He traveled aboard the space shuttle Discovery as part of a NASA study on health problems associated with aging.

4642. Due to the lack of gravity in space, astronauts tears coagulate in the eyes and end up stinging. In 2011, astronaut Andrew Feustel got some anti-fogging solution stuck in his eye and tears weren't going to get it out, so he had to rub his eyes on the foam inside of this helmet.

4643. Astronaut Buzz Aldrin was requested to fill out a military travel voucher for reimbursement for his mission to the moon; he was actually reimbursed $33.31.

Sports

4644. The longest tennis match in history lasted eleven hours and five minutes, took three days, and consisted of 183 games. It was between Frenchman Nicolas Mahut and American John Isner at the 2010 Wimbledon Championships. John Isner was the winner.

4645. In order to renew its contract as the official beer of the NFL through to the 2022 Super Bowl, Anheuser Busch InBev paid $1.4 billion. They have been the official beer of the Super Bowl since 2011, when they replaced Coors Light.

4646. The first person in the sixty one years of balloting to win the NBA MVP Award by unanimous vote was basketball star Stephen Curry.

4647. Polo shirt collars were originally designed to be flipped up to block the neck from exposure to the sun in tennis courts.

4648. Ludivine, a hound dog living with her owner in Elkmont, Alabama, snuck out of her backyard and ran after some runners who were participating in a half marathon in January, 2016. Ludivine unintentionally completed the entire race, finishing in seventh place.

4649. In 1947, Wataru Misaka was the first ever non-white player to join an NBA team. He was a Japanese-American from Utah, and he played for the New York Knicks.

4650. Approximately twenty two cow hides are needed just to make enough balls for the Super Bowl. For the regular NFL, they need over 3,000 hides to make enough footballs for the season.

4651. Only 3% of the 2.9 million female high school athletes are cheerleaders, but that one activity accounts for over 65% of all serious injuries among athletic high school girls.

4652. Sugarpova is a candy company founded and owned by famous tennis star Maria Sharapova.

4653. In 1964, Nike was founded by CEO Phil Knight and Oregon head track coach Bill Bowerman. It was originally named Bill Ribbon Sports, or BRS. The name was later changed to Nike.

4654. The Rio 2016 Paralympics' medals feature a tiny device that makes a noise when the medal is shaken, so visually impaired athletes can know if they won gold, silver, or bronze.

4655. There is a 17% chance you can play for the NBA if you are an American male, seven plus feet tall, and between the ages of twenty and forty.

4656. Joggling is a sport where you jog and juggle at the same time. His inventor, Bill Giduz, would juggle balls on a running track to increase his coordination when he realized that the pace of the three-ball juggling pattern easily matched a wide range of running cadences, thus creating the sport.

4657. The world's oldest board game was found by a team of archaeologists in a 5,000 year old Bronze Age burial site in Turkey. Board games are believed to have originated in Egypt in the Fertile Crescent.

4658. On April 24, 1849, the first baseball hats were worn by the New York Knickerbockers. They were made of straw.

4659. Jousting is the state sport in Maryland, US. It became their sport back in 1962 and has been held there ever since colonial times.

4660. Prince Constantine II, who ended up being the last king of Greece, won a gold medal in sailing during the summer Olympics of 1960, the first for the country since 1912.

4661. A professional pole vaulter called Sergei Bubka, who was active from the late 1980's to early 1990's, managed to break the high jump world record thirty five different times, each time beating his earlier record by a tiny amount, because he wanted to get paid bonuses from setting a new record as many times as possible. They say that we won't ever truly know how high Bubka could really jump.

4662. Of the top thirty fastest Olympic one hundred meter sprints in history, only nine aren't tainted with doping, and they were all set by Usain Bolt.

4663. The Memorial Stadium at the University of Nebraska can hold 85,458 people when it's at full capacity. That's higher than the population of any city in Nebraska, apart from Lincoln where the university is, and Omaha. This means that when the stadium is full, it temporarily becomes the third largest city in Nebraska.

4664. FIFA has more member countries than the United Nations. FIFA currently has 212 members, while the UN only has 193 member countries.

4665. Starting in 2007, a few days before the official NBA draft, the Harlem Globetrotters always have their own draft where they've chosen people like Usain Bolt, Tim Tebow, and Gal Gadot, however none of these people have ever actually played for the team, or joined it.

4666. During the Summer Olympic Games hosted in St. Louis Missouri in 1904, lots of bizarre things happened during the marathon event. One runner covered most of the distance in a car, another one took rat poison as a stimulant and had to be carried away from the course, and third, a person ate rotten apples from an orchard along the course, fell sick, napped for a while, and still ended up being the fourth to finish the race.

4667.   Curling stones are made of granite and weigh around forty four pounds (twenty kilograms) each. Most curling stones in the world and all of those used in the Olympics come from an uninhabited 220 acre island just off the coast of Scotland.

4668.   Women were not allowed to compete in ancient Olympics, married women weren't allowed to be in the stands to watch, and only young women and virgins were permitted. In fact, fathers used to bring their daughters in hopes that they would marry one of the champions.

4669.   Baltimore Raven, the popular American football team, were named in honor of Edgar Allen Poe's classic poem "The Raven."

4670.   There is a hybrid sport called chess boxing that combines the mental battle of chess and the physical struggle of boxing. Performers have to learn how to balance their strategy on the chess board with the plan of attack in the boxing match.

4671.   There is another variation of soccer where three teams face off against each other at the same time.

4672.   In 1919, due to a Spanish flu outbreak, the Stanley Cup final in Seattle was canceled. It was the first time ever that the finals were canceled.

4673.   During the 2000 Australian Paralympics, the Spanish Paralympic basketball team was forced to give back the gold medals they won after finding out that almost all players were not disabled.

4674.   The world record for the most medals won at a single summer Olympic Games is held by the United States. At the 1904 Olympics, which took place in St. Louis, Missouri, they won seventy eight gold medals, eight two silver medals, and seventy nine bronze ones, for a total of 239.

4675.   There is a sport known as "archery tag" which is similar to dodgeball, however, foam-tipped arrows are shot instead of throwing foam balls.

4676.   Up until the 1990's, the halftime show at the Super Bowl was just a break that included marching bands and drill teams. The intention was to simply fill in the time so that fans and TV viewers could go to the concession stand, get snacks, or just go to the bathroom.

4677.   Buzkashi is the national sport of Afghanistan. It consists of a headless carcass of a calf or goat that is kept in the center of a field while two opposing teams on horseback try to get hold of the carcass and carry it to the goal area. The game can sometimes last for days.

4678.   Even though the UK calls it football, the term soccer came from Britain in the 1800's.

4679.   The first time in Olympic history that a South American country hosted the games was at the 2016 Olympics in Rio, Brazil.

4680.   Usain Bolt found Chinese food to be rather odd when he was there for the 2008 Olympics so he only ate chicken nuggets. He still went on and won three gold medals.

4681.   John F. Kennedy's older sister, Rosemary Kennedy, was lobotomized at the age of twenty three; the surgery failed and left her permanently incapacitated. The incident, however, inspired her sister, Eunice Kennedy Shriver, to launch the Special Olympics.

4682.   Brazilian soccer great Pele was actually convinced by US politician Henry Kissinger to play in the United States.

4683.   In the early 1900's, "Tug of War" used to be an Olympic sport.

4684.   Before the game, all NHL hockey pucks are frozen so that they glide smoother and faster during the game.

4685.   In South Korea, winning gold at the Asian Games or any medal at the Olympics will exempt any able-bodied males from the country's mandatory military service.

4686.   Based on a report published in the Wall Street Journal in 2010, during a one hour regulation football game, the total of all plays averaged just eleven minutes.

4687.   Top soccer player Cristiano Ronaldo was asked to donate his cleats for a charity auction. The auction aimed to raise money for ten month old Erik Ortiz Cruz, who had a brain disorder that could cause thirty seizures a day. Cristiano didn't donate the cleats, but he instead paid for the child's surgery, some $83,000.

4688.   In the first National Collegiate Athletic Association (NCAA) tournament, only eight teams participated. Since 2011, the number of teams has increased to sixty eight.

4689.   As a way to honor Jamaican sprinter Usain Bolt, he was given Berlin's twelve foot (3.6 meter) high piece of the Berlin Wall. It weighed nearly three tons.

4690.   When the Aboroginal Canadians played lacrosse, the teams had anywhere between a hundred to a thousand people while the fields were 1,500 to 9,000 feet (500 to 3,000 meters) long. Some games went for as long as three days.

4691.   During the opening ceremony of the Olympic Games, the procession is always led by the Greek team. Then all other teams follow in alphabetical order with the exception of the last team to enter, which is the team that is hosting the event.

4692.   In 2017, Adam Rolston and his friend and caddie, Ron Rutland, played the longest hole of golf in history. They teed off on June 29, on the Western end of Mongolia, and travelled across the country, covering 1,249 miles (2,000 kilometers), hitting a golf ball all the way. They arrived at their destination in Ulan Bator, Mongolia's capital city, eighty two days later, thus completing their course. Rolston shot a 20,093, although it was estimated to be a par 14,000.

4693.   When the popular song "Take Me Out to the Ball Game" was written by Albert Von Tizler and Jack Norworth in 1908, neither of them had ever been to an actual baseball game.

4694.   Fifty five year old Scott Entsminger was a Cleveland Browns super fan, and prior to his death on July 4, 2013, he asked if six members of the team could be his pallbearers, because he wanted the Cleveland Browns to let him down one final time.

4695.   The NBA logo features a silhouette of a player, which was originally inspired by a photo of Jerry West, an all-star who played for the LA Lakers between 1960 and 1974. That logo rakes in three billion dollars annually in licensing today.

4696.   Tires used by NASCAR race teams are pumped with nitrogen unlike regular tires which use air. It's because nitrogen expands and contracts more consistently, giving the car better handling and traction than it would have if it used regular air.

4697.   Basketball star Shaquille O'Neal was the first of all athletes to get verified on Twitter. He also used a Twitter video to announce his retirement from professional basketball way before the NBA knew he intended to retire.

4698.   On October 7, 1916, Georgia Tech beat Cumberland College 222-0, setting the highest scoring college football game ever.

4699.   Between 2003 and 2005, Philip Eckmans, a Belgian who was living in Spain, developed a new sport called "Bossaball." The game combines the elements of volleyball, football, and gymnastics with music, and is played between two teams on an inflatable court that has a trampoline on each side of the net.

4700.   LeBron James, the NBA superstar, turned down a $10 million sponsorship deal from Reebok at age eighteen, because he knew Adidas and Nike would come along with better offers. A short while later, Nike offered him $90 million, which he accepted.

4701.   Barcelona Football Club has a sponsorship deal with UNICEF where it actually donates one and a half million euros a year while wearing its logo.

4702. At the Wimbledon championship, players are only allowed to wear all white. This dress code dates back to the 1800's when it was frowned upon and considered inappropriate to have visible sweat stains.

4703. During a spring training game between the Arizona Diamondbacks and San Francisco Giants on March 24, 2001, pitcher Randy Johnson hit a pigeon while pitching, resulting in the bird exploding in the air.

4704. Wales holds a world mountain bike bog snorkeling championship. Contenders have to ride a mountain bike as fast as they can along the bottom of a bog, which has a 6.5 feet (two meter) deep, water-filled trench. To make it more difficult, the bikes that they use have led-filled frames, the tires are filled with water, and the competitors wear led weight belts so that they don't float off of their bikes.

4705. A red card was once given just after three seconds of a football match commencing when a player yelled "Eff me, that was loud," when the whistle was blown.

4706. After the Patriots won the Super Bowl 51, NFL player Tom Brady became the first player ever to win four Super Bowl Most Valuable Player awards.

4707. In preparation for the 2008 Olympics in Beijing, 1.5 million people were evicted from their homes.

4708. The Carolingian Community in Kenya only makes up 0.06% of the human population, but it has produced about 70% of all elite long distance running medalists. During the Berlin Marathon in 2013, male Kenyan runners won first, second, fourth, and fifth place, while female Kenyan runners won first, second, and fourth place.

4709. Originally, golfer Tiger Woods was named Eldrick Tont Woods. In his early golfing days, a few reporters started calling him Eldrick "Tiger" Woods. After gaining fame, he ditched the name Eldrick.

4710. In Brazil, there is a stadium called "Zerao" that's positioned right over the equator. When matches are played there, technically each player is in a different hemisphere.

4711. Japanese golf players buy an odd kind of insurance that covers them in case they get a hole in one. It's a tradition there, you have to buy drinks for friends if you get a hole in one, so the insurance pays out up to $3,000 to cover that expense.

4712. Edward Hedrick, who invented Frisbee golf, wished that when he died, his ashes would be molded into a new line of Frisbees. His last wishes were honored, and a series of Frisbees containing his ashes were sold, ensuring that he would be thrown around forever.

4713. In the eight year span of Kareen Abdul Jabbar's high school and college basketball career, he managed to win 212 matches, and only lost eight. He also won the championship every single year where he was eligible.

4714. In 2016, for the first time in 108 years, the Chicago Cubs won the World Series.

4715. In 1923, an American jockey named Frank Hayes suffered a fatal heart attack and died mid-race. His body remained on the horse until crossing the finish line in first place. It was actually the first race he won.

4716. Although Michael Jordan has never played for Miami Heat, the number twenty three was retired by the team.

4717. Although wearing a wooden prosthetic leg, gymnast George Eiser won three gold medals, two silver, and a bronze in the 1904 Summer Olympics.

4718. The largest feet in the NBA go to Bob Lanier and Shaquille O'neal. They both have size twenty two feet. Bob Lanier has a height of 6 feet 8 (2.08 meters) while Shaq is seven feet (2.13 meters).

4719. On April 18, 1981, the longest professional baseball game took place between the Pawtucket Red Sox and the Rochester Red Wings. It lasted thirty two innings before being stopped to be resumed on June 23 when one more inning was played.

4720. In the yearly Yale-Harvard football game of 2004, the students of Yale tricked the Harvard crowd to hold up cards that formed the words "we suck," by telling them it would spell "go Harvard." Yale still ended up losing the game.

4721. In 1892, Gallaudet University, an all deaf school, invented the football huddle to prevent opposing teams from seeing their sign language.

4722. Research in 2014 showed that the average football player runs seven miles (11.2 kilometers) each game.

4723. Mike Tyson, the legendary heavyweight boxing champion, was taking a tour of the zoo in 1989 with Robin Gibbons, his wife at the time, when he saw an alpha male gorilla harassing other apes. Tyson asked the zookeeper to let him into the cage so he could fight the gorilla. The zookeeper declined, even after Tyson offered him $10,000.

4724. During the 2000 Summer Paralympics Games, Spain cheated by making everyone believe that ten out of the twelve players on their roster were mentally disabled, when they actually had no disability at all.

4725. It was found that 70% of US athletes have a rare gene variant in their heart, known as ACTN3, making them great sprinters. In fact, 75% of all Jamaicans have this gene.

4726. Famous soccer player Cristiano Ronaldo is the athlete with the most Instagram followers in the world with over 214 million followers.

4727. The annual Yukon Quest is regarded as the most difficult sled race worldwide, and it's held in February. It starts in Fairbanks in Alaska, and ends in White Horse, the Yukon Territory Capital (in Canada), which is 1,000 miles (1,609 kilometers) away. The event is really dangerous because of the extreme freezing weather, and the fact that participants can't seek assistance. Hans Gatt and his dogs set the record as the fastest team ever to complete the race, when in 2010, they finished the whole course in just nine days and twenty six minutes.

4728. The first woman to play for the Harlem Globetrotters was Lynette Woodard, in 1985. Since then, she has played in the WNBA and has been inducted into the Basketball Hall of Fame and Women's

Basketball Hall of Fame.

4729. In the 1960's and 1970's, professional bowlers were seen as international celebrities. They even made twice as much money as NFL stars at the time.

4730. When NBA superstar Michael Jordan was at high school, he was actually cut from his Laney High School varsity basketball team.

4731. Even though NBA superstar LeBron James is left-handed, he shoots the ball with his right hand. Similarly, Hall of Famer Larry Bird of the Boston Celtics was a player who was left-handed, but he shot the ball with the right.

4732. Brent and Wayne Gretzky hold the record for most points in the NHL by a pair of brothers. They totaled 2,861 points with Brent scoring four of those points and Wayne scoring the other 2,857.

4733. On August 25, 2014, Alexandru Duru achieved the farthest flight on a hoverboard in Quebec, Canada, which was 905 feet (276 meters).

4734. Andre the Giant left home at the age of fourteen years old to find work. When he returned home at nineteen, he had grown so much that his parents didn't recognize him. They did recognize him from wrestling on television, but they did not know that he was their son.

4735. Originally, hockey pucks were made of cow dung.

4736. Baseball umpires earn more money annually than referees in the other three major American sports leagues with incomes of up to $350,000 a year. NFL referees on the other hand earn up to $70,000 per season, NBA referees earn up to $300,000 annually, and NHL referees earn up to $255,000 annually.

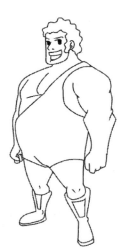

4737. In 1947, Austrian tennis player Hans Redl got to the fourth round of the men's singles event at Wimbledon. This was a great achievement given that he only had one arm. He lost one arm during World War II and competed at Wimbledon until 1956.

4738. During the 1961 to 1962 NBA season, Wilt Chamberlain averaged a mind-boggling 50.4 points per game for the Philadelphia Warriors. He also scored 100 points in a game during the same season on March 2, 1962.

4739. In the 1908 Olympics, American sprinter Forrest Smithson ran the 110-meter hurdles while carrying a Bible in his hand, winning the gold medal. He apparently did this as a way to protest against the decision to run the finals on Sundays. The truth however was that he was so religious that he often ran with a Bible.

4740. Since 1967, Tiffany has manufactured the Vince Lombardi trophy, which is awarded annually to the winners of the Super Bowl. The 20.7 inches (52.7 centimeter) tall trophy is a football standing upright on a three-sided stand, and is made completely of sterling silver. It weighs just over 6.6 pounds (three kilograms) and is worth over $25,000.

4741. In June 2011, the first pinball-inspired skate park was built by Mountain Dew in Henderson, New Zealand. It's named the Mountain Dew Skate Pinball Park which features an interactive skate park with sensors triggering lights, sounds, and skill level scoring on the top board.

4742. For Yao Ming's debut game in the NBA, his team promoted the game by giving out over eight thousand fortune cookies. Yao Ming wasn't offended at all since he'd never seen one before in China, and thought it was an American invention.

4743. Two radio stations in San Francisco had to ban Lorde's hit song "Royals" during the World Series in 2014, when the Kansas City Royals were pitted against the San Francisco Giants, because angry Giants fans called in and emailed the stations to complain about the song.

4744. When bobsledding was developed in the 1880's, the earliest participants in the sport would bob their heads trying to gain speed, and that's how it got its name. As it turned, bobbing one's head didn't really help people gain speed, but the name stuck anyway.

4745. In several places, drinking alcohol is prohibited before firearm shooting competitions because alcohol is regarded as a performance enhancing drug in that sport. Drinking calms the nerves, so it can literally steady the hands of a competitive shooter.

4746. Two years after being retired, 78% of all former NFL players become bankrupt or under financial stress. For NBA players, 60% of them are broke within five years of retirement.

4747. Because boxer Muhammad Ali didn't want the name of Muhammad to be stepped on, his star on the Walk of Fame was actually placed on the wall.

4748. Famous NBA superstars Stephen Curry, of the Golden State Warriors, and LeBron James, of the Los Angeles Lakers, were both born in Akron, Ohio.

4749. During the London 2012 Olympic Games, a specially designed radio-controlled Mini was used to transport javelins, hammers, shots, and discus around the field. The mini Minis were thirty nine inches (ninety nine centimeters) long and could carry loads of up to forty pounds (eighteen kilograms).

4750. Many basketball starters have donated millions of dollars to the Muhammad Ali Exhibit at the Smithsonian, some including Lebron James, Michael Jordan, and Magic Johnson.

4751. Mike Tyson, the former heavyweight champion, has a hectic daily workout schedule. He gets up at four in the morning, jogs for three to five miles, then performs 2,000 sit-ups, 500 dips, 500 pushups, and 500 shrugs.

4752. During World War II, the Pittsburgh Steelers and the Philadelphia Eagles were combined to make one team, the Steagles, as many players were called to duty.

4753. At the 2008 Olympics in Beijing, in order to protect the athletes from food poisoning, white mice were fed twenty four hours in advance with the same food given to the athletes. If there was a problem, the food could be traced and destroyed before being fed to the athletes.

4754. The record for the shortest NBA player of all time is held by Mugsy Bowes at 5'3" (1.61 meters).

4755. The first AFL/NFL World Championship game was the official name of the first Super Bowl.

4756. On December 7, 1963, instant replay was used for the first time in sports, during a football game between the Army and Navy at Municipal Stadium in Philadelphia. The first replay aired after a simple one-yard touchdown run.

4757. Although Bobby Bonilla retired in 2000, the New York Mets are still paying him $1.19 million a year. When the team wanted to cut him and pay him the rest of his contract, Bonilla's manager made an agreement with them to pay him $1.19 million for twenty five years, starting in 2011.

4758. Currently, Michael Jordan makes more money each year than he earned in salary during his fifteen year NBA career.

4759. In Wimbledon, players are not allowed to swear. That's the reason why line judges have to learn curse words in other languages.

Technology, Internet & Videogames

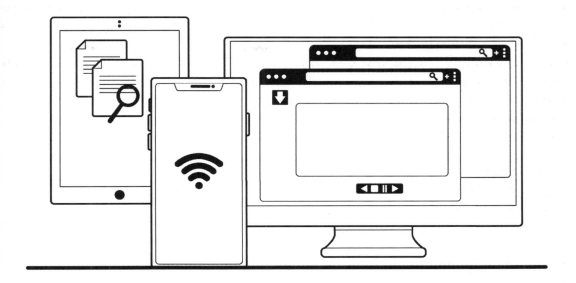

4760.   A ten year old boy from Finland discovered a bug in Instagram's programming, which people could use to delete others' comments. This happened in 2016, and Facebook paid him $10,000 for discovering it.

4761.   Lego bricks were used to construct the first ever server racks used at Google. The toy construction bricks were thought to be cost effective at the time, and it was also an easy way to expand these structures compared to permanent structures.

4762.   Studies indicate that when you study, work, or do anything productive, your motivation, focus, and productivity can improve if you listen to music. Additionally, video game music has been identified as the best kind when it comes to keeping your mind energized.

4763.   There is no significant link between mass shootings and playing video games with violence, despite what some politicians claim. In fact, many mass shooters don't play any video games.

4764.   Over half of smartphone users download zero apps every month.

4765.   Jerry's Guide to the World Wide Web was originally the name given to Yahoo, after one of its creators, Jerry Yang. The site was officially introduced on March 2, 1995, and it was the leader before Google began.

4766.   It took Apple a whole year to sell ten million iPhones in 2008 and only a week to sell thirteen million in 2015.

4767.   Instead of being woken up by a normal alarm clock, you can be woken up by a complete stranger from anywhere on the globe with an app called "Wakie."

4768.   New Zealand is often chosen by many tech companies as their test market for new products. The country has a diverse group of people and most of them speak English. Should the technology be a failure, the islands are isolated enough so it won't have as much of a negative impact on the whole brand.

4769.   On average, iPhone owners unlock their device around eighty times per day.

4770.   The channel CTFxC holds the Guinness World Record for the most consecutive personal video blogs posted on YouTube, with more than 3,057.

4771. Because of the September 11 attacks on the United States, Microsoft changed the advertising slogan for the Windows XP operating system from "Prepare to Fly" to "Yes You Can" in 2001.

4772. In 2016, a group called OurMine hacked Mark Zuckerberg's Twitter and Pinterest accounts. Apparently, his password was simply "dadada."

4773. Some bathrooms in Japan have a button that plays the flushing sound when pushed in order to mask the sound of your business.

4774. Theringfinders.com is an online site where you can find metal-detecting experts you can hire for a fixed fee to search for and find items of jewelry that you may have lost. They've successfully recovered 3,000 items worth over $5.2 million.

4775. Pillow Talk is a wristband created by Company Little Riot, based in London, England. The device picks up your heartbeat and sends it in real time to your loved one. It allows you to hear their heartbeat in your pillow and they can hear yours in theirs.

4776. Within the first three days of its release, Grand Theft Auto V made a billion dollars in sales, making it the fastest selling piece of entertainment property.

4777. A report from polygon.com shows that the video game industry actually makes a lot more cash annually than the music and film industries combined. For instance, in 2014, the industry made $83.6 billion from across the world, and by comparison, the films made just $36.4 billion, and music made $15.6 billion.

4778. Because of the codename for the Power Macintosh 7100, Apple was sued in 1994. Internally, it was referred to as Carl Sagan, in honor of the renowned astronomer, but after the suit was filed, they codenamed it BHA, meaning Butt Head Astronomer.

4779. Technically, Google is considered one of the five biggest computer manufacturers in terms of volume, just because of the fact that they make their own servers.

4780. The "Like-A-Hug" jacket gives you a hug whenever a friend clicks the like button on one of your Facebook posts.

4781. In February, 2017, a robotic coffee brewing kiosk called Cafe Ex opened in downtown San Francisco, the first of their kind in the United States. The drinks are served by barista bots, which are robotic arms designed by Mitsubishi.

4782. Nearly 14.5 billion messages account for spam each day around the globe; that's 45% of all emails. Some research companies estimate that spam email may escalade up to an even greater portion of global emails to 73%. The United States is the number one generator of spam email followed by Korea.

4783. Based on a survey done by Oxford University, the average Facebook user has about 155 friends, but only four of them are close enough to whom they would be willing to turn to in a crisis.

4784. Photographer Antoine Geiger creates images of cell phones sucking out people's faces. The images intend to reflect our self alienation and constant use of mobile devices.

4785. There are over a billion people on Facebook and over ten thousand die each day. This means that there will be more dead users on Facebook than living members and it could become a digital graveyard by the year 2065.

4786. The government in the United States can legally read any emails that you have that are over 180 days old without a warrant. Even though the Electronic Communications Privacy Act was enacted long before everybody had email, the government states that the law still allows them to do this.

4787. In 2014, Markus Notch Persson, the creator of the video game Minecraft, sold the business to Microsoft for $2.5 billion.

4788. When Gmail came out on April 1, in 2004, everyone thought it was an April Fools' joke when they were offering a whopping one gigabyte of storage compared to Hotmail's two megabytes.

4789. Founded in late 1889, Nintendo was originally a playing card company. It was based in Kyoto, Japan, and produced and marketed a game called Hanafuda. Today, Nintendo continues to manufacture playing cards in Japan and even organizes its own tournament called the Nintendo Cup.

4790. Twelve hours after starting his Instagram account, Pope Francis broke a record by hitting one million followers. He christened the account on a Saturday with a photo of him kneeling in prayer with an accompanying message that said "Pray for me," in nine languages. The previous record was set by David Beckham at one million within twenty-four hours.

4791. In 2006, a mummified human skeleton was placed on sale on eBay by a woman named Lynn Sterling, from Michigan, US. The online company removed the posting because it violated their policy against selling human remains.

4792. Susan Wojcicki, the current CEO of YouTube, rented her garage to Larry Page and Sergey Brin in 1998 when they were creating Google.

4793. On July 3, 1999, the first perfect Pac-Man score of 3,333,360 was achieved by Billy Mitchel at the Fun Spot Family Fun Center in New Hampshire. He also held world records in Ms. Pac-Man, Donkey Kong, Donkey Kong Jr., Centipede, and Burger Time.

4794. Viewing all the pictures shared on Snapchat in the last hour alone would take you around ten years to complete.

4795. Twitter users have a limit of messages per day, which is 24,000 tweets and 1,000 direct messages.

4796. In 2004, Google anonymously posted math equations on billboards in Harvard Square and Silicon Valley. Those who solved them were led to a website with another equation; if the last equation was solved, they allowed you to submit your resume.

4797. In February, 2017, a new dating app called "Hater" was released. It matches people based on their mutual dislikes. Some topics covered are Donald Trump, gluten-free, camping, marijuana, butt selfies, and Taylor Swift.

4798. Snapchat founder Evan Spiegel's net worth was $1.5 billion at the age of only twenty four, making him the world's youngest billionaire at the time.

4799. After playing World of Warcraft for three days straight, a Chinese avid computer gamer nicknamed Snowy actually died of fatigue in 2005. A service was held for her in a virtual cathedral inside the game, where over a hundred gamers visited her. In fact, she holds the Guinness World Record for the most people at a virtual funeral.

4800. Ayan Qurishi is a child genius who passed Microsoft's IT exam at the age of five, making him the youngest computer specialist in the world.

4801. The video game character Mario from the Super Mario Bros franchise was originally named Mr. Video. Later he was renamed as Mario after the owner of Nintendo's first warehouse Mario Segale. Meanwhile, Mario Segale earned himself the nickname of Mr. Video.

4802. Apple Computers was actually founded by three people and not two, as it's usually believed. Ronald Wayne was the third co-founder, but shortly after the company's creation, he decided to pull out, selling his 10% on April 12, 1976, for $800. Today that stake would be worth $62.93 billion.

4803.   According to the annual ranking of the best global brands generated by the management firm Interbrand, in 2016 Apple was number one for the fourth year in a row, with a brand value of $178 billion, and Google was number two with a brand value of $133 billion.

4804.   If you go to the website Freerice.com, you can answer multiple choice questions and have ten grains of rice donated to charity for every right question you answer.

4805.   The head designer at Apple, Jonathan Ive, was responsible for the products such as iMax, iPhone and iPod. He also helped design the character EVE from the movie Wall-E.

4806.   Blind people tend to forget more memories than those who can see as they don't have visual imagery and can't look at photos to trigger old memories. There is a company named "Touchable Memories" that prints 3D objects from old pictures that help the blind touch, feel, and relive their cherished moments like never before.

4807.   The Apple desktop interface was inspired by the company Xerox.

4808.   In 1971, the first email ever was sent by computer engineer Ray Tomlinson. He sent messages to himself from one machine to the other.

4809.   The first autonomous, untethered, and entirely soft robot has been created by researchers at Harvard University. It is a small, 3-D printed robot and it was nicknamed Octobot.

4810.   The term "bug" for computers began because there was an actual bug inside a computer in 1947, when a moth short-circuited a computer in the US Navy.

4811.   "Too Good to Go" is an app that connects users to local restaurants in the United Kingdom that want to sell perfectly good leftover food at a much cheaper price.

4812.   A discovery made by the University of Wisconsin has led to the replacement of toxic and non-biodegradable materials in smartphones such as microchips. They have found a replacement material that's made from wood pulp that is both transparent and flexible.

4813.   Given the continual complaints from customers about their phones catching on fire, Samsung had to stop the production and sales of its Galaxy Note Seven Smartphone. Even when they attempted to replace the battery supplier, customers still reported the same issues. They were forced to recall 2.5 million phones.

4814.   The very first message sent between two computers over the Internet was back in 1969, and it was "lo." The complete message was supposed to be "login," but the computer crashed after the first two letters.

4815.   In 2014, a mobile game was released called "Run Forrest Run," based on the movie Forrest Gump, where you run through Forrest's entire life.

4816.   Rick Astley became an Internet sensation in 2007 with his video "Never Gonna Give You Up," when it became part of an Internet prank known as "Rickrolling." Unfortunately, he didn't claim ownership of his work and earned only $12 in royalties off of his nearly 150 million YouTube views.

4817.   The Rosetta wearable disk is an archive of over 1,000 languages compressed using nanotechnology onto a less than one inch (2.54 centimeter) device pendant, created by the Rosetta Project. You can only read it with the use of a microscope and you can only get one if you donate $1,000 to the foundation.

4818.   The IOS game "Clash of Clans" was making a remarkable one and a half million dollars a day at its peak.

4819.   There is a device that allows monkeys to control robotic wheelchairs by sending signals with their brains. It was developed by scientists at Duke University with the aim of helping the elderly and people with disabilities.

4820.   If a big disaster or a hacking group causes the Internet to crash, there are seven people in the world who have key cards that can reboot the system when five of the keys are used together. These people literally hold the keys to the worldwide Internet security.

4821.   There is a Japanese robotics company called Fanuc that can be run for thirty days without any supervision and the robots there can build fifty other robots in the course of a day.

4822. Markus Notch Persson created the first version of the popular video game Minecraft in just six days, originally calling it "cave game." To date the game has sold over 144 million copies.

4823. It's possible to buy a 4K motion activated Wi-Fi camera for your bird feeder called "Bird Photo Booth." The device allows you to take close-up pictures and videos of the birds that drop in for a meal.

4824. Approximately 80% of YouTube views occur outside the United States. In fact, YouTube exists in over eighty eight countries, under seventy six different languages, which covers about 95% of the Internet's population.

4825. The way Google maps shows that there is a traffic jam is by how many android phones are in that area.

4826. Interscatter is a way of communication developed by Engineers at the University of Washington that converts Bluetooth signals into Wi-Fi signals. This way of communicating would allow contact lenses and brain implants to send signals to your iPhone.

4827. Jump Man was originally the name of Super Mario.

4828. The most common "how to" search on YouTube from 2012 to 2015 was how to kiss, followed by how to tie a tie, how to draw, and how to get a six pack in three minutes.

4829. The Cult Awareness Network described scientology as dangerous, ruthless, terrorist, and in response, the religion sued the network, forcing them to go bankrupt. A little later, some scientologist bought the remaining assets of the network to keep them silent.

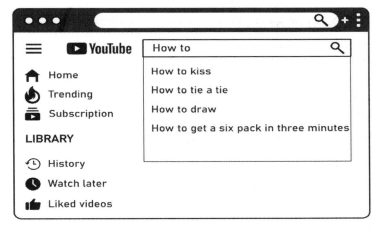

4830. In the United States, the first Copyright Infringement case to ever go on trial happened in 2009, and it involved Jamie Thomas-Rasset, a thirty two year old woman. She was found guilty of downloading twenty four songs from the web. She was fined $80,000 for every song, or $1.9 million in total.

4831. In 2014, the music video for Psy's Gangnam Style became the first video to surpass two billion views on YouTube, forcing them to upgrade from a thirty-two-bit integer system to a sixty-four-bit one.

4832. Mark Zuckerberg, the creator of Facebook, spent thirty million dollars in 2013 buying four houses around him so he could have some peace and quiet.

4833. NASA's Internet speed is ninety one gigabits per second, around 13,000 times faster than the average Internet speed in the United States, which is about 6.6 megabits per second. This is because they operate on what's called a shadow network; it's like the Internet, but it only connects a few research facilities and organizations worldwide.

4834. The largest jackpot payout in an online slot machine game, according to the Guinness World Records, was over $20 million. It was won on October 6, 2015, by Jon Heywood in Cardiff, UK, playing micro gaming's Mega Moolah on Betway's website.

4835. Kim Kardashian's emoji app was making $1,000,000 a minute at one point after its launch.

4836. George Hotz was the first person to unlock a first-generation iPhone; he was only seventeen years old when he did so. He sold the iPhone for a Nissan 350Z and three locked phones.

4837. The University of Wisconsin Green Bay is using Snapchat to inform the students that they have been accepted at the university.

4838. Google actually hires camels to carry its trekker camera in order to get street views of deserts.

4839. In the video game Super Mario Bros that was made for the first Nintendo Entertainment System, the white clouds above and the green bushes below were basically the same, they were just colored differently.

4840. A homeless man called Leo Grand met a programmer called Patrick McConlogue who asked him to choose between a hundred dollars and sixteen coding lessons back in 2013. Leo took the coding lessons, and he ended up creating an app called "Trees for Cars." The app aims to reduce carbon dioxide emissions by lowering the number of cars in traffic through carpooling.

4841. To commemorate its twentieth birthday in 1997, Apple released the TAM (Twentieth Anniversary Mac), a limited edition computer specifically marketed to executives. It cost $7,500 and it looked futuristic. Apple had it hand-delivered to customers in a limo by an employee wearing a tuxedo.

4842. With average speeds of 3.54 Mbps, the Philippines is the country with the slowest Internet in the entire Southeast Asia as of 2014. In comparison, Singapore's Internet speeds average at roughly sixty-five Mbps, and it's the second fastest in the region.

4843. In 2007, the Government of Australia spent eighty four million dollars creating a porn filter for the Internet, but a sixteen year old student at a private school in Melbourne was able to crack the code and get through that filter within thirty minutes. The boy said that the filter could be deactivated with just a few clicks.

4844. Brian Acton failed to get a job he had applied for at Facebook in 2009, but that might be the best thing that could have happened to him. Five years after that, in 2014, Facebook bought Acton's company WhatsApp for $19 billion. From his profits, Acton took $50 million and invested it into a WhatsApp competitor called Signal. On March 20, 2018, he sent out a tweet urging everyone to delete Facebook.

4845. "Ancient Earth" is an interactive digital map on the Internet that can indicate to you where the ground you are currently standing on would have been on the planet at any time in the last 750 million years.

4846. A player-vs-player fight on the video game Eve Online called Battle B-R5RB is deemed the largest battle in the history of the Internet. It went on for twenty one hours, and it involved over 7,548 player characters.

4847. As a general rule, there must be some form of food within 150 feet (forty five meters) of all parts of Google offices.

4848. Steve Jobs wanted actor Jeff Goldblum to voice Siri, but when Goldblum received the request from Jobs on the phone, he thought it was someone else, and he turned down the offer.

4849. In a link posted to their Facebook page as an April Fools' Day prank in 2014, NPR (National Public Radio) accused Americans of not reading things anymore. Outraged people quickly posted slews of comments, but the few who actually clicked the link and read the content found a congratulatory message. NPR proved that many people commented on posts without actually reading them, even when the topic was about reading.

4850. The original version of Pac-Man, the classic arcade game, was designed to never end. However, for those proficient enough to get to level 256, the game would go haywire and that made the level impossible to win.

4851. The standard Google logo was replaced by a Google doodle, which was some kind of out-of-office message, for the first time on August 30, 1998. It was a stick figure of a Burning Man that was meant to let users know that Google founders Sergey and Larry weren't available to fix any issues or bugs because they had gone to Nevada for the Burning Man Festival.

4852. In 2016, a year of unlimited data was given by T-Mobile to all its customers to play Pokémon GO. Additionally, they offered 50% off mobile accessories such as portable power packs and other items because so many people's phones were dying.

4853. The term "CAPTCHA" means Completely Automated Public Turing Test to Tell Computers and Humans Apart.

4854. As of February 2020, over two billion iPhones were sold by Apple.

4855. According to the results from an online survey, 11% of Americans think that HTML is a type of STD.

4856. The word "SIM" in SIM card stands for Subscriber Identification Module.

4857. The oldest blogger in the world is 105 year old Swedish woman Dagny Carlsson. She took a course in informatics at ninety nine years old and has been blogging ever since.

4858. "Backrub" was the name originally given to Google.

4859. In June of 2016, a massive theft of Twitter usernames and passwords took place, affecting almost thirty three million customers. According to the security company LeakedSource, more than 120,000 people had used the password "123456."

4860. "Got It" is a Silicon Valley-based company that has developed an app with the same name. If a student gets stuck on a question, they can submit it to the app and get tutors to bid for an answer. When the student accepts the bid, which generally costs about a dollar, they get a ten-minute long tutoring session by text.

4861. The letter "I" in Apple products, such as iPod, iPad, and iMac, stands for Internet. When the iMac was first introduced in 1998 by Steve Jobs, he explained this.

4862. Madden NFL, the video game franchise, is older than half the players who currently play in the NFL today.

4863. Before manufacturing mobile phones, Nokia Corporation originally manufactured pulp and paper, including toilet paper.

4864. A Russian folk song from the 19th century about a meeting between a peddler and a young girl is actually the theme song for the game Tetris. In the song, he offers the girl his wares and goods in exchange for a kiss.

4865. It has been proved that people who play action games are better learners. As they excel at predicting the sequence of upcoming events, they become better learners by playing fast-paced games.

4866. The former CEO of the renowned virtual website "Neopets" was a Scientologist who used the org board method for his company. The method was actually designed by Scientology creator L. Ron Hubbard, making it the business model for his followers.

4867. "LuDela" is a smart candle that can be lit and extinguished using a smartphone app.

4868. In 2002, actor Steve Carell provided commentary track on the sports videogame known as Outlaw

Golf, while comedian Dave Attell did the commentary for Outlaw Golf 2.

4869. YouTube has over one billion active users monthly. In comparison, Facebook has 1.8 billion, Instagram has 600 million, Twitter has 319 million, and Snapchat has an estimated 301 million.

4870. Before the Internet, hacking groups in the 1960's would take over phone lines using toys from cereal boxes. The whistles in Cap'n Crunch boxes could be played at 2,600 Hertz, creating a tone that could commandeer people's phone lines, allowing the hackers to make as many long distance phone calls as they wanted.

4871. In 1976, Ronald Wayne designed the very first Apple computer logo which was of Sir Isaac Newton sitting under a tree just as an apple is about to hit him on the head.

4872. Susan Bennett, a voice actor and former backup singer for Roy Orbison, is the female voice of the original Siri. A company called "ScanSoft" hired her to record gibberish. Technicians then took those recordings and combined them to form sentences and phrases, which ended up on all those devices.

4873. If you have the Galaxy Note 7, Samsung Pay allows you to pay for things with just your retina.

4874. Every year, over two million job applications are received by Google from around the world. As of February 2019, they had more than 114,000 employees.

4875. In London, there is a music ticketing app called "Dice" that allows their employees to call out of work for being too hungover. They simply send a message to their boss with beer, music, and sick emoji. Each employee is permitted to take four hangover days a year.

4876. The military channel voiceover for the 2005 videogame "Call of Duty 2: The Big Red One" was done by actor Mark Hamill.

4877. There is a mobile game called "Send Me to Heaven" that consists of throwing your phone as high as you can in the air. The inventor made it with the aim of destroying as many iPhones as possible, but Apple immediately banned it from the app store.

4878. Microsoft lowered their flags to half-mast when Apple's founder Steve Jobs died in 2011, as a sign of respect to him.

4879. In the spring of 2017, facial recognition technology began being used by the Canadian Border Services Agency at major Canadian airports. To keep out alleged terrorists and other criminals, the technology compares images of people arriving in the country with photographs of suspects on watch lists.

4880. In 1999, the company "Excite" turned down the offer to buy Google for one million dollars. Even when Google reduced the price to $750,000, they still rejected the offer. Today Google's market cap stands at $320 billion.

4881. A totally waterproof MP3 player was released by Sony in 2013. They sold each one fully submerged in a water bottle in order to prove the underwater capabilities of the device.

4882. Nintendo 64 wasn't always known by that name. It was first called Project Reality, then later renamed to Nintendo Ultra 64, until the name was finally shortened to Nintendo 64.

4883. Google Chrome's dinosaur Wi-Fi error message is also a game. Next time you see the dinosaur, just press the spacebar and you will see your T-rex jump. Try not to let him land on the cactus or it'll be game over.

4884. The music from the videogame "Sonic the Hedgehog Three & Knuckles" was composed by the late Michael Jackson, who refused to take credit for the work when he heard how it sounded after it was mixed into the game.

4885. In 2015, around 2,200 pounds (1,000 kilograms) of gold were recovered by Apple from recycled iPhones, iPads, and Macs, which was worth over $40 million. Gold is highly averse to corrosion and an excellent conductor of electricity, which is why it's often used in consumer electronics. Even though silver is actually the best conductor, it corrodes more easily.

4886. When Apple began designating numbers to employees, Steve Jobs was not happy that Steve Wozniak received number one while he got number two. He believed that he should be second to no one, so he took number zero instead.

4887. "Pick a Melon" is an app that helps you pick a ripe watermelon. The way it works is that you place the microphone of your smartphone on the watermelon, knock on the melon until all three test lights are glowing, and wait for the result.

4888.

4889. In May 2017, a couple from Cardiff, Wales, named Martin Sherbington and Eliza Evans, got married in virtual reality, on a social network called Alt Space VR. The wedding took place at a virtual nightclub called "The Spire" and around 150 of their friends and family attended the event, many of whom wouldn't have been able to make it to a real life wedding in Cardiff.

THE APP SAID THIS IS THE RIPE MELON.

4890. The longest videogame marathon playing ever recorded was achieved by Hecaterina Kinumi Iglesias who played World of Warcraft for twenty nine hours and thirty one minutes on March 29, 2014, in Vigo, Spain.

4891. Math Pics is an iOS app that can answer math equations in seconds. The way it works is that you take a picture of a hand-written math problem and it will give you the answer as well as step by step directions on how it got there.

4892. Although his Twitter account has roughly eighteen million followers, Pope Francis has never actually been on the Internet once in his life.

4893. Nintendo started back in 1889 as a playing card maker, and its products became a hit with the Yakuza, of all people. The criminal organization ran gambling parlors, and they ordered lots of cards from Nintendo, making them their main supplier. Were it not for the vast sums of money they got from supplying the Yakuza, Nintendo might not have grown to be the big video game company we know today. In an ironic turn, after Nintendo started making their popular Super Nintendo Entertainment Systems (SNE's) and video games, the Yakuza started robbing their daytime shipments, and the company was forced to start transporting their products at night.

War & Military World

4894. After the Revolutionary War in 1785, the US Navy was actually disbanded with the last ship being the Alliance. In 1794, it was brought back mainly to fight pirates.

4895. During the Cold War, blood type tattoos were used in Indiana and Utah to enable rapid transfusion. Even school children were tattooed to facilitate emergency transfusions, in case an atomic attack happened.

4896. It's traditional to leave a coin on a military headstone to show the family of the fallen soldier that someone else came to the gravesite to pay their respects, and different coins mean different things. A penny says that someone visited. A nickel says that the visitor trained together with the deceased at the same boot camp. A dime says that the visitor served with the deceased. A quarter means the visitor was present when the soldier died.

4897. Audie Murphy, who fought in WWII when he was just twenty one, was the most decorated American soldier during that war. He is credited with killing 240 German soldiers, and he received thirty three medals and awards. He later became a film star.

4898. The codename for the atomic bomb that was detonated by the United States over the Japanese city of Nagasaki on August 9, 1945, was "Fat Man."

4899. The St. Ermin's Hotel was the base for secret British Spies and the wartime intelligence community during World War 2. The complete top level of the hotel was full of explosives put there by the British Secret Intelligence Service, while hotel guests used the rest of the building having no clue.

4900. At least 500 canvased dummies were dropped on D-Day away from the Normandy Beaches to distract from actual drop zones. The dummies, which were called ruperts, were just under three feet (less than one meter) tall; they came with battle sounds and were made to self-destruct upon landing so that the Germans couldn't find them.

4901. When America built the SR-71 Blackbird, the fastest manned plane that was virtually undetectable during the Cold War, the CIA set up a bunch of dummy corporations to purchase titanium from the Soviet Union. This means Russia was basically supplying materials used to make planes that spied on them.

4902. As the Second World War raged on, there was high demand for penicillin and limited supply, so doctors decided to recycle it by collecting urine from people who had taken the antibiotic, extracting penicillin that had gone all the way through those people, and giving it to other patients.

4903. America's last official declaration of war was in 1942, against Romania, Hungary, and Bulgaria.

4904. In 1943, a Second World War naval destroyer called the USS O'Bannon defeated a Japanese Submarine by hauling potatoes at it. They created a plot to commemorate the ingenuity of the crew but someone stole it in the 1970's.

4905. The government of Switzerland was concerned about being invaded during the Cold War, so they set up a plan to defend their borders by wiring several roads, bridges, and railways with explosives. They prepared more than 3,000 points of demolition, and the bombs were ready to go off at any moment. Lots of the bombs were hidden in mountainous areas, and they could have caused rock slides that would devastate the invaders.

4906. Whenever he met with his war cabinet during World War II, Winston Churchill would insist that only noiseless typewriters should be used in the meeting because he couldn't stand the noise.

4907. Only an estimated 14-19% of kamikaze aircrafts managed to hit their marks during World War II. Most of the aircrafts got shot down and they never got close to the vessels that they intended to destroy.

4908. Yakoc Stalin, Joseph Stalin's son, was captured while fighting with the Nazis in 1941. Yakov ended up dying in captivity because Stalin refused to trade a marshal for a lieutenant.

4909. At a certain point during the 1985 Geneva Summit, Reagan and Gorbachev agreed to pause the Cold War if an alien invasion would take place on Earth.

4910. The city of Kyoto in Japan was originally at the top of the atomic bomb target list during World War II. The city name was personally removed from the list by the US Secretary of War, Henry L. Stimson, because he had previously been there during his honeymoon and loved the city.

4911. The Mongol army invaded Japan twice, and both times they were saved by the harsh storms that crippled the Mongols. They called these storms "kamikaze" or "divine winds."

4912. Oskar Speck, a German canoeist, kayaked from Germany to Australia between 1932 and 1939. After arriving in Australia, he was declared a prisoner of war due to the outbreak of World War II.

4913. When at war, the Philippines hang their flag upside down. In 2010, the flag was accidentally displayed upside down behind its president when meeting with President Obama and other leaders of the Assembly of Southeast Asian nations. It caused great confusion and tension as everyone thought it was an act of war.

4914. Canada and Denmark are in dispute over a territory called Hans Island. The military forces of both countries regularly visit the island and remove the other country's flag leaving a bottle of Danish schnapps or Canadian whiskey.

4915. The US Air Force accidentally dropped two nuclear bombs in North Carolina in January, 1961, when a bomber broke in two mid-flight. Luckily neither of the bombs went off. If they had, they would've been more devastating than the Nagasaki and Hiroshima incidents combined.

4916. During the Cold War, the United States used to send textbooks filled with violent images and militant Islamic teachings to Afghan schoolchildren, as covert attempts to spur resistance of the Soviet occupation.

4917. When the Nazis invaded Paris in 1940, French soldiers cut the elevator cables to the Eiffel Tower. They thought that if Hitler wanted to erect their flag on the top of the tower, they would have to climb hundreds of stairs to get there.

4918. To locate and mark the locations of sea mines, the US Navy uses dolphins and sea lions. Dolphins have the most sophisticated sonar known to man while sea lions have exceptional low light vision and underwater directional hearing capabilities, which makes them the perfect animals for the job.

4919. During the Vietnam War, the external fuel tanks of the US fighter jets were dropped over Vietnam when they were empty or the pilot needed more maneuverability. A lot of these tanks were reused later by Vietnamese farmers as canoes.

4920. In 1957, a convoy of five B-52 fighter jets from the United States flew around the Earth as a way to prove that they could drop a nuclear bomb anywhere. The convoy traveled more than 40,000 kilometers (24,840 miles) without landing to refuel, during forty five hours and nineteen minutes. It was called Operation Power Flite.

4921. In order to protect the country's ports during World War II, the US Navy partnered with the mafia. For decades however, the US government has denied its collaboration and not just in relation to the Second World War.

4922. In 2015, the British government finally finished paying for World War I, almost one hundred years after the debt was issued.

4923. Honduras and El Salvador actually went to war over soccer, on July 14, 1969. Although it only lasted one hundred hours, it took 6,000 lives and 12,000 people were injured.

4924. During the Afghanistan War, British Corporal Sean Jones ordered his men to affix bayonets to their guns and charge across 264 feet (eighty meters) of open ground against the Taliban forces as their men were ambushed, outnumbered, and under fire. It actually worked; enemy forces scattered fleeing the fight, due to the unexpected move.

4925. The Spanish town of Huescar declared war on Denmark in 1809, then forgot about it for 172 years. During that time, not a single shot was fired and no one was killed. A peace treaty was finally signed in 1981 when a historian found the official declaration and realized that the war was still running.

4926. The first technical fatality of the Civil War occurred during a 100-gun salute. It happened when a cannon prematurely discharged, killing Private Daniel Hough of the First US Artillery.

4927. The Soviets built an A-40 Krylya Tanka, a tank that had wings during the Second World War. Luckily it didn't work.

4928. During the Nigerian Civil War in 1967, both sides agreed to a forty eight hour ceasefire to be able to watch a soccer game. They wanted to watch famous player "Pele" play, without having to worry about the war.

4929. There is a tradition among military commandos in Lebanon of eating live snakes in order to display their strength and courage.

4930. The reason why Napoleon Bonaparte wore his black felted beaver fur hat sideways, instead of with the points at the front and back, was so that he could be easily spotted on the battlefield.

4931. D-day was originally set for June fifth, but due to bad weather, it had to be postponed by twenty four hours.

4932. Swarm boats are US Navy boats that don't require a captain. They are developed by the Office of Naval Research. They use a radar system to communicate with one another and are designed to overwhelm and confuse the enemy.

4933. If you were recruited during the American Civil War, you could pay someone $300 to go in your place. This was called commutation and it was intended to raise money for the war effort. However, it was often deeply criticized as it was better at raising money than troops.

4934. The most armed country in the world is the US with almost ninety guns per one hundred people.

4935. The last man to be executed in the US by a firing squad was James W. Rogers. The last request from him was a bulletproof vest.

4936. During the Second World War, the Nazis had planned to kill Sir Winston Churchill with a bar of exploding chocolate. The explosive device was coated with a thin layer of dark chocolate by Hitler's bomb makers and it was packaged in an expensive-looking black and gold paper. Fortunately, British spies discovered the plan.

4937. Canada declared war on Japan after Pearl Harbor, the first western nation that did so. The US declared war the day after.

4938. During World War II, Germany used guns that had a curved barrel device that was clamped onto the end of an MP 44 rifle. The guns allowed soldiers to shoot over obstacles without exposing themselves to return fire.

4939. There was a bear named Wojtek that fought in the Polish army during World War II. His name meant "he who enjoys war." He carried shells to the front line and was taught to salute; he became a mascot for the soldiers and even developed a habit for drinking beer and smoking cigarettes. He survived the war and lived the rest of his life in the Edinburgh Zoo.

4940. Soldiers during the First World War would fire hundreds of random shots over their trenches to boil the coolant water in their machine guns, just so they could make some tea.

4941. During World War I, invisible ink was made using semen because the common techniques of detection didn't cause it to react.

4942. Twice as many people died of disease in the American Civil War than they did as a result of fighting. Acute diarrhea was one of the biggest problems the soldiers had. It was such a serious issue that they had an unwritten rule that said that soldiers shouldn't fire on or kill enemy combatants while they were answering nature's call.

4943. Napoleon wanted a form of communication in the early 19th century that would not require sound or light. It was created and named "tactile military code" which became the basis for Braille.

4944. An officer aboard the Titanic named Charles Herbert Lightoller was trapped under water when the vessel sank, but fortunately, a boiler exploded and that propelled him back to the surface. He later rescued 130 soldiers from Dunkirk during the Second World War.

4945. The last person to be killed during the First World War was an American soldier called Henry Gunther. He was shot dead at 10:59 am, just one minute before the armistice that stopped the war.

4946. Project Mogul was an operation conducted by the US Air Force to help detect nuclear weapons tests conducted by the Soviet Union. They mounted microphones onto high-altitude hot air balloons which were used to detect long range sound waves.

4947. Otto Frank, (Anne Frank's father), Adolf Hitler, and the great fantasy writer J.R.R. Tolkien, were all soldiers who fought at the Battle of the Somme during the First World War.

4948. There is a town in Normandy called Terville, which is the only one in France to never have lost one single person in the last five wars in which the country was involved. This included WWI and WWII.

4949. Golden eagles have been trained by the French military to destroy terrorist drones so that they don't have to shoot them down.

4950. The shortest war in history was the Anglo-Zanzibar War, which only lasted thirty eight minutes.

4951. During World War II, Japan launched balloons with bombs into the jet stream. Five picnickers found one of these balloons and attempted to move it; the bomb went off and killed them. This is known as the only mainland attack in the US. The locations of many of the balloons are still unknown.

4952. Ambrose Burnside was a general in the American Civil War known for his unusual facial hairstyle, and is where the term "sideburns" come from.

4953. During the Boshin War, a female soldier called Nakano Takeko didn't want enemy soldiers to take her head as a trophy, so her dying wish was for her sister to chop it off and bury it.

4954. At just twelve years old, Calvin Graham was the youngest American serviceman in the Second World War. He received the Bronze Star, and Purple Heart medals, and in 1978, he was honorably discharged. He passed away in 1992 at age sixty two.

4955. The Berlin Holocaust Memorial Project had to be stopped in 2003, after it was discovered that the company contracted to make a coating that would prevent graffiti on the monument was the same exact company that was contracted to manufacture the gas used to murder millions of Jews in concentration camps during the Second World War.

4956. Radford Army Ammunition Plant, a top secret military explosives manufacturer in Virginia, had to take some additional precautions when in July, 2016, people started sneaking onto their property while playing the phone game Pokémon GO. There was a rumor that a Charizard had been spotted on the premises, but it wasn't true.

4957. Instead of using periscope controllers in their submarines, the US Navy is now using Xbox 360 controllers, and that has cut the training time for operators from several hours to only a few minutes.

4958. An American congressman named Andrew May remarked during a press conference in June, 1943, that American submarines were able to survive Japanese attacks because the enemy was setting depth charges at shallow depths. The Japanese heard his comment and started modifying their depth charges, and this resulted in the loss of 800 American lives.

4959. Commanders in British Trident Submarines were told during the Cold War that if the BBC Radio 4 program "Today" was off the air for three recurring days without any explanations, they should assume that Britain had been destroyed, and act accordingly. If that happened, the commanders were to open sealed envelopes and follow the instructions outlined by the Prime Minister.

4960. For people in Finland, saunas are such an integral part of life that in the Second World War, their soldiers used the logs and natural terrain to build saunas inside war zones. These saunas were only used at night time to avoid attracting the enemy.

4961. Gustav the pigeon flew 150 miles (241 kilometers) to Britain during the Second World War to inform them about the Normandy invasion, and he was awarded the Dickin Medal of Honor for his contribution.

4962. Originally, M&M's were only sold to the US Military and it was part of soldiers' rations in wartime.

4963. The US Airfare was conducting military exercises near Tybee Island near the state of Georgia, on February 5, 1958, when a B47 bomber collided with an F86 fighter in midair, and a Mark 15 nuclear bomb was subsequently lost. The nuke was not active to prevent detonation, and the military did extensive searches. It was not found and it remains lost in the Atlantic Ocean to date.

4964. The longest civil war in world history is still going on. It's called the Karen Conflict, and it started in Karen State, Burma, in 1949, now known as Karen State, Myanmar. Currently, Karen State nationalists are engaged in a fight with Myanmar Armed Forces, and they want independence.

4965. As German and Russian soldiers were fighting during the First World War in the winter of 1916 to 1917, they were attacked by a massive pack of starving wolves. Things got so bad that the two enemy sides agreed to work together temporarily, just to survive the vicious animals.

4966. Natalia Karp was born in Poland and was sent to a concentration camp in 1943 after losing her husband in a bombing raid. At the camp, she saved hers and her sister's lives by skillfully playing Nocturne in C Sharp Minor by Chopin on piano, and impressing the camp's commandant who chose to spare the two.

4967. Hiroo Onoda, an imperial Japanese army officer, remained at his jungle post on the island of the Philippines for twenty nine years as he refused to believe that World War II was over. He finally returned to Japan in 1974 and was welcomed as a hero.

4968. Up to 4% of the sand on the beaches of Normandy today are made of shrapnel from the D-Day fight that took place in 1944.

4969. During the First World War, to conceal observation posts on the battleground, soldiers used camouflage trees. Camouflage artists sketched actual battle damaged trees in the battlefield. They were made behind lines by cutting down a real tree at night and replacing a battle worn tree with the replica. This provided a surveillance point where there was usually a flat exposed area.

4970. During the American Civil War, some soldiers had wounds that glowed blue. These soldiers had a better survival rate compared to others, so the glow was called "Angel's Glow." The luminescence was actually due to bacteria that produced antibiotics that live inside nematodes, and these nematodes have made homes in the soldiers' open wounds.

4971. During World War II, a band on the USS Arizona called the USS Arizona Band were all killed during the bombing of Pearl Harbor.

4972. In 1864, during the US Civil War, the Battle of Cherbourg took place. It involved a single ship battle between the Union warship USS Kearsarge and the Confederate warship CSS Alabama. The battle happened off the coast of France, in the English Channel. The CSS Alabama eventually lost and sank.

4973. On June 17, 1955, a land mine that was planted during World War I, in 1917, was struck by lightning and killed a cow. The rare event made the cow a casualty of war thirty eight years later.

4974. The man who murdered John F. Kennedy Jr., Lee Harvey Oswald, was a US marine. He defected, however, and joined the Soviet Union in 1959, where he met his wife and had a child. In 1962, after deciding that he made a mistake moving to Russia, Oswald moved back to the US with his family.

4975.   Andorra does not have an active military, so every citizen in the country should own a rifle by law. In fact, the police force will offer a firearm to citizens if it's needed.

4976.   The Soviets thought that women were the best to fit in sniper duties as they need to be patient, careful, and deliberate. They would also avoid hand to hand combat and need higher levels of aerobic conditioning than other troops.

4977.   Being clean-shaven became popular in the US after the troops returned home as heroes from World War I. Soldiers had been required to shave so that gas masks could securely fit on their face.

4978.   The "335 Years War" is considered the longest war ever recorded in human history. It happened between 1651 and 1986, and it involved the Isles of Scilly and the Netherlands. There were however no deaths or injuries, and not even one shot was fired.

4979.   A Polish doctor created a fake typhus epidemic in World War II which prevented the Nazis from sending 8,000 Jews to concentration camps as they had phobias about hygiene.

4980.   In 1956, the Canadian Army put on an exhibition to show a bazooka type of weapon during a fair. The testing resulted in a bad incident, so they didn't use it any more.

4981.   When the Confederate Army was running out of gunpowder, bat's poop was the solution. Bat guano's high nitrate content provided a key ingredient for the production of gunpowder.

4982.   If somebody is considered unfit to serve in the US Military, they are given a 4F classification. This term came about a long time ago during the American Civil War and it literally meant the person lacked the four front teeth, which were necessary to open packs of gunpowder. Some young able-bodied men would avoid service by pulling out their front teeth.

4983.   The record for the longest confirmed kill shot in history was done by a Canadian special forces sniper, shooting an IS militant dead from 11,611 feet (3,540 meters) away.

4984.   Soldiers with mentally low IQs were recruited into the military for the Vietnam War. Unfortunately, they were three times more likely to die than any other soldiers.

4985.   In 1950, Himalayan and American black bears were used as test subjects by the United States Air Force when testing their ejector seats for the B-58 Hustler. The bears were sedated and strapped into the seats. Despite some of them suffering broken bones, all of them survived until they were euthanized and dissected.

4986.   As of 2018, the United States Department of Defense employs 2.86 million people from military, National Guard, and civilian backgrounds. The annual budget for the Department of Defense is $7.17 billion US.

4987.   In 1794, George Washington founded the Springfield Armory in Massachusetts. The company manufactured weapons for every major war in US history, from the war of 1812 until the Vietnam War in 1968.

4988.   Between 1860 and 1916, it was mandatory that every soldier in the British Army had a mustache. If someone shaved it, he would be disciplined or even imprisoned. In battle, facial hair has its advantages as it protects the soldier's face from the cold elements.

4989.   The United States spends more money on the military than the rest of the world combined. There are 8,400 attack helicopters around the globe and 6,400 of them reside in the US.

4990. In the United States, if you are missing a toe, you will not be allowed into the armed forces. To join, it's mandatory that you have both feet totally intact, despite the fact it's possible to run even without your big toe.

CONGRATULATIONS, YOU CAN JOIN THE ARMY.

4991. Fazal Din, a twenty three year old Indian soldier was in Burma, commanding an attack on Japan's bunker position when, on March 2, 1945, at the height of the Second World War, he found himself stabbed all the way through by a Japanese sword. As the enemy soldier pulled it out to move on, Din grabbed the sword from his hand, then used it to kill him and another soldier. He waved the sword in the air to inspire his platoon, then he walked twenty five yards to the platoon headquarters, bleeding along the way, where he calmly gave his report upon arrival, before he collapsed and died a hero.

4992. The United States Playing Card Company in collaboration with the American and British intelligence agencies created a very special deck of cards during World War II with the intention of helping prisoners of war escape from German POW camps. The deck was called the "map" deck and it was made by hiding maps of top secret escape routes between the two paper layers that make up regular playing cards. When the cards were soaked in water, they could be peeled apart to reveal hidden maps that allowed escaping prisoners to find their way to safety.

4993. During World War II, the Nazis attempted to teach dogs how to talk and read, and even had special academies for trainees, according to Dr. Jan Bondeson, from Cardiff University. It was reported that one dog said the words "mind furor" when asked who Adolf Hitler was.

4994. After the First World War, much of the battlefield was barren and the red poppy was among the few plants that grew on the land, which is why it became the remembrance symbol that's been worn for decades.

4995. US Navy torpedo motors used 180 proof grain alcohol as fuel in the Second World War, and naval officers often stole the fuel and added pineapple juice to make an alcoholic beverage they called torpedo juice. The authorities started mixing poisonous chemicals into the fuel to discourage this practice, but the ingenious sailors always figured out ways to remove the poison from the alcohol.

4996. In June 1959, 3,000 letters on the Postal Service were mailed by the US Navy via a guided missile, which was fired towards an air station in Mayport, Florida. The attempt was successful and reached the station in twenty two minutes.

4997. Adolf Hitler gave a methamphetamine-based pill called pervitin to German soldiers. It was marketed as a pickup pill that supposedly reduced stress and fatigue, and brought on euphoria.

4998. The highest-ranking officer to be killed during the US Civil War was General Albert Johnston. He didn't pay much attention to a wound he got on his leg and eventually died from losing too much blood.

4999. During World War II, fashion designer Coco Chanel was a spy for the Nazi Party and an advocate during the Third Reich. She shared the idea that Jewish people were a threat to Europe.

5000. On July 20, 1944, Colonel Claus Von Stauffenberg, Chief of the Army Reserve, tried to assassinate Adolf Hitler. He planted a bomb in a briefcase which he placed near Hitler under a table, then left quickly. Another Colonel inadvertently moved the bomb further away from Hitler. When it was detonated, Hitler was injured but he survived.

Did you enjoy the book or learn something new? It really helps out small publishers like Scott Matthews if you could leave a quick review on Amazon so others in the community can also find the book! You can do so by scanning the QR code below which will take you straight to the review page.

Printed in Great Britain
by Amazon

20306760R00196